WOMEN TRANSFORMING CONGRESS

Edited by
CINDY SIMON ROSENTHAL

UNIVERSITY OF OKLAHOMA PRESS : NORMAN

Published with the assistance of the National Endowment for the Humanities, a federal agency which supports the study of such fields as history, philosophy, literature, and language.

Library in Congress Cataloging-in-Publication Data

Women transforming Congress / edited by Cindy Simon Rosenthal.
    p. cm. — (Congressional studies series; v. 4)
    Includes bibliographical references and index.
    ISBN 0-8061-3455-0 (alk. paper) — ISBN 0-8061-3496-8 (pb.: alk. paper)
    1. Women in politics—United States.   2. Women legislators—United States.   3. Women—Government policy—United States.   4. United States. Congress.   I. Rosenthal, Cindy Simon, 1950–   II. Series.

HQ1236.5.U6 W6675 2002
327.73'0082—dc21

2002019422

Women Transforming Congress is Volume 4 in the Congressional Studies Series.

The paper in this book meets the guidelines for permanence and durability of the Committee on Production Guidelines for Book Longevity of the Council on Library Resources. ∞

1 2 3 4 5 6 7 8 9 10

To my parents, Margarete and Clarence,
who inspired and encouraged me.

CONTENTS

Photographs

Tables and Figures

TABLES

FIGURES

Foreword

RICHARD F. FENNO, JR.

The U.S. Congress has long held a special fascination for students of American politics. Its purposes and its performances are as complex as the country itself, and sooner or later, most all of the country's serious problems end up (or begin) in its deliberations and decisions. The endless variety of its activities has attracted and tested a similarly wide range of scholarly interests, theories, and approaches. Like the ever-changing institution itself, political science inquiry never stands still—not in abstract theorizing, not in substantive focus, not in investigative technique.

In the forty-odd years that I have been studying Congress, the hallmark of this scholarly diversity has been an enduring sense of community among scholars. The idea of a common, open-ended enterprise is strong, and each new contribution is welcomed and valued—not as truth, but as a constructive effort to advance knowledge and understanding. From that time-honored perspective, *Women Transforming Congress* is a welcome and constructive addition to the community research effort. As a participant in the Carl Albert Center conference that launched this enterprise, I experienced the same intellectual excitement that has motivated other subcommunities of congressional scholars.

The impetus behind this new look at Congress is obvious: there is an interesting new group of legislators to look at. And clusters of new members, we know, frequently become the engines of institutional change. The number of female members of Congress has been gradually increasing—to the critical point where their behavior can now be aggregated and systematically evaluated. Who are they? How did they get there? What have they been doing? And, most important, what difference have they made?

In this book, 23 political scientists—19 of them women—have tackled these puzzles from various angles. Collectively, they have presented a strong case for using a gendered looking glass when examining congressional behavior. Their case is well grounded in political science research. To a relevant degree, as yet unspecified, congresswomen do think and act differently from congressmen. And because they do, Congress—to a degree yet to be well specified—is a changed institution. On the road to increased specification, the authors have laid down a careful, wide-ranging, and stimulating research marker. The collection is noteworthy, too, for the sheer scope of its original data collections and for the large increase they bring to our Congress-centered knowledge base.

Consider, for example, these data collections—each of which has been subjected to careful and illuminating analysis: 674 television commercials from 39 congressional election campaigns; 1,772 *New York Times* articles, over a 16-year period, on nine women's organizations; 82 lengthy personal interviews with women members of Congress in two Congresses; data on two health issues taken from 4,183 news stories, and 75 congressional hearings over a 48-year period; 13,000 cosponsorships on 1,700 women's rights bills; all floor speeches on five pieces of legislation in a single Congress; primary sponsors of 1,079 women's issue bills in two sessions of Congress; individual-level data on 2,707 committee staffers on 22 congressional committees and subcommittees supplemented by interviews with same; answers to a mail survey of 140 personal and career questions from 430 men and women members of 15 state legislatures, and also from 224 former members of Congress.

Some of the essays in this volume concentrate on the behavior of women only; some compare the behavior of men and women; some direct attention to institutional processes and their gendered impact. Altogether they leave little doubt that women members of Congress have brought with them distinctive policy interests, and, further, that they have made differences of scope and content in pushing those policy interests onto the national legislative agenda. In studies centering on interest group activity, on bill sponsorship, and on floor debates, women's perspectives and their influence clearly register—in substantive policy areas as specific as reproductive rights and breast cancer, and in areas as general as social welfare.

Influencing the policy agenda and the policy debate does not, however, automatically translate into influencing policy outcomes. The studies of committee and staff activity show that women members are increasingly positioning themselves on relevant committees and subcommittees in policy areas of special concern to them. There, however, as several authors demonstrate, evidence of influence is less compelling—as matters such as party, seniority, procedure, and traditional patterns of decision making come into play. In this inside setting, the impact of women as a group tends to diminish, and the impact of the individual woman legislator tends to increase. Indeed, the studies that focus on electoral presentations, on committee participation, and on changes in cohort makeup over time do describe a set of politicians becoming increasingly strategic in their behavior.

As this book was on its way to press, a historic, capstone women's event occurred: Nancy Pelosi's election as the second most powerful Democrat in the House of Representatives. Her story is, no doubt, partly the story of a woman politician and partly, also, the story of a strategic politician. As such, her triumph captures the unfinished, ongoing story of women transforming Congress—and of Congress transforming the activities of its female members. Taken as a whole, the 17 chapters of this book capture that same developmental sense—that the accomplishments and adjustments of congressional women are very much in flux, and that the scholarly specification of their accomplishments and adjustments remains incomplete. This collection, therefore, comes at a challenging point in time for female members of Congress—and for political science scholars and students as well. For students who want to learn about these important contemporary politicians, *Women Transforming Congress* eminently qualifies as their most reliable primer and their most stimulating guide.

Preface and
Acknowledgments

This volume grew out of the first-ever national research conference focusing exclusively on women and the U.S. Congress. The symposium was convened and hosted by the Carl Albert Congressional Research and Studies Center at the University of Oklahoma in April 2000. The purpose of the conference was to assess the impact that women have had (and might yet achieve) on the U.S. Congress. The conference succeeded beyond our dreams, bringing together a remarkable group of scholars to present new research, to debate the findings, and to explore avenues for future research. Together, congressional and gender scholars from around the country engaged in a stimulating and profitable series of discussions. The conference also assessed the state of research on women and the institution, a topic generally not well developed in the field of legislative studies. A substantial body of research focuses on women's roles in state legislatures; however, much less research has used gender as an analytic lens to understand the U.S. Congress. Indeed, much of the "mainstream" congressional scholarship has neglected the insights to be gained through gender analyses.

One conference event in particular drove home the critical importance of heightening awareness of the contributions of women in Congress. Five former congresswomen, who collectively served 78 years in the U.S.

Congress and who witnessed institutional changes spanning four decades, engaged in a wide-ranging conversation about their experiences. The conversation included Susan Molinari (R-NY), who was elected by her colleagues to the eight-person Republican majority leadership team in 1994, making her the highest-ranking woman in Congress; Cardiss Collins (D-IL), who represented the Seventh District in Chicago for 24 years, a record of tenure that makes her the longest-serving African American woman in the U.S. Congress; Margaret Heckler (R-MA), who served for 16 years and helped found and initially cochair the Congressional Caucus for Women's Issues; Barbara Kennelly (D-CT), who was the first woman to serve on the House Committee on Intelligence, to serve as chief majority whip, and only the third woman in history to serve on the 200-year-old House Ways and Means Committee; and Barbara Vucanovich (R-NV), who served seven terms and became the first Nevadan to be elected to a leadership position in the U.S. House of Representatives when in the 104th Congress she was chosen by her colleagues as House Republican Conference secretary. These women engaged in a roundtable that quickly took on the intimate character of a frank, front-porch chat focused on the bonds of friendship and common experience that brought them together. In spite of their geographic, partisan, ideological, and age differences, they shared the fundamental commitment to women being a part of the U.S. Congress and having a place at the table where issues are discussed.

At the heart of this book is the simple point that being at the table matters. Sharing a commitment to that vision are the scholars who contributed research to this volume. Through its publication, this book moves that discussion to another venue and furthers the Carl Albert Center's commitment to professional scholarly research that improves understanding and appreciation of the quality of representation and the challenges of representative democracy as embodied in the U.S. Congress. Bringing together the research in a thematically coherent way will be, I believe, a significant contribution to scholars, teachers, students, and those interested in the intersection of women's interests, representation, policy making, and the U.S. Congress.

The collective nature of an enterprise such as this produces many rewards and debts. This whole project could not have been successful without many participants who gave generously of their time, energy, and interest to the conference and then provided support and encouragement to see this volume published. In particular, I am indebted to two colleagues at the Carl Albert Center—Gary C. Copeland, the current director and curator of the Center, and Ronald M. Peters, Jr., director and curator of the Center at the time of the conference. Ron Peters continues to provide advice and guidance as the general editor of the University of Oklahoma Press's Congressional Studies Series. Their commitment to the project has been essential and enthusiastic. Others at the Center made invaluable contributions: conference coordinator Julie Raadschelders, archivist Carolyn Hanneman, who assembled the original photos documenting the history of women and the U.S. Congress, and several undergraduate research assistants, including Jennifer Mulhall, Bryan Pepper, and Misty Wetmore. One undergraduate research assistant, Brett Murphy, deserves special recognition for his careful and diligent work on the bibliography and book notes. Martha Garuccio provided invaluable editorial and expert assistance at the crucial stage of bringing the chapters into a coherent and engaging manuscript. She proved to be an insightful reader, a careful and patient editor, and an excellent sounding board. I convey thanks to Catherine Bark, OU Gaylord College of Journalism librarian, for her gracious assistance with last-minute research.

For the illustrations, we are particularly indebted to source material from Foerstal's *Biographical Dictionary of Congressional Women*, Kaptur's *Women in Congress*, Washington's *Outstanding Women Members of Congress*, and Congressional Quarterly's *Politics in America*.

I am grateful to the authors not only for their intellectual contributions and insights but also for their patience, cooperation, and good cheer in the process of revisions. Through their participation in the project—individually and collectively—I have learned a great deal, and I am honored by their association with this book. Less visible to the readers of this final volume but crucially important to me were the contributions of Richard Fenno, Charles Bullock III, Ronald Keith Gaddie, Rick K. Wilson, and Randall Strahan, who served as discussants at the conference and later offered suggestions to revise and strengthen the manuscripts. Two anonymous reviewers for the University of Oklahoma Press offered very helpful suggestions to guide the manuscript toward its final form, and for that I am greatly appreciative.

The University of Oklahoma Press and its staff have provided excellent assistance to this project. Inspiration for the Congressional Studies Series came from Kim Wiar, formerly senior acquisitions editor for the press. Jean

Hurtado, current acquisitions editor for the series, has been an enthusiastic supporter of the project, and Alice Stanton, managing editor, and the production staff have been a source of professionalism and expertise. John Mulvihill proved to be a patient, capable, and attentive copy editor.

I must finally thank my family—Jim, Catie, and Aaron—for their support and patience as this project grew and evolved. Sharing a household with someone who leaves a trail of page proofs and manuscripts, is harried by one deadline after another, and neglects the routines of a well-functioning home requires extra reserves of good cheer. They gave full measure, and I owe them one.

WOMEN TRANSFORMING CONGRESS

CHAPTER ONE

Introduction

CINDY SIMON ROSENTHAL

transform: to change in composition or structure, to change the outward form or appearance of, to change in character or condition, to change in form, nature, or function. Synonyms: TRANSMUTE *a change into a higher element or thing;* CONVERT *a change to a new or different use or function,* TRANSFIGURE *a change that exalts or glorifies.*

A re women transforming the U.S. Congress? Good social science research must be guided by clear definitions and an unambiguous question, and thus this book begins with a question. But perhaps the question is premature and unrealistic. After all, since March 4, 1789, when the first session of the U.S. Congress convened, only 200 women have ever served as members, less than 2 percent of the total number (11,590 persons) who have shouldered that responsibility and had that honor. For the first 128 years, women never graced the halls of the Capitol as members of the national legislature. A highly visible few women may be thought to alter the appearance of an institution, and yet those few can also go largely ignored, unnoticed, or marginalized as different and irrelevant.[1] Indeed in the year 2000, more than 200 years after the convening of the first Congress, the reality of women's underrepresentation still haunted the nine women serving in the U.S. Senate. In a book they wrote together, these women noted one of their key lessons: "Change takes time. As Patty Murray has joked, 'Some pundits still think change in the Senate means brightly colored dresses in a sea of gray suits.' But the true task of passing on the opportunity—of reaching out to the next generation of women so that they can build on your success—is a long, gradual process."[2]

Are women transforming Congress? Perhaps the question is unfair to ask. After all, Senator Rebecca Latimer Felton, the first woman ever to serve in the U.S. Senate, promised on taking the oath of office that future congress-women would bring "integrity of purpose" and "unstinted usefulness," but she served only two days.[3] In the 107th Congress (2001), women made up only 13.6 percent of the House membership and only 13 percent of the Senate. The U.S. Congress's traditions and norms of seniority and apprentice-ship endow leaders and committee chairs with additional powers. Women hold an even smaller share of these positions. Before 2002, no woman ever successfully held one of the top three party leadership positions in either house, and only a dozen women (10 in the House and 2 in the Senate) ever chaired full committees.[4] What impact could so few (often serving so briefly) have on the character, practices, and policy decisions of an institution?

Are women transforming Congress? Perhaps the question is ill-conceived. After all, women's lives, concerns, and interests are complex, not mono-lithic or unidimensional. The rich diversity of women's experiences and interests certainly cannot be represented easily by so few. On one level, one woman in Congress may be said to represent all women citizens. In that sense, to transform a representative body might be readily accomplished only if what is represented is simple, categorical, and straightforward. Polit-ical theorist Hanna Pitkin asserts, however, that political representation "means acting in the interest of the represented, in a manner responsive to them."[5] Can 60 House members or 13 U.S. senators truly be said to repre-sent—to act for the political interests of—nearly 143 million American women? Alternatively, do the men in Congress serve women's substantive interests? A transformation might, in one sense, be accomplished only if all women feel their interests are adequately represented.

We assert in this book that the question is not premature, unrealistic, unfair, or ill-conceived. When we ask, Are women transforming Congress? we learn something new about one of the most studied and analyzed insti-tutions of lawmaking and political representation. Using gender as a lens of analysis, we learn not only about women and their experiences but also about the extent to which gender defines political institutions and shapes their norms, behaviors, and history.[6] Using gender as the basis for an analytic appraisal of Congress reveals clearly the gendered dimensions of this foremost legislative body. As many have argued, political institutions have largely been constructed by men, often to serve men's interests. The U.S. Congress is no different.

Using gender to analyze congressional life, this volume attempts to marshal new insights about the U.S. Congress and the men and women who serve in it. But before examining the evidence, some review of the literature on women in legislatures is not only useful but also helpful to distinguish the particular contributions offered by this collection.

WOMEN IN LEGISLATURES

It has been assumed that an increase in the descriptive representation of women contributes to an increase in the substantive representation of women. Scholars have sought to prove that assumption by exploring empirical evidence from the 50 state legislatures and the U.S. Congress. Political theorist Mary Hawkesworth argues that because men and women come from different backgrounds, a legislature with equal proportions of men and women will expand the character and content of legislative debate.[7] Barbara Burrell adds that women's presence in a legislative body is likely to change what issues rise to the level of political question, since men do not encounter the same life experiences as women and may never think to propose certain laws or policies.[8] Members of Congress themselves suggest that legislative outcomes would differ substantially if the composition of the membership were altered. In the 1977 House floor debate on the Hyde Amendment, Elizabeth Holtzman (D-NY) asserted precisely this point: "Mr. Chairman, someone once said that if the membership of this House were different, this decision would not even be before us today. I think that this is very true. After listening to the debate, I would say that if there were 417 women in this House instead of 417 men, and if there were 18 men instead of 18 women in this House, that we would not be faced with this amendment today."[9]

There are a number of reasons to assume that female legislators will support and raise women's policy concerns in legislative forums. As women, female legislators may have themselves experienced the problems that their legislation seeks to ameliorate. Representative Margaret Heckler (R-MA), author of the Equal Credit Opportunity Act of 1974, recalled the motivation for her own legislative initiatives to curb economic discrimination against women:

> All of us have our own stories. . . . I was the only woman in my law school class and when I looked for a job in Boston, although I was honored on the Law Review, I couldn't even get an interview. These were in the very early days of professional women in our society. I experienced that discrimination, which was a searing experience and absolutely unforgettable. . . . There was a time when, regardless of their income, women could not use that income to obtain a home mortgage. I introduced a bill that banned discrimination based upon marital status or gender for granting home mortgages. . . . We had clear needs in those days—we had to get the right to credit. Imagine not being able to have credit in your own name.[10]

Women in office may believe they have a responsibility to rectify the historic inattention to women's interests by policy makers. Their conception of their role may include a particular commitment to representing women in their own district or American women more generally. For example, female legislators who have survived breast and ovarian cancer report a special commitment to women's health issues.[11] Representative Barbara Vucanovich (R-NV) recalls that

> many of us had to be role models for other women, but we also had to speak up in committees and on the floor. . . . I'm a breast cancer survivor, but before I had cancer, I really didn't pay much attention to it. But Cardiss [Collins, D-IL] was ahead of me and introduced legislation to cover mammograms for women aged sixty-five. What a fight! I remember Bill Natcher [D-KY], one of the most gracious, charming men that I ever knew, but he just simply couldn't understand. He was Chairman of the Appropriations Committee, and he just couldn't believe that this was something we needed.[12]

Similarly, former representative Marjorie Margolies-Mezvinsky (D-PA) explains that "it is because of our own experiences, and those of our mothers, sisters, daughters, and granddaughters, that we have a vested interest in the outcome of gender-specific issues. Only a woman can viscerally know the nightmarish connotations that accompany the word *mastectomy*; only a woman can truly imagine the very personal ramifications of not having the legal right to make her own reproductive choices."[13]

Counterbalancing the reasons why women legislators might be advocates of women's issues are considerations that might temper the activism of women officeholders. For example, female legislators may have reasons to avoid women's rights issues and minimize differences that would thwart their efforts to fit into established norms. To be sure, both men and women vary in their enthusiasm for women's rights policies, and not all women embrace such issues as abortion rights and the ERA.[14] Jeane Kirkpatrick notes that some pioneering political women in the 1970s intentionally stayed away from women's rights policies in order to avoid controversy.[15] Nonetheless, some women legislators, identified by Debra Dodson, who initially avoided women's issues for fear of being stereotyped, later acknowledged the necessity of their own advocacy.[16]

Given competing speculations about the policy interests of women legislators and moving beyond anecdotal evidence,[17] many scholars have attempted to assess more rigorously whether women legislators differ from their male colleagues. One line of congressional studies has explored whether women are generally more liberal than their male colleagues in terms of roll-call voting behavior; the results are clearly mixed.[18] Sex of the member does predict a significant association with voting for specific women's issues such as abortion or family and children's issues.[19] Previous roll-call voting research found that female lawmakers at both the state and national level are more supportive of feminist public policies.[20] Partisanship, however, also influences roll-call voting, with Democrats more clearly associated with feminist public policy since the 1970s.[21] Gender divisions over support for feminist legislation and women's policy concerns remain significant within the parties, though some studies report only small or insignificant differences between levels of support from Democratic men and Republican women.[22] Nonetheless, analyses of roll-call voting only scratch the surface of how gender shapes legislative participation. As political scientist Richard Hall notes, the intensity of a legislator's position or preferences can be understood only by seeing how members of Congress dedicate their time.[23]

Women in Congress are distinguished by their willingness to invest additional time on behalf of feminist legislation. Karin Tamerius finds that women are much more likely than men to make a greater investment in activities (e.g., cosponsorship, floor speeches, and sponsorship) that require more time and commitment than roll-call voting—the more the investment of time required, the greater the difference between men and women.[24] The Center for American Women and Politics (CAWP) has developed detailed legislative histories of a series of issues in the 103rd and 104th Congresses, which demonstrate that women were instrumental in the passage of several women's issue bills, including the Freedom of Access to Abortion Clinic Entrances Act and the Violence Against Women Act.[25]

Prior to the data accumulated in this volume, the strongest evidence of policy differences and impact by women legislators came from investigations of state legislatures, where women are more numerous. Sue Thomas and other scholars show that on issues dealing with women, children, and families, women legislators are likely to introduce more bills, to identify those bills as priorities, and to achieve a higher rate of passage of those priority bills.[26] The state research suggests that variation in the participation of women across legislatures is explained by whether the number of women in the legislature approaches a *critical mass* and whether the legislature has a women's caucus.[27]

If the evidence regarding policy impact has been at least suggestive of women's impact on legislative agendas, evidence of women's influence in changing norms of behavior is sketchier. Some scholars have focused on legislators' orientations to and exercise of power. Many feminist theorists have argued that women officeholders are more likely to embrace strategies of empowerment rather than power as dominance over others.[28] Again the little empirical work that has been done focuses on women in state legislatures. Beth Reingold, examining male and female legislators in Arizona and California, finds few sex differences in power strategies and concludes that both men and women claim to practice "power to" politics.[29] Based on survey research, committee observations, focus groups, and interviews, my own research suggests that women as committee chairs are likely to use their leadership roles differently than their male colleagues, though institutional norms encourage men and women to conform to many similar strategies. Women chairs are more likely to be motivated by a desire to involve people in legislative deliberations, to use committee management practices that are inclusive of others, to report a preference for more collaborative and accommodative conflict resolution styles, to be less comfortable with competitive or dominating leadership styles, and to demonstrate greater patience and better listening skills needed to work out differences of opinion.[30] State legislative scholars Malcolm Jewell and Marcia Whicker have found a male proclivity to command styles and a female proclivity to consensus style, with most legislative leaders embracing what Jewell and Whicker call a coordinating style.[31]

Other empirical studies of legislative behavior suggest other differences. Lyn Kathlene's innovative study of discourse in the Colorado legislature reveals gendered patterns of speaking behavior—men talk first, talk longer, take more speaking turns, and interrupt others four times more often.[32] By contrast, women use their fewer turns to be more facilitating. Analyzing U.S. Senate committee hearings, Laura Winsky-Mattei finds that women as witnesses encounter greater hostility, are cut off more often by male members, and are accorded less credibility.[33] Other behavioral differences in legislatures have been noted in terms of speeches on the floor, approaches to thinking about political issues and problems, and strategic use of committee position to block pro-life legislation.[34] Recently, scholars have explored whether or not the presence of women changes the behavior of men in legislatures. Based on a content analysis of the House floor debates on the Hyde Amendment from 1974 through 1997, Dena Levy and colleagues find that women have altered the terms of debate and influenced the way men talk about abortion.[35]

LIMITATIONS OF PREVIOUS RESEARCH

Against this background, this volume attempts to extend our understanding of gender in legislative institutions. In several ways we attempt to overcome the limitations of previous research. First, until recently the numbers of women lawmakers have led scholars to focus more on the states than on the U.S. Congress as a venue of study. As Georgia Duerst-Lahti argues effectively in her chapter, gender has simply not been a part of "the realm of debatable topics" considered by legislative, and particularly congressional, scholars. We rectify this neglect and engage the field of congressional studies in all of its aspects—normative, interpretive, and empirical.

Second, for the most part, previous research has concentrated on women in office after the late 1960s, what Barbara Burrell has called the "feminist era."[36] The focus on the feminist era coincided with a surge in the number of female political scientists and female political officeholders, the impact of feminism on the social sciences, and a new interest in questions relating to women and politics. In the case of Congress, women of the earlier period entered office via widow's succession and were assumed to be controlled by their husband's advisers and to lack a legislative agenda of their own.[37] While the focus on the feminist era offered important insights, gender has always been present in congressional operations. Thus, we attempt to take as long a view as possible in these investigations.

Third, most scholarship has emphasized women officeholders, which tends to render a less than complete picture of women in their interactions with Congress. Clearly, to understand fully the gendered dimensions of the U.S. Congress, it is essential to look beyond the individual members to consider the contributions of congressional staff, interest groups, media, policy advocates, and voters. Thus in this volume, we seek to understand the impact of gender as a societal construct that informs interest group dynamics, social movements, and voters as well as institutional actors, both elected and nonelected.

Fourth, and perhaps substantively most important, the earlier research also focused on the discovery of differences between men and women and tended to neglect the importance of institutional norms and dynamics that shaped behavior of both men and women.[38] As political scientist Sally Kenney points out, "To say that an institution is gendered, then, is to recognize that constructions of masculinity and femininity are intertwined in the daily culture of an institution rather than existing out in society or fixed within individuals which they then bring whole to the institution."[39]

As Duerst-Lahti notes, gender analysis exposes how structures, practices, and institutional history produce an ethos about men and women and masculinity and femininity in institutions that operates in both conscious and nonconscious ways. Examination of gendered institutions draws attention to the fact that individuals often conform to norms and behaviors in spite of their predilections or predispositions. Eschewing differences but acknowledging institutional norms is implicit in the sentiment expressed by U.S. Senator Barbara Mikulski: "I didn't want to be one of the boys. I *did* want to be one of the gang."[40] The power of institutional norms is also implicit in the silence heard from congressional colleagues of U.S. Representative Pat Schroeder (D-CO) and Representative Ron Dellums (D-CA) as the two suffered the indignity of sharing a single chair ("cheek to cheek") on the Armed Services Committee as Chairman F. Edward Hebert (D-LA) expressed his disapproval of "a girl and a black" being named to his committee.[41] The story confirms not only the formal power of committee chairs but also underscores the institutionalized behaviors—acquiescence and conformity—that allow organizations to resist change that might otherwise result from demographic transformations.

REEXAMINING CONGRESS AS A GENDERED INSTITUTION

What then do we learn by using gender as a lens of analysis to understand the institution of the U.S. Congress? How do those insights help to answer the question of transformation of our national lawmaking institution? First and foremost, our analysis exposes new insights about the U.S. Congress as a gendered institution.

What is revealed by extending our focus on women's interactions with the Congress beyond the "feminist" era? In general, these chapters provide a two-part answer—both yes and no—to the initial question: Are women transforming the U.S. Congress? In the affirmative, these chapters illustrate that women, though few in number and relatively new to positions of institutional power, are transforming our understanding of the nature of representation and are dramatically reshaping the agenda and the representation of interests in Congress. In the negative, however, the evidence of institutional change as a result of increased participation by women is far more cautionary. One cannot, as yet, conclude that women have converted Congress into a different form. Significant change in the gendered structure, the fundamental norms and practices, and established assumptions about legislatures and legislative behavior has not happened. As this volume shows, the transformation has occurred mainly in the processes of representation, but not in the basic institution or its traditions. More specifically, the following five major themes emerge from this volume.

Gender Analysis and Congress

Perhaps most importantly, gender as a lens of analysis tells much about the U.S. Congress and offers new ways to approach legislative studies. First, Georgia Duerst-Lahti points out that political science has failed to provide the necessary language to identify gender as an ideology at work in legislative institutions. In her chapter, Duerst-Lahti attempts to rectify the inadequacies of language and provide vocabulary with which to speak about gender as ideology. Rather than accepting that only feminist women operate under the influence of gender ideology, she advocates naming gender as a proto-ideology and delineates a spectrum of conservative to liberal forms of *masculinism* and *feminalism*. Most importantly, Duerst-Lahti demonstrates and explains the ideological premises of masculinity that influenced designers of institutions of American democracy, especially the U.S. Congress. Her insight into this institutional history reveals gendered aspects of representation woven into the founding design of our national legislature.

Gender and the Nature of Representation

Second, we learn something about the nature of representation. In chapter 3, Susan Carroll presents empirical evidence of what political theorist Jane Mansbridge calls *surrogate representation*. Carroll draws from 77 in-depth interviews with women members of the 103rd and 104th Congresses and argues that women members feel a special responsibility to represent women beyond the geographic boundaries of their districts. One striking aspect of Carroll's research is the near unanimity, even across party lines, with which women members of Congress express this obligation and sense of duty to represent all women.

Cindy Simon Rosenthal and Lauren Cohen Bell expand the discussion beyond the elected members by looking at the demographics and positional power of congressional staff. Their analysis broadens the picture of representation in Congress quite compellingly when they show that underlying the relatively few visible female members of Congress exists a formidable presence of women as staff. In Congress as in other gendered workplaces, however, women staff tend to concentrate in certain issue areas and consequently are generally underrepresented on staffs of committees or subcommittees unless there is a woman staff director. Perhaps most important, Rosenthal and Bell show how under the right circumstances and when interest groups demand, committee staffers may be called on to "stand in" for their bosses and engage in substantive representation of women's interests in policy deliberations. In the modern professional legislature, representation is not unmediated; staff clearly play representational roles.

The Power of Institutional Norms

Third, this volume provides important evidence of how members operate in the crosshairs of powerful institutional norms to conform, even while their individual backgrounds and goals may offer the possibility of transformation. For example, the long view of women representatives from 1916 to the present reveals the important emergence of congresswomen as strategic politicians. Irwin Gertzog demonstrates how women who present themselves for election and win campaigns to the U.S. Congress are politically experienced, skillful and resourceful, and rational in their office-seeking calculations. Most prominent among the women who have emerged as strategic politicians are African American women. The hegemonic model that emerges from Gertzog's chapter is one of a congressional career where ambitious professionals and, especially, women are fitting into and being transformed by institutional norms rather than the reverse.

On the campaign trail, a much more complicated story of transformation and congressional norms is apparent from Dianne Bystrom and Lynda Lee Kaid's analysis of political campaign communication. Looking at television advertisements of U.S. Senate races during the 1990s, they find shifts in the behavior of men to embrace more feminine issues and videostyles. Both men and women appear to be balancing masculine and feminine messages, images, and verbal and nonverbal strategies in their campaign appeals. Of note, however, women running in U.S. Senate races were more likely than men to use negative attacks throughout the 1990s. In effect, Bystrom and Kaid show how pressures of gender transformation work on men to soften their video styles and work on women to compete on traditional masculine terms.

In committee settings, the story of transformation is also a complex one, confirming powerful institutional norms as well as individual opportunities. Laura Arnold and Barbara King provide a well-nuanced analysis of the fate of the women who entered the U.S. Senate in 1992—the so-called Year of the Woman. Arnold and King show how the aftermath of the Thomas-Hill spectacle created opportunities for women to move more quickly into prestigious committee assignments. As a result, the 1990s were distinguished by the presence of women on almost all Senate committees and in some leadership roles on subcommittees. Arnold and King carefully analyze committee appointments in subsequent years, however, and reveal the reemergence of traditional Senate appointment processes in which seniority prevails over consciousness of the need for diversity in committee representation.

In her study of House committees, Noelle Norton exhibits the potential for policy transformation when the demographic makeup of committee leadership changes only incrementally. Her analysis underscores this well-established institutional lesson: committee position matters. By examining reproductive policies from 1969 to 1998, Norton traces the impact that relatively small numbers of women with increasing committee seniority and leadership roles had on these policies. Adding an analysis of welfare reform legislation in the 104th Congress, Norton shows how women inside House and Senate committees were instrumental in advancing child care and child support enforcement provisions as part of welfare reform. The caveat to this transformation is that pivotal committee roles in the rest of Congress remain principally the domain of men and will continue so given the excruciatingly slow incremental rate of change in descriptive representation in the institution.

Gender Influences on Congressional Policy Making

Fourth, this volume offers substantial evidence of the dramatic contributions of women in reshaping the congressional agenda. Christina Wolbrecht offers powerful analysis of women's rights legislation both before and after the second wave women's movement of the 1970s. As she considers more than 1,700 women's rights bills between 1953 and 1992, she shows how the contours of the agenda changed over this 40-year period. More importantly, she illustrates the extent to which men and women members of Congress have participated in shaping that agenda and in contributing new ideas or policy solutions to the agenda. Women are central to these agenda changes and to the introduction of new initiatives.

Similarly, Michele Swers's chapter explores gender dynamics in congressional agenda-setting. Swers examines bill sponsorship in the U.S. House before and after the dramatic reversal of party fortunes between the 103rd and 104th Congresses. In looking at the last Congress of Democratic party control and the first Congress of Republican party dominance in the 1990s, Swers asks whether a shift in majority and minority party status affects a member's willingness to expend political capital on the pursuit of women's issue legislation. She finds evidence that the contributions of both men and women House members to the congressional agenda track with rational calculations driven by party status. Nonetheless, the tendency of congresswomen to take the lead on women's issue bills endures, suggesting that gender cannot be dismissed with the assumptions of universality that rational choice theory demands.

Gender analysis of floor debate reveals the importance of women's voices to changing the content of policy discourse. Katherine Cramer Walsh argues that women are transforming congressional debate by enlarging the range of perspectives represented. Specifically, her content analysis of four floor debates in the 104th Congress points to important differences in the content and framing of policy issues and demonstrates how women members of Congress speak more often on behalf of underrepresented groups. While floor debate is seldom decisive in persuading members of Congress in their final vote decision, floor debate can serve as a highly visible link between descriptive and substantive representation. Walsh's analysis offers clear evidence of difference in legislative behavior by men and women.

While policy making depends on the activities of members of Congress during bill introduction, the role of interest groups also appears to hold gendered significance. By analyzing media advocacy strategies of prostate and breast cancer groups, Karen Kedrowski and Marilyn Stine Sarow trace how breast cancer groups paved the way for increased congressional funding and attention to breast cancer research and treatment. This analysis clearly shows the dramatic effect interest groups have on congressional decision making. More meaningful is that Kedrowski and Sarow demonstrate how breast cancer groups brought a formerly private issue to the arena of policy discourse. Furthermore, prostate cancer patients, whose interest groups were less well organized and visible than breast cancer groups, were significant beneficiaries of women's activism. In a gender significant example of the classic logroll of congressional politics, breast cancer activism in Congress resulted in equal opportunity policies for both cancers.

Also looking at media coverage and women's interest groups, Anne Costain and Heather Fraizer examine how the second wave of the women's movement transformed into a community of interest groups increasingly focused on the institutions of the U.S. Congress and the presidency. Congress's policy concerns most closely reflect those interest groups' priorities during this transitional period. Costain and Fraizer's analysis offers the striking discovery that protest and tactics of violence—often discarded by the leaders of social movements as they become more established actors within the policy process—continue to plague the climate around women's interest groups. The reason, Costain and Fraizer discover, is that the women's groups are targets, not perpetrators, of protest and violent tactics.

Barriers to Future Gender Transformation

In sum, we might conclude from the research in this volume that women are transforming the composition or outward form and appearance of the U.S. Congress. Clearly, they are also changing the form and character of its primary output of substantive representation, which is public policy. Women are present in the institution in a myriad of roles: they are participating, they are on all of the Senate committees, they are sources of ideas and policy proposals as active members and as staff, they are on the floor and in committee, and they are engaged in debate. But the institution and its norms remain powerful bulwarks against change. Policy has been transformed, but the necessary re-forming of the structure, function, and nature of the institution remains on the horizon. How far distant is the promise or possibility of institutional change? Clearly, some aspects of institutional change will not occur until more women take their place as members of the U.S. Congress.

What are some of the barriers to a more dramatic shift in the social demography of the Congress? Four chapters in this book offer a glimpse of the potential in the future. Richard Matland and David King's analysis of congressional elections and voters' responses to women candidates under controlled experimental conditions reveals a significant barrier for women running on the Republican party ballot. Even when offered identical candidate profiles that vary only in the sex of the candidate, Republican voters attribute more liberal leanings to women candidates. Bolstered by Matland and King's analysis of primary and general elections in the post–World War II period, this simple attribution helps explain why Republican women have faced a formidable barrier in securing primary election nominations in recent years.

Sue Thomas, Rebekah Herrick, and Matthew Braunstein identify another critical barrier to a more gender-balanced Congress. Drawing on surveys of state legislators, which is the largest single recruitment arena for future congressional members, and of former U.S. representatives, Thomas, Herrick, and Braunstein illustrate the extent to which men envision political careers at an earlier age while women face substantially greater duties of family and household that make political office-seeking difficult. This analysis suggests that family and societal norms continue to limit the pool of female candidates who might alter more significantly the representative face of the U.S. Congress.

Looking abroad for a comparative perspective, Joyce Gelb examines the recent influx of women in the British House of Commons. Gelb asks what conditions gave rise to the dramatic transformation in the House of Commons membership and whether such an abrupt change in descriptive representation can be envisioned for the U.S. Congress? Arguably, the House of Commons is as institutionally masculine, if not more so, than the U.S. Congress—after all, the House of Commons has a shooting range but no child care unit. While tracing the fascinating story of gender representation in the House of Commons, Gelb underscores the fundamental importance of institutional rules and party processes in producing representation. The institutional conditions of elections and parties that might lead to a similar transformation of social demography in the U.S. Congress are clearly not present, nor do they appear on the immediate horizon.

Finally, Cindy Simon Rosenthal speculates on the impact that women in congressional leadership might have on the future. While Representative Nancy Pelosi (D-CA) made history in 2002 by becoming the first woman elected as party whip and thus breaking into the top ranks of congressional leadership, the prospects for institutional transformation through leadership are clouded. Rosenthal argues that leadership influence is constrained by a congressional system that still values the norm of seniority. The harsh reality is that transforming Congress will require *both* a critical mass of like-minded congresswomen *and* senior women in key committee and leadership roles.

In the end, this is a cautionary tale about a very important institution, the U.S. Congress, and how it represents all the U.S. population. Through gender analysis of the U.S. Congress, much can be learned about its history, members, other actors, various constituencies, and future. Old lessons can be interpreted with new meanings and possibilities. The hope is that this volume is the beginning, rather than the end, provoking new research that employs the rich perspective and revealing lens of gender analysis.

NOTES

1. Kanter, *Men and Women of the Corporation*.

2. Mikulski et al., *Nine and Counting*, 190.

3. Karen Foerstel, *Biographical Dictionary of Congressional Women*, 88.

4. Ibid., 2.

5. Pitkin, *Concept of Representation*, 209.

6. Duerst-Lahti and Kelly, *Gender Power, Leadership, and Governance*, ch. 1.

7. Hawkesworth, *Beyond Oppression*, 184.

8. Burrell, *Woman's Place*, 7.

9. *Congressional Record*, 17 June 1977, 19708.

10. Roundtable discussion, "Reflections on Congressional Life," Women Transforming Congress conference, Norman, Oklahoma, 14 April 2000.

11. Dodson, "Representing Women's Interests."

12. Roundtable discussion, "Women and Reflections on Congressional Life," *Extensions*, spring 2000, 6.

13. Margolies-Mezvinsky and Feinman, *Woman's Place: The Freshmen Women*, 90.

14. Klatch, *Women of the New Right*.

15. Kirkpatrick, *Political Woman*.

16. Dodson, "Representing Women's Interests."

17. Other memoirs and insider accounts of congressional activities include Margolies-Mezvinsky with Feinman, *Woman's Place: The Freshmen Women*; Boxer, *Strangers in the Senate*; Dodson et al., *Voices, Views, Votes*; Gertzog, *Congressional Women*, 2nd ed.; Foerstel and Foerstel, *Climbing the Hill*; and Bingham, *Women on the Hill*.

18. Leader, "Policy Impact of Elected Women Officials," 265–84; Gehlen, "Women Members of Congress," 304–19; Frankovic, "Sex and Voting in the U.S. House"; Welch, "Are Women More Liberal Than Men"; Burrell, *Woman's Place*, ch. 8; McCarty, Poole, and H. Rosenthal, "Income Redistribution and National Politics."

19. Tatalovich and Schier, "Persistence of Ideological Cleavage," 125–39; Burrell, *Woman's Place*, ch. 8; Swers, "Are Women More Likely to Vote for Women's Issue Bills?"

20. Swers, "Are Women More Likely to Vote for Women's Issue Bills?"; Burrell, *Woman's Place*, ch. 8; Leader, "Policy Impact of Elected Women Officials"; Poole and Zeigler, *Women, Public Opinion, and Politics*; Saint-Germain, "Does Their Difference Make a Difference?"

21. Gertzog, *Congressional Women*, 2nd ed.; Wolbrecht, *Politics of Women's Rights*.

22. Thomas, "Voting Patterns"; David Hill, "Women State Legislators"; Leader, "Policy Impact of Elected Women Officials"; Swers, "Are Women More Likely to Vote for Women's Issue Bills?"

23. Richard Hall, *Participation in Congress*.

24. Tamerius, "Sex, Gender, and Leadership."

25. Dodson et al., *Voices, Views, Votes*.

26. Thomas, *How Women Legislate*; Dodson and Carroll, *Reshaping the Agenda*; Saint-Germain, "Does Their Difference Make a Difference?"

27. Saint-Germain, "Does Their Difference Make a Difference?"; Thomas, *How Women Legislate*.

28. See, for example, Ruddick's *Maternal Thinking* for an explanation that women's maternal roles shape a worldview distinct from that of men, or Deutchman's "Feminist Theory and the Politics of Empowerment" for an argument that women as traditional outsiders are more likely to define power as empowerment.

29. Reingold, *Representing Women*. Reingold's work affirms earlier work by Diane Blair and Jeanie Stanley, "Personal Relationships and Legislative Power."

30. C. Rosenthal, *When Women Lead*.

31. Jewell and Whicker, *Legislative Leadership*.

32. Kathlene, "Power and Influence in State Legislative Policymaking"; Kathlene, "Position Power vs Gender Power."

33. Winsky-Mattei, "Gender and Power in American Legislative Discourse."

34. Tamerius, "Sex, Gender, and Leadership"; Kathlene, "Position Power vs Gender Power"; Berkman and O'Connor, "Do Women Legislators Matter?"

35. See Levy, Tien, and Aved, "Do Differences Matter?" whose research confirms similar shifts in use of language and discourse. For example, O'Connor and Segal examined Supreme Court Justice O'Connor's impact on her male colleagues in sex discrimination cases, while Fox, *Gender Dynamics in Congressional Elections*, investigated the effect of women in campaigns on the behavior of their male challengers.

36. Burrell, *Woman's Place*.

37. Gertzog, *Congressional Women*, 2nd ed.; Gertzog, "Matrimonial Connection"; Werner, "Women in Congress: 1917–1964"; Frankovic, "Sex and Voting in the U.S. House"; Gehlen, "Women Members of Congress"; Gehlen, "Legislative Role Performance of Female Legislators."

38. Exceptions to this claim include work by Duerst-Lahti and Kelly, Rosenthal, Kathlene, and others who tend to explore the constraints imposed on individual actors by norms of masculinity.

39. Kenney, "Field Essay: New Research."

40. Mikulski et al., *Nine and Counting*, 115.

41. Pat Schroeder, *24 Years of House Work*, ch. 2.

CHAPTER TWO

KNOWING CONGRESS AS A
GENDERED INSTITUTION

Manliness and the Implications of Women in Congress

GEORGIA DUERST-LAHTI

ender as a subject of inquiry has tended to constitute more of an enclave within the subfield of legislative studies rather than being a widely acknowledged and accepted dimension for all to know. As evidenced by programs at political science meetings and a perusal of the writings of top legislative scholars, gender research is segregated into the research area of women and politics rather than integrated into research on Congress and legislatures.[1] My main argument in this chapter asserts that gender analysis should be part of institutional analysis of legislatures. The reasons are several: Gender is more than sex difference and includes men and masculinity as well as women. Gender incorporates socially induced practices performed by individuals, and these practices become part of institutions precisely because institutions have been constructed by individuals over time. Gender also has normative dimensions and functions at a protoideological level, with masculinism proving potent in most public institutions.[2]

A lack of awareness about gender, whether masculine dominance or the presence of women, has been the largely unquestioned norm in congressional scholarship. For example, in looking at texts on Congress written by 12 top scholars prior to 1990 I found no mention of topics critical to gender, such as women and representation, democracy, power, even member characteristics, although occasionally women members receive a paragraph, or women's suffrage a sentence. For example, Congressional Quarterly's Origins and Development of Congress (1976) never mentions male hegemony of the membership, women, the 19th Amendment, or Jeannette Rankin. George Galloway's History of the House of Representatives (1976) offers a mere paragraph about the handful of women who served up to that time. None cover men or masculinity in gendered terms either. This absence of focus on gender goes without question and thereby shapes scholarly knowledge, which is a critical point.

Barbara Hinckley's Stability and Change in Congress offers one modest exception, when she notices women in analytic ways, such as "something screens women out" as candidates.[3] In The New Politics of Congress (1974), Thomas P. Murphy offers a good example of early gender analysis. He details the women who have entered Congress, investigates the implications of the women's caucus, and locates women's institutional power possibilities within congressional structures such as the Democratic Study Group.

Since 1990, scholarly books outside the women and politics enclave show the slow addition of women into congressional study, although none has yet moved to gender analysis, especially analysis beyond simple sex difference approaches. The long-running mainstay text by Lawrence Dodd and Bruce Oppenheimer, Congress Reconsidered (1977 to 2001), did not add a chapter on women and blacks until the sixth edition in 1997. Similarly, in a study of U.S. House elections from 1946 to 1986, Gary Jacobson gives two pages to the "Year of the Woman" but misses the gendered implications for the 1992 election and the "angry white males" of the 1994 election. In The Dysfunctional Congress? (1999), Kenneth Mayer and David Canon offer a few sections related to descriptive representation, but turn to race rather than gender. Interestingly, they could not have pursued their line of reasoning about the collective dilemma and the link between descriptive and substantive representation had they used gender instead of race. First, they rely on the Supreme Court's opinion in Shaw v. Reno and the creation of black-majority districts. The Court has never taken up a case concerning the underrepresentation of women in the drawing of districts. Such would be unlikely because women are a numerical majority in most districts. Second, because women are the majority, to pursue "their" interests would presumably be to pursue the majority interest and hence should produce a centralizing force in Congress as well as an electoral advantage for individual female candidates. As many chapters in this volume detail, women's interests have generally been marked as distinct from majority interests and so do not function fully by the commonly used collective logic despite women's majority status. More than sheer numbers create the "collective" in the collective dilemma. Most important, women are woefully numerically underrepresented in Congress. Had the authors used gender, men's self-interest in maintaining a near monopoly on congressional posts would have immediately become apparent. Further, they do not consider the extent to which men must represent the substance of women's interests, and the converse, as an antidote to the problem of the collective dilemma, much to my point here about the need for gender analysis.[4]

In one of the best developments, Paul Herrnson systematically includes female candidates in *Congressional Elections*, although he is only beginning to incorporate the burgeoning literature on gendered strategies in messages and advertising. While these texts constitute progress, many other texts on Congress remain devoid of any gender analysis. In one telling measure, from 1990 to 1998, only 8 of 233, or 3.4 percent, of all articles in the journal *Legislative Studies Quarterly* dealt with women or gender. To draw from Mary Fainsod Katzenstein's award-winning study of institutional change, part of what defines collectivities "is agreement on what requires debate."[5] To the extent legislative scholars constitute a collectivity, they have not yet agreed to debate gender.

My purpose is to put gender analysis into the realm of debatable topics because it is relevant to political institutions, perhaps especially Congress. I will argue for a renewed embrace of institutional analysis rooted in organization theory, a once vital tradition that has been overshadowed by formal theory, rational choice, and game theoretic approaches.[6] While Michele Swers's chapter in this volume shows how rational choice theory can be linked to gender analysis, the dominance of these approaches in political science squeezes out questions not answerable from their methods. Particularly problematic is the use of the "representative individual" whose demographic characteristics, social statuses, and cultural orientations are deemed irrelevant because only a singular rationality exists.[7] Further, the ahistorical orientation of most "rational" new institutions analysis renders past constructions mere artifacts of the present institutions. Historical aspects also require more attention.

FROM GENDER DIFFERENCES TO GENDERED ORGANIZATION THEORY TO GENDERING NEW INSTITUTIONS

Although the work of Nancy Chodorow, Carol Gilligan, Nancy Hartsock, and other feminist scholars is intended to explain, describe, and interpret gender difference, they all begin from the premise that such differences result from social structures, socialization, normative gender strictures, and life experiences rather than biological imperatives.[8] Separate spheres are not necessary. To the extent that differences matter (even if entirely socially determined), they serve as a foundation for beliefs about gender that become implicated in gender ideology.[9] In turn, these gender differences inform alternative approaches to organization, including the organization of Congress.

An extensive literature has mapped out many points upon which gender differences occur. Table 2.1 lists several of the sex-gender differences attributed to the masculine and the feminine and associated with judgments about human nature and the ideal distribution of power and resources. These differences have been extracted from many germinal studies of gender, and they can be understood as some of the differences in gender preferences that help construct ideological perspectives.

TABLE 2.1

Proto Attributed Gender Differences

MASCULINE	FEMININE
Individuation	Connection
Instrumental	Contextual
Rule focused	Relationship focused
Dominate	Collaborate
Power over	Power to
Competition	Cooperation
Hierarchy	Web-Center
Speak out	Listen well
Public sphere	Home sphere
Breadwinning	Caregiving

One would be hard-pressed to overstate the influence of Chodorow and her observation that men tend to individuate and women tend to connect. Said another way, males create stronger ego boundaries in order to be masculine, while females have reason to develop more permeable ego boundaries and to value relationships to others more. Men, then, generally try to get themselves noticed by separating through speaking out and standing out, women by building relationships, attending closely, and integrating well. Many attributes related to Chodorow's conclusions also have been developed by Gilligan. These include men's instrumentality, which is contrasted to women's propensity to contextualize information and problems, and men's faith in and adherence to rules in contrast to women's view that rules have relative value in each particular circumstance. Further, the work of Hartsock focuses on men's concept of power as "domination and control over." As a result, women must contend with men's propensity to organize hierarchically and always compete for position within the hierarchy. A single leader commands from the top. In contrast, women are more likely to view power as a capacity that enables—power to do some desired end. The organization that follows is a web of connections that links everyone involved cooperatively. The leader may shift depending on function, although leaders become communication hubs coordinating from the center. Men assume dominance is at stake; women assume cooperation can follow. These differences both create and derive from the long-standing judgment that men supposedly should occupy the public sphere of politics and commerce while women tend the home fires and care for children. Men become breadwinners, women become caregivers—because they are believed to be better suited to separate spheres. When women cross into the public sphere, beliefs about sex-gender differences tend to accompany them.

These assumed gender differences can be found in alternative perspectives on "proper" organization proffered by Frederick Taylor and by Mary Parker Follett, contemporaries but not collaborators throughout much of the first half of the 20th century.[10] Frederick Taylor's highly influential "scientific management" and Mary Parker Follett's "art of management" approach contributed intellectual orientations to very different perspectives on organization theory. In brief, Taylor made famous the "triangle," a hierarchical, rational, adversarial command approach, while Follett espoused the "web," a flexible, creative, collaborative wholeness approach. The com-

TABLE 2.2

Gendered Organization Theorists: Taylor and Follett Compared

Image	Triangle with Taylor at apex	Web of human relations
Basis	Science	Art
Values	Rationality, productivity, efficiency	Creativity, productivity, efficiency
Centers on	Work at hand	The worker as person
Organizational Orientations	Top down command and control Standardization Centralized authority Hierarchical structure	Nature of work dictates the process Flexibility Wholeness Interpersonal relations
Management/ labor relations	Adversarial Managers know best	Collaborative Workers part of something; can teach too
Worker as	Interchangeable parts, "hands" Insufficient mental capacity	Multidimensional Complex beings
Human nature	Lazy, lacks ambition	A doer, needs purpose
Emphasis	Time and motion, parts	Wholeness, relationality
Power	Power over	Power to

SOURCE: Adapted from the work of Newman and Guy (1988).

parison of them in table 2.2 is at least strongly suggestive of the same gendered pattern as evident in table 2.1.

For Taylor, the emphasis was on controlling work by breaking tasks and human labor into optimal parts. The relationship of management to workers was adversarial because workers' human nature was judged to be lacking in ambition. This laziness derived from their singular desire to avoid effort, which itself followed from weakness of mind. To surmount the challenges of getting rational and efficient work performed by inadequate humans, wise managers needed to command unwilling workers through hierarchy bolstered by centralized authority and optimally standardized tasks. Because individual workers were believed to be motivated solely by the paycheck, rules about standardization were needed. To control competition between workers and the leader, hierarchical structures were needed to facilitate a leader's dominance.

In contrast, Follett emphasized the worker as a person. Relations could be collaborative because the workers' nature was judged to be complex and multidimensional, and workers were believed to want to do, to need a purpose. The orientation of the organization then could be based on interpersonal relations, with flexible approaches to work that holistically and creatively involved work and the workers. In Follett's organization, leaders collaborate in building power to accomplish a purpose within a web of human relationships. Individuals (both leader and worker) are embedded in a context that inevitably involves complex relationships, where collaboration and cooperation make sense as they collectively strive toward a larger purpose. A leader accomplishes ends by knowing the whole person, matching functions to personal strengths, and taking care to utilize the whole person. As suggested by table 2.2, a leader does this best by being in the middle of things and listening well.

The way in which masculine attributes correspond with Frederick Taylor's approach and feminine attributes correspond with Mary Parker Follett is striking. While no evidence presented here can directly link their respective approaches to attributed gender differences, the consistency in assumptions and preferences entices and leads to a distinct hypothesis: *If founding mothers rather than founding fathers had organized Congress originally, and dominated it throughout its evolution, Congress likely would be a very different institution.* Precisely how that difference in gender dominance would play out is not straightforward, however. One possible evolution might be found in James March and Johan Olsen's notion of aggregating and integrating institutions, shown in table 2.3.[11]

March and Olsen are concerned with assessing "real political institutions" and with making them function as "appropriate instruments of democracy" capable of producing democratic equality. The ideas of new institutions are long familiar to and used by scholars of executive branch institutions because the subfield public administration has always employed the organization theory used by March and Olsen. Sociology also has tended to connect organizations and institutions, with organizational culture and institutional power structures forming the central nexus of the research. W. Richard Scott, for example, likens new institutions theory to open systems in organization theory.[12] It is perhaps surprising that legislative scholars have not used more organization theory in their research, especially considering its strong appearance in earlier decades.[13] Legislative scholars

TABLE 2.3

Contrasting Aggregative and Integrative Institutions

ASPECT	AGGREGATIVE	INTEGRATIVE
"The People"	A collection of individuals qualified to be treated as citizens	A group extending backward into history and forward into the future
Citizens are	Rational	Reasoning
Citizens seek	Self-interest	General welfare
Method to discover people's will	Political campaigns and bargaining with majority rule	Deliberation within a context of shared values
Order based upon	Rationality and exchange	History, obligation, and reason
Leadership involves	Brokering coalitions among interests	Trusteeship for social traditions and future needs; an educative role
Primary outcome of political process	Allocation of resources	To develop a polity with shared purpose and trust
Process emphasizes	Instantaneous response	Slower adaptations to protect against momentary passions and rationalities
Majority control	Supremacy of majority rule	Majority rule within framework of institutional rights and norms
Driving logic	Exchange	Unity

should be genuinely concerned with the need for "appropriate" institutions, since, arguably more than any other major political institution, legislatures are critical instruments of democracy. Hence, they need to be appropriate if democracy is to thrive. The relative merits of aggregating and integrating institutional forms deserve scrutiny, especially as these forms implicate gender predilections.

Aggregating institutions limit citizens to certain qualities, seeing citizens as rational and self-interested. They rely on campaigns and bargaining to discover the people's will and base order on rationality and exchange, with exchange serving as the driving logic. Leaders then broker coalitions among interests such that the primary outcome of politics is the allocation of resources, fast responses, and majority rule. Integrating institutions understand the people to be embedded in history and to have a future.

Current citizens reason about the general will and rely on deliberation within the context of shared values to determine the people's will. Leaders act as trustees for the past and future and educate in order to achieve the primary outcome of shared purpose and trust, with unity serving as the driving logic. Therefore majority rule operates within rights and norms to curtail momentary passions.

Table 2.3 invites comparison to table 2.2. Taylor's scientific management would accord well with aggregating institutions. In aggregating institutions, adversity and competition are assumed, as are rational and self-interested humans. The majority operates by "power over" minorities in order to allocate resources with time and motion efficiency. In contrast, Follett's views fit comfortably with integrating institutions. Her view of humans as complex, purposive, and part of a whole corresponds well with the contextualized, reasoning, sharing citizens of integrative institutions who have concern for the general welfare. The majority needs "power to" act as trustees who care about the past and for future citizens, because relationships matter and wholeness counts.

Can the correspondence of attributed gender differences with gendered organization theory, and, in turn, with aggregating and integrating institutions be demonstrated empirically? Unfortunately, since women currently constitute less than 15 percent of Congress, they have limited effect on the "rules of the game," and they have scant control over leadership positions or influence on institutional processes. Fortunately, however, research on state legislatures demonstrates a connection. Cindy Simon Rosenthal's pathbreaking book *When Women Lead* finds that female chairs of state legislative committees adopt integrating leadership styles compared to the aggregating preferences of their male counterparts.[14] Her finding is consistent also with analysis by Malcolm Jewell and Marcia Whicker on gender and legislative style in which they find some evidence that state legislators are increasingly using "feminized" styles regardless of whether the legislator is male or female.[15] Given the decentralized power and structure of legislatures, which emphasizes functional expertise, a congruence between approaches such as Follett's and legislatures should not come entirely as a surprise. Women might be predicted to do better in state legislatures and Congress than in the presidency, which relies on the single great leader.[16]

Yet, gender analysis understands that gender is not necessarily tied to sexed human bodies; men can act in accord with integrative institutions.[17]

Clearly some have and do.[18] Gender analysis would predict that integrative institutions might emerge in somewhat different forms under masculine or feminine dominance. Further, with a critical mass of women, integrative institutions arguably are far more likely to come to fruition.

CONGRESS AND A FRAMEWORK FOR INSTITUTIONAL GENDER ANALYSIS

This volume demonstrates how congressional research can employ gendered institutions theory. Most "new institutions" analyses of Congress focus on structures and rules and norms, or what might be called practices. I propose a framework that also includes gender ethos and gender power arrangements of Congress.[19] Gender power refers to the multiple distributions of social and political influence and resources within an institution and the dynamics resulting from people performing gender within the normative boundaries that gender imposes. The framework includes an understanding of how gender operates as a protoideology to influence behavior, preferences, and policy choices. The gender ethos framework also attends to structures and rules or practices, but both formal and informal aspects are considered, including implicit expectations. Further, the framework considers exogenous or societal factors as well as the endogenous or internal institutional factors. Unlike most political science approaches to new institutions research, the gender ethos framework also focuses on an institution's social demography and history. The representative individual of most formal theory renders social demography irrelevant, whereas in gender analysis it obviously figures prominently. Further, because institutions build on decisions of predecessors, particularly the preferences of founders, history is important to all categories. However, certain historical features of an institution prove "remarkably sticky," and history must be considered in its own right as well as being recognized as pervasively important.[20]

Feminalism, Masculinism: Gender as Protoideology

Gender ideology is more than feminism, and feminism is more than one unified political ideology. The implications of these facts are threefold. First, not only feminists adhere to a gender ideology; all humans do. To recognize this fact is to break free of the notion that feminism is the only gendered political ideology, a recognition that opens the door to more complete analysis. Part of this process is made easy by looking at feminism, which has always incorporated hyphenated and distinctive strands such as radical feminism and liberal feminism. Adherents can share the notion of feminism while diverging on ideological components that create a radical compared to a liberal outlook. Second, this approach to gender ideology recognizes that men have gender too, and that masculinity has an ideological foundation of its own. Like women and feminism, men can agree on masculinism but diverge on liberal or conservative ideology. Awareness of this fact is necessary for gender analysis of Congress and other political institutions created by men. Third, both men and women hold views that run the ideological spectrum, about governing *and* about gender.

While most congressional scholars assume that liberal to conservative governing ideology subsumes gender ideology, the approach I proffer here instead holds that a male and a female representative may be close partisans—moderate Republicans, for example—and therefore share a moderate conservative ideology about governing and government; however, they may well differ in their guiding beliefs about gender ideology. On issues driven by gender ideology, congresswomen may share more views with one another than they do with the congressmen with whom they otherwise agree. Certainly, men and women in Congress may agree fully on gendered matters, but empirical research in this volume and elsewhere demonstrates frequent and predictable divergence along sex lines. The approach I employ means that it is fully possible for a male and female member of Congress to share views about governing but not about gender; for two males or two females to share views about gender but not about governing; and many permutations in between. In other words, not all congresswomen are feminist, but they often come together around issues in ways distinctive from males who are their closest partisans on other matters. Not all men are antifeminist, but they still may share ideological orientations rooted in their masculine existence. For these reasons, the idea of feminalism, which reaches across women's ideological orientations, can greatly enhance analysis much as the use of patriarchy or masculinism has done.

Moving to this mode of thinking about gender requires a model that treats gender ideology as a protoideology. Protoideology can be defined as a parent or source ideology from which other political or governing ideologies emanate.[21] At a protoideological level, gender has two prominent and equivalent modes, masculinism and feminalism. *Masculinism* is defined as an ideology that begins from, and generally prefers, that which is associated with masculinity, the masculine and males. It can be understood as the ideological aspect of what feminists have called patriarchy, but in this usage, the emphasis is on males and masculinity, not the subordination of women. Masculinism improves upon the term patriarchy because it breaks clear of any confusion lingering over the patriarchal ideology debated by John Locke and Sir Robert Filmer. The term also clearly denotes its ideological nature with its "ism" suffix.

Feminalism is defined as an ideology that begins from, and generally prefers, that which is associated with feminality, the feminale and females. My aim is to further analysis of institutional norms, practices, assumptions, and preferences rather than to examine, relative to men, the subordination or superiority of women and their ways, assumptions, and preferred modes of conduct. I use the term feminalism, which derives from the word *feminale*, or qualities associated with females, rather than feminism, or another logical term, femininism, because conservative women's political thought can then be incorporated into a single woman-based framework that also includes feminist women.[22] Using the term feminalism also avoids the confusion inherent in two words that look and sound very much alike. Additionally, a term based on biological delineations rather than social practices associated with femininity improves theoretical potential, despite the danger of essentialism. In this framework, men's ideologies can then be juxtaposed to women's ideologies, thereby creating conditions of theoretical equality as well as conceptual accuracy and clarity.[23]

Most importantly, the use of gender as protoideology makes it possible to account for *both* shared and divergent ideological orientations among women, among men, and between women and men. This framework compounds traditional understandings of liberal and conservative governing ideologies with gender ideologies. Such an approach helps explain why congresswomen align with like-minded congressmen for some policies and break into gendered groups on others. Table 2.4 portrays similarities between masculinism and feminalism as well as differences within and among men and women who hold various compounded ideologies.

The use of compounded gender ideology provides explanations and interpretations that are both possible and desirable. This framework provides a more nuanced way to account for identifiable differences in perspectives. For example, in this volume, Susan Carroll traces how both liberal

TABLE 2.4

Strands of Compounded Gender Ideology in U.S. Governing

CONVENTIONAL IDEOLOGY	CRITICAL DIMENSIONS	FEMINISM	MASCULINISM
Social democrat (neoleft)	Gender as structural system of oppression Compassionate active state Prohumanist, redistributive similarity	Social-democrat feminism	Enlightened left masculinism (radical profeminist men)
Social liberals	Acknowledged opportunity difference State resources and services needed State as enforcer of social contract	Social-liberal feminism	Liberal masculinism (profeminist men)
New (neo) liberalism	Autonomous individual, equal as the same Freedom to achieve with selective help Legal protections, public-private partnerships	Liberal feminism	Neofraternalism
Libertarian (neo) conservatism	Autonomous individual, equal as the same Forced to be free, failure as personal Equal opportunity, private solutions	Equality/corporate feminism	New paternalism
Traditional conservatism	Socially desirable complementarity, pragmatic State-supported separate spheres, private solutions Gender as rooted in biology but open to socially derived contingencies	Traditional maternalism	Traditional paternalism
Social conservatism (new right)	Difference divinely and biologically ordained Strong state, masculine public power Separate spheres, fixed-gender complementarity	New right feminism	New patriarchalism

and conservative congresswomen can see themselves as surrogate representatives of women. Similarly, Swers shows the distinct partisan patterns of male sponsorship of legislation related to traditional "women's issues" and what she terms "antifeminist" legislation. Richard Matland and David King's chapter reveals how gender ideologies subconsciously lead Republican voters to attribute philosophical positions to women candidates that they do not explicitly hold. Recognizing the feminalist perspective means recognizing its counterpart, masculinist perspective. This recognition opens the door to various analyses, institutional analysis among them, predicated on gender as protoideology.

Formal and Informal Structures

Institutional structures include formal ones such as committees, political parties, and institutional leadership, as well as informal structures like the regular dinners that female senators hold or male members' basketball teams. Oftentimes informal norms can lead to formal structures and formal rules can lead to informal structures. For example, the informal norm of seniority frequently determines the formal composition of committee leadership, while parliamentary rules can foster informal alliances to circumvent the rules. Exogenously, structure also shapes relationships to the executive branch and judiciary, as well as with voters, the press, and interest groups. Within the literature that melds gender and legislatures, structures for decisions, power, change, and other networks have received some attention already.[24] Less research has tapped informal structures, probably in part because access to reliable data is problematic. The nexus between formal and informal structures is at the heart of Laura Arnold and Barbara King's exploration of committee assignments in the U.S. Senate contained in this volume. Committee assignments obviously denote the Senate's formal division of labor, power, and expertise, but the process of aligning members' interests with available positions is cloaked in mystery. In the Arnold-King analysis, the particular fate of women elected to the Senate in the so-called Year of the Woman reveals the resistance of institutional structures to gendered challenges.

Structure directly influences power arrangements. Sue Thomas, who explicitly explored attempts to reform legislatures in her earlier work, demonstrates how March and Olsen's "ad hoc reforms" and "mundane adaptiveness" can be employed by women to transform the institution.[25] In Congress, however, decentralized power through multiple and overlapping sources fosters individual power bases that can be exploited to deter transformation. Avenues for changes in the distribution of gender power necessarily confront masculinism, which would predict that resources and preferences accrue to men more often, and more readily, than to women. That conclusion is supported by Kedrowski and Sarow, who show in their chapter of this book how the structure and use of media power by breast cancer groups produced congressional policy benefits for less active prostate cancer interest groups. Similarly, Joyce Gelb's chapter on the gains of women in the British Labour party reveals how political opportunity structures can simultaneously benefit descriptive representation and yet limit substantive representation. The consequences of these power structure arrangements for women and men require attention, as does the historical encoding of institutional meanings "constructed in the process of becoming."[26]

Practices: Rules, Norms, and Expectations

To explore masculinism in legislatures, in large part, is to explore rules, norms, and expectations, and legislative studies have long concentrated on these aspects of institutional performance. The mere preoccupation with rules, or unanimous conduct, is itself important. Other institutional practices include seniority, the lack of space for female members until recent changes, and expectations about spouses. Beyond the expectations imposed on members are the norms and rules confronted by other institutional actors. For example, the chapter by Cindy Simon Rosenthal and Lauren Cohen Bell reveals how norms of conduct and unwritten practices operate on congressional staff to produce opportunities or obstacles for gender representation.

Exogenous practices are also numerous. Outside of Congress, gender norms are experienced daily by most Americans, and societal expectations shape who is assumed to be the family caregiver and who the breadwinner. Sue Thomas, Rebekah Herrick, and Matthew Braunstein, in their chapter, directly implicate societal norms of household responsibilities in explaining who runs for legislative office and how members of Congress balance their public duties and family expectations. The extent to which women self-select into or out of Congress due to agreement with norms and practices is a key question. Certainly, election and effectiveness pressures enforce considerable compliance with current (aggregative) norms, rules, and expectations.

Scholars have already uncovered numerous findings related to masculinism in legislatures. Jewell and Whicker find leadership styles to be increasingly "feminized," or at least pulled in more collaborative directions, even while men maintain power dominance and women in legislative leadership posts struggle not to be marginalized.[27] Beth Reingold finds the fewest differences between women and men in the most professionalized of state legislatures.[28] Presumably then, in Congress, the most professional of all U.S. legislatures, women and men would also be the most alike. And indeed, one consequence of professionalization, Rosenthal argues, is that competitive and aggregative styles of leadership are more common among committee chairs whether male or female.[29]

Gender power analysis taps into the relative power advantages derived from gender practices. One such practice is legislative discourse. As Lyn Kathlene has shown, women in formal positions can be talked over by male committee members regardless of superior positional power.[30] The norms of masculine speech styles can be seen not only in committee discourse but also on the campaign trail, as Dianne Bystrom and Lynda Lee Kaid demonstrate in their chapter on candidates' videostyles. Gendered norms also are evident on the floor of the House as Katherine Cramer Walsh uncovers in her chapter analyzing perceptual frames employed by members during floor debate. Practices, however weakened, of seniority and comity also may work against women inside legislatures. For example, Noelle Norton's analysis of reproductive policy in this volume shows how one or two strategically placed senior members can thwart the policy efforts of congresswomen working on abortion-related issues. Some practices, such as potential deference to women on "feminine" policy areas, might work conversely to women's advantage. As the research in this volume demonstrates, however, the balance of gender power tips toward norms of masculinity rather than the reverse.

Social Demography

Intimately involved with an institution's history, structures, and rules is the social demography of those who occupy Congress. Clearly gender power also affects extra-institutional actors—voters, pressure groups, issue networks, political parties, as well as those in the presidency, executive branch, and the judiciary. Specifically, the ratios of men to women along with the valuation and the access to organizational power must be considered. Arnold and King's analysis in this book does just that, revealing how the social demography of Senate committees includes two dimensions— the breadth of descriptive representation across all committees, as well as the power garnered through positions on key committees.

Basic demographic data about those who have occupied legislatures over time show that men have been present almost to the exclusion of women. Nonetheless, women have held legislative office (see Irwin Gertzog's chapter), women have served as staff (see Rosenthal and Bell's chapter), and women constitute a majority of many constituencies (see Anne Costain and Heather Fraizer's chapter.) These scholars focus on the differing social circumstances that produce the Congress's particular social demography and the resulting assets of gender power. For example, Gertzog's analysis underscores how marginalization defined the congresswomen who initially gained office (i.e., often by widow's succession) and how over time congresswomen, especially African Americans, have become strategic politicians very much like their male colleagues.

Important for Congress is the prominence of lawyers, a gateway profession. Around half of the founders were lawyers, and although the proportion has declined in recent years, lawyers continue to be the plurality occupation for members of Congress. The legal profession is also important for understanding the demography of congressional staff. Rosenthal and Bell show that while women hold professional committee jobs in proportions similar to those among attorneys, the percentage of women in law lags behind the percentage having other analytic training (e.g., economics or public administration) who might assist committee deliberations. Important then has been the fierce historic defense of the legal profession as a bastion for men. In a notorious 1894 case brought by Belva Lockwood, the state of Virginia denied her the right to practice law on the grounds that "any person" meant "any man."[31] Nonetheless, the dramatic rise of the number of women in law school bodes well for the regendering of Congress.

Social demography provides an area integral to regender and reinscribe gender power. Frequently, however, areas in which women advance first, as legislative caseworkers for example, provide an opening into the institution for women, but then also become less valued.[32] Worse yet, the intrusion of women into masculine institutions can provoke backlash, as Costain and Fraizer's chapter confirms in documenting the increase in violence directed toward groups at the heart of the institutionalizing women's movement.

Gender power can be assessed by looking to the relative number and influence of men and women inside legislatures along with their subsequent contributions to substantive representation. Karin Tamerius, for example, has demonstrated critical ways in which females in Congress, much more than males, invest in legislation for women throughout the policy process.[33] In this volume, Christina Wolbrecht shows that men in Congress cosponsor legislation on women's issues, but the initiative for agenda setting and producing new policy solutions is largely borne by congresswomen. Swers, likewise, shows that a handful of men author the lion's share of antifeminist legislation. Such studies bear directly on the adequacy of representation and the overall gender distribution of preference.[34] If dominance of the masculine in preferences is found, then the nonpreferred— women—will have been "encoded as novelties."[35] Like anyone different from the dominant demographic group, women could still face difficulties in terms of trust, a key ingredient of effective working relationships.

Institutional History

According to March and Olsen, history is encoded into institutions.[36] Similarly, gender ethos is shaped by an institution's history, its founding members, characteristics of the early and prominent leadership, and purposes and functions originally and over time. Virginia Sapiro has observed that male bodies have created legislative bodies,[37] so it is reasonable to expect masculinity and manliness to be reflected in legislative bodies. History's effects would be embedded most permanently in a legislature at the time of its initial design. Because the Constitutional Convention was decidedly masculine, the distribution of power would likely be so as well.[38] If the initial "distribution of preferences" favored the masculine, then the masculine would, of course, continue to control power until reform or redesign changed it. The research task is to unearth gender ideological aspects in legislative foundings.

What would indicate a masculinist preference in the history of Congress? In the next section, I scrutinize several aspects. First is the simple question of who is judged preferable to wield public power. A second aspect asks what language is invoked to describe the institution. Third, as March and Olsen reiterate, is the examination of the initial distribution of preferences that determines an institution's capacity to function as "an appropriate instrument of democracy" capable of delivering political equality. The norms and beliefs central to the founders of an institution constitute what March and Olsen refer to as "preferences." As institutions evolve over time these beliefs are reinforced, and future individuals shape and are shaped by the institution.[39]

The masculine character of Congress seems undeniable and sets its "culture and folkways," and by extension its rules, processes, values, and norms. In fact many scholars have written about the men and manly virtues assumed as part of the founding and history of Congress—Louis Hartz who proclaimed Locke's individualism freed all men to become heroes, Bernard Bailyn on manly virtue in republicanism, Nelson Polsby on the men who institutionalized Congress, Stanley Elkins and Eric McKitrick on "young men of the Revolution." But none of these scholars have, however, agreed that their observations about masculinity require debate, nor do they recognize that masculinity has meaning for the nature of the institution. Similarly, male leaders of Congress have not entered into debate about the manly culture of Congress that challenges women's full participation.[40] In other words, they have failed to acknowledge that such manly influence matters, or that Congress is a gendered institution.

In sum, gender analysis provides new insight on the defining features of institutions. Institutions have been defined as "persistent and connected sets of rules (formal and informal) that prescribe behavioral roles, constrain activity, and shape expectations."[41] Or, as "the formal rules, compliance procedures and standard operating procedures that structure the relationship between individuals in various units of the polity and economy."[42] Important for purposes of gender analysis is one further distinction. "Institutions, like organizations, have structures, functions, and rules. Unlike organizations, however, institutions are denoted by a set of norms and beliefs shared among a given population.... Institutions do more than structure people's daily routines; they also assign value to what people do, and they shape the very self-definitions people come to hold."[43] If the people matter, then social demography must be considered, and gender indisputably is one important social dimension. Institutions evolve as normative environments whose prominent aspects can be revealed by their history.

INSTITUTIONAL GENDER ETHOS:
FINDING MANLINESS IN CONGRESS

A cursory analysis of the founding period of the Congress can draw together these theoretical frameworks and illustrate the insights that analysis of gender ethos can bring to understandings of institutions. In the case of the United States, the founders made judgments about human capacity based on gender. Their decisions naturalized a split between the public and private domains, insisted on a need for a single head of household, reinstated coverture, and created exclusionary suffrage laws.[44] The boundaries between public and private domains were very rigid at the time, more so even than in western Europe according to Michael Kimmel.[45] Such values and beliefs meshed comfortably with "common sense" and the shared empirical reality of the 18th century that resulted in men as the sole political agents. Hence, the founding fathers, "young men of the Revolution,"[46] continued the system of patriarchal privilege, even if that masculine system shifted to "one national brotherhood" plagued by some "fraternal fratricide."[47]

Not all men were included, of course. Gordon S. Wood clearly believes that the colonies' elite men would not have willingly allowed the lower-class men of the "meaner sort" to become officeholders, and only grudgingly to be voters. Benjamin Franklin particularly was among the aggrieved, having spent his life achieving the requisite "gentleman" status needed to hold high office and that conservative elites held particularly dear while creating the Senate especially.[48] Only gentlemen possessed adequate morality and "had the natural capacity and the leisure to be fully virtuous, . . . [and the] 'greatness of soul' in which 'the public's greatest good' stood foremost among their concerns."[49] No women possessed such greatness.

Mark Kann explicates the intensive use of "a grammar of manhood" by the founders to "encourage American men to reform themselves, to restore order to the hierarchical ranks of men, and to foster social stability, political legitimacy, and patriarchal power."[50] The founders inherited laws, institutions, and values that portrayed politics as an exclusively male enterprise, and they accepted that system much to their own advantage. Clearly, John

Adams knew it was a "masculine system" they created.[51] The founding fathers indeed left their "gendered legacy" on U.S. political institutions.[52] According to E. Anthony Rotundo in *American Manhood*, "nineteenth-century men and their concepts of manhood helped to define the character of many important American institutions." They sought sufficiently "virile systems" as they developed these institutions: "Many of the customs and folkways of the United States Congress have their origins in the early nineteenth century, when not only the federal government but the capital city itself were virtually all-male settings; continued years of male dominance in Congress have only elaborated the masculine culture established in the early 1800s."[53]

Finally, at the time of the founding, Congress was the superior institution of the three branches of government. Legislatures offered more promise for republican democracy than the executive or judiciary. Further, given the colonial experience, Congress was vested with much more power than the presidency, and state legislatures were extremely important, perhaps the most important units of government.[54] Most colonial executives had been appointed by the king, whereas colonies created their own legislatures. Not surprisingly, upon independence, James Wilson observed that toward the executive and the judiciary "the people behaved like stepmothers. The legislature was still discriminated by excessive partiality; and into its lap, every good and precious gift was profusely thrown."[55] Further, legislatures were cast in the role of "provider," with the other two branches being "left dependent upon the legislative for the subsistence."[56] In both of these views, the founding legislature was the most virile and masculine of the branches.

Two empirical accounts illustrate my larger point: *Congressional Dynamics*, by Calvin Jillson and Rick K. Wilson, and *The Washington Community, 1800–1828*, by Sterling Young. The former is a "rational" new institutions analysis of the Continental Congress, the latter a recounting of the power structures of the early Constitutional Congress.

Jillson and Wilson pursue the usual institutional dilemmas of "rational" new institutions research: the problems of coordinating shared interests, of collective action (free rider and tragedy of the commons), and of collective choice. They contend members of the Continental Congress created few rules to constrain choice and force collective decisions, refused to institute a stable leadership structure to manage daily business, and were "always

more willing to live with incoherence than to grant disproportionate powers to any individual or group." Yet, along with the inevitable conflict over
both means and ends, they assume the decision makers were purposeful
and acted in a fashion that best enabled them to achieve goals. The members, they claim, did not desire an "orderly, stable, and efficient . . . policy-
making institution." Instead, their goals were the protection of two incom-
patible principles, state sovereignty and unanimity. Debate was unlimited
and super majorities were required, especially after 1781. "They were willing to live and tinker with an institution *that they understood*, one that *pro-
tected their individual independence* and state sovereignty, rather than solving
the fundamental institutional problems plaguing the Congress."[57]

Jillson and Wilson offer explanations for the Congress's failure, including the interest of the members and the institutional structure. They make
a persuasive case within the confines of their argument. What they fail to
probe, however, is why autonomy, both as individual independence and
as state sovereignty, was so understandable and so powerful a goal that
members were willing to let the institution fail, and possibly endanger the
Revolution, rather than to abandon the principle. To understand the nature
of the institution, its structures and rules, the social demography of the
members should be recalled. Those members were exclusively men. Therefore, masculine gender and gender ideology, masculinism, must be considered for a complete analysis. Gender provides some explanation for their
hyperfocus (fixation) on autonomy as an overriding goal.

The analysis returns to table 2.1, which contends that autonomy has been
a primary preoccupation of masculinity because individuation is the key
to successful masculinity, to manliness. As many feminist theorists have
noted, liberalism, including Locke's, was predicated upon a particularly
atomistic concept of individuals, one preoccupied with separating in order
to be fully autonomous.[58] Further, and consistent with other protogender
attributes, members of the Continental Congress insisted on speaking out
through unlimited debate. This institutional practice might well be a man-
ifestation of separating, of standing out as an individual. Further, living in
an era in which the masculine political system was transformed from Sir
Robert Filmer's traditional patriarchy to "liberal patriarchy," the members
could be understood as operating in opposition to or in fear of a potential
return to the system of a tyrannical father.[59] Such a system would have produced a leader who would again dominate others in a hierarchical order of

men. These men would compete to better themselves, to rise, instrumentally working to improve their standing in the public sphere. Therefore, institutional arrangements that denied any individual disproportionate power, even power to manage daily business better, made sense. Doing so ensured that no one would be able to dominate. Similarly, the practice of unanimity ensured no group could come to wield power over others.

Because these men understood *man's* nature, they devised a decision-making system that achieved their *collective* goal of *individual* independence. This system operated inside masculinism as paternal power gave way to a fraternal order.[60] Jillson and Wilson conclude that "the balance was struck decidedly in favor of autonomy."[61] Predictably, the democratic rhetoric of equal brothers and the goal of achieving fraternal equality produced institutional arrangements such as those of the Continental Congress.

One of the Congress's main problems, according to these authors, was that it could not aggregate the individual interests of members or of the states they represented. Attending to such interests and appetites was essential if the new government was to persist. "Possessive individualism," as both Louis Hartz and Gordon Wood agree, would become the means to calm the beast in American men.[62] A new set of institutional arrangements was needed, and the Constitutional Convention produced them.

Sterling Young approaches Congress after the new arrangements have been established, concentrating upon the formative years of 1800 to 1828. Using gender analysis to reinterpret his account reveals how masculinity, and masculinism as protoideology, emerges. Because few brought their families, most members of Congress lived in boardinghouses. According to Daniel Webster, "boardinghouse society was for the most part one of 'unvarying masculinity.'"[63] In the boardinghouses, senators mixed with representatives, young with old, newcomers with old- timers, and so on, as members sought others of similar social origin and acculturation. These fraternities were the main social structure of Congress. More importantly, they became the "basic units of its political structure."[64] Young demonstrates that these fraternities voted as blocs to a high degree, regardless of majority size and political parties. In fact, the fraternities stood in the way of achieving coordinating mechanisms through political parties.

Care was taken within the boardinghouses to enact egalitarian practices. The antipathy to a single great leader remained. Congressional spokesmen for the president were not seen as party leaders; they were known instead as the "palace troops" and the "ministerial phalanx,"[65] in essence presidential warriors. Tension continued over being seen as a "leading man," with the talent and standing to claim a singular place above others. Men who acted as the "single presidential 'leader' in Congress" faced innuendo and derision.[66]

In 1811, Henry Clay won the post of House Speaker with overwhelming majorities. In classic aggregative fashion, his strategy for success involved parceling out two votes on every committee to each of the fraternities, thereby attending to members' primary goals of fraternity power and aggregating individual interests through boardinghouse fraternities rather than states or parties. As a result, fraternities achieved dominion by attaining committee chair positions, a practice that splintered Congress further. The strategy also probably led to the establishment of the norm of seniority, which helped bring stability to leadership, but also reinstituted privilege for older men. Ironically, but necessarily due to the constraints of hegemonic fraternalism of the boardinghouse culture, Clay may have "foreclosed any real leadership for himself" due to the strength of, and competition among, fraternities.[67] Nonetheless, attending to the goal of maintaining fraternity power on committees arguably led to the system of standing committees, which in turn allowed Clay to centralize his individual power as the one who appointed committee members.[68]

The framework for studying gender ethos in organizations and institutions explains phenomena in terms quite distinct from "rational" new institutions research, and in a way that calls into question the soundness of the "representative individual." As this brief exploration suggests, the structures and practices of an institution can be explained quite readily when protoideological concerns rooted in social demography are considered. Further, the historical dimensions of an institution gain meaning as the "remarkably sticky" remnants of past institutional transformations reappear and are reinstituted.[69] Such initial preferences thereby carry forward through many iterations of reform. Women who enter Congress confront the initial preference for masculinity as it has transformed over time.

BEYOND CONGRESS AS THE "FIELD OF DREAMS"

With the initial preferences distributed in a decidedly masculine manner, the stickiness of prior features, and the ongoing super-majorities of men in

Congress, Congress is ill-formed as an instrument of democracy capable of producing gender equality. Although many reforms and changes in both structures and practices have occurred since Henry Clay was speaker, a fraternity atmosphere was said to exist as recently as Dan Rostenkowski's reign on Ways and Means.[70] Also, most contemporary accounts by women in Congress are replete with examples of manly assumptions and masculine orientations that suggest research on the gender ethos of Congress is sorely needed. Just adding more women to the mix will be inadequate, according to Kimmel, because "the increasing numbers of women in organizations has been more than counterbalanced by the gendered nature of the institutions themselves." The "field of dreams" fallacy—if women are welcome, without discrimination, then they will come into the institution—is based on the assumption that when they arrived, women would act just like men.[71] To some extent, congresswomen have been forced to perform the masculine in order to succeed, and however successful they may be, the masculine character then persists despite the female presence. Such does not make for gender equality.

Certainly, legislative scholars have been prominent in new institution research, with much of their attention being directed toward a search for more appropriate institutions through proposed reforms.[72] As Mary Katzenstein illustrates, with the exception of "the newer analyses of gender and organizations . . . institutional studies do not ask who benefits and who loses as a result of particular institutional arrangements, how power is allocated, or what might cause different groups to gain or relinquish institutional control."[73]

Unfortunately, few scholars of gender and legislatures have explicitly embraced the new institutions mode of analysis, especially that which can incorporate analysis of gender ethos.[74] In a fine overview of aspects of such research, Sally Kenney emphasizes that numbers affect power in and the culture of institutions; gender is oppositional and hierarchical and is continually reinscribed; masculinity is fiercely defended; and institutions will try to contain progressive change including change in gender.[75] She concludes that "political institutions are in a very real sense constructed on the basis of women's exclusion."[76] One might think legislative scholars would be eager to investigate this claim.

Institutional analysis of gender in legislatures inevitably challenges existing inequities. However, for change to occur, in Congress and among those who study it, the "old bulls" in leadership need to recognize masculinity in Congress, rather than assume it as universal or inconsequential.[77] We know reconstitutive change comes to Congress when the pressures and opportunities created by political parties, the electorate, and the national governmental agenda meet with institutional vision and institutional activism. In her study of reconstitutive change in Congress, Elaine Swift concludes that ideas matter.[78] Without the theoretical ideas about what change is needed and how change should come about, the vision proves inadequate for activists. Those inside Congress who want more gender balance need the ideas from scholars to shape a vision.

Democracy demands legislative institutions capable of fostering equality. The inequality of the initial distribution of preferences in the first Congresses in favor of the masculine must be given meaning and importance for today's continuing gender inequalities. But to provide a vision, the collectivity of Congress and the collectivity of scholars of legislative institutions must agree that manliness, masculinity, and masculinism require debate. Until such time as masculinist preferences are debated, women in Congress will continue to perform the masculine well—by necessity—if they are to be effective. Women, professional legislators in the most professional of legislatures, will adapt, and gender equality will be slowed as a result. Nonetheless, their feminalist presence makes women in Congress unwitting activists and constitutes a challenge to masculine dominance whether or not they struggle consciously for reconstitutive change.[79] If women persist, a new order can emerge. How soon and how great a transformation remains for the future.

NOTES

1. Malcolm E. Jewell stands out as one exception among "top" scholars through his pathbreaking work on legislative leadership with Marcia Whicker. Arguably, some scholars, Sue Thomas perhaps most notably, who have specialized in women or gender in legislatures also have entered the ranks of the "top"; however, their work seems to be cited more often in gender research than legislative research.

2. See *Gender Power, Leadership, and Governance*, Duerst-Lahti and Kelly, eds., for more background on gender.

3. Hinckley, *Stability and Change in Congress*, 60.

4. Mayer and Canon, *Dysfunctional Congress*, 112–13.

5. Katzenstein, *Faithful and Fearless*, 35.

6. Much of the new institutions analysis on organizations other than legislatures bears a striking correspondence to scholarship done through organizational theory, especially theory about organizational cultures. This fact should not be surprising given the history of James G. March and Johan P. Olsen, whose contributions have been central to the field of organization theory at least since 1950 and are most clearly articulated in *Rediscovering Institutions*, 1989. Indeed, many scholars of legislatures—Joseph Cooper prominent among them—have drawn directly on organization theory to study legislatures, especially in the early 1980s. (See, for example, Joseph Cooper and Calvin McKenzie, *The House at Work*.) A simultaneous development in organization theory has been the study of gender in organizations. Rosabeth Moss Kanter pioneered the field in 1977. In public administration, organization theory has been well analyzed for its gendering by Stivers in *Gender Images in Public Administration*. Others contributing to such analysis are Kathy Ferguson, *A Feminist Case against Bureaucracy*; Hale and Kelly, *Gender, Bureaucracy, and Democracy*; Hearn et al., *The Sexuality of Organization*; Joan Acker, "Gendered Institutions"; and Mills and Tancred, *Gendering Organizational Analysis*.

7. See the work of Peregrine Schwartz-Shea for an outstanding feminist critique of formal and game theoretic approaches.

8. The literature on sex-gender difference is now enormous, and so is the critique of it. Only a few of the more influential sources for this sex-gender theory as it pertains to U.S. politics are cited here. These include Chodorow, *The Reproduction of Mothering*; Gilligan, *In a Different Voice*, with Nancy Loevinger and Kohlberg cited within; Whicker and Jewell, "Feminization of Leadership"; Thomas, *How Women Legislate*; C. Rosenthal, *When Women Lead*; Elshtain, *Public Man, Private Woman*; Hartsock, *Money, Sex, and Power*.

9. Butler, *Gender Trouble*.

10. Newman and Guy, "Taylor's Triangle, Follett's Web." See also *Prophet of Management*.

11. March and Olsen, *Organizational Basis*, especially 118–26.

12. Scott, *Institutions and Organizations*. In terms of Scott's "three pillars" of institutional theory, gender analysis involves the normative and cognitive pillars ideologically and the regulative pillar in praxis.

13. For example, see the work of Nelson Polsby, Ronald Peters, Randall Strahan, Elaine Swift, and Joseph Cooper.

14. C. Rosenthal, *When Women Lead*.

15. Jewell and Whicker, *Legislative Leadership*.

16. Borrelli and Martin, *Other Elites*.

17. The relative standing of a masculinist version of integrative institutions may depend on the particular features of a moment in history's dominant masculinity. Masculinities compete for hegemony. See Connell, *Gender and Power* and *Masculinities*.

18. Early in his post as chair of the Ways and Means Committee, Wilbur Mills seemed to operate in an integrative fashion as described by Strahan, *New Ways and Means*.

19. Duerst-Lahti (1987) first developed this approach to researching gender ethos; Guy and Duerst-Lahti (1992) and McGlen and Sarkees (1993) have also conducted gender organizational analysis with this approach.

20. Jillson and Wilson, *Congressional Dynamics*, 299.

21. I thank Kenneth Hoover for suggesting protoideology as an improvement on the term I had been using, much to my dissatisfaction—metaideology.

22. See Duerst-Lahti, Johnson, and Norton, *Making Masculine Mothers: Gender Ideology in Welfare Reform*, in progress, for further explanation. The concept is akin to the term *womanist*, which Alice Walker coined to describe black women's relationship to themselves and feminism.

23. Kathy Ferguson speaks to the utility of creating instances of theoretical equality as a means of achieving equality in praxis; see *The Man Question*, especially ch. 1.

24. C. Rosenthal, in *When Women Lead*, Norton, in "Women, It's Not Enough to Be Elected," and Thomas, in *How Women Legislate* are among legislative scholars who have empirically examined the ways formal structures such as standing committees in Congress or official leaders of state legislatures are shaped by gender.

25. March and Olsen, *Organizational Basis*, 57; Thomas, *How Women Legislate*.

26. March and Olsen, *Organizational Basis*, 40.

27. Jewell and Whicker, *Legislative Leadership*.

28. Reingold, "Conflict and Cooperation." This point also has important bearing on the norms aspect below and shows the interactive effects across these research domains.

29. C. Rosenthal, *When Women Lead*, 163.

30. Kathlene, "Power and Influence."

31. As described in Rotundo, *American Manhood*, 213.

32. Women may get such posts because they are less valued in the first place, or because they are more readily gendered to the feminale; that is, dealing with crying or upset constituents is something women are thought to do better than men. See Foerstel and Foerstel, *Climbing the Hill*, especially ch. 4.

33. Duerst-Lahti and Kelly, *Gender Power, Leadership, and Governance*.

34. Adequate is a slippery term in regard to political representation. A minimal measure would be ready reelection of incumbents or lack of civil unrest or petition of redress. Of course the founding, in March and Olsen's terms, distributed the "preference" that suffrage be granted to propertied white males, which matters greatly for access to adequate representation.

35. March and Olsen, *Organizational Basis*, 34.

36. Ibid., 56.

37. Sapiro "Gender Politics, Gendered Politics."

38. March and Olsen, *Organizational Basis*, 143–44.

39. Ibid., passim.

40. Women in Congress would find direct challenge difficult because their immediate effectiveness would be undermined if Congress were like state legislatures. See

Thomas, "Women in State Legislatures." Presumably, conditions in Congress would be a heightened form of conditions in state legislatures because it is most professional of all; self-selection and election screens out those most likely to object to the institution itself, and more is at stake.

41. Robert O. Keohane, as cited in Katzenstein, *Faithful and Fearless*, 185 n. 41.

42. Peter Hall, as cited in ibid.

43. Katzenstein, *Faithful and Fearless*, 33.

44. Much has been written about these facets by feminists. See, for example, Elshtain, *Public Man, Private Woman*; Kerber's *Women of the Republic, Toward an Intellectual History of Women*, and *No Constitutional Right to Be Ladies*. On women's political importance throughout, see Evans, *Born for Liberty*.

45. Kimmel, *Manhood in America*.

46. The phrase is from historians Stanley Elkins and Eric McKitrick, as cited in Milkis and Nelson, *American Presidency*, 10.

47. Kann, *Republic of Men*, 125–29.

48. Polsby, "Institutionalization in the U.S. House," 145, as cited in Elaine Swift, *Making of an American Senate*, 15.

49. Thomas E. Cavanagh, as cited in Swift, *Making of an American Senate*, 15.

50. Kann, *Republic of Men*, 1.

51. In a letter to his wife, Abigail, April 14, 1776, John Adams wrote, "Depend upon it, We know better than to repeal our Masculine systems. Altho they are in full force, you know they are little more than Theory," in Rossi, ed., *Feminist Papers*.

52. Kann, *Republic of Men*, especially ch. 7.

53. Rotundo, *American Manhood*, 8.

54. See Harris and Hain, *America's Legislative Processes*, ch. 1.

55. In Charles C. Thach, Jr., *Creation of the Presidency, 1775–1789*, as cited in Milkis and Nelson, *American Presidency*, 4.

56. Jefferson about Virginia, quoted in Milkis and Nelson, *American Presidency*, 4.

57. Jillson and Wilson, *Congressional Dynamics*, 6, 5, 10, 133, 144, 290 (italics added).

58. See especially Christine DiStefano, *Configurations of Masculinity*, 1991.

59. Mark Kann, *On the Man Question*, especially the introduction and ch. 7 and 8.

60. Pateman, *Sexual Contract*.

61. Jillson and Wilson, *Congressional Dynamics*, 298.

62. Mark Kann, *On the Man Question*, 12, claims both scholars agree. He goes on to explain that David Hume insisted that habitual civic virtues and prior loyalty to the notion of public good also were necessary.

63. Young, *The Washington Community, 1800–1828*, 101 n. 52 and 53. I thank Irwin Gertzog for telling me of this book.

64. Ibid., 99.

65. Ibid., 129, which draws on the *Memoirs*, I:403–404, of John Quincy Adams.

66. Ibid., 127–32, see especially n. 48, 49, 51.

67. Ibid., 134.

68. Gamm and Shepsle, used by Mayer and Canon, *Dysfunctional Congress?* 114. Mayer and Canon also write, consistent with David Mayhew, about "credit claiming" behavior (7). This behavior is consistent with individuation and is of particular distaste to many women in Congress; see, for example, Mikulski et al., *Nine and Counting.*

69. Jillson and Wilson, *Congressional Dynamics,* 299.

70. Strahan, *New Ways and Means.* I thank Randall Strahan for drawing this to my attention.

71. Kimmel, series editor's introduction, vii–viii.

72. For example, Shepsle and Weingast, "Institutional Foundations of Committee Power."

73. Katzenstein, *Faithful and Fearless,* 34–35.

74. Thomas, *How Women Legislate,* C. Rosenthal, *When Women Lead,* and Reingold, *Representing Women* stand as clear exceptions and as leaders of gender institutional analysis of legislatures. Theorists Wendy Brown, *Manhood and Politics,* and Carol Pateman, *The Sexual Contract,* contribute important theoretical insights to this effort.

75. Kenney, "Field Essay, New Research," encapsulates insights from emerging research that integrates gender and institutional research.

76. Ibid., 462.

77. The term "old bulls" is taken from a news article about congressional leadership by Guy Gugliotta, "Playing Musical Chairs in the House," *Washington Post,* 30 March 1998, p. 12, national weekly edition.

78. Elaine Swift, *Making of an American Senate,* especially ch. 3.

79. This is a reformulation of Katzenstein, *Faithful and Fearless,* 163.

CHAPTER THREE

REPRESENTING WOMEN

Congresswomen's Perceptions of
Their Representational Roles

SUSAN J. CARROLL

A considerable body of research has documented that women representatives at both state and national levels are more likely than their male colleagues to support feminist positions on so-called women's issues, to actively promote legislation to improve women's status in society, and to focus their legislative attention on issues such as health care, the welfare of families and children, and education.[1] For the most part, however, research has not investigated the beliefs that undergird and ground women representatives' seemingly greater concern for and commitment to these issues.[2] This chapter explores the perceptions of women members of Congress regarding women as a category and examines how these perceptions affect their sense of themselves as representatives.

Much of the literature on women serving in Congress and the state legislatures is framed in terms of descriptive representation and its relationship to substantive representation.[3] Women representatives descriptively represent, or "stand for," women in the general population by virtue of their inclusion in the societal category called "women." However, most activists who work to increase the numbers of women in office and most scholars who study the effects of those increasing numbers are concerned about substantive representation as well. They presume that increased descriptive representation will lead to increased substantive representation; women representatives not only will "stand for" women, but also will "act for" them.

This formulation, however, fails to specify the geographic location of women who are to be represented. Is a woman representative presumed to "act for" only the women who live within the boundaries of the district she represents, or is she expected to "act for" women outside her district as well?

In recent work, Jane Mansbridge has drawn attention to a form of representation that she calls *surrogate representation*.[4] Surrogate representation occurs when a representative acts for the interests of voters beyond the boundaries of the representative's district. The represented voter cannot cast a vote for the surrogate representative, and thus accountability in an electoral sense is absent. Instead, the relationship between the surrogate representative and the voter usually rests on a shared ideological perspective or a common group identity.

As a result, surrogate representation can take place through descriptive representatives who share critical aspects of their identities with particular groups of voters and consequently see themselves as having common interests with those voters. As Mansbridge has explained: "Surrogate representatives do not have to be descriptive representatives. But it is in this surrogate process that descriptive representation often plays its most useful role, allowing representatives who are themselves members of a subordinate group to circumvent the strong barriers to communication between dominant and subordinate groups."[5]

This concept of surrogate representation is of potential significance for considering how the presence of women representatives may be altering the institution of Congress and its policy agenda. To the extent that women members of Congress see themselves and act as surrogate representatives for women outside the geographic boundaries of their districts, they bring something distinctive to their roles as representatives, something that most men do not bring.

This chapter assesses the extent to which women members of Congress do, in fact, perceive themselves to be surrogate representatives for women who may live beyond the borders of their districts. It examines whether women members of Congress feel a special responsibility to represent the interests of women within the institution and explores their ideas about the commonalities among women that could constitute the basis for surrogate representation.

DESCRIPTION OF THE STUDY

This chapter draws on 82 in-depth, semistructured interviews with women members of Congress conducted by the Center for American Women and Politics as part of a larger project on the impact of women members of Congress on various policy areas during the 103rd and 104th Congresses.[6] The first round of interviews was conducted between June and October 1995,[7] with 43 of the 55 women[8] who had served in the 103rd Congress (38 representatives, 5 senators; 31 Democrats, 12 Republicans). The second round of interviewing took place between October 1997 and March 1998,[9] with 39 of the 58 women[10] who had served in the 104th Congress (36 representatives, 3 senators; 27 Democrats, 12 Republicans).

The interviews, which were taped and conducted mostly in person, ranged in length from about 15 minutes to more than an hour. Interviews with the congresswomen were done "on the record" so that their names could be attached to quotes from their interviews. The fluid and flexible nature of the semistructured interviews prevented exact duplication of questions to each of the congresswomen interviewed. Consequently, the analysis presented in this chapter is qualitative in nature.

CONGRESSWOMEN'S PERCEIVED RESPONSIBILITY TO REPRESENT WOMEN

Mansbridge has suggested that "in practice, it seems that legislators' feelings of responsibility for constituents outside their districts are considerably stronger when the legislature features few, or disproportionately few, representatives of the group in question. . . . The sense of surrogate responsibility is also particularly strong when the surrogate representative shares experiences with surrogate constituents in a way that a majority of the legislature does not."[11]

Women as a category are underrepresented in Congress, holding only 73, or 13.6 percent, of the seats in the 107th Congress. Women held even fewer seats in the 103rd and 104th Congresses.[12] The contemporary women's movement has widely popularized the belief that women share experiences, ranging from disproportionate child-rearing responsibilities to discrimination in the workplace, which are not shared by most men. As a result, consistent with Mansbridge's speculations, a strong sense of surrogate responsibility could be expected to be widespread among the women who serve in Congress.

Indeed, it is. Congresswomen were asked whether, in addition to representing their districts, they felt a further responsibility to represent women. Almost all the women answered affirmatively and explained in some detail why they felt a special obligation to represent the interests of women. For example, Senator Barbara Boxer (D-CA) articulated the extra responsibility she feels to be a surrogate representative:

> There are still so few women in Congress. . . . So you really do have to represent much more than your own state although my state is huge. . . . Women from all over the country really do follow what you do and rely on you to speak out for them on the issues of women's health care, reproductive choice, condition of families, domestic priorities, environment, . . . equal pay for equal work. . . . I even had that in the House of Representatives, which was incredible because I just came from a small district. So it is a pretty big burden. And I remember when I came [to the Senate], Barbara Mikulski said, "Oh, my god, thank god, someone I can share this with," because she carried the load for so long as the only Democratic woman in the Senate.[13]

Some of the congresswomen talked, as Boxer did, about the need to represent women from all across the country. Others, like Representative Eva Clayton (D-NC), focused on the responsibility they feel toward women in their home states: "It is inescapable that women will communicate with you in a more vivid way of their hopes for their lives. . . . And it doesn't limit itself to my district. I have women all over the state say, 'You are my congresswoman. . . .' They identify with my presence here. And that adds, I think, an extraordinary opportunity, but I think it also adds a worthy burden that one has to be responsive [to] and responsible for."[14]

Representative Louise Slaughter (D-NY) offered yet another perspective, discussing the obligations she felt to be a surrogate representative for women in congressional districts that were represented by men or were less progressive than her own: "I do feel an obligation to all women in the country. In many cases, they don't have us [women representatives]. A lot of women are probably represented by some man. . . . [O]ne of the most important things for me . . . is . . . to make sure that all those women have equal opportunity and equal access to what we have. . . . I think we have an obligation . . . to make sure that the other women in the country aren't left behind."[15]

Some women members described how their perceived responsibility to represent women affects the way they consider legislation and conduct business in Congress. Representative Nancy Johnson (R-CT) provided a particularly compelling example of this:

> We need to integrate the perspective of women into the policy-making process, just like we have now successfully integrated the perspective of environmental preservation, the perspective of worker safety. . . . Whenever something comes up, we automatically think, "Gee, how will this affect the environment? How will this affect the working people at the work site?" But we don't really think, "How is this going to affect women who work at home? Women in the workplace with home responsibilities? Women who are single parents?" And so I do feel a special responsibility to participate in the public policy process in a way that assures that . . . I think through: "How will this affect women who are at home taking care of children who need to re-enter the workforce later on? How does this affect women who didn't get to go beyond high school because their family thought only boys should go to college, and now they're stuck?" I know a lot more [than congressmen] about the shape of women's lives and the pattern of women's lives, so I need to look and see: How will the public policy affect those patterns? And how will they help or hurt?[16]

Some women came to Congress with histories of advocacy on behalf of women and consequently easily assumed the role of surrogate representative. For example, Delegate Eleanor Holmes Norton (D-DC), who had been chair of the Equal Employment Opportunity Commission (EEOC) in the Carter administration, observed: "By the time I got to Congress, my view on women and my feeling of responsibility for pressing forward their demands was very well formed. . . . This was just another place, another forum, to act on them."[17]

However, other women did not come to Congress with the intent of serving as surrogate representatives for women. Instead, they became advocates for women while serving in Congress. In fact, their sense of responsibility to women often developed as a response to the neglect of women's interests within the institution. Representative Patsy Mink (D-HI), for example, recalled:

> When I first came to Congress in 1965, I had a notion that my basic responsibility was to my constituents and my state. And gradually as I took my place here, I realized that I had a far greater role to play and that it extended far beyond just caring for the constituents' needs— that I had to speak for all the women in America. And so it was not something that I came to Congress understanding, but certainly it hit me very quickly after I arrived that I had a voice that was far more important in the Congress than just the voice as a representative from Hawaii.[18]

Some of the veteran congresswomen on the Republican side of the aisle offered similar descriptions of how they came, over time, to take on the responsibility of representing women's interests within the institution. Representative Marge Roukema (R-NJ) insisted that she "hadn't wanted to" take on women's and family issues. She had "fought it." But she had been "shocked to my toenails to realize . . . the indifference of the men in Congress and . . . the callousness of them to some of these issues." She described her evolution as an advocate for women's interests as follows:

> When I first came to Congress, . . . I really didn't want to be stereotyped as the woman legislator. . . . I wanted to deal with . . . things like banking and finance. But I learned very quickly that if the women like me in Congress were not going to attend to some of these family concerns, whether it was jobs or children or equity . . . then they weren't going to be attended to. So I quickly shed those biases that I had, and said, "Well, nobody else is going to do it; I'm going to do it."[19]

Veteran congresswomen were not alone in assuming responsibility for representing women only after entering the institution. Some of the congresswomen first elected in the 1990s described experiences similar to those of Mink and Roukema. For example, Representative Leslie Byrne (D-VA), elected in 1992, observed: "Most of us didn't come in as women's issue people, but what we . . . found . . . is that if we didn't step in, those issues weren't addressed. I have always said that all issues are women's issues. But there are particular issues that affect women in greater proportions than others that don't seem to get the attention, and those are the ones you find yourself looking at just out of an issue of fairness."[20]

With few exceptions, a commitment to representing women was widely shared by congresswomen regardless of their party, ideology, race or ethnicity, tenure in office, or institutional position. For the most part they talked about this responsibility in similar ways. However, the more senior and influential women in Congress, especially those who had attained a position of leadership within their party, often saw an additional component of their responsibility to represent women—a responsibility to ensure other congresswomen's success as effective institutional players so that the perspectives of women would be voiced at all levels within the House and Senate. Senator Barbara Mikulski (D-MD) described her efforts to help five new Democratic women senators entering the 103rd Congress have an immediate impact on the institution:

> When the Democratic women came, I had a series of empowerment workshops for them on how to get started in the Senate, how to get committee assignments, and how they could move to be full partners in the Senate. And I took everything that I had learned in my first six years and really condensed it into a series of memos and . . . then a workshop. . . . You know, in all of American history until the 5 Democratic women came, only 19 of us [women] had served, less than a half a dozen in our own right. So I was determined as the dean of the Democratic women that the women, once they came, would be able to make their mark very quickly.[21]

Representative Barbara Kennelly (D-CT) spoke in similar fashion of the commitment she felt to help other women members advance within the House of Representatives: "I've felt it was important for me to open doors here, and I have. And that takes a lot of time, as well you know. I haven't reached the top of leadership, but I have opened the doors for it. Others will reach the top."[22]

Like some of the women who were more senior and influential, women of color talked in somewhat different ways about their feelings of responsibility for representing women. Women of color were as likely as white women to see themselves as surrogate representatives for women, and there were strong similarities between women of color and white women in their perceptions of their responsibility to help women. However, some differences also were apparent.

For example, some women of color expressed the inseparability of their identities as, and their responsibilities to, people of color and women. Senator Carol Moseley-Braun (D-IL) observed: "I jokingly use the old Popeye 'I am what I am.' And that means I'm an African American; I'm a female. Neither of those particular constituencies have traditionally had much of a voice here in the United States Senate and particularly with regard to policymaking and lawmaking. So to the extent that I bring those experiences to the mix, I think that not only does that help and enhance . . . the efficacy . . . of women in our policymaking process, but it also helps the body as a whole."[23] Similarly, Representative Cynthia McKinney (D-GA) noted: "I am an African American woman who has a certain set of life experiences that differentiate me from the typical male member of Congress. Therefore, I bring that to the institution, and the institution is changed and enhanced because of the difference I bring."[24]

Several Democratic women of color expressed a particular sense of responsibility to represent the interests of poor and working-class women. Representative Patsy Mink (D-HI) explained her feeling "that poor women . . . have no representation in Congress, other than women who feel a sense of commitment to represent their causes."[25] Similarly, Representative Eva Clayton (D-NC) suggested that African American women often bring the perspectives of poor and working-class women to bear on congressional debates: "To the extent that African American women would know more women who come from a disadvantaged community . . . or women who are living on limited means, I think our voices would put those faces in debates. . . . It would not be just articulating about the middle-class woman who is struggling to go from college to graduate school, but a woman who is struggling [to go] from high school to college, or one who has no high school education at all."[26]

Finally, a few women of color expressed the belief that their responsibility to represent women extended beyond the borders of the United States. Taking a global view of the surrogate representative role, Representative Nydia Velazquez (D-NY) suggested that women legislators "have a responsibility that goes beyond women in America. . . . We have a responsibility to protect women elsewhere."[27] Representative Carrie Meek (D-FL) gave specific examples of situations where her sense of responsibility to women extends beyond the borders of the United States: "A woman who is raped in Bosnia by the troops who were there, or a woman who is raped in Haiti by the coup members over there, a woman who has her genitalia mutilated in certain African societies. . . . I am partially responsible for that, for some amelioration of that, if at all possible."[28]

In the end, only a very small minority of congresswomen did not perceive themselves as having a responsibility to represent women. While these few congresswomen were more focused on other dimensions of their representative roles, considerations about women still sometimes entered into the picture. For example, Representative Helen Bentley (R-MD) explained: "Well, I felt a real responsibility for representing America, representing American industry, representing American jobs. . . . All economic issues are women's issues as well, and certainly if jobs are there and the economy is going well, there are jobs for women as well as for men. And if they're not, women will be the first ones cut out. So my whole strength throughout my years in Congress was on the issue of jobs, keeping jobs in this country, of fair trade."[29]

Similarly, Representative Barbara-Rose Collins (D-MI), who saw herself more as a surrogate representative for the working class, acknowledged:

> I felt my biggest responsibility was to represent the working class, whether they were in my district or not because they were the people who were the least represented in Congress. . . . I mean GM could afford million dollar lobbyists, right? But the people who worked at GM couldn't afford a lobbyist to look out for their interests. . . . So . . . most of my emphasis was on . . . the people who form the bedrock, the foundation of America, who toiled ceaselessly in the vineyards, but yet were left out of most of the tax benefits. So those were the ones I made my top criteria. For women, I more or less used myself as a litmus test on how it would affect me, and that's when I would go to bat for women's issues such as with breast cancer. I mean, women's issues were almost like African American issues—you just automatically supported them without thinking about it. . . . I didn't feel it was a responsibility; it was just more or less given that that would be a part of my agenda.[30]

Although women like Bentley and Collins did not consciously choose to act as surrogate representatives for women, they nevertheless saw their legislative actions as beneficial to women.

"THE TIES THAT BIND"

The perceived obligation that most congresswomen feel to act as surrogate representatives for women seems to be rooted in their beliefs that there are underlying commonalities among women. When congresswomen were asked if they believed women in the general society had anything in common as a group, almost all of them, regardless of party or ideology or race or ethnicity, expressed a belief that there are shared concerns that bind women together across divisions of geography, philosophy, class, and color. Rosa DeLauro (D-CT) exemplified the sentiments expressed by most congresswomen: "I've always thought that there was probably more that women had in common [than not], whether they're people from urban areas, inner cities, or suburban areas, or people who are from rural and farm districts. . . . There are what I call 'the ties that bind.'"[31]

Women members of Congress described a wide range of qualities and experiences that they believe women share. The vast majority of these perceived commonalities can be roughly grouped into four categories: caregiving, shared life experiences, discrimination, and work style.

Perhaps the most frequently mentioned commonality had to do with women's roles as caregivers and nurturers. Representative Sue Kelly (R-NY) reflected a point of view common among the women members of Congress: "I think women bring a very different view to lawmaking. . . . Women are the nurturing people in the nation. Women are the people who get called by their parents when there is a problem. Women are the people who get called by their kids when there is a problem. We are the people who do the nurturing and have to think: How do we fix this?"[32] Representative Marcy Kaptur (D-OH) gave another version of a caregiving response:

> I think that women in general are more life-giving. And I remember reading a quote after the Vietnam War . . .—that men always believe that there is something worth dying for, and the difference is that women believe there is something worth living for. And I've thought about this a lot. . . . I think that women in society have not been able to achieve a point yet . . . where their desire to give life and to nurture living things is given precedence in the body politic. So I think that women can also be great peace givers, given the opportunity. I don't think that they are as predatory [as men]. At least, I hope not.[33]

Yet another example of a caregiving response was offered by Representative Carrie Meek (D-FL): "I think that we have an attunement, as a group, that men don't have. I think it's because of the role we have had all of our lives—the child-bearing role, the nurturing role—that we are more sensitive to social issues. . . . We get to the core of things. Our intuition for these kinds of things, in my opinion, is something that women just normally have—that deep, instinctive feeling."[34]

Many of the women in Congress believed that women in society share other life experiences beyond their caregiving responsibilities. Representative Susan Molinari (R-NY) elaborated on what she saw as some of these other shared experiences: "From just a physical standpoint, the way we have to dress, what happens to our bodies, having a period, having a baby, walking through life under those circumstances, having to wear stockings every day, high heels at certain points—these are things that just bring women together."[35]

Representative Elizabeth Furse (D-OR) suggested that what women have in common is "a *not-male* experience," explaining, "the fact that we are not male is a very important experience, given that so much that happens in this world is driven through a male perception."[36] And Representative Tillie Fowler (R-GA) pointed to "just growing up as a woman," being in "Girl Scouts or Brownies or Junior League or YWCA or whatever." She noted that "there are organizations and activities that, as women, you have participated in or had life experiences in that were because you were a woman."[37]

A number of women members of Congress also pointed to the experience of discrimination as a common bond shared by women. Representative Barbara Vucanovich (R-NV), for example, explained her belief that all women "face some discrimination . . . whether it's in business or whether it's in the legislative situation just simply because it has been a man's world."[38] Similarly, Representative Karan English (D-AZ) suggested that the experience of discrimination binds women together: "They [women] have something in common in that they have been treated similarly for centuries, and the United States is no different. Without a voice or the opportunity to vote, their participation and their representation and their services are going to be different than men, and that puts us all in a similar category."[39]

Representative Louise Slaughter (D-NY) echoed English's observation that women have "been treated as a category" and further noted, "We've always made less money, regardless of the fact that we went to the same universities and got the same degrees."[40] Finally, Representative Nydia Velazquez (D-NY) talked about how the experience of discrimination was a bond that transcended race: "Every study that has been conducted in terms of women's achievement and gaining parity in every level of our lives—government, workplace . . . access to health care—we find out that there is common ground for all women to come together. We are facing, no matter our race, the same type of stigma, the same type of battles, that every single woman faces in this nation, no matter what race or color she is coming from."[41]

Perhaps most surprising was the frequency with which women members of Congress pointed to aspects of women's work styles as a common bond. Numerous congresswomen talked about women's approach to problem-solving, their interest in achieving consensus, their concern with details, and other work-style qualities as areas of commonality among women. Senator Olympia Snowe (R-ME), for example, described a number of qualities related to work style she believes women have in common:

> Women are focused on outcomes, results, and getting the job done. Basically women don't spend a lot of time on the periphery of a problem. They generally like to delve into it . . . and figure out what's the best way to achieve that outcome. . . . I think women are just basically that way, whether they're working in community affairs or their own professions or being at home. . . . Another thing I think women pay attention to is . . . details. And another thing is always trying to do their very best. . . . I see that as a trait that is common among a lot of women.[42]

Senator Blanche Lambert Lincoln (D-AR) also saw similarities in women's work styles, suggesting that "women are good at compromising, . . . realizing that sometimes it's better to get a step ahead than just stay in the same place for 14 years." She further explained that women have learned "how to work as team members because they have had so many responsibilities in the past with children, with family budgets, with household duties and things like that. They knew that they couldn't get everything they had to do at the church done by themselves, so they had to form committees. So women are used to working on teams; they're used to working together."[43]

Similarly, Representative Sue Myrick (R-NC) expressed her belief that women "are more prone to try to find ways to work together, to bring people together. We do it with our kids, to get along with one another."[44] Several congresswomen also noted that women are more likely than men, in the words of Representative Jan Meyers (R-KS), to "want to develop consensus more than fight it out."[45]

COMPLICATING THE PICTURE:
THE FORCES THAT DIVIDE

While the congresswomen perceived several ties that bind women together, they also were acutely aware of the differences that separate women and drive them apart, particularly in the context of the legislature. Women in the general society are divided by such markers as class, race, party, and ideology, and these divisions play themselves out in the congressional setting as well. Several of the congresswomen noted that although women, in their view, have much in common, they are not monolithic. The congresswomen recognized both that there are commonalities among women *and* that women also are often divided from one another.

Congresswomen's perceived responsibility to represent women is filtered through their other differences. Some of the major divisions among the congresswomen are those of party, race and ethnicity, district, and ideology.[46] Of these, district and ideology stood out in the interviews as particularly likely to influence the degree to which, and the ways in which, the responsibility that congresswomen feel to represent women is translated into behavior on public policy.[47]

First and foremost, every member of Congress has the responsibility to represent her or his district. Any member who does not do this well is likely to have a short tenure in office. Congresswomen were well aware that district considerations often lead women to favor different policies and to vote in different ways from one another. As Representative Tillie Fowler (R-GA) explained: "we are each individuals and we represent different districts. . . . And so since our districts are different . . . we're going to have some different interests at times."[48]

Many of the congresswomen felt fortunate to have a good match between their personal ideologies and the ideologies of their districts. Representative Jan Meyers (R-KS), for example, observed: "I was extremely fortunate in that I am very compatible with my district. . . . I didn't have to be looking over my shoulder all the time. I won with significant majorities, and I think it was because my district agreed with me on most things. . . . There was not a lot of tug and pull between my district and my conscience."[49]

However, some women members, especially those from marginal districts, very clearly experienced a tug and pull between their own preferences and those of their district. Representative Karen Shepherd (D-UT), a Democrat who served from 1992 to 1994 in a district previously and subsequently held by Republicans, explained:

> I didn't take the same kind of leadership role on those [women's and social] issues when I was in Congress, because in my district here, which is a very conservative district, those are politically charged issues that . . . would have been harmful to me. So the way I did it there was by working in the Women's Caucus, by helping in every way I could, and whipping the bills and getting the votes and making the right votes. But my very good, close friend Lynn Woolsey, for example, got on the committee I would have sold my soul to be on—the Education and Labor Committee—because she cares, as I do, about those issues. But if I would have been on that committee, it would have been a political liability.[50]

Similarly, Representative Karen Thurman (D-FL), who had a history of being pro-choice but opposed Medicaid funding for abortions, described the frustration of not being able to appease both the constituents of her fairly conservative district and the women's groups with whom she felt a kinship: "Medicaid funding for abortions is a difficult issue for me. And we got blasted by women's groups. . . . There are times that I think people have to step back. . . . I mean, . . . who is my replacement going to be? . . . Give me a break here! . . . I think women's groups have to come further [in understanding that congresswomen from conservative districts may not always be able to support feminist positions] than where they are."[51] Thus, as both the Shepherd and Thurman examples illustrate, a congresswoman's responsibility to represent her district can come into conflict with her ability to represent women's interests as she perceives them.

Although the 104th Congress was polarized along partisan lines, many of the women in Congress had worked together across party lines in the 103rd and previous Congresses and continued to do so on a more limited basis in the 104th. Perhaps as a result, Democratic women and moderate Republican women alike tended to see the major dividing line among women not as party, but rather as ideology. In particular, they saw several of the women in the cohort of conservative freshmen elected in 1994 as ideological outliers who, in Georgia Duerst-Lahti's conception of compounded gender ideology (this volume, see table 2.4), might be categorized as social conservatives and new right feminalists. For example, Representative Cynthia McKinney (D-GA) observed of the cohort of women elected in 1994, "Some [of these] women are bad old girls who want to be good old boys, and that's a shame."[52] This sentiment was echoed, among others, by Representative Elizabeth Furse (D-OR):

> I think many of them [women in the class of '94] . . . come from a much more right-wing, Christian viewpoint. . . . They are not feminists, and in fact, are proud not to be feminists. And I think if you eliminate the feminist experience or feminist understanding, you eliminate a lot of common ground. . . . We . . . know from the 104th Congress that just having females is not the answer to pushing the women's agenda because [some of the new women] . . . are not there for women. They're there for a right-wing agenda.[53]

Representative Deborah Pryce (R-OH), a moderate Republican first elected in 1992, characterized the ideological differences among women in a somewhat different manner:

> I think that some women members feel that they . . . must play up the women's issues for the women's groups back home, for a constituency that really helped them get elected. And so perhaps they get known for those issues more than other things. But in this Congress, especially with this new pack of women, they only shy away from that type of thing, and they want to be known as representatives and not women representatives, and [they believe] that all issues are their issues. . . . I'm in the middle. But I can see the two extremes pretty clearly.[54]

Several of the women members saw abortion as the issue that produced some of the sharpest divisions among women on ideological grounds. When Representative Connie Morella (R-MD), a moderate pro-choice Republican, was asked if she saw a difference between the ability of women to work together in the 103rd and 104th Congresses, she replied: "I see a difference, and I think it basically has to do with the abortion issue and the perception of the abortion issue as a divider because certainly women care about osteoporosis and women's health issues in general. They care about equity in the workplace. But the abortion issue has somehow clouded the thinking of some of the new women. They've seen this as sort of a barrier."[55]

Representative Ileana Ros-Lehtinen (R-FL), a more conservative Republican, shared Morella's view that the abortion issue, in particular, sharply divided women ideologically: "I think that we [women in Congress] have a common bond. Unfortunately, we have not paid enough attention to what unites us, and we tend to dwell on what divides us, like abortion or funding for some controversial health programs. Those kinds of issues, as important as they may be to certain members, . . . are divisive. But there are a lot of issues that we could unite and rally around, and we just don't seem to pay enough attention to those family-type issues."[56]

Ideological differences not only divide women in Congress, they also affect the way congresswomen perceive women's interests and thus the way in which the responsibility they feel to represent women is translated into behavior on public policy. For example, Representative Barbara Vucanovich (R-NV), who identified herself as pro-life, explained that on legislation dealing with abortion, "I felt like I should represent the women who felt that way [pro-life]."[57] While Vucanovich was interested in representing women, her interpretation of representing women on the abortion issue, consistent with her pro-life views, was very different than, for example, the interpretation of fellow Republican Connie Morella, who is strongly pro-choice.

Similarly, Representative Nancy Johnson (R-CT) characterized the different ideological interpretations she saw among some Republicans and Democrats in representing women's economic interests:

> I think the Republican women feel a greater responsibility to attend to the issue of economic opportunity for women. Now the Democratic women tend to look at social services for women. That's important, but if those social services end up disempowering women, then they are a . . . negative in their lives. You have not then done them [women] a service; you've done them a disservice. The Republican women have been trying to turn that around—to look at service to women as a lever to empower them to fulfill their own potential.[58]

As Johnson's example illustrates, the ideological filters of congresswomen can lead them to very different interpretations of how to best represent women's interests.

CONCLUSIONS AND DISCUSSION

Congresswomen's views about women and their representational responsibility to women are potentially significant for considering how the institution of Congress is changed by the presence of women among its members. While a few exceptional male members of Congress may feel a responsibility to represent women outside their districts, for women members of Congress this responsibility seems to be the norm, rather than the exception. Being a surrogate representative for women is, I suggest, part of what it means to be a woman member of Congress at this particular historical moment. When congresswomen perceive of themselves and act as surrogate representatives for women outside the geographic boundaries of their districts, as they clearly often do, they bring something distinctive to their roles as representatives, something that most men do not bring.

Women members of Congress perceive several common bonds among women in the general population. Congresswomen see women in the population as sharing the experiences of caregiving, gender-based discrimination, and the everyday occurrences of growing up and living as a woman in a male-dominated society. These shared experiences among women provide the women members with a set of gender-related interests and a sensitivity that they feel an obligation to consider and bring to bear in their work as legislators.

Many women members also perceive that women have a work style that grows out of their gender-related experiences and that differs from the dominant work style of men. To the extent that women members, as representatives of women, bring this perceived work style to their own work in Congress, they may, over time and as their numbers increase, help to bring about changes in the way business is conducted within the institution.

While most women members of Congress perceive of themselves as surrogate representatives for women and share some common perceptions about the experiences and ties that bind women together, they differ in the districts they represent, their own ideologies, their partisan commitments, and their racial and ethnic backgrounds. All of these differences, and perhaps other differences as well, can influence how congresswomen translate their perceived responsibility to represent women's interests into actual policy decisions. As a result, even when women members of Congress act in ways that they perceive as representing women, their actions may not always look the same. They may vote differently, offer different amendments, or favor different legislative solutions. Consequently, the changes in policy making that result from congresswomen's surrogate representation of women's interests will not always be unidirectional, straightforward, or uncomplicated.

NOTES

1. For example, Dodson and Carroll, *Reshaping the Agenda*; Carroll, "The Politics of Difference"; Thomas, *How Women Legislate*; Tamerius, "Sex, Gender, and Leadership"; Flammang, *Women's Political Voice*.

2. An exception is the work of Reingold, in *Representing Women* and "Concepts of Representation," although her work differs from mine in focusing on state legislators and their perceptions of women as a constituency within their districts.

3. For a theoretical discussion of descriptive and substantive representation, see Pitkin, *Concept of Representation*.

4. Mansbridge, "Many Faces of Representation"; Mansbridge, "Should Blacks Represent Blacks and Women Represent Women?"

5. Mansbridge, "Should Blacks Represent Blacks and Women Represent Women?" 642.

6. The study was made possible by the generous support of the Charles H. Revson Foundation and the Ford Foundation.

7. One interview was conducted after these dates (Senator Barbara Boxer in February 1996).

8. This number includes Eleanor Holmes Norton, delegate from the District of Columbia.

9. One interview was conducted after these dates (Senator Carol Moseley-Braun in April 1999).

10. This number includes Eleanor Holmes Norton, delegate from the District of Columbia.

11. Mansbridge, "Many Faces of Representation," 11.

12. Center for American Women and Politics (CAWP), "Women in the U.S. Congress 2001."

13. Interview with Barbara Boxer, 20 February 1996.

14. Interview with Eva Clayton, 25 July 1995.

15. Interview with Louise Slaughter, 24 October 1997.

16. Interview with Nancy Johnson, 3 December 1997.

17. Interview with Eleanor Holmes Norton, 24 August 1995.

18. Interview with Patsy Mink, 19 October 1995.

19. Interview with Marge Roukema, 20 July 1995.

20. Interview with Leslie Byrne, 9 August 1995.

21. Interview with Barbara Mikulski, 20 July 1995.

22. Interview with Barbara Kennelly, 20 July 1995.
23. Interview with Carol Moseley-Braun, 29 June 1995.
24. Interview with Cynthia McKinney, 29 October 1997.
25. Interview with Patsy Mink, 19 October 1995.
26. Interview with Eva Clayton, 4 November 1997.
27. Interview with Nydia Velazquez, 25 July 1995.
28. Interview with Carrie Meek, 31 October 1997.
29. Interview with Helen Bentley, 2 August 1995.
30. Interview with Barbara-Rose Collins, 18 February 1998.
31. Interview with Rosa DeLauro, 30 June 1995.
32. Interview with Sue Kelly, 22 January 1998.
33. Interview with Marcy Kaptur, 19 July 1995.
34. Interview with Carrie Meek, 27 June 1995.
35. Interview with Susan Molinari, 28 June 1995.
36. Interview with Elizabeth Furse, 24 July 1995.
37. Interview with Tillie Fowler, 28 June 1995.
38. Interview with Barbara Vucanovich, 19 September 1995.
39. Interview with Karan English, 15 September 1995.
40. Interview with Louise Slaughter, 24 October 1997.
41. Interview with Nydia Velazquez, 25 July 1995.
42. Interview with Olympia Snowe, 29 June 1995.
43. Interview with Blanche Lambert Lincoln, 17 November 1997.
44. Interview with Sue Myrick, 25 February 1998.
45. Interview with Jan Meyers, 14 September 1995.
46. The variables of party, race and ethnicity, district, and ideology are, of course, highly interrelated. Liberal women tend to be African Americans, non-Cuban Latinas, or white Democrats from liberal districts. Conservative women tend to be white Republicans elected from conservative districts.
47. The research staff who conducted the interviews with congresswomen were white. Unfortunately, it is not possible to know whether this affected the degree to which possible racial differences were expressed.
48. Interview with Tillie Fowler, 28 June 1995.
49. Interview with Jan Meyers, 18 November 1997.
50. Interview with Karen Shepherd, 8 August 1995.
51. Interview with Karen Thurman, 20 June 1995.
52. Interview with Cynthia McKinney, 29 October 1997.
53. Interview with Elizabeth Furse, 24 July 1995.
54. Interview with Deborah Pryce, 28 September 1995.
55. Interview with Connie Morella, 22 June 1995.
56. Interview with Ileana Ros-Lehtinen, 18 July 1995.
57. Interview with Barbara Vucanovich, 18 November 1997.
58. Interview with Nancy Johnson, 3 December 1997.

CHAPTER FOUR

CONGRESS AND THE
TRANSFORMATION OF THE
WOMEN'S MOVEMENT

ANNE COSTAIN AND HEATHER FRAIZER

The cause of American women's suffrage required nineteen campaigns before nineteen Congresses before it succeeded. Elizabeth Cady Stanton wrote of her testimony before the Senate Committee on Privileges and Elections in 1878:

> In the whole course of our struggle for equal rights, I never felt more exasperated than on this occasion, standing before a committee of men many years my junior, all comfortably seated in armchairs. . . . The peculiarly aggravating feature of the present occasion was the studied inattention and contempt of the chairman, Senator Wadleigh of New Hampshire. . . . He alternately looked over some manuscripts and newspapers before him, and jumped up to open or close a door or a window. He stretched, yawned, gazed at the ceiling, cut his nails, sharpened his pencil, changing his . . . position every two minutes, effectively preventing the establishing of the faintest magnetic current between the speakers and the committee. It was with difficulty that I restrained the impulse more than once to hurl my manuscript at his head.[1]

This account contrasts sharply with the way members of Congress treated women nearly one hundred years later: "It was toward the end of

1982, after the failure of sufficient states to ratify the ERA [Equal Rights Amendment], that Senator Dole realized that Republicans should provide some leadership role in the enactment of pension equity legislation. . . . The pension issue was selected by the Republican leadership as *the* women's issue on which to concentrate, partially so they could go home and say they did something for women."[2]

It is tempting to characterize women's journey from shunned outsiders to sought-after constituency group as an example of American democratic inclusion—which it is. "You've come a long way, baby." Yet, it must equally be acknowledged how rarely groups relegated to the semipolitical status of social movement are able to transform themselves, as women did, into an institutionalized lobbying and voting bloc. The American women's movement throughout this long period is most usefully thought of as a single movement, first emerging in the mid-1800s and continuing into the 21st century.[3] Its periods of most intense activity have been characterized by historians as waves, with the first being the attainment of woman suffrage (first wave),[4] the second the massive effort to win ratification of the Equal Rights Amendment to the Constitution (second wave),[5] and the current wave being building on the new institutionalized position of women as a lobbying and voting bloc to unite women across lines of color and class, yet not relinquishing the option of taking their cause to the streets when gains are threatened (third wave feminism).[6]

Throughout the movement's history, many of its successes and failures have pivoted around congressional action and inaction. Congressional approval was required to place the "Anthony"[7] amendment before state legislatures to gain women's suffrage. The 70-year struggle for women's right to vote, which began in Seneca Falls, New York, led ultimately to a dramatic vote on the floor of the U.S. House of Representatives in January 1918 and reluctant U.S. Senate approval more than a year later. More recently, the U.S. Congress has also been a key political arena as women's groups have organized and lobbied successfully for landmark legislation such as the Equal Pay Act of 1963, Title IX of the 1972 Education Act Amendments, the Pregnancy Discrimination Act of 1978, and the Family Leave and Medical Leave Act of 1993. Congress has also been the site of elusive, bittersweet legislative battles, such as the Equal Rights Amendment approved by Congress in 1972 some 50 years after its original introduction, but not renewed for an extended ratification period in 1983. The interactions between the women's movement and Congress have produced a distinctive history of transformation and institutionalization.

Research on social movements identifies institutionalizing as a distinct phase that comes toward the end of a movement's life cycle. Institutionalization occurs when a social movement is willing to engage the state by working within its structures (e.g., through electoral politics, legislative lobbying, or carrying test cases to the courts for resolution).[8] For many social movement scholars, institutionalization marks the end of the movement phase and thus crosses over to interest group or electoral research.[9] Yet, as Ronald Aminzade, using the case of the French Revolution, has argued, institutionalization is often confused with formalism.[10] Formalism occurs as a social movement starts to devote an increasing share of its resources to organizing formal groups, which may include interest groups or political parties. Formalism frequently precedes movement abandonment of protest politics. But, although Aminzade acknowledges that increasing involvement with institutional politics tends to push movements in the direction of formalism, he insists that it is more of a tactic than a result. Perhaps because of the frequent confusion between institutionalization and formalism, few movement scholars have made systematic efforts to document this end stage of a movement's entry into the larger fabric of politics.[11]

Our study recognizes the unique opportunity the women's movement offers to better appreciate institutionalization. In the second wave of the movement, women were able to reemerge as major actors on the national political stage, using lobbying and electoral politics. This occurred even after their movement's initial phase as outsider and challenger of the status quo had largely passed, but while direct action and protest remained important parts of their repertoire of contention. The ability to achieve such a transformation was almost certainly tied to the movement's public image and to the way that group leaders projected that image. Social movement scholar Doug McAdam has warned of the fragile balance that insurgent movements must adopt to succeed: "For the movement to survive, insurgents must be able to create a more enduring organizational structure to sustain insurgency. Efforts to do so usually entail the creation of formally constituted organizations to assume the centralized direction of the movement previously exercised by informal groups."[12]

McAdam goes on to note that setting up formal organizations puts the movement at risk of initiating three processes, any one of which can cripple the movement's efforts to bring about more social change. These are hierarchy and oligarchy, where leaders come to value their own positions in a group more than the goals of the movement; co-optation, where state structures or other external supports of the movement come to dominate its agenda; and, finally, the fading of indigenous support, where the groups giving rise to the movement feel so distant from its formal organizations that they no longer mobilize nor contribute to its support.[13] The women's movement has been unusually successful in creating organizations leading it on the path from social movement to institutional actor, while retaining the ability to mobilize a large grassroots constituency.

In this volume's consideration of the impact that women have had on Congress, it is important to recognize and trace the progression of the women's movement through its evolution from social movement to interest group and finally to a voting bloc that no elected official can safely ignore. It seems that the most unusual aspect of this movement's success is its ability to escape the trap of formalism, in which increasing commitment to organization saps the strength and the resources of movement activists, as the movement becomes more institutionalized. As is true of most movements, the women's movement contains a number of organized groups that played key roles in institutionalizing. We focus on these groups—what they were like and how they appeared to the public. This provides important clues concerning the movement's ability to sustain both institutionalization and protest politics.

This focus on organized groups, while rejecting formalism, makes sense in the context of social movements. For, when movements enter the political arena, both organized groups within them and the leaders of these groups become more visible and better known to the public than the movements' more loosely structured and numerous sympathizers, activists, and attentive publics. Most people react to a movement's leaders and organizations more than to its goals or mass of followers, because these offer the representations of the movements' goals and agendas that the public is accustomed to seeing in news outlets.[14] The media normally interview spokespersons and cover group actions via spokespersons rather than exploring the public policy critiques of the movement in the abstract. In response to public and media attention, social movement group leaders may aggressively seek this specialized attention from the press and political institutions as one strategy to get airtime for their issues. Other group leaders simply become the focus of media and institutional attention because of who they are—protest leaders are more likely than most other political figures to be charismatic, and charisma has been shown to be another effective strategy for rebellious groups to use to overcome collective action problems.[15] Consequently, group leaders' actions and statements often play a disproportionate role in defining the movement's image and issues for the public as well as for institutions of government, including the U.S. Congress and the presidency.[16]

To understand the image and actions of the formal groups within the second wave of the movement, we used media coverage to isolate patterns of interaction between U.S. political institutions and women's movement groups between 1980 and 1996. The data set consists of all articles (1,772 total) published in the *New York Times* between January 1, 1980, and December 31, 1996, that mention at least one of nine nationally visible second wave women's organizations. We chose these nine second wave feminist groups, based on their high level of political activism[17] and the wide range of feminist styles and issues they cover, to represent the very public phase of the women's movement emerging in the mid-1960s. Each group emerged and, in some cases, disbanded in the period between 1966 and 1982. They are the National Organization for Women (NOW); National Women's Political Caucus; Women's Equity Action League (WEAL); Federally Employed Women (FEW); Congressional Caucus for Women's Issues; Society to Cut Up Men (SCUM); Redstockings; Older Women's League (OWL); and National Abortion Rights Action League (NARAL). We used neither coders nor the *New York Times Index* for this project, but entered the names of each group directly into the LexisNexis search engine, which found all articles appearing in the *New York Times* mentioning one or more of the groups. During the years searched, 1980 to 1996, the *Times* published between 55 and 168 articles annually that referred to at least one of these groups. A small number of the articles, which we manually dropped from the data set, simply reported that the group was holding a meeting, listing place and time. The other articles all contain substantive discussions of either the groups, or issues, or political events with which the groups were involved.

Although we focus on actions of second wave women's movement groups, the period covered encompasses parts of both second and third waves. This is a time when the movement most visibly transformed itself from protester to institutionalized political actor. For the many movements that plunge from protest to obscurity, we believe this transition provides valuable lessons. Third wave groups appear to represent a new stage of movement presence; so we elected to examine the transformation process undergone by the second wave rather than the reemergence of the movement in the third wave.

WAVES OF HISTORY IN THE WOMEN'S MOVEMENT

Before analyzing the institutionalizing phase initiated by the second wave of the women's movement, it is important to place this wave within the context of the tactics and gains of the movement as a whole. The first wave of the suffrage movement initiated woman's quest for a social and political role comparable to man's—at a time when women were expected to remain outside the public sphere.[18] Women were seen as the center of home and family life, men as the proper occupants of public space. Women began to assert a right to a public role by mobilizing behind two highly morally charged issues, slavery and temperance. Suffrage groups did picket the White House, adopting the perspective that until women possessed the vote, they would blame the party controlling the presidency for women's continued exclusion. However, most of their efforts were directed toward Congress. First wave feminist groups included the National Woman Suffrage Association, the American Woman Suffrage Association, the Congressional Union, the American Association of University Women, the General Federation of Women's Clubs, the League of Women Voters, and the National Woman's Party. Supported by pressure from these and other suffrage groups, amendments to the Constitution giving women the right to vote were introduced in nineteen successive Congresses before receiving majority votes from both chambers. When women at last gained suffrage in federal elections in 1920, they did so largely on the grounds that they would clean up politics, bringing a new, less self-interested sensibility to political affairs. As politics continued to carry with it the taint of power, women were largely dismissed as important political actors, setting the stage for second wave feminism.

The women's movement that reemerged in the mid-1960s was initially seen as an offshoot of the black civil rights movement, echoing often-heard demands in the sixties for equality and democracy.[19] By its second year, NOW and much of the movement were urging adoption of the unfinished agenda of the first wave women's movement—endorsing an Equal Rights Amendment to the U.S. Constitution as well as continuing women's historic opposition to force and violence.[20] By the mid-1970s, the American movement had reached its zenith in press coverage and activism, only to lose ground following the 1982 defeat of the Equal Rights Amendment (ERA).[21] Yet, while the highly mobilized protest phase of the women's movement lost momentum, the movement, instead of disappearing from public view, began to transform itself into a more institutionalized, but nonetheless successful, actor in the arenas of interest group and electoral politics.[22]

The third wave movement gained attention in the 1990s as a more conventionally structured women's movement asserting grassroots activism, including protest politics, and inclusion of previously marginalized groups of women. Among its objectives are the protection and preservation of gains made during the movement's protest period, coupled with the goal of building electoral clout to further women's ability to influence the national institutions of government. Also, and critically, the third wave mobilized to address more adequately the linked issues of race, class, and gender. Its groups include Third Wave, the Fund for a Feminist Majority, Human Rights Campaign, the National Organization of Pan Asian Women, Gender Pac, Women's Action Coalition, and Women's Health Action Mobilization (WHAM).

Congress and the presidency have been important targets of all three feminist waves. Various scholars have traced the ability of a small, underfunded lobby to stimulate passage of the Equal Credit Opportunity Act, add "sex" to the executive order on affirmative action, pass Title IX of the 1972 Education Act Amendments and the Pregnancy Discrimination Act, to promote the Equal Rights Amendment in many states, and to equalize pension and other retirement benefits between women and men.[23] These policy gains, along with numerous other legislative and executive branch victories on women's issues have substantially reshaped American public policy toward women.

But, women's success in contributing to the attendant transformation of Congress is largely due to their social movement-linked lobby. Although Jo Freeman raised the central question of what it means to be a social movement lobby in America in her pathbreaking book *The Politics of Women's Liberation* (1975), the question has never satisfactorily been answered. To

investigate the transformation of the women's movement into an institutionalized political actor, we draw together data on the process of social
movement institutionalization and responses from key political institutions.

Institutionalization accelerated following rejection of the ERA by state
legislatures. This defeat was such a serious blow to the women's movement
because it meant the loss of the most popular issue within the movement
as well as one of the few issues capable of uniting groups across the movement. In the wake of, and contributing to this loss, the presidency appeared
to slip away from its earlier support of movement goals. Ronald Reagan,
elected in 1980, became the first president since the emergence of the second wave women's movement to oppose ERA and legalized abortion. So,
in the face of diminished protest activity by the early eighties, and a decidedly less friendly executive branch, women's groups changed tactics and
began to institutionalize. They applied pressure on a far greater range of
issues during this era and aggressively took on countermovement groups,
such as Randall Terry and Joseph Scheidler's anti-abortion Operation Rescue, using the legal process and passage of new laws to thwart Operation
Rescue's coercive tactics to stop abortions from being performed.[24]

DATA AND METHOD

Although the impetus for institutionalization came from within the
women's movement, we believe that institutionalization of the movement
during this period was based largely on the perception that the public
approved of movement activities, including, most significantly, the activities of the organized groups within the movement. We used coverage
between 1980 and 1996 by the *New York Times*[25] to test this perspective.
Using LexisNexis, we downloaded 1,772 articles (figure 4.1), entering all
the articles into QSR Nudist, a content analysis program, which permits
searches for word patterns within texts. Our purpose was to disclose the
image of the movement and its groups conveyed through the elite press.

We chose 1980 as the initial year to measure movement institutionalization for two reasons. The first was that social movements historically have
become most involved in conventional activity after their peak period of
political engagement is past. Consequently, it made sense to begin the data
set in a year when the social movement representing women faced mounting and sustained obstacles. In the 1980 election, women's vote divided

FIGURE 4.1

Article Totals by Year in the New York Times, *1980–1996*

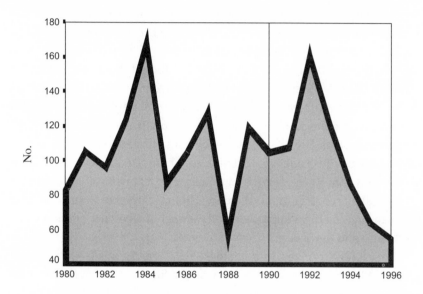

narrowly between sitting president Jimmy Carter and challenger Ronald Reagan, while men elected Republican Ronald Reagan overwhelmingly. The entire decade posed difficult political challenges for the women's movement, with Republicans holding the White House and opposing many key women's issues—most notably legalized abortion and the ERA.

The women's movement also ran into tough times politically in the 1990s, with a steady decline in press coverage of women's issues and court-upheld limitations on access to abortion in the wake of the *Webster v. Reproductive Health Services* (1989) decision. For although *Webster* failed to overturn *Roe v. Wade* (1973), it made it possible for states to restrict access to abortion to such an extent that women's constitutional right to have an abortion, pronounced so powerfully in *Roe*, was in danger of being overwhelmed by state regulations discouraging women from choosing to have abortions. Finally, the hottest "women's" political issue in the 1990s was sexual harassment, introduced to the mass public during the Clarence Thomas hearings in 1991, continuing in the Robert Packwood (R-OR) ethics hearings in the Senate in 1995, and in the allegations directed at President Bill Clinton throughout his presidency, culminating in an impeachment trial in the Senate where he was accused of having lied to a court about his sexual relations with a young White House intern. These issues were particularly damaging to the women's movement because politicians such as Packwood and Clinton had been valuable allies of the movement in many of its legislative battles, yet the private conduct of these men seemed to replicate the male abuses of power that the movement had so long attacked. Although 1992 was heralded as the "Year of the Woman" in politics because of impressive gains in the number of women officeholders both in Congress and in statewide offices, this seemed insufficient to counterbalance a decade filled with challenges to feminism. There is, perhaps, a sweet irony in the view that the arrogant and dismissive treatment of law professor Anita Hill by senators in the Clarence Thomas Supreme Court confirmation hearings led to an unprecedented number of women winning seats in the House and the Senate.[26]

The second reason for choosing these years was the availability and reliability of the data. Nineteen-eighty was the first year in which the entire printed version of the *New York Times* was available for direct download as opposed to scanning or typing in articles. The time period chosen offered the best opportunity for accuracy, because manual entry greatly increases the chance of introducing error during the inputting of data.

Using this data base, it is possible to contrast the issues, tactics, and coverage of women's groups as the various organizations interacted with Congress and with the president. In order to divide the articles initially, we used *Congress* and *congressional* to locate the subset of legislative materials and *president* and *presidential* in word searches for executive branch content. The use of *president* created coding problems not encountered in the *Congress* search. *President* falsely identified a number of articles discussing the presidents of interest groups, labor unions, boroughs in New York City, and foreign leaders. Also, *president* picked up a large number of references to U.S. vice presidents and vice presidential candidates. To correct for these false finds, we read through the language surrounding *president* and removed articles making no reference to current or former American presidents.

To understand the issues bringing women's movement groups together with institutions, we searched for words allowing us to find mentions of abortion, civil rights, education, and jobs and employment. Abortion articles were isolated rather easily using the terms *abortion* and *anti-abortion* in a pattern search. For education, we used *school, teacher*, and *education*. The workplace, economy, and jobs were traced using *employ, job, work*, and *economic*. Finally, civil rights stories were identified with the terms *civil rights, equal rights*, and *discrimination*.

Finally, because there are a variety of types of political interactions with institutions, we broke out the articles mentioning lobbying and electoral involvement with the words *lobby, lobbying, campaign, pressure*, and *pac*. Protest was targeted through *protest, picket, confront, strike, disrupt, rally, boycott, riot*, and *sit-in*. Violent actions were separated by *violence, violent, injury, destroy*, and *injure*.

WOMEN'S MOVEMENT GROUPS AS POLITICAL ACTORS

Comparing the number of articles featuring women's groups, the Congress, and the president, figure 4.2 shows the levels of interactions between the institutions and movement groups during this period of institutionalizing. In general, approaches to the legislative and executive branches track pretty closely. There are two exceptions. In 1984, for the first time, a major American political party nominated a woman candidate for vice president—Representative Geraldine Ferraro (D-NY). Unsurprisingly, women's movement groups had far more contacts with the executive branch, including the presidential campaign, than in any other year in the period. The second exception to comparable levels of interaction between the two branches and movement groups is predictable as to year, 1992, but unusual in its institutional link—which was to the presidency. That year was widely heralded as the "Year of the Woman" because so many women were elected to Congress and to state offices. However, the greatest number of articles featuring second wave women's groups and the presidency dealt with the presidential campaign. Leaders of many of the women's groups weighed in to criticize President George Bush for his veto of the Family Medical Leave Act and for his strong opposition to abortion. A *New York Times* article from October 21, 1992, explained that, "According to a NOW study on female legislators and social policy, 71 percent of women––but only 52 percent of the men—in Congress sought to override a Presidential veto of the Family Medical Leave Act."[27] A story from June of that year reported that

FIGURE 4.2

Women's Group Articles Referring to Congress and the President

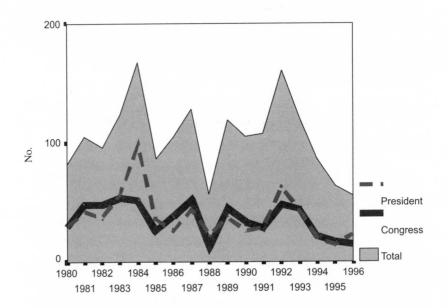

these groups [the Mid-Fairfield County Citizens for Choice, the Coalition of Citizens for Choice, the Greater Bridgeport Coalition for Choice, and the Danbury Coalition for Choice, a branch of the Danbury area National Organization for Women] are made up of Connecticut residents, many of whom have never been involved in a political cause or joined an activist group. Their members are becoming galvanized by the immediacy of the impending Supreme Court decision [*Planned Parenthood of Pennsylvania v. Casey*], and are growing increasingly angry at President Bush's staunch opposition to abortion rights.[28]

Although there were some articles about women's groups pleased with Bill Clinton's nomination by the Democrats, criticism of Bush's stands on issues affecting women far outweighed praise of Clinton.

The *New York Times* referenced NOW far more than any other second wave group. The National Organization for Women has always occupied a special place as the largest membership organization to emerge out of the second wave women's movement. The breadth of its interests brings it

FIGURE 4.3

Congressional Issues

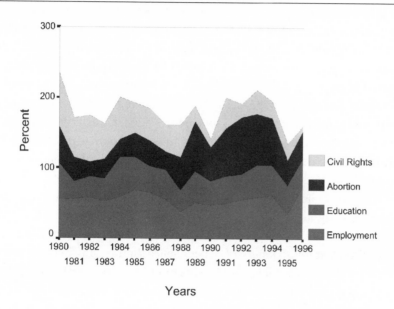

more attention than more narrowly focused issue groups such as FEW, NARAL, and OWL. NOW is also noteworthy for its frequent success in selecting media-savvy presidents, stretching from Betty Friedan, who was its first, through Eleanor Smeal and Jill Ireland, both of whom became household names nationally as feminist leaders. Throughout this period, NOW routinely accounted for close to half of the coverage of second wave women's groups.[29]

In reviewing these articles on second wave groups and political institutions, we were especially interested in which issues and events brought the movement into closest contact with the institutions of government. Figure 4.3 shows the proportion of stories mentioning frequently referenced issues and Congress. (The totals add up to more than 100 percent because articles frequently include more than one subject.) Throughout these decades, employment and jobs was the subset of issues most consistently discussed. The two least stable issue areas for congressional deliberation were civil rights, which stimulated numerous articles throughout the 1980s, and abortion, which became a major focus in the 1990s. The issue of education, while less volatile than civil rights or abortion, varied more than employment and jobs. While NOW worked on virtually all women's issues, most of the other groups focused on a narrower subset of issues. The National Women's Political Caucus directed much of its attention at getting greater numbers of feminist women, and sometimes male allies, elected, appointed, and involved in promoting women's issues. Women's Equity Action League worked to improve the opportunities for women in education and business. FEW, as its name suggests, promoted the well-being of women who were government employees. The Congressional Caucus for Women's Issues organized and lobbied within Congress to encourage passage of bills beneficial to women. SCUM and Redstockings were radical feminist protest groups. OWL targeted the double disability of being a woman and being old. NARAL, as its full name makes obvious, took a leading role in defending abortion rights.

Presidential issues followed a path similar to those handled by Congress, suggesting a common pattern of issue salience (figure 4.4). There are, however, two clear differences. First, education became a noticeably more important topic for presidential consideration in the 1990s. The other difference was that civil rights continued as an executive focus throughout this period of institutionalizing, while shrinking to virtual insignificance in Congress. President Bill Clinton took on a range of civil rights issues, ranging from ending bias based on sexual orientation, supporting continued affirmative action to promote diversity, and continuing the call for an equal rights amendment to the constitution. Wade Henderson, executive director of the Leadership Conference on Civil Rights, was quoted in the *New York Times* as saying about Clinton, "His record stands with the best of recent Presidents, with the possible exception of Lyndon Johnson."[30] The breadth of Clinton's support for civil rights was shadowed for some of his supporters by his compromise on gays in the military, where the "Don't ask, don't tell" policy replaced Clinton's initial pledge to end discrimination against gays. Likewise, his abandonment of Lani Guinier, whom he had nominated to be assistant attorney general for civil rights, when conservatives dubbed her the affirmative action "quota queen," led many to doubt the strength of his commitment. By contrast, Congress dealt with few civil rights issues in the mid-1990s. After the state of California ended its affirmative action programs, a conservative Congress did little to halt movement away from earlier civil rights initiatives.

FIGURE 4.4
Presidential Issues

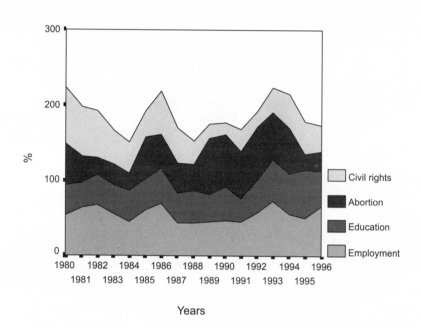

Years

Overall coverage of second wave women's groups by the *Times* displays a similar pattern to coverage of these groups' interactions with Congress (figure 4.5). In the 1990s, proportionally more articles focus on abortion and fewer on civil rights. Employment and education are fairly consistent throughout the period. Rising presidential discussion of education is reflected in the overall figures. In the context of this volume on transformation in Congress, one important finding is that Congress appears to provide a more accurate reflection of the issue priorities of second wave women's movement groups than the executive branch—suggesting that the "popular" branch of government still retains a strong representative role in democratic government.

WORKING WITH INSTITUTIONS

It might reasonably be hypothesized from a formalist perspective that second wave groups gained success by adopting mainstream lobbying

FIGURE 4.5

Proportional Issue Coverage in the New York Times

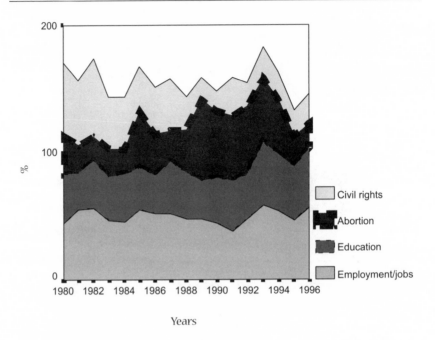

Years

tactics. These tactics include testifying before Congress; contributing funds to legislative campaigns; going from office to office to persuade representatives and their staffs to support the group's position; organizing coalitions of interest groups to apply coordinated pressure on Congress; and using the courts to win favorable interpretations of legislation coming out of Congress. Part of this "mainstreaming" would be abandonment of noninstitutional means of rallying political support. According to this common wisdom, social movements institutionalize themselves by giving up their tactics of protest politics. By contrast, Aminzade would hold that although there is a positive relationship between more conventional political means and institutionalization, it is far from a one-to-one correspondence. In other words, social movement organizations may institutionalize while still engaging in protest and unconventional political tactics.

FIGURE 4.6
Congress: Lobbying versus Protest

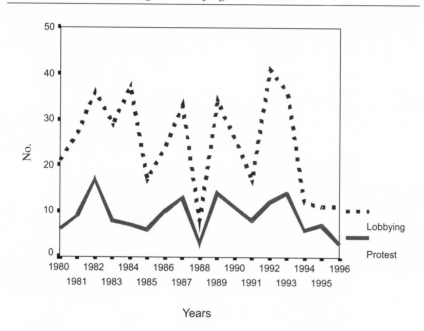

Figure 4.6 compares the numbers of protest activities versus conventional lobbying interactions when women's organizations engaged political institutions. As most scholars would predict, there were many more articles written about lobbying than protest activities in the 1980s and 1990s as institutionalization proceeded apace. Since the mass media frequently portray movements as radical and threatening to public order, thus coloring the public's view of them, it is unsurprising given women's success that their groups are portrayed as largely unthreatening. Comparing the interactions of second wave women's groups with Congress and the president, coverage of lobbying as compared with protest is quite similar for the two institutions (figure 4.7). With campaigning incorporated as one part of the measure of lobbying coverage, two elections stand out. The vice presidential candidacy of Geraldine Ferraro clearly drew the participation and comment of second wave women's groups. The congressional elections of 1992, the "Year of the Woman," also engaged women's groups, with cheerleading from Clinton as Democratic party presidential nominee. The parties,

FIGURE 4.7

President: Lobbying versus Protest

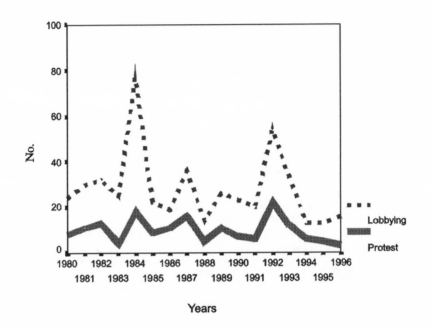

particularly the Democrats, featured women candidates in these elections to stretch their electoral edge with female voters.[31] Well-known women candidates such as Dianne Feinstein and Carol Moseley-Braun also played a role in perpetuating a gender gap.

Just as lobbying covers several different types of political activities, so too does protest politics, which ranges from the peaceful and noninvasive to the violent and destructive. It makes sense that protest invoking violence or destruction of property would be seen differently by the media and the public than protest involving peaceful demonstrations. Dividing peaceful protest from violent protest shows the former occurring more frequently than the latter (figure 4.8). For a movement engaged in a sustained effort to become an institutionalized political interest, this is what one would expect. Virtually all social movement scholars have observed that institutionalization moves those social movement groups engaging in it away from the use of violence.[32] In fact, movement splits frequently grow out of the efforts of more extreme groups to escalate violent confrontation in the hope of

FIGURE 4.8

Women's Group Articles Focused on Protest and Violence

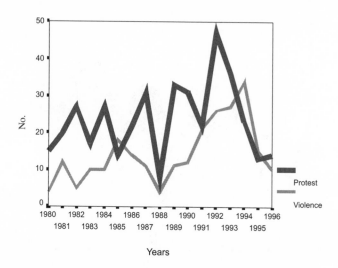

pressuring more moderate groups to move away from institutionalizing. In the same way that lobbying activity became relatively more important during the 1980s and 1990s, violent protest should become rarer as institutionalizing proceeds. Yet, this is not the pattern that emerges. Figure 4.9, which shows the percentage of articles by year broken down according to mentions of lobbying, protest, and violence, indicates that violence increased along with protest. Nor is the pattern one in which more extreme second wave groups such as SCUM or even NOW initiate violence to slow or reverse the efforts of moderate groups such as WEAL and the National Women's Political Caucus to institutionalize. Violence is a feature of these protests not because it occurs there, but because the protest itself is staged in opposition to violence. As one example, in 1996, an official of the New York chapter of NOW responded to news that the New York Giants had signed a college athlete with a history of arrests for violence against women by stating that her organization would not protest the signing at this time, but may decide to protest at a later time.[33] In 1995, in the aftermath of Nicole Simpson's death, all the protest articles reported in the *Times* that mentioned violent behavior dealt with domestic violence. In 1994, domestic violence and anti-abortion violence dominated the protest news.

FIGURE 4.9

Percentage of Articles according to Type of Political Act

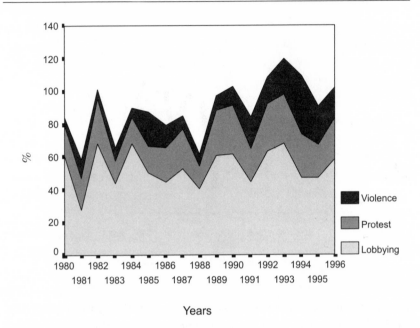

Years

Women's groups protested these types of violence with candlelight vigils, marches, and other forms of nonviolent protest. For example, "Take Back the Night" marches, which originated in San Francisco in 1978, have spread across the country as annual events bringing together demonstrators across racial, gender, and class divides to show their outrage that women cannot safely travel alone at night in most American cities.[34] Countermovement violence against women was reported in the language of a dissenting Supreme Court opinion: "Justice [John Paul] Stevens said, the [anti-abortion] demonstrators' aim was 'to deny every woman the opportunity to exercise a constitutional right that only women possess' by combining 'massive defiance of the law with violent obstruction of the constitutional rights of their fellow citizens.'"[35]

At a news conference outside of Madison Square Garden, the New York Mets' manager was denounced by individuals and group spokespersons for responding to a question about how he deals with a losing season with the quip that he beats his wife. Diane Welsh, president of the New York chapter of NOW, which arranged for the protest, stated, "When sports celebrities joke with impunity about domestic violence, ordinary men begin to believe that abuse of their wives is normal."[36] In only a very few instances was it suggested that feminists engaged in violent protest. One example concerned Senator Robert Packwood (R-OR), accused of sexual harassment. "Protests, relatively small but vigorous to the point of violence, have greeted Mr. Packwood at several stops. Women's groups say they are infuriated that Mr. Packwood, a Republican long considered a staunch supporter of their issues, has refused to meet with them."[37]

Despite the unanticipated finding that women's involvement in protests linked to violence increased along with institutionalization, the long-held role of women as critics of force and violence provides the explanation. Women's groups in virtually all instances were organizing or speaking out in opposition to violence, not using it as a tactic. This is confirmed since, overall, the women's movement received positive and sympathetic coverage throughout the period of backlash and regrouping after defeat of the ERA. From 1980 to 1996, favorable articles about second wave groups and their issues consistently outnumbered critical ones by 15 to 25 percent.[38] This puts the question of the role of violence for the institutionalizing of a movement into a different category. Just as it seemed that citizens became increasingly willing to have institutions make room for the interests of African Americans in the aftermath of violent efforts to exclude them from politics, women may actually have gained in seeking an institutional role because of the efforts by countermovement activists to block their access to constitutional rights—whether to seek an abortion or to be free from violence. Figure 4.10 shows that although abortion was the greatest single issue drawing violent opposition, other women's issues similarly attracted violent reactions.

The president and Congress were part of the coverage of roughly the same number of violent acts (figure 4.11). Both institutions condemned the most blatant acts of violent aggression, such as murders of doctors who conducted abortions and bombings of clinics where abortions were available. More significantly, Congress in 1994 passed the Violence Against Women Act, mandating interstate enforcement of judicial orders protecting individuals from repeated or threatened violence, establishing a National Domestic Violence Hotline, training state and federal judges in the handling of domestic violence, and providing civil rights remedies for some

FIGURE 4.10

Violence by Issue

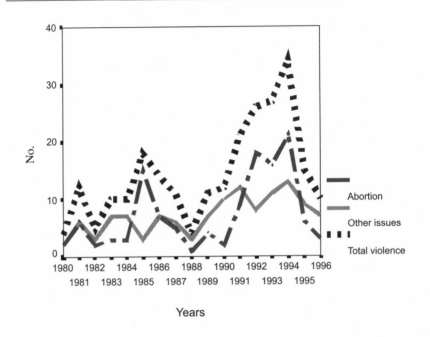

gender-linked crimes.[39] Yet, given the nature of the threats, women's organizations and the social movement they are tied to offered a more thorough and wide-ranging critique of social and political violence than did the institutions of government.[40]

CONCLUSIONS

The evidence presented suggests that social movement groups may make tactical choices that both aid the process of institutionalizing movements within mainstream politics and sustain strong ties to the larger movement. The most visible national groups growing out of the second wave of the American women's movement have continued to exert a presence in the news, through both conventional lobbying and a range of protest activities, even as overall press coverage of their actions has waned. While the protest presence, including its linkage to social and political violence, at first seems contradictory (since continued challenges to the political system, while

FIGURE 4.11
Institutions and Violence

Years

heavily involved in working within it, have long been thought to alienate the public), the nature of the protest suggests why it has not exacted this kind of a political cost. Not only has protest by these groups been nonviolent, but it has consisted primarily of countering violent attacks by their opponents. This reinforces a public perception of women both as nonviolent and as victims of violence.

Institutionally, Congress more than the presidency has accurately mirrored the issue concerns of women's groups during this transformational period. Civil rights as a focus, following the defeat of the ERA, gave way to a more varied set of issues, including employment and jobs, abortion, and education. The relatively large amount of continuing press coverage, even in the wake of regrouping following the defeat of the ERA, reinforces the point made by Karen Kedrowski and Marilyn Stine Sarow's chapter in this book, which is that a lobbying effort may effectively stimulate press coverage to achieve a particular policy goal.

A larger point from the women's movement case is that the increasingly institutionalized role of social movement organizations does not necessarily alienate or significantly weaken the social movement as a whole. In fact, the women's movement provides a convincing example that retaining protest behaviors while movement organizations develop as electoral and lobbying blocs may be a viable path to sustaining the momentum of movements while institutionalizing within democratic political structures.

NOTES

1. Eleanor Flexner, *Century of Struggle*, 173.
2. Gelb and Palley, *Women and Public Policies*, 189–90.
3. Ryan, *Feminism and the Women's Movement*.
4. For detailed discussions of first wave feminism, see Flexner, *Century of Struggle*; DuBois, *Feminism and Suffrage*; O'Neill, *Everyone Was Brave*; and Cott, *Grounding of Modern Feminism*.
5. For analyses of second wave feminism, see Freeman, *Politics of Women's Liberation*; Costain, *Inviting Women's Rebellion*; and Ryan, *Feminism and the Women's Movement*.
6. See, for example, Ferree and Hess, *Controversy and Coalition*.
7. The amendment was widely called this at the time to honor suffragist Susan B. Anthony.
8. Meyer and Tarrow, "Movement Society," 21, offers the following definition: "Institutionalization is defined by the creation of a repeatable process that is essentially self-sustaining . . .; it is one in which all the relevant actors can resort to well-established and familiar routines. For political movements, institutionalization denotes the end of the sense of unlimited possibility. . . ." One aspect of Meyer and Tarrow's discussion of institutionalization differs from ours. They assume that co-optation, which they describe as "challengers alter their claims and tactics to ones that can be pursued without disrupting the normal practice of politics" (21), is a normal part of institutionalization. We believe that there are circumstances in which it can be avoided.
9. Burstein, in "Interest Organizations," 39–56, points out that disciplinary divisions, relegating some stages of movement activity to sociological study and other stages to analysis as political science, are more likely to obscure political behavior than to uncover it.
10. Aminzade, "Between Movement and Party," 40–41.
11. Tarrow, "Very Excess of Democracy"; Mark Traugott, *Repertoires and Cycles*.
12. McAdam, *Political Process*, 54.
13. Ibid., 55–56.
14. The media do track public opinion about large, politically active movements as well, reflecting sympathetic views of followers along with the broader public

perspective on salient aspects of the movement. For a discussion of the links between movements and public opinion, see Burstein, *Discrimination, Jobs, and Politics*, and Costain and Majstorovic, "Congress, Social Movements and Public Opinion."

15. Olson, *Logic of Collective Action*; Muller and Opp, "Rational Choice and Rebellious Collective Action"; Muller and Opp, "Rebellious Collective Action Revisited."

16. The media greatly influence the content of American political discussion. See McCombs and Shaw, "Agenda Setting Function"; Page and Shapiro, "Educating and Manipulating the Public"; and Gamson, *Talking Politics*.

17. The literature on women's organizations identifies each group as politically active (Carden 1974; Costain 1978, 1979, 1981, 1983, 1992; Gelb 1995; Gelb and Palley 1977, 1982, 1987; Katzenstein 1987, 1990, 1995; Schlozman 1990; Spalter-Roth and Schreiber 1995).

18. Elshtain, *Public Man, Private Woman*.

19. Ryan, *Feminism and the Women's Movement*; Freeman, *Politics of Women's Liberation*.

20. Costain, *Inviting Women's Rebellion*, 46; Costain, "Women's Movements and Nonviolence."

21. Costain, *Inviting Women's Rebellion*, 79–99.

22. Gelb and Palley, *Women and Public Policies*, rev. ed.; Costain, "Women's Lobby"; Costain, *Inviting Women's Rebellion*; Schlozman, "Representing Women in Washington"; Spalter-Roth and Schreiber, "Outsider Issues and Insider Tactics."

23. Gelb and Palley, *Women and Public Policies*, rev. ed.; Costain, "Eliminating Sex Discrimination in Education"; Costain, "Struggle for a National Women's Lobby."

24. Spalter-Roth and Schreiber, "Outsider Issues and Insider Tactics."

25. We initially intended to use the *New York Times* along with several less elite newspapers from other regions of the country. Because the *Times* had so many articles featuring second wave women's groups, we decided to examine all the coverage in the *Times* rather than comparing partial coverage from several different papers.

26. McGlen and O'Connor, *Women, Politics, and American Society*, 2nd ed., 14–15.

27. Catherine Manegold, "Women Advance in Politics by Evolution," *New York Times*, 21 October 1992, p. A:1.

28. Abby Newman, "Activists Are Bracing for U.S. Abortion Ruling," *New York Times*, 14 June 1992, sec. 13CN:4.

29. Costain and Fraizer, "Media Portrayal of Feminist Groups," 163–65.

30. Steven Holmes, "On Civil Rights, Clinton Steers Bumpy Course between Right and Left," *New York Times*, 20 October 1996, p. A:16.

31. E. Cook, Thomas, and Wilcox, eds., *Year of the Woman*.

32. Tarrow, "Very Excess of Democracy," 148–49.

33. Mike Freeman, "Risking Protests, Giants Sign Troubled Husker," *New York Times*, 16 November 1996, p. A:33.

34. Ferree and Hess, *Controversy and Coalition*, 100, 192.

35. Linda Greenhouse, "Supreme Court Says Klan Law Can't Bar Abortion Blockades," *New York Times*, 14 January 1993, p. A:1.

36. "Green Quip Angers Women," *New York Times*, 5 August 1993, p. B:12.

37. Timothy Egan, "Harsh Homecoming for Senator Accused of Harassment," *New York Times*, 27 January 1993, p. A:1.

38. Costain and Fraizer, "Media Portrayal of Feminist Groups," 159.

39. Gelb and Palley, *Women and Public Policies*, rev. ed., 230.

40. Costain, "Women's Movements and Nonviolence."

CHAPTER FIVE

Women's Changing Pathways to the U.S. House of Representatives

Widows, Elites, and Strategic Politicians

IRWIN N. GERTZOG

To the casual observer of politics, the election of Missouri's JoAnn Emerson and California's Lois Capps and Mary Bono to succeed their husbands in the U.S. House of Representatives during the late 1990s may seem very much like business as usual. After all, widows have been replacing their husbands in Congress since 1923. However, a closer look at the pathways women have followed to gain seats in the House reveals that widow's succession, while once relatively frequent, is now the exception. Consequently, most contemporary congresswomen have little in common with their earliest predecessors. Differences in background characteristics have contributed to variations in the style and product of their performance.

This chapter focuses on the changing background characteristics of women elected to the House of Representatives from 1916 to 2000. It documents the decline in the election of politically inexperienced women—including those who either succeeded their husbands or those whose victories were closely linked to their elite socioeconomic status—as it traces the increase in the proportion of women who are *strategic politicians*. Considering the increasing number of minority women who have contested House seats in recent years, special attention has been given to the incidence of strategic politicians among African American women.

The chapter then examines the potential influence of strategic politicians once they are elected to Congress, and points out that the ambitions of an increasing number of these women transcend service in the House. The chapter concludes by exploring the impact women strategic politicians are having on the Congressional Caucus for Women's Issues.

THE ELECTION OF CONGRESSIONAL WIDOWS

Between 1917, the year the first elected woman representative, Jeannette Rankin, took the oath of office, and 2000, 43 wives received Democratic or Republican nominations to succeed their husbands in the House. They were disproportionately from the South—18 ran in that region—and 37 of the 43 won.[1] During the 84-year period under review, 412 House members died before their terms expired, but only 298 could have been succeeded by wives—after bachelors, widowers, and husbands of incapacitated wives are removed from consideration.[2] This means that the wives of only 14 percent of the men who died in office were nominated to succeed their spouses.

Given the often extensive media attention devoted to a widow's prospects each time a House member dies, these figures seem small. On the other hand, elected widows once made up a startlingly high percentage of all the women serving in the House. Among the 30 congresswomen elected through 1942, 14 (46 percent) had succeeded their husbands. Even by 1962, almost 45 percent of all female House members had been congressional widows. Of course, these percentages reflect obstacles conventional female candidates have faced as much as they measure the efficacy of the matrimonial connection.

The background characteristics of these widows have a number of similarities with those of the socioeconomic elites discussed in the following section. Most congressional widows, like Frances Bolton of Ohio and Louisiana's Lindy Boggs, were born into families whose men were part of their state's socioeconomic and political elites. Many, like Florence Prag Kahn of California and Marguerite Stitt Church of Illinois, graduated from the best colleges then open to women. Others were products of exclusive finishing schools. These women were often prominent philanthropists, progressive educators, respected community leaders, dedicated social workers, and Democratic and Republican county and state committeewomen. When their husbands were elected to the House, several, like Margaret Chase Smith and Sala Burton, became their spouses' political secretaries, campaign managers, and principal cheerleaders.[3]

In short, most of the women who ran to succeed their husbands had established impressive track records on the periphery of politics, but had never entered its vortex before their own unplanned pursuit of a congressional seat. During the first half of the 20th century, marriage to a budding politician, along with gender-related obstacles, were powerful disincentives to candidacy for any office. Even in the latter half of the century, the political careers of their husbands were oppressively restrictive. For virtually all Americans, there was room for only one ranking public official in a nuclear family, although the occasional exception did exist.[4]

The recent successes of three congressional widows in rapid succession—JoAnn Emerson, Lois Capps, and Mary Bono—have reinforced perceptions that the matrimonial connection provides a well-traveled route to Congress. One might infer from these three events that the election of congressional widows is common, and that we should expect more of the same in the years ahead. But the number of widows who come to the House is likely to be smaller, rather than larger in the foreseeable future. To understand why, it helps to look at spousal succession in historical perspective.

Table 5.1 presents the incidence of widows' nominations from 1917 to 2000, controlling for South and non-South variations, and breaking the 84 years into four time periods. Between 1917 and 1940, widows of 9 percent of deceased House members nationwide were nominated to replace their husbands. The practice was more common in the South (14 percent) than outside that region (6 percent). These percentages increased over the next two time periods, with more than one-half (55 percent) of the deaths in the South followed by widows' succession between 1965 and 1982.

The regional gap narrowed during the most recent time period, with the upward trend continuing outside the South, while the frequency with which southern widows were nominated declined to one in three. Not shown in table 5.1 is that during the last decade of the century, the widows of 8 of the 12 House members who died could have conceivably been nominated to replace them. Only 3, in fact, succeeded their husbands; 4 others were mentioned prominently as possible successors, and 1 of the 4, Marta Brown of California, narrowly lost a bitter 1999 Democratic primary.

TABLE 5.1
Widows Receiving Nominations as a Percentage of House Vacancies Created by Married Members' Deaths, 1917–2000

TIME PERIOD	SOUTH			NON-SOUTH			TOTAL		
	VACANT POSITIONS	WIDOWS NOMINATED	%	VACANT POSITIONS	WIDOWS NOMINATED	%	VACANT POSITIONS	WIDOWS NOMINATED	%
1917–1940	42	6	14	99	6	6	141	12	9
1941–1964	18	5	28	79	11	14	97	16	16
1965–1982	9	5	55	23	4	17	32	9	28
1983–2000	6	2	33	16	4	25	22	6	27

The principal inference to be drawn from these figures is that the *percentage* of congressmen who are being replaced on the ballot by spouses following their deaths is as high as it has ever been, about one in four, but the *number* of women given an opportunity to take this route to the House is declining. The latter trend can be explained in a number of ways. Perhaps the most obvious is that advances in medical science have dramatically reduced the number of congressmen who die in office—from an average of 17 deaths each term between 1917 and 1940 down to about 2 deaths per term during the last decade of the century.[5]

The sharp decline of one-party politics in the South may also explain the fact that fewer spouses are nominated to succeed their husbands. There are fewer districts in which leaders of the dominant party have the luxury of anointing a caretaker to run in a special election and to serve until party leaders and primary voters can select a House member whose political credentials are weightier than the widow's. Widows who succeed husbands in southern districts have rarely been reelected following their initial term, usually stepping aside voluntarily.[6]

Finally, we are likely to see fewer women nominated to succeed their husbands because the percentage of women serving in the House is growing. The larger the number of women members, the smaller the number of male members whose deaths could occasion succession by a wife. In the 2000 election, 59 women were elected to the House, a development that may increase the chances of "widower's" succession. This event almost occurred in 1981, when Representative Gladys Noon Spellman died and her husband, Reuben, narrowly lost a Democratic primary to succeed her. But no married congresswoman has died in office since then.

The continued high *percentage* of women nominated to succeed their husbands is more difficult to explain. A widow who inherits her husband's name and campaign funds is a potentially more formidable candidate for increasingly expensive House races. It is also possible that because life experiences of today's women more nearly approximate the experiences of men, contemporary women make better politicians than their predecessors. Wives' involvement in their spouse's campaign and careers may have come to be a legitimate qualification for public office. Moreover, the increased attention devoted to candidates' private lives may induce party leaders and voters to more readily link a wife's candidacy with her husband's personal and political achievements.[7]

THE ELECTION OF SOCIOECONOMIC AND POLITICAL ELITES

Three women House candidates with major party endorsements ran in 1916, but only one, Jeannette Rankin, was successful. Over the next quarter-century, 13 additional nonwidows of congressmen captured House seats. What distinguished these women was that, with few exceptions, their families could be described as belonging to the country's socioeconomic elite, giving them the advantages and life experiences associated with the privileged family circumstances that had long facilitated men's elections to national office.

These women can be grouped into three overlapping categories. A handful were social elites, women whose families were among the most respected citizens in their communities and states, in some cases enjoying national reputations. For example, Nan Honeyman of Oregon was the daughter of a distinguished West Point officer. She attended private finishing schools, studied music for three years in New York City, established a close friendship with Eleanor and Franklin Roosevelt, and married into one of Portland's leading families.

A second overlapping group benefited from significant wealth. Ruth Pratt, for instance, was the daughter of a well-to-do manufacturer, attended Wellesley College, and married the millionaire son of an oil company executive. The third group is the largest—women who profited from political connections—and includes women who share characteristics with the first two groups. Ruth Hanna McCormick, the daughter of Republican senator and president-maker Marcus Hanna, married Medill McCormick, who served in the Illinois state legislature and later in both the U.S. House and Senate. Ruth Bryan Owen was the daughter of William Jennings Bryan; and Winnifred Mason Huck was the first (and, thus far, the only) woman to replace a deceased father in the House.

The social, economic, and political resources at the disposal of these women almost certainly helped them receive major party nominations and win elections. They stood to benefit from the reputations their families enjoyed, from their widespread name recognition, from the prior political success of husbands, fathers, or other male relatives, and from their wealth, a tangible instrument for aggregating other resources.

According to table 5.2, the next quarter-century witnessed a decline in the proportion of congresswomen who could be described in this way,

TABLE 5.2

*Socioeconomic and Political Elites among Nonincumbent Women
Elected to the House, 1916–2000**

PERIOD	No. OF WOMEN ELECTED	No. OF SOCIOECONOMIC AND POLITICAL NOTABLES	% OF SOCIOECONOMIC AND POLITICAL NOTABLES
1916–1940	14	12	86
1942–1964	26	13	50
1966–1982	30	6	20
1984–2000	78	10	13

*   Women who ran to succeed their husbands are excluded from this table.

although as many as one-half fit the pattern. Among the 13 are women who achieved a national and international celebrity rarely matched by congresswomen elected in the years that followed. Out of the theater and entertainment fields emerged such luminaries as Clare Boothe Luce and Helen Gahagan Douglas. Social elites included Reva Beck Bosone, whose mother was a descendant of both the Mayflower Pilgrims and 1847 Mormon pioneers, and Emily Taft Douglas, whose father was an internationally known sculptor, whose cousin was William Howard Taft, and whose husband, Paul, had his political aspirations interrupted by World War II before he returned to civilian life and a career in the U.S. Senate.

Among the six notables elected between 1965 and 1982, two were able to capitalize on substantial wealth, and four were the beneficiaries of male relatives' political success. Moreover, Millicent Fenwick was a multimillionaire state legislator, Olympia Snowe succeeded her husband in the state legislature following his death, and Louise Day Hicks and Barbara Kennelly both held elective office before coming to Washington and were daughters of powerful New England politicians. What differentiates these four women from their elite predecessors is that they came to the House of Representatives having been twice blessed—once by virtue of their elite status, a second time because they had already seized the opportunity to conduct an election campaign, serve a constituency, and claim the attention that commonly accompanies officeholding.

As is reported in table 5.2, the significant increase in congresswomen elected since 1983 has been accompanied by a decline in the proportion of those whose social, economic, and political circumstances constitute an elite status. Among the 10 elite congresswomen are the daughters of professional politicians—Susan Molinari, Lucille Roybal-Allard, Elizabeth Patterson, Cynthia McKinney, and Shelley Moore Capito—and three multimillionaires from California—Nancy Pelosi, Jane Harman, and Ellen Tauscher.

This assemblage of elites represents just over 1 in 10 of the women elected to the House during the last 18 years, which indicates that social status, affluence, and a political pedigree are no longer the dominant assets associated with successful campaigns for the House. Other background characteristics, notably prior electoral success, have come to replace widowhood and elite membership as the principal passports to congressional service.

The implications of this development are significant. It means that those who nominate and elect House members—both party leaders who dominated the process during much of the 20th century and primary voters, whose role in candidate-centered campaigns has increased significantly—are less interested in women's attributes that have little to do directly with their political skills. These characteristics once provided inexperienced candidates with a cachet that helped them claim credibility as politicians.

Such resumes are apparently less serviceable today. Women who in the past depended on family social status, significant wealth, or political reputations established by male relatives when mounting a race for the House now face a more daunting task. Their ranks have shrunk, although an increasing number of recently elected congresswomen combine such a background with an impressive precongressional political career of their own. And voters appear to be relying more than ever on the political achievements of women candidates. Consequently, the successes of modern congresswomen are linked at least as much to their track records in public office as to their political pedigree, and they come to Washington with all of the qualities we expect in strategic politicians.

STRATEGIC POLITICIANS

The term *strategic politician* is associated with the works of Gary Jacobson, among others, and has been employed to help explain the extent to which the president's party loses House seats in midterm congressional elections.

The qualities of such politicians emerge from the literature on political recruitment and legislative elections. First and foremost, strategic politicians are *ambitious*. Their principal goal is to win public office, and, in the case of *progressive* politicians, to use lower levels of office as springboards to higher office.[8] They are also unlikely to be "conscripted" by party leaders to run in a hopeless election unless they do not have to give up the office they presently hold. In that case, their decision to exploit a losing campaign is made to position themselves for a promising future contest. Strategic politicians are also unwilling to allow themselves to be "co-opted" by party leaders should they enjoy a celebrity status.[9]

Strategic politicians are *skillful* and *resourceful*,[10] able to be articulate, and to present an appealing physical and temperamental presence. They conduct effective campaigns, carefully selecting relevant issues to capitalize upon. Their networks of friends and supporters tend to be extensive and diverse, which enhances their ability to cultivate and maintain the loyalty of state and local party leaders. These features of their candidacy, coupled with a formidable ability to aggregate financial resources, inhibit serious opposition in primary elections.[11]

Those who qualify are also *experienced, professional* politicians. They already hold, or recently held, public office when they seek higher office.[12] Occupying office allows them to establish rapport with constituents, and to deal with state and local bureaucracies.[13] Strategic politicians are likely to be task-oriented professionals, who realize future victories depend on valid claims of legislative achievement. Therefore, they publicly take responsibility for policy change and policy reinforcement.[14] Successful campaigns for lower office help them develop the confidence they need to seek higher office.[15]

Finally, strategic politicians are *calculating* and *rational*. The chances of their securing their party's nomination are carefully considered, and entry into a race is based on the likelihood of success.[16] They calculate how victory or defeat will affect their careers,[17] and, more often than not, they wait for an incumbent to retire or otherwise leave an office before seeking the office.[18] Political decisions, particularly those about whether to run and which office to seek, are made dispassionately, only after the advantages and drawbacks of each course of action are subjected to rational calculation.[19]

WOMEN STRATEGIC POLITICIANS

Recent literature on gender and politics makes clear that contemporary political women are no less likely than men to be strategic politicians. Women serving in state legislatures are as ambitious as male legislators, with more of them considering politics a career than their male colleagues, and a larger proportion stating plans to seek reelection.[20] Among those who run or seriously consider contests for the House, women weigh both strategic and personal factors, not automatically allowing gender, marital status, or the psychic costs of running to deter candidacy. Moreover, there is evidence that in recent years more women with children are running for office in spite of their motherhood.[21] In short, contemporary women politicians are as ambitious as men.[22]

Women strategic politicians today are also skillful and resourceful, with no significant gender difference in the ability to raise funds.[23] Contributions to their campaigns from political action committees are as generous as those bestowed on men, and party and other support systems are as accessible to female candidates as they are to male candidates.[24] In fact, women have the added advantage of receiving funds from PACs that confine their contributions to female candidates. And, as early as the 1970s, voters reportedly considered gender a relatively unimportant factor affecting their choices.[25]

Much of the literature concludes that women lawmakers are more task oriented and more policy oriented than their male colleagues, and women lawmakers are considered more sensitive to constituent needs.[26] The number of women in elective office has increased significantly, and the eligibility pool may be approaching a critical mass,[27] with more of them obtaining leadership roles in city councils and state legislatures,[28] positioning themselves to run for higher office.

Finally, women are more likely than men to make rational decisions on whether to run based on how well they are "positioned" to seek higher office, and based on their perception of vulnerability.[29] Consequently, they are more likely than men to delay decisions to run until they believe they have sufficient financial resources and the support of community organizations.[30] Moreover, women are no less likely than men to run if they think they can win,[31] and their campaign organizations and support systems are put together with more care and forethought.[32]

Contemporary congresswomen who fit this description include Republican Jan Meyers of Kansas and Democrat Patsy Mink of Hawaii. Meyers was elected to the Overland Park City Council in 1967, rose to the presidency of the council in 1970, and was elected to the Kansas state senate in 1972. After 12 years in the state senate, she won an open seat in Congress, served 12 years, and retired from politics in 1996. Mink graduated from the University of Chicago Law School, served in the Hawaii House for two years, the state senate for four years, and won an open seat in the U.S. House in 1964. In 1976, she left the House to run unsuccessfully for an open seat in the U.S. Senate. Mink returned to Honolulu, where she served on the city council before reclaiming her seat in the U.S. House in a 1990 special election. With her reelection to the 107th Congress, she began her 13th term in the House.

As these two examples suggest, two synoptic indicators may be employed to conflate qualities characteristic of strategic politicians. First, strategic politicians hold or recently held elective public office before contesting a House seat. Successful campaigns for public office and fulfilling the responsibilities of that office allow them to express the ambition they harbor, to acquire and demonstrate political skills, and to exercise resourcefulness when aggregating funds, establishing political networks, and building coalitions.

Second, strategic politicians contest *open* House seats only. They are interested in winning elections and holding public office. They are unlikely to invest scarce resources in a contest for a seat they have little chance of winning simply for the purpose of promoting policy goals or sending a message. Consequently they will risk their careers only when rational calculation suggests that their chances of winning are promising.

This study restricts the definition of strategic politician to these two readily observable, unambiguous variables—occupying an elective public office and contesting an open seat when running for the House—an approach that is seductive in its simplicity.[33] Moreover, each of the two conditions implies a fundamental component of the recruitment process—*availability* and the *political opportunity structure*. Candidates are *available* when they are positioned to run for office, and there is no better springboard to one public office than another public office. The *political opportunity structure* accommodates a candidate when the seat she is seeking can be won without having to defeat an incumbent.

TABLE 5.3

Strategic and Nonstrategic Women Politicians Elected to the House, 1916–2000

TIME PERIOD	ALL NON-INCUMBENT WOMEN ELECTED TO THE HOUSE*	STRATEGIC POLITICIANS ELECTED TO THE HOUSE	
		N	%
1916–1940	14	3	21
1942–1964	26	10	38
1966–1982	31	18	58
1984–2000	78	52	67
Total	149	83	56

* Women who ran to succeed their husbands are excluded from this part of the analysis. The four women who served nonconsecutive terms (Rankin, Woodhouse, Mink, and Harman) are counted each time they won as nonincumbents.

Within the context of these guidelines, it is clear that the proportion of strategic politicians among the women elected to the House has increased steadily over the years. Findings reported in table 5.3 reveal that whereas only about 2 in 10 (21 percent) of the nonincumbent women elected to the House before World War II qualified as strategic politicians, two in three (67 percent) did so in elections held since 1984. The small number of women reflected in the figures during the earlier years means that the percentage point differences distort the amount of change that has taken place. Nonetheless, it is clear that a larger number of ambitious, skilled, experienced women are coming to Washington prepared to pursue political careers.

This inference is reinforced by the figures in table 5.4, which compares the percentages of successful and unsuccessful women strategic politicians who ran for the House between 1916 and 2000. Although the number of candidates appearing in the earliest period is small, one cannot help but be struck by the dramatic increase in the number of politically experienced women nominated for open seats between 1984 and 2000. As many as 31 were defeated, but in the nine elections between 1984 and 2000, an average of 9 were nominated every two years, with 52 elected to the House. Their candidacies have become commonplace enough for them to run against one another.[34]

TABLE 5.4

Strategic Women Politicians Nominated by Major Parties to
Run for the House as Nonincumbents, 1916–2000

TIME PERIOD	TOTAL NON-INCUMBENT WOMEN NOMINATED	WINNERS		LOSERS	
		N	%	N	%
1916–1940	5	3	60	2	40
1942–1964	18	10	55	8	45
1966–1982	28	18	64	10	36
1984–2000	83	52	63	31	37
Total	134	83	62	51	38

While women who are strategic politicians won a majority of contests they entered, never dipping below 55 percent, their success rate during the last two decades, 63 percent, means that larger numbers have, over time, made relatively good use of the prevailing political opportunity structure. Moreover, the election of 2002 bodes well for female strategic politicians because reapportionment and redistricting following the 2000 census will produce a bonanza in open seats—although the huge gains made by women House candidates following the 1990 census will be difficult to duplicate.

That congresswomen who are strategic politicians have come gradually to replace, first, widows of congressmen, and, second, women whose principal resource was the sociopolitical and economic status of their families is an important development. It means that prior election to state and local office has become a more important component of the credentials women rely on to secure seats in the House. At the same time, the House has become increasingly populated by female politicians who, unlike many of their predecessors, are unafraid to address controversial social issues affecting women directly,[35] who are prepared to fight for prized committee assignments[36] and party leadership positions,[37] and who are driven by political ambition.

No subgroup of congresswomen has contributed to this trend more materially than African American House candidates. The increasing number of African American women serving in Congress is due to a combination of factors that include the impact of the 1965 Voting Rights Act and the growing numbers of strategic politicians in their midst. This trend warrants separate analysis.

AFRICAN AMERICAN WOMEN AS
STRATEGIC POLITICIANS

The first African American women elected to the House was Shirley Chisholm, a New York City school teacher who served in the state assembly before her Brooklyn constituents sent her to Washington in 1968. Since then, 17 additional black women have been elected to the House, and they make up 10 percent of all congresswomen who have ever served in that chamber.[38]

Among the seven elected through 1990, all but one, Barbara Jordan of Texas, represented districts in or near cities outside the South, including New York, Los Angeles, Chicago, and Detroit. In 1992, five southern black women were elected to the House, almost certainly a consequence of the Voting Rights Act of 1965. The enormous increase in black voter registration and turnout in that region led to election of black state and local officials who were then positioned for congressional candidacies.[39] Four of the five elected in 1992 were state legislators; the fifth, North Carolina's Eva Clayton, was a county official. Four of the five represented districts in peripheral southern states—Florida, Texas, North Carolina—with only Georgia's Cynthia McKinney serving a Deep South constituency. Other Deep South states, South Carolina, Alabama, Mississippi, and Louisiana, have yet to send an African American woman to Congress.

During the decade of the 1990s, the percentage increase of black women in the House was marked, even as their number remained small. Between 1990 and 2000, 13 new African American women were elected, representing non-South constituencies in California, Michigan, Indiana, and Ohio. Surprisingly, no other African American woman has been elected from the northeast since Shirley Chisholm's initial victory in 1968. Twelve are incumbents at this writing, and they make up 32 percent of all African Americans in the 107th Congress. By contrast, the remaining 47 women constitute 12 percent of nonblack representatives.

The backgrounds of black congresswomen have been significantly less diverse than those of other women who have served in the House. First, all ran as Democrats. Second, compared to the 36 (23 percent) nonblack women who replaced their husbands, only one (6 percent), Cardiss Collins of Illinois, succeeded her husband following his death.[40] This fact should not come as a surprise inasmuch as there were so few black congressmen whose wives could conceivably have succeeded them. Third, only one

African American congresswoman, Cynthia McKinney, was brought up in a politically active family, as the term has been defined here. Again, this should not be surprising since during most of the 20th century, the incidence of politically oriented, elite African American women was almost certainly limited to a handful of communities nationwide.

Table 5.5 reports the success rates of black women who have run for the House. Astonishingly, *all but one* of the African American women who qualified as strategic politicians won, and *all but one* of the African American women who were not strategic politicians lost.[41] (For a complete list of African American women who have run for election to the House, see www.ou.edu/special/albertctr/wtc.) Just why this has been the case is difficult to say. It is conceivable that black women officeholders exercise more caution than nonblack women when choosing an open seat to contest. It is also possible that because a number of these women sought the Democratic party nomination in districts specifically crafted to return an African American representative (including the district that sent Shirley Chisholm to Washington), winning the Democratic primary was tantamount to a victory in the general election. African American women officeholders who sought the Democratic nomination for an open seat but lost in the primary election are not included in the table.

TABLE 5.5

Strategic and Nonstrategic Black Women Politicians
Who Ran for the House, 1968–2000*

| TIME PERIOD | NONSTRATEGIC POLITICIANS | | STRATEGIC POLITICIANS | | |
	WON	LOST	WON	LOST	TOTAL
1968–1986**	0	8	4	0	12
1988–2000	1	42	13	1	57
Total	1	50	17	1	69

* Cardiss Collins, having succeeded her husband, is excluded from this analysis.
** Two time periods were used not for analytic purposes, but because information for the earlier time period is incomplete. The period 1968–1986 includes all candidates who won, but the race of a few women who lost has not been fully documented. Information about the race of women candidates running after 1986 is complete.

Whatever the underlying reasons, the number of black women in the House is likely to grow at a slower pace in the immediate future than it did in the 1990s. Anything more than an incremental increase is likely to come at the expense of black male candidates, since black candidates have difficulty winning majorities in districts that do not have a black majority or a significant plurality.[42] And because of the limited number of such districts, and the fact that virtually all are currently represented by black House members, black men and black women who are House aspirants will clash within these districts, competing in a zero-sum game.[43]

If African American women were to affiliate with the Republican party and build political bases in districts that are primarily white and primarily Republican, they could increase their numbers. Though this is an unlikely scenario, it is the pathway followed by the only African American Republican males to serve in the House since the 1930s, Gary Franks and J. C. Watts.

CONGRESSWOMEN'S INFLUENCE IN THE HOUSE

The 1990s were good to strategic women politicians, who now make up more than three-quarters of the House's female membership. This development was years in the making. During the 1970s, one-fifth of all open-seat House *primary elections* featured a woman contestant. This increased to one-third during the 1980s.[44] And between 1992 and 1998, as much as two-fifths of open-seat *general elections* featured at least one woman candidate. In 2000, 32 House members retired or sought other offices. Thirteen of their seats were contested in November by at least one politically experienced woman.

The proliferation of female politicians is all but certain to increase the influence of both strategic and nonstrategic women in the House. This inference is based, in part, on the assumption that strategic women, by definition, are ambitious and skilled, qualities that are precursors to power in Congress. But it is also linked to the lower House retirement rate among women as compared with men. Between 1972 and 1980, an average of 20 percent of congresswomen left the House every two years, compared with a departure rate of 17 percent among congressmen.[45] During the next five-election cycle, turnover decreased to 12 percent for men and 14 percent for women. In the 1990s, the departure rate decreased slightly for women, to

13 percent, but increased to 16 percent for men. Following the 2000 election, 10 percent of male members did not return to the 107th Congress compared with 9 percent of congresswomen.

This has meant that congresswomen have been incrementally increasing their seniority levels vis-à-vis men (one reason some opponents of the seniority system might reconsider their objections), and many of these career politicians are now poised to claim powerful committee positions. Between 1993 and 2000, two women chaired two minor House committees, Small Business and Ethics, and two women served as ranking members on the Government Reform and Small Business Committees. During the same period, women chaired or were ranking members of almost a score of subcommittees in each Congress, including panels on Ways and Means, Judiciary, Resources, Science, and Appropriations. Their numbers on the five most sought after House committees increased from an average of 20 in the 103rd and 104th Congresses to an average of 25 in the 105th and 106th. There are 29 in the 107th.[46] Marcy Kaptur, Nancy Pelosi, and Nita Lowey are among the Democratic women on Appropriations who are in line to bear the oxymoronic title "Woman Cardinal" in the event the Democrats gain control of the House in the 108th Congress.

Contemporary congresswomen are also demanding more recognition from party leaders. Barbara Kennelly was elected to a midlevel Democratic leadership post (defeating New York's Louise Slaughter) before leaving the House to run for governor, and, in 1993, former Speaker Newt Gingrich helped engineer selection of two congresswomen, Susan Molinari and Barbara Vucanovich, to secondary leadership positions in the House Republican Conference. When the two left the House, they were replaced by two other women, Jennifer Dunn and Deborah Pryce, each of whom defeated male challengers.

Democratic leaders have supported women for similar slots, and when the start of the 106th Congress saw no congresswoman occupying a visible leadership position, minority leader Richard Gephardt created a new one and helped elect Rosa DeLauro to fill it. Nita Lowey broke new ground when she was elected chair of the Democratic Congressional Campaign Committee in the 107th Congress, a position that, given the intense, partisan competition characterizing House dynamics in recent years, carries far more responsibility than was once the case. But the most significant breakthrough to date was the selection of Nancy Pelosi as Democratic whip late in 2001, after Michigan's David Bonior relinquished the position to launch his gubernatorial campaign.

The practice of tokenism once employed with impunity by both parties in the leadership selection process has been abandoned for the most part. It fell victim to the ambitions of highly motivated congresswomen who seized opportunities to exploit resources of their own to secure top leadership positions.

CONGRESSWOMEN AS PROGRESSIVE POLITICIANS

For some strategic women, the House itself may lose its luster, in which case there is always a higher office to contemplate. Two such offices, state governor, and U.S. senator, have been sought routinely by male House members over the years. Only five women who served in the House have run for governor, and only one, Ella Grasso in 1974, prevailed.[47] Grasso and three of the remaining four contested open seats, with only Barbara Kennelly facing an incumbent. This 20 percent success rate is slightly lower than the one in four ratio compiled by male representatives during the last 30 years.[48]

But more telling than the difference in these proportions is the fact that so few congresswomen sought nominations for governor. It is possible that women consider state legislatures and statewide offices more useful springboards to the governorship. That four of the five gubernatorial contestants came to the House as strategic politicians, and that four of their five election contests occurred since 1994 are not robust enough reasons to conclude that very many congresswomen will soon occupy governors' mansions.

More congresswomen have run for the Senate, however, and the progressive ambitions of these House members is one reason the upper chamber is losing its predominantly male character. As table 5.6 makes clear, during the half-century after Jeannette Rankin unsuccessfully sought her party's nomination for the Senate, the proportion was about 1 in 10. Since 1965, it has been 1 in 4. Women first elected between 1965 and 1982 show the highest level of progressive ambition, although it should be noted that 6 of the 10 congresswomen initially elected during this period did not run for the Senate until the 1990s.[49] Women's success rate since 1966 has been respectable, matching the 40 percent figure compiled by male House members who ran for the Senate during the last 35 years.

TABLE 5.6

Female Representatives Who Ran for the Senate, 1916–2000

Year of Initial Election	No. of Women Elected to the House	Ran for the Senate		Election Outcome	
		N	%	Won	Lost
1916–1940	27	3	11	1	2
1942–1964	38	5	13	0	5
1966–1982	34*	10	29	3	7
1984–2000*	26*	5	19	3	2
Total	125*	23	18	7	16

* Female representatives serving in the 107th Congress are excluded inasmuch as their prospects for future Senate campaigns cannot be determined.

Unreported in the table is that in 14 of the 23 races, congresswomen contested seats defended by incumbents. All but two, Debbie Stabenow and Maria Cantwell, lost. (See listing at www.ou.edu/special/albertctr/wtc.) This suggests that strategic women House members may be well advised to delay a bid for the Senate until they can face a nonincumbent. Lengthy service in the lower chamber may be needed to gain statewide visibility and to raise the large sum of money required to finance a viable campaign for the upper chamber. The strategic calculations leading to a House victory are not very different from considerations ambitious politicians give to running in a more high-stakes, Senate election. Growth in the number of seasoned women who are prepared to make these calculations promises a palpable increase in the number of congresswomen running for the Senate during the first decade of the new millennium.

STRATEGIC POLITICIANS AND THE FUTURE OF THE WOMEN'S CAUCUS

The Congressional Caucus for Women's Issues (CCWI) began as the Congresswomen's Caucus in 1977 after several failed attempts. Its creation during the 95th Congress coincided with increasing lobbying by national feminist groups whose strategies included making their goals heard in the national legislature. (See Costain and Fraizer, this volume.) Initially, the caucus provided congresswomen with the opportunity to refine their appeal to constituents and identify aspects of legislation of special concern to women. The group also offered social and emotional support for women in the male-dominated legislature. It is probably no coincidence that the changing strategies of women's organizations paralleled the changing inclinations of women to affiliate with the caucus. Earlier, some congresswomen, especially Republicans, believed they would lose the respect of male colleagues and suffer at the polls if they identified too closely with the feminist agenda.[50]

Increases in the number and proportion of congresswomen who are strategic politicians have made the future of the CCWI problematical. The influence of this catalyst for women's rights has waxed and waned over the years. And then, in 1995, the new Republican House majority stripped it and 27 other legislative service organizations of much of their resources. Ever since, CCWI's efficacy and visibility have been attenuated. Many new strategic congresswomen are members in name only, and most do not subscribe to the biweekly and quarterly reports published by the group's research subsidiary, Women's Policy, Inc.[51]

The access these women have to consequential committee and leadership positions, coupled with a level of ambition unmatched by most of their predecessors, has led them to invest fewer resources in an informal group that is largely peripheral to House decision making. Monthly caucus meetings have become less prominent on the schedules of women whose frenetic weekly routines are replete with increased committee responsibilities and interactions with party leaders, in addition to the legislative and representative tasks all members fulfill. Estrangement from caucus activities is especially characteristic of women harboring progressive ambition inasmuch as active membership in the CCWI competes for time with the conduct of statewide campaigns.

Congresswomen's diminished interest in the caucus flows not from hostility toward a feminist agenda or a fear that constituents and colleagues will conclude that they are fixated on feminist priorities. Rather, their distance from the caucus stems from a belief that if they want to promote feminist values, they can be more effective in legislative settings that are integral to House decision making.[52] They are as ardently feminist as the solid core of caucus activists, but, as modern-day strategic politicians, they have less of an incentive to manifest the cooperative, sororital spirit evidenced by the women who created and sustained the caucus in years past. They are more likely to be entrepreneurs exerting influence directly on House colleagues than agents of a marginal women's collective whose resources have been cut back drastically, whose influence has been largely indirect, and whose track record is mixed.

The changing orientations of congressmen toward women politicians and their changing perceptions about the centrality of women's experience in the policy-making process have had the effect of weakening further the ties strategic women establish with the CCWI. Discourse among male lawmakers has come to include as a matter of course the impact legislation is likely to have on women—as women—in all walks of life. Consequently, strategic women politicians have come to rely less than they did in the past on the catalytic services once available primarily through affiliation with the CCWI.

Moreover, as the number of congresswomen has grown, the diversity of constituencies they represent has also increased, leading to sharper differences in the value orientations congresswomen reflect on matters central to women's lives. This helps explain why more of them have exhibited limited enthusiasm about promoting women's rights, with several initially rejecting invitations to join the CCWI. Six of the seven first-term Republican women did just that in 1995, as the 104th Congress got under way. The dilution of caucus inclusivity, in turn, has threatened one of the caucus's principal objectives—the need to be seen as legitimately representing all American women.

In short, the ambition, entrepreneurial spirit, and ideological diversity characteristic of contemporary congresswomen have tended to discourage many of them from taking an active role in CCWI activities. Paradoxically, the increasing numbers of feminists who are also strategic politicians has had the effect of atrophying the informal House group most devoted to women's interests.

NOTES

1. See appendix B in Gertzog, *Congressional Women*, for information about widows nominated through 1995.

2. Other congressmen removed from consideration are those who had announced their retirement or had been defeated in a primary before their death. Those succeeded by a brother, son, or nephew, and those who committed suicide were also excluded. Sources of information about congressmen who died and their families include the *Congressional Record*, especially eulogies about the deceased, and the *New York Times* obituaries.

3. Sources for biographical information about congresswomen include Chamberlin, *A Minority of Members*; *Current Biography Yearbook*, 1940–98; *Biographical Dictionary of the American Congress, 1774–1989*; Edward T. James, ed., *Notable American Women, 1607–1950*; and items appearing in the *New York Times*, the *Washington Post*, *Congressional Quarterly Weekly Report*, and *Roll Call*.

4. Richard and Maureen Neuberger are a well-known exception to the rule. In the 1950s Richard was in the Oregon state senate while Maureen was in the state assembly. Later, she succeeded him in the U.S. Senate, following his death.

5. One recent study suggests that installation of a new ventilation system in the Capitol during the 1930s helped prolong members' lives. Maltzman, Sigelman, and Binder, "Leaving Office Feet First."

6. Of the 15 southern widows elected to succeed their husbands, only one, Lindy Boggs of Louisiana, was reelected for terms of her own.

7. This tendency was most recently reflected in Missouri's 2000 Senate contest, when the name of a deceased candidate, Governor Mel Carnahan, could not be removed from the ballot because his death occurred too close to the November 7 election date. Voters cast ballots knowing his wife, Jean, would be appointed to the Senate should he receive a majority—which is precisely what happened.

8. Schlesinger, *Ambition and Politics*, 6.

9. The terms conscription and co-optation are defined and employed by Seligman et al., *Patterns of Recruitment*, 7.

10. Krasno and Green, "Preempting Quality Challengers," 921.

11. Bond, Covington, and Fleisher, "Explaining Challengers Quality," 513.

12. Jacobson, "Strategic Politicians and the Dynamics of House Elections," 776.

13. Bond, Covington and Fleisher, "Explaining Challengers' Quality," 513.

14. David Mayhew, *Congress: The Electoral Connection*, ch. 1.

15. Krasno and Green, "Preempting Quality Challengers," 921.

16. Maisel and Stone, "Determinants of Candidate Emergence," 79; Moncrief, "Recruitment and Retention in U.S. Legislatures," 178.

17. Biersack and Herrnson, "Political Parties and the Year of the Woman," 167.

18. Bianco, "Strategic Decisions," 361; Levitt and Wolfram, "Decomposing Sources of Incumbency Advantage," 57.

19. Schlesinger, *Ambition and Politics*, 6.

20. Carey, Niemi, and Powell, "Are Women State Legislators Different?" 100; Dolan and Ford, "Are All Women State Legislators Alike?" 79.

21. Dolan and Ford, "Change and Continuity among Women State Legislators," 147; Gertzog, *Congressional Women*, 47; and Maisel and Stone, "Determinants of Candidate Emergence," 92.

22. Burrell, "Presence and Performance of Women Candidates," 499.

23. Burrell, "Campaign Finance: Women's Experience," 127.

24. Biersack and Herrnson, "Political Parties and the Year of the Woman," 172.

25. Bernstein, "Why Are So Few Women in the House," 155.

26. Carey, Niemi, and Powell, "Are Women State Legislators Different?" 90.

27. Chaney and Sinclair, "Women and the 1992 House Elections."

28. Dolan and Ford, "Change and Continuity among Women State Legislators," 145.

29. Bledsoe and Herring, "Victims of Circumstances," 217.

30. Duerst-Lahti, "Bottleneck: Women Becoming Candidates," 22.

31. Bledsoe and Herring, "Victims of Circumstances," 217.

32. Carey, Niemi, and Powell, "Are Women State Legislators Different?" 89.

33. Conventional definitions of strategic politicians are usually applied to candidates who run for the House in midterm elections. They may challenge incumbents or contest open seats. For the purposes of this study, strategic politicians may run in presidential election years, as well as in midterm contests, and they contest open seats only.

34. In the 2000 election, for example, two strategic politicians, Betty McCollum and Linda Runbeck, contested Minnesota's Fourth Congressional District. Democrat McCollum won. The successful House candidacies in 2000 of California's Hilda Solis and Susan Davis indicate that the definition of strategic politician employed here may need modification. For the purposes of this analysis, neither qualified. But both state legislators faced term limits and, had they not challenged incumbents—Solis in a primary, Davis in a general election—their political careers probably would have been interrupted, their ambitions at least temporarily unrequited.

35. Gertzog, *Congressional Women*, 259–60.

36. Ibid., 136.

37. Ibid., 137

38. A special election in June 2001 sent one more black woman to the House—Democrat Diane Watson of California. All women who serve or served in the House as nonvoting delegates are excluded from this analysis.

39. In 1969, 131 among the 520,000 elected officials in the United States were African American women. Almost one-half were school board members. The number had increased to 337 in 1973, and African American women constituted 12 percent of all elected African American officeholders. See Bryce and Warwick, "Black Women in Electoral Politics," 395.

40. Curiously, the first black woman to serve in a state legislature, Mrs. E. Howard Harper of West Virginia, succeeded her husband following his death in 1927. See Bryce and Warwick, "Black Women in Electoral Politics," 399.

41. The strategic politician who lost is Republican Joan Johnson, who attempted to replace Rick Lazio when the Long Island Republican ran for the Senate against Hillary Rodham Clinton in 2000. Johnson conducted an indifferent campaign, and her prospects were almost certainly damaged by the candidacies of conservative, Right to Life, and Independence Party House aspirants who together captured 18 percent of the vote. Carol Cheeks Kilpatrick is the lone nonstrategic politician who won. The Detroit Democrat was a member of the state legislature when she successfully challenged incumbent Barbara-Rose Collins in the 1996 primary, following revelations of misuse of public funds by Collins. This analysis and the figures

in the table 5.5 do not include the June 2001 winning candidacy of California's Diane Watson, and the losing candidacy of Virginia's L. Louise Lucas in special elections. Both are strategic politicians.

42. David Lublin, "Election of African Americans and Latinos," 276.

43. Such a confrontation (although it did not involve an open seat) took place in a Brooklyn, New York, 2000 primary election. The contest pitted an African American city councilwoman, who, because of term limits, could not run again for the council, against an African American male incumbent Democrat. The woman, Una Clark, was defeated by Congressman Major Owens.

44. Burrell, "Presence and Performance of Women Candidates," 500.

45. Included in this group are those who retired, died, lost a bid for reelection, or ran for another office. The figures were aggregated from stories appearing in *Congressional Quarterly Weekly Report*, 1972–2000.

46. The five most prestigious House committees are Appropriations, Budget, Energy and Commerce, Rules, and Ways and Means. Among the 18 GOP women representatives in the 107th Congress, 11 serve on one of these committees.

47. The others were Helen Bentley, 1994, Patricia Saiki, 1994, Jane Harman, 1998, and Barbara Kennelly, 1998. Saiki had left the House in 1990 to run (unsuccessfully) for the Senate.

48. Information about candidates and election results in this portion of the chapter has been derived from *Congressional Quarterly Weekly Report*, 1965–2000.

49. Elizabeth Holtzman and Geraldine Ferraro ran for the Senate twice, Holtzman in 1980 and 1992, Ferraro in 1992 and 1998. Each candidacy is considered separately in this analysis.

50. Gertzog, *Congressional Women*, 166–69.

51. Gertzog, *Congresswomen in the Breech*, ch. 7.

52. Ibid.

CHAPTER SIX

WOMEN AS CANDIDATES IN CONGRESSIONAL ELECTIONS

RICHARD E. MATLAND AND DAVID C. KING

In 2000, an intensely fought battle for the Republican nomination for an open seat in Arizona's 2nd Congressional District found Susan Bitter Smith, the only woman in the race, finishing a distant third to Jeff Flake. At the start of the campaign Bitter Smith was the favorite. She had several years of experience on the local city council, the backing of the local newspaper, and was seen as a rising star in the Republican party. By the end of the race she was embroiled in a nasty shouting match over who was more willing to use dirty politics to win and she had faded badly. Flake went on to win the traditionally conservative district handily in the general election. In a distinctly different race and district, the Democratic primary in the Fourth Congressional District of Minnesota, Betty McCollum ran against three other candidates to succeed Congressman Bruce Vento, who retired due to illness. McCollum was the favorite, and despite a few rough spots she won the primary by a comfortable margin, with 50 percent of the vote. Her closest opponent (a man) had 23 percent of the vote. In the fall she won a comfortable victory in the traditionally Democratic district to become one of the five newly elected female members of the House of Representatives.

We know voters evaluate candidates based on their party, their stands on specific issues, and their perception of the candidate's ideology, character, and competence. An issue that remains latent is whether a candidate's sex has an indirect effect on perceptions of issues, ideology, character, or competence or whether a candidate's sex may directly affect the vote. This chapter considers whether a candidate's sex matters to the person's electoral chances. We believe that sex has a limited effect in general elections. The independent effect of sex appears to be limited by more salient characteristics of an election, such as candidate's party label, incumbency, and the current dominant issues of the day. Party labels are likely to be especially relevant when considering low-information elections, such as elections to the House of Representatives.[1] Furthermore the reality of congressional elections in much of the country, including the suburban Phoenix, Arizona, district that Susan Bitter Smith ran in and the urban St. Paul, Minnesota, district that Betty McCollum represents, is that certain districts lean heavily toward one party or the other. The true competition in these districts is in the party primaries, especially when a seat opens up because an incumbent retires, runs for higher office, or dies in office.

While primary and general elections differ on several central characteristics, relatively little work has been accomplished that considers how the possible effects of candidate sex may differ between general and primary elections. This is surprising since primaries are precisely the point at which we would expect descriptive characteristics such as sex to be most relevant. Since the most salient of all political cues, political party, does not distinguish between primary candidates, other cues are given more opportunity to influence voters' decisions. Another issue we analyze is one that has received virtually no prior consideration: whether candidate sex affects voters differently in Republican and Democratic primaries.

Evidence of emerging gender gaps in party identification and female representation in the U.S. Congress suggests the effect of candidate sex on voters may work differently in the two parties. As figure 6.1 shows, historically there has been a relatively small difference in the proportion of Democratic and Republican members of Congress who were female. The earliest period shows women tended to do slightly better in the Republican party. Women were a higher percentage of the Republican delegation than the Democratic delegation in all but three Congresses from 1916 to 1954. From the mid-1950s to mid-1960s the parties traded in terms of which had a higher proportion of women, while from the mid-1960s until 1980 women were always a higher proportion of the Democratic delegation. For every

FIGURE 6.1
Percentages of Women in Congress by Party

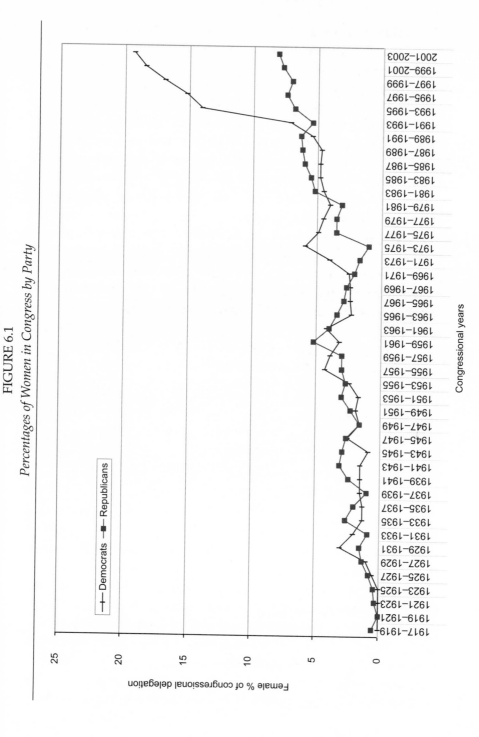

Congress in the 1980s, however, there was a higher proportion of women in the Republican than in the Democratic delegation. This was true despite the developing gender gap in voting showing women favored the Democratic party at the time. Finally in 1990 women started doing better in the Democratic delegation, and the gap has grown markedly in the 1990s to the point that it is now quite striking. At the start of the new millennium, the 107th Congress has the widest gap yet seen, with women constituting 19 percent of the Democratic delegation compared to only 8 percent of the Republican delegation.

This chapter first outlines existing research on women candidates in general elections, then presents new evidence based on experimental and historical data on the possible effects of sex on candidate evaluations in primary elections. The results are suggestive rather than definitive. The evidence presented offers the distinct possibility that the effect of candidates' sex functions differently in the two major parties. First, however, let us look at the existing evidence on the effect of candidate sex in general elections.

THE EFFECT OF CANDIDATE SEX IN ELECTIONS: PREVIOUS RESEARCH

Elizabeth Cook notes three ways to assess the effect of candidate sex on voters' decision making: actual election results, public opinion surveying, and experiments.[2] Each of these research methods has its strengths and weaknesses. We consider the election results and survey data quickly, but as we will be presenting the results of an experiment we will spend slightly more time presenting a review of the experimental results.

Election Results Evidence

Actual election results offer an obvious starting place. Richard Seltzer, Jody Newman, and Melissa Voorhees Leighton sum up the success of female candidates in general elections from 1972 to 1994 with the following statement. "When women run, women win . . . as often as men do."[3] What should be added to that statement is that women win as often as men do *when we compare similar candidate types.* If one merely compares male and female candidates running for the U.S. Congress, men do win more often than women. This occurs, however, not because they are men, but because of incumbent advantage. Table 6.1 shows that when we compare similarly

TABLE 6.1

Summary of Success Rates, 1972–2000, U.S. House, General Elections

U.S. HOUSE CANDIDATE TYPE	SUCCESS RATES	
	MEN	WOMEN
Incumbents	95.2% (5,289)	95.7% (376)
Open-seat candidates	51.6% (1,206)	43.6% (163)
Challengers	5.6% (4,364)	4.0% (569)

situated candidates in general elections, there is little difference in how men and women do.[4]

Candidates for the U.S. House are of three types. They are either (1) sitting incumbents, (2) running for an open seat, that is, a seat where there is no incumbent running, or they are (3) challengers. Looking at table 6.1 we see there are no significant differences in success rates for incumbents and challengers. The gap between male and female House candidates for open seats does meet the standard of statistical significance. Closer inspection reveals that the 8 percent gap in winning percentage is driven largely by a significant difference in how women have fared in winning open seats in the mid-1990s and onward, a period in which they have done much worse than men. From 1972 to 1994 the rates of victory were statistically equivalent. Since then women's victory rates have dropped dramatically: 47.9 percent of women won from 1972 to 1994; only 32.6 percent of women won from 1996 to 2000.[5] Clearly victory rates in open-seat elections are a trend that warrants careful attention to determine whether the results of the last three elections were a minor blip or if they indicate a broader trend against women. Candidate class, that is, whether the candidate is an incumbent or challenger, plays a far more significant role in explaining the overall difference in representation levels between men and women. Incumbents, whether they are male or female, have an extremely good chance of winning reelection. The very low legislative turnover in the U.S. Congress has been emphasized as a significant reason for the low levels of women's representation.[6]

The rough numbers are just a first cut at these issues. Table 6.1 merely indicates that those women who make it through to the general elections tend to do as well as the men who make it through to the general election. However, if serious barriers to entry exist, many women may never make it as far as the general election ballot. If women whose skills and talents are superior to most men are the only women who win general elections, then goals of equality have not been met. If superior women are merely doing as well as average men, that isn't equality. Furthermore, the election results data do not help us to understand whether candidate sex affects voting calculus. Additional tools are needed to get a handle on these questions, and therefore we turn to the survey evidence.

Survey Evidence

A battery of questions measuring beliefs in gender equality in politics have been included in the General Social Survey from the early 1970s to the present. Stephen and Linda Bennett have developed an Index of Political Gender Roles that measures traditional versus modern attitudes toward women in politics.[7] As a cohort replacement effect has occurred, with older generations disappearing and being replaced by newer voters, we have seen a dramatic drop in the proportion of voters who cling to a traditional perspective on women's role in politics. While 30 years ago the ratio of modern to traditional voters was approximately two to one (65 percent to 33 percent), today that ratio has expanded to seven to one (86 percent to 12 percent). The overall trend is clearly in the direction of accepting changing roles for women in politics.

To look at women as candidates more concretely, several researchers have used national election surveys of voters to assess how female candidates have done. While the results are not unanimous, the consensus is that women candidates do at least as well and perhaps slightly better than male candidates. What is clear is that "on average, women have been slightly more likely than men to vote for women candidates."[8] While this is true, it can have several explanations. The most obvious is that most female candidates in the past decade have been Democrats and most of the Democratic voters in the past decade have been women. The more technically sophisticated vote analyses seem to indicate, although not uniformly, that women voters will cross over to support women from the other party.[9] The same is not true of male voters, who show no evidence of crossing party lines simply to support men.

Thompson and Steckenrider used a quasi-experimental design to test for an effect of candidate sex.[10] They ran hypothetical elections, collected from a mail survey, where the amount of information provided about candidates varied from one election to the next. They included (or consciously withheld) information on gender, party, and position on one issue (abortion). They found that party and issue cues were overwhelmingly used as the most relevant cue to voting. There was a subsection of voters, however, who voted for women candidates based on gender contrary to their party affiliation. While this subsection of voters was not large, they could make a difference in a tight congressional race where the ability to attract independent and crossover votes is crucial.

Experimental Evidence

Both actual election results and survey analyses are "over-identified"; so many factors occur simultaneously that may plausibly affect the vote that it is very difficult to determine whether being female or male had a direct effect on people's voting decision. Experiments allow for precise estimates of how candidate sex affects the vote. In the general format of experiments designed to study the effects of candidate sex, a candidate is described—or a speech is read—and respondents are asked to rate the candidate on several issue dimensions and/or say whether the candidate would get their vote. What makes the process an experiment is that while everyone reads the same description or speech, half of the sample, chosen at random, is told the candidate is a woman while the other half is told the candidate is a man. Since all other stimuli are exactly the same, and given that respondents are randomly placed into treatment and control groups, any statistically significant differences between the two subsamples must occur because the candidate's sex affects the way respondents assess the candidates.

Since 1975, 15 experiments aimed at understanding how gender affects the perceptions of political candidates have been reported in political science and social psychology journals. These experiments are summarized in the appendix to this chapter. The experiments can be sorted into two categories. The first category tests whether "changing" a candidate's gender affects the votes for the candidate. The second category focuses on whether male or female candidates are thought to be more competent in dealing with specific policy areas.

The most common approach for assessing whether gender directly affects voting is to present respondents with descriptions of two candidates in a hypothetical election situation. Respondents are then asked to mark a ballot.[11] The results of these studies are fairly consistent: only two studies found differences in levels of support depending on the candidate's gender; all the other studies (8 of 10) fail to find any direct effects at the ballot box.[12]

A second approach, focusing on whether female or male candidates are seen as better at handling issues in specific policy areas, has found much stronger gender effects. Respondents evaluated a candidate based on either a short description or a speech, with the candidate's sex manipulated.[13] These studies show there are general categories of public policies (such as "nurturing" and "compassion" issues) in which female candidates are deemed better.[14] "Education," "helping the poor," "supporting the arts," and "health" are all issues where in one experiment or the other voters have been shown to believe female candidates are better at handling the issue.

Concerning issues that male candidates are thought superior at handling, the experimental results are ambiguous. Neither Mark Leeper nor Kim Fridkin Kahn report any issue areas in which male candidates have an assumed advantage in terms of competence.[15] Virginia Sapiro finds males were considered better on farm issues, while both Sapiro and Leonie Huddy and Nayda Terkildsen find that being male provided a positive effect for presumed competence on military issues.[16] The studies done by Rosenwasser and her colleagues find that male candidates are seen as stronger than female candidates on a "masculine task" scale that is dominated by military issues.[17] Significantly, both male and female advantages in competence appear only for issues that are not directly discussed in the speech or descriptions to which the respondents react.

Several experiments have explored the effect of gender on how voters view a candidate's character. Sapiro, Leeper, and Kahn all report that female candidates are seen as more honest or better able to maintain integrity in public office.[18] Scholars have also tested whether traditionally male or female traits affect evaluations of candidates or legislative effectiveness.[19] These experiments show that male traits are generally seen as more desirable and are associated with being a more effective legislator. What these studies fail to do, however, is prove that male candidates automatically have higher levels of these "male traits"—such as being articulate. Regardless of sex, we expect most candidates to be articulate. We are therefore reluctant to ascribe stereotypical male and female "traits" among the general public to the highly selective group of people who run for Congress.

We have a couple of concerns with these experiments. First, 14 of the 15 experiments we review use students as subjects, almost all college undergraduates.[20] University students are atypical of the national population on a host of factors, and therefore it can be difficult to generalize results to the voting public. University students' political values are less clearly established. They are less likely to vote and be actively engaged in politics. They tend to be more liberal on social issues, including the proper role for women in society. These characteristics may leave us with a weaker effect for a candidate's gender in college-based laboratory experiments than in the population as a whole.

Our second concern is that several of the experiments have given respondents very little information with which to evaluate candidates, and this calls into question the generalizability of previous results. Most important, 14 of the 15 published experiments fail to include *any* information about a candidate's partisanship as a possible cue to voters, even though a candidate's political party is the best predictor of how voters will mark their ballots. In general elections it is entirely possible that party identification, both the voter's and the candidate's, will overwhelm any gender effects, making gender virtually irrelevant. For primaries we might assume that the experimental results, where party was not defined, hold, but it is at least as plausible that gender interacts with party so that perceptions of female candidates will differ across the two parties. Unfortunately, because previous experiments have failed to build information on political party into their design, we can only speculate.

The impoverishment of information in previous experiments has also led to contradictory results when scholars have tested for affinity effects.[21] A gender-based affinity effect is present when voters support candidates who are similar to themselves: men are more likely to vote for male candidates or women are more likely to vote for female candidates. One might expect to find an affinity effect in answers to statements such as "This candidate shares my concerns" or "This candidate cares about people like me." When those sentiments are turned into a vote for a specific candidate, however, male-male and female-female affinity effects may cancel each other out, leaving no real impact on who is elected. Five previous experiments explicitly tested for affinity effects. The two studies reporting pervasive affinity effects, however, not only failed to provide respondents with information on the candidate's party, they provided very little substantive information of any kind to use in evaluating the candidates.[22] The three other studies provided respondents with considerably more background on the candidates, and affinity effects disappeared under most model specifications.[23]

Previous experiments have provided political scientists with several valuable insights. Gender differences do not lead directly to significant differences in male and female candidates' vote-getting abilities. Voters, however, view male and female candidates differently. There are indications that male and female candidates' competencies are thought to differ across issues, and depending on what issues are engaged in an election campaign, women may be helped or hurt. Experiments have come to these conclusions while giving respondents sketchy candidate descriptions. We do not take issue with this except to note that affinity effects and differential evaluations of expertise may fade as voters learn more about candidates. The relevance of these experiments is, however, strengthened by the fact that most studies of congressional elections show voters know relatively little about the political candidates they vote for. They do, however, know the partisan affiliations of these candidates, and the failure of earlier experiments to include partisanship is a serious omission.

INCLUDING PARTISANSHIP IN A VOTING EXPERIMENT

The experiment described below presents results from a national survey sponsored by the Republican Network to Elect Women (RENEW). A random sample of 820 adults from throughout the United States was polled December 6–8, 1993. The survey—designed to conform to an experimental methodology—was conducted by Public Opinion Research, one of the country's leading political polling firms. Each respondent was read the same candidate description, and in the descriptions half of the respondents were told the candidate was a male, while the other half were told that the candidate was a female. Each respondent heard the following:

I am going to read you a brief description of a potential candidate for Congress in this area. After I read this, I will ask you to evaluate [him/her]. The candidate is a Republican [man/woman] who has never run for office before, but has been active in the community. [She/He] is a businessperson who is running because [he/she] says that Congress "just doesn't get it" and wants to bring a common sense business approach to government. [His/Her] first priority is to work to reduce government spending and waste.

After the candidate was described, respondents evaluated the candidate on a number of traits and on the likelihood they would support the candidate. Ideally, we would also have results where we compare male and female Democrats, but this experiment was designed to evaluate only Republican candidates. Nevertheless, as one of only two experiments to include information on candidate sex and the crucial party label, this experiment presents important information. It allows us to present preliminary evidence of what the consequences of candidate sex might be both in the Republican primary and in terms of the feasibility of getting cross-party votes.

What do we expect? Our first concern is whether a candidate's gender affects the likelihood that voters will support or oppose the candidate. We have argued that gender-based affinity effects and issue differences probably diminish in information-rich elections. We expect that once a party label is added to a candidate the candidate's gender will not affect how our respondents evaluate the candidate. Our presumption is that party is a much more powerful cue when evaluating candidates.

A second set of expectations involves perceived candidate characteristics. Social psychologists have shown there are consistent gender stereotypes subscribed to by both men and women.[24] Women are generally seen as more nurturing, more supportive, less confrontational, and in some cases more honest. Men, on the other hand, are seen as more decisive, stronger, and better able to deal with crises. Based on findings from previous experiments, we assume the more masculine factors—such as being well qualified and a strong leader—would favor the male candidate, while being able to "share my concerns" (which suggests an ability to empathize) and being "trustworthy" would favor the female candidate.[25]

Our first analyses consider the effects of gender affinity and partisan affiliation. If there is a gender-based affinity effect, males should be more likely to vote for male candidates, and females should be more likely to vote for female candidates. The data indicate a slight, though not statistically significant ($p = .32$) affinity effect among male voters (see table 6.2). Of male respondents, 42.3 percent who were told the candidate was male said they were very likely to vote for him, while 35.3 percent of males who

TABLE 6.2

Tests for Affinity Effects: Respondents' Likelihood of Voting for Candidate

	VERY LIKELY	SOMEWHAT LIKELY	NOT VERY LIKELY/ NOT LIKELY AT ALL
Male R's/male candidate	42.3%	34.0%	23.7%
	(66)	(53)	(37)
Male R's/female candidate	35.3%	44.1%	20.6%
	(60)	(75)	(35)
Female R's/male candidate	32.4%	42.3%	25.4%
	(69)	(90)	(54)
Female R's/female candidate	31.2%	51.1%	17.8%
	(72)	(118)	(41)

NOTE: $x^2 = 3.5$ $p = .32$ (male R's); gamma = .05
$x^2 = 6.0$ $p = .11$ (female R's); gamma = –.07

SOURCE: Public Opinion Research, for RENEW, December 1993, N = 820. Sample size in the table is 770 because "don't know" and "refused to answer" responses were dropped.

were told the candidate was female were very likely to vote for her. The results show candidate sex has no such effect for female voters: 32.4 percent of female respondents would be very likely to vote for the male candidate, and 31.2 percent were very likely to vote for the female candidate. At the other end of the scale, female respondents were somewhat less likely to dismiss the possibility of supporting a female candidate (17.8 percent) versus male candidates (25.4 percent), although for neither male nor female respondents did any of these effects reach statistically significant levels.

Table 6.3 shows the effects of partisanship: responses to the question asking if respondents were likely to support the candidate are broken down by party identification. Not surprisingly, party identification has a dramatic effect. Among Republican identifiers, 47.1 percent said they were very likely to support the candidate, while only 9.2 percent saw it as not very likely or not likely at all. On the other hand, only 19.6 percent of the Democrats said they were very likely to support the candidate, while 36.2 percent saw it as not very likely or not likely at all. Independents held opinions between those of the party identifiers.

TABLE 6.3
Party-ID and Respondents' Likelihood of Voting for Candidate

	VERY LIKELY	SOMEWHAT LIKELY	NOT VERY LIKELY/ NOT LIKELY AT ALL
Republicans	47.1%	43.8%	9.2%
	(144)	(134)	(28)
Independents	35.1%	44.4%	20.5%
	(60)	(76)	(35)
Democrats	19.6%	44.2%	36.2%
	(52)	(117)	(96)

NOTE: $x^2 = 79.7, p=.000$
SOURCE: Public Opinion Research, for RENEW, December 1993, N = 820. Sample size in the table is 770 because "don't know" and "refused to answer" responses were dropped.

While we found strong evidence of a party affiliation effect and little evidence of a direct gender-based affinity effect, we are especially interested in how a respondent's party identification and a candidate's gender interact. For example, do Democrats view female Republican candidates more favorably than otherwise identical male Republican candidates? In the first four rows of table 6.4, we report the difference, based on gender, in the percentage of respondents who state the candidate is "very well" or "somewhat well" described by the indicated characteristics (as opposed to "not very well" or "not very well at all"). A positive percentage difference indicates the female candidate has an advantage over an otherwise identical male candidate.

In the full sample, all respondents consider the female Republican more trustworthy and more likely to share their concerns than a similarly described male Republican. The bottom row of table 6.4 shows that on the crucial aspect of voting, the sample as a whole is more likely to vote for the female candidate. The percentage differences on these three questions are statistically significant, but what is especially noteworthy is how the differences break down across party groups. For example, among Democratic voters, the advantage for the female candidate on "trustworthiness" tops 19 percent. Her advantage among Democratic and Independent voters on empathy ("shares my concerns") hovers near 10 percent. The female

TABLE 6.4
Percentage Evaluating Female Candidate More Favorably

Question This candidate ...	All Respondents (N = 781)	Republican Respondents (N = 319)	Independent Respondents (N = 184)	Democrat Respondents (N=278)
... can be trusted[1]	8.61%***	3.15%	7.82%	19.14%***
... shares my concerns	6.38%**	1.60%	11.87%*	9.89%*
... is a strong leader	1.26%	-7.24%*	8.44%	5.41%
... is qualified	0.02%	-5.73%	1.28%	4.79%
Respondent Very Likely or Somewhat Likely to Vote for the Candidate	5.42%*	-0.11%	10.53%*	9.63%*

$*p < .10, ** p < .05,$ and $*** p < .01$ on a two-tailed test
[1] The differences presented in the table are based on answers to the following ques‍tion: "Now, based *just* upon what you have heard in the brief description I read, pleas‍tell me how well you believe each of the following descriptions fit this candidate"
Source: Public Opinion Research, for RENEW, December 1993, N = 820. Sample size in the tabl‍varies because "don't know" and "refused to answer" responses were dropped.

candidate's advantage in terms of likely support is 10 percent among Inde-pendent and Democratic voters. A 10 percent swing to the Republican can-didate from Independents and Democrats could easily be the difference between winning and losing in a competitive House race.

IMPLICATIONS FOR GENERAL ELECTIONS

The analysis above provides us with several useful and interesting results. First, there are no significant gender-based affinity effects. To confirm these results, we tested for affinity effects on multiple subsets of the population, including working women, black women, wealthy and poor women, and so on. We also looked for affinity effects among male respondents. We found none. The experimental evidence purporting to show a gender-based affinity effect has always been problematic, and it has disappeared in pre-vious experiments that provided relatively rich cues about candidates. It does so in this case also. Voters are not automatically drawn to candidates simply because they are of the same sex; party and political positions are of greater concern when choosing a candidate to vote for.

In interpreting table 6.4 it is important to remember that Democrats and Independents are consistently less likely to believe that the Republican candidate (regardless of the candidate's gender) "shares my concerns," "is qualified," "can be trusted," or "is a strong leader" than Republicans. Republican candidates begin with a big disadvantage among Democrats and Independents. What table 6.4 shows, however, is that the Republican female candidate can make up for some of the skepticism created by their Republicanism. Women are consistently advantaged by their gender, when being evaluated from the perspective of Democrats and Independents. Most importantly—from the perspective of the Republican leadership—Democrats and Independents are more likely to vote for the female Republican.

What characteristics are important for a candidate to have when running for office? The political science literature suggests several features associated with successful candidates. The characteristics measured in table 6.4—such as trust, empathy, and leadership skills—figure prominently in evaluations of which candidates voters think are "qualified."[26] Among Independents and Democrats, a Republican woman rates more highly on this quality than a Republican man does. Trust in government and politicians has been steadily declining in the United States and most Western democracies.[27] Republican female candidates are less likely to be seen as professional politicians. In the RENEW experiment, when asked how well the term "typical politician" described the candidate, Independents and Democrats made a clear distinction, based on gender.[28] A candidate who looks physically different from those who are now in power is more convincing as an agent of change. Women candidates have that advantage.

While trustworthiness, qualifications, and leadership skills are important, *votes* are paramount. Regardless of a candidate's gender, partisan predispositions are barriers that may block crossover votes. The "bottom line" in table 6.4 is that female Republican candidates are more likely than male Republican candidates to get votes from Democrats and Independents. Strategically speaking, the Republican party would advantage itself by running more women candidates. As figure 6.1 shows, however, the greatest gains for women have been largely occurring in the Democratic delegation and not the Republican delegation.

IMPLICATIONS FOR PRIMARY ELECTIONS

To this point our analysis has concentrated on the impression Republican male and female candidates might make on Democrats and Independents in a general election. Before a Republican woman can get that opportunity, however, she must face a Republican primary electorate. It matters little if a female Republican candidate is able to win crossover votes in the general election if she is unable to win her primary.

When we concentrate on Republican voters and consider the dynamics of a primary race, the results are not encouraging for a Republican female candidate. Looking at table 6.4 we see that the Republican respondents, unlike the Democratic respondents, do not see the female Republican candidate as someone who is more likely to share the characteristic of "can be trusted." While both the Democratic and Independent respondents saw the Republican female as stronger in terms of "sharing my concerns," such an advantage was not given to the Republican female by Republican respondents. Strikingly, when it comes to seeing the candidate as a "strong leader," the Democrats and Independents perceive the female candidate as stronger (albeit the effect is not significant), while the Republicans see the male candidate as stronger. We see a similar, although nonsignificant effect in terms of being well qualified. On every one of these characteristics, the Republican respondents, when compared to the Democratic and Independent respondents, are more sympathetic to the male candidate. The one saving grace appears to be that there is no less of a hesitancy to support the female candidate. Let us, however, take a second look at the question of willingness to support a candidate.

In political survey research work a battery of questions is used to identify where a respondent's political leanings lie along a seven-point scale from strong Republican to strong Democrat. Table 6.5 shows the percentage of respondents "very likely" to vote for the male and female candidate across the standard seven-point party identification scale.[29] The results are unmistakable. While strong Democrats are much more supportive of a female Republican than a male Republican, strong Republicans are much less supportive of the female candidate. The Republican female candidate is at her biggest disadvantage among respondents who consider themselves "strong Republicans." Sixty-six percent of strong Republicans who evaluated the male candidate were very likely to vote for him; only 51

TABLE 6.5

Percentage of Respondents "Very Likely" to Vote for Candidate

Voter's Party-ID	Female Republican Candidate	Male Republican Candidate	Female Candidate's Advantage (+) or Disadvantage (–)
Strong Republican (n = 143)	50.68	65.71	–15.03*
Republican (n = 94)	34.09	36.00	–1.91
Leans Republican (n = 80)	29.78	42.42	–12.64
Independent (n = 183)	35.42	29.89	+5.53
Leans Democrat (n=91)	18.37	21.43	–3.06
Democrat (n = 75)	16.33	15.38	–0.94
Strong Democrat (n = 109)	26.42	14.29	+12.13*

$* p < .10$ on a two-tailed test

SOURCE: Public Opinion Research, for RENEW, December 1993, N = 820. Sample size in the table varies because "don't know" and "refused to answer" responses were dropped.

percent of strong Republicans who evaluated the female candidate were likely to vote for her. This is especially problematic since "strong" partisans are far more likely to contribute time and money to a campaign and are much more likely to vote in primaries. Given that strong party identifiers are the most active slice of voters in primaries, our experimental data suggest that female Republicans will have a more difficult time getting nominated.

Why should staunch Republicans be more skeptical of a female candidate? Monika McDermott suggests that gender provides a low-cost social information cue as to the ideological bent of a candidate. She provides some evidence that voters perceive female candidates as more liberal. We test for a similar effect. Our respondents were asked how well the term "conservative" described the candidate being evaluated.[30] The results are instructive. For Democrats and Independents there was very little difference in evaluations. Thirty-two and three-tenths percent of those evaluating the male candidate and 34.1 percent of those evaluating the female candidate said the label "conservative" described the candidate "very well," a trivial difference. For Republicans, however, while 42.4 percent of those who evaluated the female candidate said the label described her "very well," the equivalent response for the male candidate was over 15 percent higher, at 57.7 percent. In addition, for Republicans the evaluation of how "conservative" the candidate was directly affected the vote. Seventy-one percent of those who said the conservative label described the candidate "very well" said they were "very likely" to vote for the candidate, while only 27 percent of those who did not believe the conservative label fit "very well" were "very likely" to vote for the candidate. Being a woman appears to send a cue to Republican voters, but not to Democratic or Independent voters, that the candidate is less conservative than the men she may have to compete against in a party primary. To the extent that conservatives are active in primaries, the impression that female Republicans are more liberal than otherwise identical male candidates works against women trying to win votes in the Republican primaries.

ADDITIONAL EVIDENCE ON THE EFFECTS OF GENDER IN PRIMARIES

The experimental results described above are thought provoking. They suggest there are systematic differences across the two major parties in the way sex interacts with candidacies. Before we extrapolate too far, however, we caution that this suggestion is at least initially built on the slender reed of evidence from one experiment. It deserves careful consideration, but more evidence must be gathered and considered. While a full-blown investigation of public opinion data and historical election results in primaries is well beyond the scope of this chapter, we can take a look at some select pieces of evidence to bring additional information to light.

First, when we consider public opinion we can look at the Index of Political Gender Roles and see if the results systematically vary by party identification. The differences are modest. There are minor differences that indicate Republican voters are somewhat more traditional. While the more traditional values of the Republican identifiers may be a small part of the explanation, we believe it is more accurate to interpret the experimental results not as Republican voters being antiwomen, but rather that they are proconservative. When little other information is provided to these conservative voters, they infer from the candidate's sex political stands that they are reluctant to support. It isn't women's active role in politics per se that troubles these Republican voters; it's their possible liberalism.[31]

As a second piece of independent data on how candidate sex affects candidate evaluations in primary elections, we can take a preliminary look at how women actually do in primary campaigns. Table 6.1 showed there were dramatic differences in victory rates across seat types. Incumbents overwhelmingly win, and challengers overwhelmingly lose. As Ronald Gaddie and Charles Bullock note, the "open seats are where the action is." There are only a couple of previous studies that have looked at whether there are differences in the likelihood of women winning open-seat primaries. Barbara Burrell looks at differences in the likelihood that a woman running for an open-seat nomination will win in the Democratic and Republican party for the 1970s and the 1980s. Gaddie and Bullock test for differences in success rates among women running for a nomination in the Democratic or Republican party in the 1980s and through 1992. Neither finds significant differences in the likelihood a woman will win.[32]

Despite these findings, we believe the data for the 1990s merit a careful look. There are at least a couple reasons. First, we use a slightly different measure of female success than Burrell and Gaddie/Bullock. They measure the percentage of all female *candidates* who succeed at winning nominations. We believe a better measure is the proportion of *districts* where women are running where the nomination is ultimately won by a woman.[33] The second reason for considering success rates in primaries in the 1990s is that there is good reason to believe that as increasing attention has been focused on the gender gap in voting, there has been an increasing message that women are more liberal than men. Voters may have become more sensitized to the possible implications of sex in a way that has not occurred in the past.[34]

Table 6.6 shows the number of districts where women ran and won the nomination for the two major parties in the 1990s and for 2000. We see there are far more districts where women are running in open-seat primaries on the Democratic side than on the Republican side (by definition the opportunities are equal since an open seat is always open for both parties). Furthermore, Democratic voters have shown a higher propensity to choose a female candidate. In 53.5 percent of Democratic primaries in open-seat districts where a woman has run, the party's voters have selected a female candidate. On the Republican side, women have won in 37.5 percent of the districts where there was a woman running. The 16-point difference in win rates is statistically significant ($p < .02$, two-tailed test). At least for the 1990s we see a significant difference in how women fare in the Democratic and Republican primaries.

TABLE 6.6

Women's Success in Winning Primaries for Open Seats to the
House of Representatives: Democratic and Republican Women

	DISTRICTS W/ FEMALE DEM. CANDIDATES	WINS	% VICTORIOUS	DISTRICTS W/ FEMALE REP. CANDIDATES	WINS	% VICTORIOUS
1990	11	7	63.6	6	2	33.3
1992	40	23	57.5	19	11	57.9
1994	21	10	47.6	19	5	26.3
1996	20	7	35.0	12	4	33.3
1998	19	12	63.2	11	4	36.4
2000	16	9	56.3	13	4	30.7
Total	127	68	53.5	80	30	37.5

CONCLUSIONS

There is no such thing as a nonpartisan election for the U.S. Congress. Candidates are partisan creatures, born of party primaries, vying for jobs in an intensely partisan institution. One implication of our results is clear. Partisan identification must be included in future experiments that consider how voters evaluate candidates, even if the primary interest is in questions of gender.[35] Unlike previous experiments, our experiment tried to take account of the central role party plays in elections. Our results show that even when the information in the environment is enriched by including party labels, gender effects still appear.

While the assertion of female advantage in congressional races is relatively new among political scientists, it infected professional political consultants a decade earlier and is now conventional wisdom on the campaign trail. "Voters trust women more than men, believe that women listen better than men, and look to women for new ideas," argues Cathy Allen, a Seattle political strategist.[36] The experimental results reported here are supportive of these assertions, and as such they are part of a growing literature suggesting that female candidates have some distinct advantages in congressional campaigns. Our study shows, however, that those advantages are mediated by partisanship. For Republicans evaluating a female Republican, gender appears to send a signal that the candidate is more liberal than a comparable Republican male. This may lead to Republican women having a harder time winning the party's nomination. For Independents and

Democrats, on the other hand, being female does not send a strong ideological signal.[37] Rather, it provides signals on a different set of characteristics. Specifically, Democratic and Independent voters are predisposed to view female Republicans as more likely to share their concerns, and to be more trustworthy and better leaders. Entire political campaigns can be built around such positive traits.

In 1986, 52 percent of the women in Congress were Republicans. Fifteen years later, that figure had dropped to only 31 percent. While there has been a significant increase in the number of women running and winning under the Democratic label, the increase among Republican women has been modest. The reason does not appear to lie with the voting public as a whole. Our results show that Republican women are likely to have some distinct advantages over Republican men as general election candidates. Representative Nancy Pelosi (D-CA), citing women candidates' ability to "identify" with voter concerns, said, "in marginal districts, women candidates have an advantage."[38] Most of the turnover in House elections occurs in these marginal districts; so the potential for change can be exploited by turning to female candidates.

Republican women, however, appear to have significant problems within their own party and especially with the most activist elements in their party. There is some danger the differences in intraparty success may exacerbate the growing gender gap in the House. The relatively high success rates of women winning nominations in the Democratic party is likely to affect the calculus of women who are potential Democratic candidates and make it more tempting to run for their party's nomination for Congress. Women's relatively low rates of success in winning nominations in the Republican party may make it less likely that female Republican candidates will run.

Women are in the process of transforming how Congress works. To this point, however, that transformation has very much occurred only on one side of the aisle. If the Republican party were more willing to turn to women as candidates, we could see a significant increase in women's representation and possibly also an increase in Republican victories.

NOTES

1. Abramowitz, "Comparison of Voting for U.S. Senator and Representative in 1978"; Hinckley, "American Voter in Congressional Elections"; McDermott, "Voting Cues in Low-Information Elections"; and Shanks and Miller, *New American Voter*.

2. E. Cook, "Voter Reactions to Women Senate Candidates."

3. Seltzer, Newman, and Voorhees Leighton, *Sex as a Political Variable*, 79.

4. The data for table 6.1 for 1972–94 are taken from Seltzer, Newman, and Voorhees Leighton, *Sex as a Political Variable*, 83. Data for 1996, 1998, and 2000 were collected from *Congressional Quarterly Weekly Report*.

5. Men's victory rates for the same two periods remained relatively stable at 51.2 percent and 53.6 percent, respectively.

6. Darcy, Welch, and Clark, *Women, Elections, and Representation*.

7. Bennett and Bennett, "From Traditional to Modern Conceptions of Gender Equality."

8. Seltzer, Newman, and Voorhees Leighton, *Sex as a Political Variable*, 102.

9. E. Cook, "Voter Response to Women Senate Candidates"; E. Cook and Wilcox, "Women Voters in the 'Year of the Woman'"; Dolan, "Voting for Women"; Paolino, "Group Salient Issues and Group Representation"; Smith and Fox, "Electoral Fortunes of Women Candidates for Congress."

10. Thompson and Steckenrider, "Relative Irrelevance of Candidate Sex."

11. Adams, "Candidate Characteristics, Office, and Voter Responses"; Ekstrand and Eckert, "Impact of Candidate's Sex"; Garrett and Brooks, "Effect of Ballot Color, Sex of Candidate"; Huddy and Terkildsen, "Consequences of Gender Stereotypes"; Leeper, "Impact of Prejudice on Female Candidates"; Riggle et al., "Gender Stereotypes and Decision Context"; Sapiro, "If Senator Baker Were a Woman"; Sigelman and Sigelman, "Sexism, Racism, and Ageism in Voting"; Spohn and Gillespie, "Adolescents' Willingness to Vote for a Woman." Riggle et al., "Gender Stereotypes and Decision Context" (1997), alters the format slightly by providing information via computer screen on several candidates and asking the respondents to select one.

12. One exception is Adams's experiment, when he found that gender effects differed depending on the level of office sought. See Adams, "Candidate Characteristics, Office, and Voter Responses," for more information. The other exception is Fox and Smith (1998), who found no bias in their sample of UC-Santa Barbara students, but a noticeable bias against women, using the same instrument, among Wyoming students.

13. Huddy and Terkildsen, "Gender Stereotypes and Perception," used a description of the candidates. Sapiro "If Senator Baker Were a Woman," and Leeper, "Impact of Prejudice," used a speech by the candidate.

14. Huddy and Terkildsen, "Gender Stereotypes and Perception."

15. Leeper, "Impact of Prejudice," and Kahn, "Does Being Male Help?"

16. Sapiro, "If Senator Baker Were a Woman," and Huddy and Terkildsen, "Gender Stereotypes and Perception."

17. Rosenwasser et al., "Attitudes Toward Women and Men in Politics"; Rosenwasser and Seale, "Attitudes Toward a Hypothetical Male or Female Presidential Candidate"; Rosenwasser and Dean, "Gender Role and Political Office."

18. Sapiro, "If Senator Baker Were a Woman"; Leeper, "Impact of Prejudice"; and Kahn, "Does Being Male Help?"

19. Rosenwasser and Dean, "Gender Role and Political Office"; Huddy and Terkildsen, "Gender Stereotypes and Perception"; Huddy and Terkildsen, "Consequences of Gender Stereotypes."

20. The exception is Kahn's "Does Being Male Help?" on U.S. Senate races. She uses adults from a single city, Ann Arbor, Michigan.

21. Ekstrand and Eckert, "Impact of Candidate's Sex"; Sapiro, "If Senator Baker Were a Woman"; Sigelman and Sigelman, "Sexism, Racism, and Ageism in Voting"; Garrett and Brooks, "Effect of Ballot Color, Sex of Candidate"; Spohn and Gillespie, "Adolescents' Willingness to Vote for a Woman"; Riggle et al., "Gender Stereotypes and Decision Context."

22. Sigelman and Sigelman, "Sexism, Racism, and Ageism in Voting"; Garrett and Brooks, "Effect of Ballot Color, Sex of Candidate."

23. Ekstrand and Eckert, "Impact of Candidate's Sex"; Sapiro, "If Senator Baker Were a Woman"; Riggle et al., "Gender Stereotypes and Decision Context."

24. Williams and Best, *Measuring Sex Stereotypes.*

25. Sapiro, "If Senator Baker Were a Woman"; Rosenwasser and Dean, "Gender Role and Political Office"; Leeper, "Impact of Prejudice"; Kahn, "Does Being Male Help?"; Huddy and Terkildsen, "Gender Stereotypes and Perception."

26. Canon, *Actors, Athletes, and Astronauts*; Fenno, *Home Style.*

27. Nye, Zelikow, and King, *Why People Don't Trust Government.*

28. The ratings are 2.12 versus 2.29 on a four-point scale, p = .04 for a one-tailed test. The question format is the same as that presented in table 6.2. Interestingly, Republican voters did not perceive a difference on this candidate characteristic (male = 2.36, female = 2.42).

29. While the bottom row of table 6.4 includes voters who are very likely or somewhat likely to vote for the candidate, table 6.5 looks only at those who are very likely to vote for the candidate. Since we are interested in the effects of sex on primary voters, it is wise to limit the evaluation to those who are most intense in their feelings.

30. The format of the question is the same as that in table 6.3.

31. It is perhaps worth noting that this belief is not without some evidence, although it is clearly subject to the problem of being an ecological fallacy. As a group, ADA scores measuring how liberal is a representative's voting record show that Republican women in the House are more liberal than Republican men.

32. Gaddie and Bullock, *Elections to Open Seats,* 137; Burrell, *Woman's Place Is in the House.*

33. The following explains the dilemma: Assume there are 10 open seats. For Democrats assume there are 5 female candidates in each district; assume further that in each of these open seats a woman wins the nomination. If we consider each individual female candidate as a case, as Gaddie and Bullock do, we report only 20

percent of Democratic women win a nomination (10 of 50). The Matland/King measure would register this as 10 districts where 10 women won all the nominations or 100 percent success for women. Now assume at the same time exactly one woman runs for the Republican nomination in each of these districts. Assume 3 of the 10 Republican women candidates win. For both the Gaddie-Bullock measure and Matland/King measure this would be registered as 30 percent of women victorious. When we compare success among Republicans and Democrats, the Gaddie-Bullock measure would find success was greater on the Republican side where 30 percent of the women running won a nomination versus 20 percent of the women on the Democratic side. The Matland/King measure would find Democratic women had greater success in winning 100 percent of the possible nominations, while the Republican side won only 30 percent. We believe individual measures don't accurately present how well women as a whole are doing in the party. Therefore, in the chart we measure the proportion of seats in which women are running where a woman wins the nomination.

34. The perception of women becoming more and more Democratic in their voting is a total misreading of the data. Historical data shows that the gender gap has largely been created by men, especially in the South, moving away from the Democratic party and toward the Republican party. (See Kaufmann and Petrocik, "Changing Politics of American Men," and Norrander, "Evolution of the Gender Gap.") Despite women being relatively stable in their political views over the last 50 years, the press, time and again, inaccurately refers to the movement of women toward the Democratic party. What has happened is that men have increasingly moved toward the Republican party.

35. We strongly suspect that the one recent study that did find a bias against women as candidates (Fox and Smith) did so not because respondents were biased against women, but because they used the sex of the candidate to impute both party and ideology to the candidates.

36. Guy Gugliotta, "At Yale, Women Give Campaigning the New College Try," *Washington Post*, 13 June 1996, p. C:1.

37. It is worth noting that the failure of a Republican woman to send a strong ideological signal is consistent with McDermott's work using the NES, where she found that being female sent a clear ideological signal for Democratic women, but failed to send a clear ideological signal for Republican women.

38. Cohen, "Gloomy Day for the GOP."

Review of Published Experiments Regarding Female Candidates

Author(s)	Office	Sample	Stimuli Source	Candidate Attributes	Gender Effects		
					Differences in Level of Support	Differences in Areas of Expertise	Other Findings
Adams (1975)	President Senate Mayor Council	135 undergrads	Ballot w/ position paper	Gender, policy positions	Contextual: Less for national & executive; more for local, esp. legislatures	Not tested	
Ekstrand & Eckert (1981)	Governor	732 undergrads	Ballot w/ long cand. descriptions	Gender, pol. experience, demographics, policy (lib. v. con.)	No direct effect. Some complex interactions.	Not tested	No affinity effect found.
Sigelman & Sigelman (1982)	Mayor	460 college students	Ballot w/ short cand. descriptions	Gender, profession, policy (lib. v. con.)	None found	Not tested	Affinity effect found.
Garrett & Brooks (1987)	Congress	96 undergrads	Ballot w/ short cand. descriptions	Gender, statement (vague)	None found	Not tested	Affinity effect found.
Spohn & Gillespie (1987)	President	705 high school students	Ballot w/ short cand. description	Gender, demographics policy (lib. v. con.)	No direct effect. A few complex interactions.	Not tested	Slight affinity effect. Also blacks more supportive of female candidates.
Huddy & Terkildsen (1993a)	President Congress Mayor	297 undergrads	Brief candidate description	Gender, varied masculine & feminine traits	None found	Not tested	Male "traits" and "issues" more important than female ones for a good president.

| | | | | | GENDER EFFECTS | | |
AUTHOR(s)	OFFICE	SAMPLE	STIMULI SOURCE	CANDIDATE ATTRIBUTES	DIFFERENCES IN LEVEL OF SUPPORT	DIFFERENCES IN AREAS OF EXPERTISE	OTHER FINDINGS
Riggle et al. (1997)	City council Senate	292 undergrads	Lengthy issue positions in issue matrix	Gender, demographics, party (on subsample)	None found	Not tested	No affinity effect. Male candidate believed to have greater ability, perseverance, & closer to voter.
Fox & Smith (1998)	U.S. House	431 undergrads	Short issue positions in issue matrix	Gender, policy positions	Pro male bias found in half tests	Not tested	Regional differences using same instrument (state culture matters): for California undergrads no bias; for Wyoming undergrads a pro male bias
Sapiro (1981/82)	U.S. House	143 undergrads	Candidate description and speech	Gender, speech (vague)	None found	Female: education,. health. Male: farm, military. (Effects only on unstim- ulated issues)	No affinity effect. Female deemed more honest; male thought more likely to win.
Leeper (1991)	Governor	142 undergrads	Long candidate speech	Gender, speech (explicit)	None found	Female: education, helping poor, arts. (Effects only on unstimulated issues.)	Female deemed more honest; male thought more likely to win.

Study	Office	Sample	Stimulus	Variables			
Rosenwasser et al. (1987)	President	286 undergrads	Brief description	Gender, demographics	Not tested		Male superior on a scale of 5 "masculine" policy areas, female superios on scale of 5 "feminine" policy areas. No difference on neutral tasks.
Rosenwasser & Seale (1988)	President	141 undergrads	Brief description	Gender, demographics ($^{1}/2$ sample read a vague speech)	Not tested	Replicates Rosenwasser et al. (1987)	"Male policy areas" more important than "female policy areas." Amount of information did not affect evaluations.
Rosenwasser & Dean (1989)	President	133 undergrads	Brief description	Gender, demographics, varied masculine & feminine traits	Not tested	Replicates Rosenwasser et al. (1987)	Male more likely to win (regardless of traits). Other results replicate 1988 study.
Kahn (1992)	Senate	117 local residents	Newspaper article	Gender, incumbency, type of newspaper coverage	Not tested	Female: education, health and "women's issues." (Effects only on unstimulated issues).	Female deemed more compassionate and honest.
Huddy & Terkildsen (1993b)	Local & national	297 undergrads	Brief description	Gender, varied masculine & feminine traits	Not tested	Female: "compassion and women's issues." Male: military issues	Male traits (instrumentality) judged superior on military, economic, & women's issues. Female traits (warmth/expressiveness) superior on compassion issues.

CHAPTER SEVEN

Are Women Candidates Transforming Campaign Communication?

A Comparison of Advertising Videostyles in the 1990s

DIANNE BYSTROM AND LYNDA LEE KAID

U.S. Senate candidate Jill Docking sits in a chair, wearing a blouse and jacket, in front of a shear white drapery with vases of flowers on either side of her. Looking squarely into the camera, she enumerates the reasons why Kansans should elect her to an open Senate seat vacated by Bob Dole, who is running for president, in 1996: "I'm Jill Docking. I'm a wife, a mom, and a businesswoman. I'm running for the U.S. Senate because we need fewer professional politicians in Washington. What we need are fresh new ideas about improving education, fighting crime, creating new jobs, and protecting Social Security. As a financial adviser, I know we need to balance the budget, but not on the backs of our children and our elderly. We must protect working families in Kansas. Professional politicians have had their chance. Now it's our turn." As the ad progresses, the camera shot widens, showing family-style pictures in a cluster to her left. The spot is titled "Home."*

Meanwhile, her opponent, U.S. Rep. Sam Brownback, is shown in a variety of shots in his ad, "Bio," while a female announcer talks about his background and accomplishments. In casual dress, he shakes hands with a group of men, some blue collar and some in suits; feeds grain to cattle with his dad; and talks to female FFA members with his arm draped over a cow. Next, he's shown in a coat and tie, talking and walking with a group of college students, mostly female. Then, it's back to the farm, where he is pictured in casual clothes, talking in a wheat field to a group of older farmers. Next, he's shown in a meeting with a group of men, wearing a coat and tie. Finally, he's pictured with his wife and children in an outdoor family setting. As the scenes change, the female announcer reads: "He's all Kansas. Raised on a Kansas farm his folks still operate. State President of the FFA. President of the K-State student body. President of his KU law class. Kansas Secretary of Agriculture. Chosen as a White House fellow. Congressman. Dad. Sam Brownback for the U.S. Senate."

With significantly more women entering the political arena, researchers are becoming increasingly interested in exploring differences and similarities in the campaign communication styles and strategies of female and male candidates. Studies investigating the role of gender in campaign communication have become more feasible, from a methodological perspective, since the 1992 election when record numbers of women sought and won political office. For example—for the decade examined in this study—the number of women seeking seats in Congress increased from 77 in 1990, to 117 in 1992, to 121 in 1994, to 129 in 1996, and to 131 in 1998. In 2000, the number of women seeking seats in Congress fell slightly to 128, although their overall representation increased from 9 to 13 in the Senate and from 56 to 59 in the House.[1] Furthermore, as the Richard Matland and David King chapter in this book illustrates, the number of women contesting seats in primary elections also has increased steadily.

Televised political ads provide an important resource for documenting the communication styles and strategies of political candidates, as they remain one of the few candidate-controlled (rather than media-mediated) communication tools of the modern political campaign. The purpose of our study was to examine whether the increasing number of women seeking political office has had an impact on the communication aspects of campaigns. Have women adapted to masculine speech styles and strategies during campaigns, or have they transformed the styles used in political campaign communication? To provide some answers to these questions, this study investigates and compares the styles, strategies, and techniques employed by both female and male U.S. Senate candidates through a content analysis of their televised political advertising during the 1990s.

The importance of television advertising to today's political campaign is underscored by the significant financial resources devoted to such communication. For example, political parties and candidates for local, state, and federal office spent $400 billion on television commercials in the 1996 election, up 34 percent from 1992.[2] Studies examining the influence of political advertising on voter perceptions of candidates and their issues and images show that this money may be well spent.[3] For example, a study of the 1992 U.S. Senate races in California found that commercials influenced perceptions of candidate recognition, favorability, electability, and voting preference.[4]

Several researchers have argued that television and the control it offers over campaign messages, especially in transmitting information on image and issues, is even more important for female candidates,[5] who are often framed in stereotypical terms by the media.[6] Media coverage of female candidates oftentimes emphasizes their traditional roles as wives and mothers and focuses on their appearance, personality, and personal lives.[7] For example, the hairstyles of former Texas governor Ann Richards and U.S. Senate candidate Lynn Yeakel, Yeakel's wardrobe, and U.S. Senator Barbara Mikulski's weight and physical appearance were subjects of media scrutiny during the 1992 and 1994 campaigns. And, in her 1992 race for the U.S. Senate, Carol Moseley-Braun was described in an article in the *New York Times* as "a den mother with a cheerleader's smile," while her opponent, Rich Williamson, was portrayed as "all business, like the corporate lawyer he is."[8] Newspaper coverage further stereotypes female candidates by associating them with "feminine traits" and "feminine issues" and according them less coverage that focuses on their viability as candidates.[9]

In light of such stereotypical treatment by the media, female candidates can use political advertising to counter such images and present themselves in their own ways and words. Through an examination of the verbal, nonverbal, and production content—collectively, the "videostyle"—of the televised political commercials of male and female candidates opposing each other for U.S. Senate seats in the 1990s, this study attempts to analyze whether women have transformed campaign communication, and in what ways, or whether women instead have adapted to traditional masculine styles and strategies.

METHOD

This chapter reports some of the results of studies conducted on the television advertising used by female and male candidates when competing against each other for seats in the U.S. Senate in the years of 1990, 1992, 1994, 1996, and 1998.[10] Mixed-gender U.S. Senate races were selected because such campaigns usually rely heavily on television advertising to provide candidate information to statewide audiences. Each of these studies used a coding process involving a codesheet and detailed codebook investigating the "videostyle"—the verbal, nonverbal, and production content—of these ads. The coding process was based on a 1986 study by Lynda Lee Kaid and Dorothy Davidson,[11] which delineated the elements of videostyle, with revisions to also include gender-based expectations discussed in communication and political science literature.

These studies coded for demographic information on the candidates along with three types of commercial content: verbal, nonverbal, and production content. Verbal content included the presence or absence of negative attacks, the issues mentioned, the image qualities highlighted, and the structure of the appeals made. Nonverbal content included the setting of the ad; who is speaking and who is pictured in the ad; and the candidate's voice, facial expressions, body movements, gestures, dress, and use of touch. Production content included the ad's format, use of special effects, and length. The extent to which male and female candidates might have adopted production techniques—such as computerized alterations, dramatizations, or editing techniques—that resulted in technological distortions in the spots also was considered.[12]

Other categories interwoven throughout the coding were designed to measure for differences between female and male candidates on several variables that have been previously associated with gender. For example, communication studies have shown that women establish more eye contact than men, use more facial expressions, are more expressive, smile more than men, and wear normative clothing to win approval.[13] In addition, certain issues, image characteristics, and appeal strategies have been identified as "masculine" or "feminine" in political science and communication literature. For example, women have been associated with such issues as education, health care, and the environment and such image traits as compassion, cooperation, and honesty. Men have been associated with such issues as taxes, the economy, crime, and defense and such images as tough, aggressive, and emphasizing their accomplishments.[14]

Sample

All advertisements analyzed in these studies were obtained from the Political Communication Center at the University of Oklahoma, which holds the largest collection of broadcast political commercials in the world. This chapter summarizes and provides additional analysis of the results of studies examining 674 commercials from 39 mixed-gender races for the U.S. Senate in the 1990s—130 ads from 7 races in 1990, 226 ads from 12 races in 1992 and a 1993 special election, 149 spots from 7 races in 1994, 102 spots from 9 races in 1996, and 67 spots from 4 1998 U.S. Senate races.[15]

Coding

The campaign spot was the unit of analysis in each study. Coders were primarily graduate and undergraduate students who were trained in the use of the coding instrument. Using Holsti's formula,[16] intercoder reliability was calculated for a randomly selected subsample of the spots in each year. Individual category reliabilities ranged from +0.80 to +1.00 in each year, and the average intercoder reliability across all categories and years was +0.87.

Data Analysis

Descriptive statistics were used to analyze the frequencies and the presence or absence of variables recorded by coders in the defined categories. Frequencies were calculated based on a candidate's sex. Chi-squares and contingency tables were used to identify significant differences in the television commercials produced for female and male U.S. Senate candidates in the 1990s.

RESULTS

An examination of the videostyles of male and female U.S. Senate candidates running against each other in the 1990s reveals the ways in which women have both transformed campaign communication and, at the same time, adapted to traditional male norms in the verbal, nonverbal, and production content of their television ads.

Verbal Content

Perhaps the most interesting development in female versus male video-styles in U.S. Senate campaigns in the 1990s was the increasing use of negative attacks by female candidates. This defies conventional wisdom that female candidates might raise the level of political discourse, rather than adapt to the increasing use of negative attacks permeating political television advertising in recent years. Table 7.1 shows that both women and men sponsored more positive ads than negative ads, in total. However, for women, the percentage of positive ads decreased from 61 percent candidate-positive in 1990–93 to 57 percent candidate-positive in 1998. Male candidates, on the other hand, used 66 percent positive ads in 1990–93 and a slightly increased 68 percent in 1998. The difference in focus was most apparent in 1996, when 73 percent of men's ads were positive compared to just 36 percent of women's ads—a difference that was strong enough to reach the critical value for significance.

This means, of course, that the percentage of negative ads for female candidates has increased from 39 percent in 1990–93 to 43 percent in 1998. And, the percentage of negative ads for women has exceeded the percentage for men in every election year—or 39 percent to 34 percent in 1990–93, 53 percent to 50 percent in 1994, and 43 percent to 32 percent in 1998, with the biggest difference in 1996, when 64 percent of women's ads were negative compared to just 27 percent of men's spots.

Even when the ad's primary focus was positive, women still tended to use some form of negative attack. The differences in attacks made by women and men were significant in 1996 (66 percent to 29 percent), 1998 (57 percent to 35 percent), and across the entire decade, with attacks occurring in 49 percent of all female candidate ads but in only 38 percent of male candidate ads throughout the 1990s.

Although female candidates were more likely to use attack strategies than their male counterparts throughout the 1990s, it should be noted that women concentrated their attacks on the issue positions of their opponents, rather than on their image traits. In 1998, for instance, 82 percent of the attacks by female candidates focused on issues, but male candidates emphasized personality traits in 67 percent of their attacks.

As far as the issue and image content of commercials, an interesting reversal occurred during the 1990s. According to table 7.1, the overall

TABLE 7.1

Videostyle Verbal Content in Male and Female Senate Ads, 1990–1998

	1990–93		1994		1996		1998		TOTALS	
	MALE (n = 205)	FEMALE (n = 151)	MALE (n = 80)	FEMALE (n = 69)	MALE (n = 55)	FEMALE (n = 47)	MALE (n = 37)	FEMALE (n = 30)	MALE (n = 377)	FEMALE (n = 297)
Ad focus										
Positive	66%[1]	61%	50%	47%	73% *	36%	68%	57%	64%	56%
Negative	34	39	50	53	27	64	32	43	36	44
Attack made in ad	35	39	55	52	29 *	66	35 *	57	38 *	49
Use of appeals										
Logical	47	48	61	45	45	51	24	23	47	46
Emotional	22	18	8	9	13	17	41	43	19	19
Ethical	31	34	31	48	42	32	35	33	33	38
Fear appeal	5	4	21	26	NA	NA	3 *	30	9[2]	14[2]
Ad type										
Issue	72	67	53	54	55	55	27 *	53	61	62
Image	28	33	47	46	45	45	73	47	39	38
Structure of reasoning										
Inductive	68	60	45	46	60	68	59	60	61	60
Deductive	32	40	53	42	35	30	41	40	38	40

* Chi-square indicates difference between men and women is significant at $p < .05$.

[1] All percentages may not add to 100 due to rounding and not applicable/not determinable categories.

[2] Excludes 1996 data; not available.

distribution of image- and issue-focused commercials for male and female Senate candidates is about the same. But this composite number masks a change that occurred during the final election cycle this study examined. In the 1990–93 races, men were more issue oriented than women, with 72 percent of male candidates' commercials devoted to issues compared to 67 percent of female candidates' commercials. This difference was not statistically significant. The issue content of male and female ads was the same in 1994 and 1996. However, in 1998, a statistically significant difference occurred in the opposite direction. In the 1998 races, while female U.S. Senate candidates still devoted more than half of their spots (53 percent) to issues, male candidates focused 73 percent of their spots on image characteristics, giving only 27 percent to issues.

When candidates did emphasize issues, however, women and men were quite similar in the topics they chose to highlight. For instance, as table 7.2 indicates, both men and women emphasize most "masculine" issues to a similar degree. For example, there is no difference in the extent to which the sexes concentrate on such "masculine" issues as the economy in general, the budget/deficit, crime, or defense/military. Only in the area of taxes could a difference be seen; and, even then, only in the 1990–93 races, when women placed significantly more emphasis on taxes (29 percent) than did men (16 percent).

On issues more often classified as "feminine," there were no statistically significant differences at all between men and women in the 1990–93, 1994, and 1996 elections. However, two "feminine" issues, health care and education, received much greater emphasis by female candidates in 1998 (see table 7.2). The increase in women's emphasis on education in ads is also the only difference to result in a strong differential comparison across the entire decade.

As for the image attributes—or personality traits—emphasized by the candidates in their commercials, few differences were found (see table 7.3). This was particularly true for the image traits classified as "masculine." Whereas men were more likely than women to emphasize such "masculine" traits as past performance/success and experience in politics, women were anxious to show that they were tough and action oriented. Although there were some significant differences between men's and women's emphasis on "masculine" image attributes, particularly in the 1996 election, these differences were not statistically significant when looking at the entire decade.

TABLE 7.2

Videostyle Comparison of Issue Verbal Content, 1990–1998

	1990–93		1994		1996		1998		TOTALS	
	MALE (n = 205)	FEMALE (n = 151)	MALE (n = 80)	FEMALE (n = 69)	MALE (n = 55)	FEMALE (n = 47)	MALE (n = 37)	FEMALE (n = 30)	MALE (n = 377)	FEMALE (n = 297)
Masculine issue mentions										
Economy	32%	36%	8%	0%	2%	2%	38%	30%	23%	22%
Taxes	16 *	29	14	12	51	53	51	30	24	30
Budget/deficit	9	9	1	1	13	19	3	7	7	9
Crime	7	6	9	6	18	13	3	17	8	8
Defense/Military	8	9	0	1	2	0	7	0	5	5
Feminine issue mentions										
Health Care	18	21	3	1	13	0	8 *	47	18	16
Education	14	19	1	0	22	34	14 *	50	12	21 *
Medicare/SS/elderly	13	12	6	5	26	17	22	33	16	13
Drugs	5	3	0	0	2	4	3	3	3	3
Women's Concerns	3	9	0	5	NA	NA	19	27	31	81

* Chi-square indicates difference between men and women is significant at $p < .05$.

[1] Excludes 1996 data; not available.

TABLE 7.3

Videostyle Comparison of Image Verbal Content, 1990–1998

	1990–93		1994		1996		1998		Totals	
	Male (n = 205)	Female (n = 151)	Male (n = 80)	Female (n = 69)	Male (n = 55)	Female (n = 47)	Male (n = 37)	Female (n = 30)	Male (n = 377)	Female (n = 297)
Masculine traits										
Performance/ success	58%	36%	0%*	45%	51%*	21%	24%	13%	41%	34%
Strength/ toughness	33	40	36	30	20	26	49	60	33	38
Aggressive/ fighter	46	38	16	30	27	30	35	47	36	37
Experience in politics	33	24	48	49	49*	21	14	10	39	29
Action-oriented	19	20	21	30	42	38	24	40	23	28
Leadership	34	36	18	0	33*	11	32	23	20	23
Competent	12	15	9	12	24	17	16	17	14	15
Knowledgeable/ intell.	16	12	1	12	6	9	8	33	11	14
Feminine traits										
Honest	19	19	29	26	31	30	59*	20	27	23
Sensitive/ understanding	27	22	16	0	16	11	30	13	23	14
Trustworthy	12*	8	0	0	20	30	41*	3	14	9
Washington outsider	11	15	14	12	7	13	16	30	11	16

* Chi-square indicates difference in men and women is significant at $p < .05$.

Perhaps more surprising is the finding that most of the "feminine" traits were more characteristic of male than of female candidate videostyle (see table 7.3). Male candidates in 1998 characterized themselves as "honest" (59 percent) significantly more often than did female candidates (20 percent). In line with this finding, in both 1990–93 and in 1998, men more overtly portrayed themselves as "trustworthy" (men 12 percent and women 8 percent in 1990–93, and men 41 percent and women 3 percent in 1998). Though these significant differences were not sustained during the entire decade, it is important to note the tendency of men to associate themselves with "feminine" traits during the period studied.

The verbal content of political candidate videostyle was also measured by the types of appeals—logical, emotional, or ethical—made to voters in ads and the structure—inductive or deductive—of the reasoning in the ads. In a logical appeal, statistics, examples, and other facts are presented to persuade viewers that the evidence is overwhelming in favor of some position (either to support the candidate or attack his/her opponent). Emotional appeals are designed to invoke particular feelings or emotions in viewers, such as happiness, good will, pride, patriotism, or anger. Ethical appeals focus on the qualifications of the candidate or attack the qualifications of her/his opponent by telling what she/he has done or is capable of doing, or how reliable she/he is.

In terms of types of appeals, there were no significant differences between male and female candidates' videostyles across the decade, although there appeared to be some differences between the election cycles themselves. In 1990–93, according to table 7.1, both male and female candidates relied primarily on logical proof to make their points, but in 1998 the dominant type of appeal for both sexes was emotional proof. Most dramatic was the difference in the use of fear appeals, or claims meant to scare the viewer about the consequences of some action—such as voting for the opponent. Although neither male nor female candidates used fear appeals substantially in 1990–93, women used a surprising number of fear appeals in 1998. Nearly one-third (30 percent) of all women's ads used some type of fear appeal in 1998, compared to only 3 percent of male spots, a statistically significant difference shown in table 7.1. Although some of the female candidates' fear appeals in 1998 spoke about their opponents' desire to cut Social Security and Medicare benefits or limit reproductive choice, most were focused on guns and violence. The following is an example of a fear appeal sponsored by Barbara Boxer, an incumbent running for reelection in California, in 1998:

> While ominous music plays, men behind bars are pictured with weapons. A male announcer says: "This is a Saturday Night Special. It's the favorite gun of street criminals. This is an assault weapon. It's the favorite gun of drug dealers." Then, Boxer's opponent is shown, sharing the split screen with a table of various weapons. "This is Matt Fong. He's the gun lobby's favorite candidate for the Senate because he's against new bans on Saturday Night Specials and assault weapons." Then, the music turns upbeat, and Boxer is pictured. "And this is Senator Barbara Boxer. She's pushing for tough bans on Saturday Night Specials and assault weapons. That's why she's the favorite Senate candidate of California's police. Barbara Boxer. The right direction for California."

There was no difference in the style of reasoning—inductive versus deductive—used by male and female candidates. Interestingly, both sexes relied predominantly (about 60 percent throughout the decade) on the feminine style of "inductive" reasoning, which is characterized by proceeding from a series of examples or specifics to draw a general conclusion, like the Boxer ad above. Deductive reasoning, of course, is the opposite (proceeding from the general to the specific) and is considered more typical of masculine reasoning.[17]

Nonverbal Content

The second aspect of videostyle involves the nonverbal components of a candidate's self-presentation. Female candidates exhibited several forms of nonverbal behaviors in their political ads—normative clothing, smiling facial expressions, and eye contact—that are associated with women in their everyday life as a means to win approval.[18] The most consistent difference in male and female nonverbal style in the 1990s relates to candidate dress: women were significantly more likely to dress formally than men, who appeared to favor casual dress (see table 7.4). Formal attire includes business or professional dresses, men's suits and women's pantsuits. Casual dress includes sweaters or casual shirts, slacks or jeans, and athletic wear.

TABLE 7.4

Videostyle Nonverbal Content of Male and Female Candidates, 1990–1998

	1990–93 Male (n = 205)	Female (n = 151)	1994 Male (n = 80)	Female (n = 69)	1996 Male (n = 55)	Female (n = 47)	1998 Male (n = 37)	Female (n = 30)	Totals Male (n = 377)	Female (n = 297)
Dress										
Formal	53%[1] *	85%	35% *	46%	45%	65%	14% *	60%	44% *	72%
Informal	47	15	41	17	55	35	54	13	47	22
Frequent eye contact	40 *	61	36	19	31	28	27	37	37	45
Smiling facial expression	29 *	56	24 *	48	16	19	27 *	48	27 *	48
Touch	20	25	—	—	61 *	34	54 *	17	25[2]	20[2]
Candidate is main speaker in ad	25 *	38	9	13	22	30	32	37	22	32

* Chi-square indicates difference in men and women is significant at $p < .05$.

[1] All categories do not total 100% because of inapplicable situations, such as candidate not present in ad.

[2] Excludes 1994 data; not available.

Women wore formal attire in 72 percent of their ads across the decade, while men dressed formally in only 44 percent of their spots. In the early part of the decade, women dressed formally in 85 percent of their 1990–93 ads, compared to 53 percent of men. Women trended away from such formality a bit over the years, dressing formally in only 60 percent of their 1998 spots; but men also drifted toward more casual clothes, since only 14 percent of the men dressed formally in that year. Men wore casual dress in 47 percent of their 1990–93 ads, compared to 15 percent for women, and in 54 percent of their 1998 ads, compared to 13 percent for women.

Women were more likely to exhibit another stereotypical "feminine" nonverbal behavior in their ads across the decade—they smiled more often than men in 1990–93 (56 percent to 29 percent), 1994 (48 percent to 24 percent), and 1998 (48 percent to 27 percent), which was significant in all periods. The difference in their facial expression for the entire decade (48 percent to 27 percent) was also significant.

Except for dress and facial expressions, the differences between women and men in the nonverbal content of their ads have not stayed the same in the 1990s. For instance, while table 7.4 shows that women were significantly more likely than men (61 percent vs. 40 percent) to maintain frequent eye contact with the viewer—another "feminine" nonverbal trait—this difference was not sustained throughout the decade. In 1990–93, women differed from men in another feminine style characteristic: they were more likely to touch others in their ads. However, by 1996, this difference had disappeared, as men co-opted this strategy. Men used touch in 61 percent of their ads in 1996 and 54 percent of their 1998 ads, whereas women used this strategy in only 34 percent and 17 percent of their 1996 and 1998 ads, respectively, a statistically significant difference.

Another subtle indicator of nonverbal style is whether the candidate actually appears and serves as the dominant speaker in an ad. While female candidates were the dominant speakers in 38 percent of their ads compared to 25 percent for men in 1990–93, this statistically significant difference had disappeared by 1998, as male candidates' style became more similar to that of female candidates (see table 7.4). However, the overall trend for the decade still shows a higher percentage for women in this category; women appeared more frequently as the main speaker in 32 percent of their ads, while men were dominant speakers in 22 percent of their spots.

Production Content

The final element of videostyle relates to the production content of spots. Production techniques are an important element of candidate videostyle as they can help determine the impression an audience gets.[19] For example, a close-up camera angle makes a candidate seem warmer and friendlier because it's more intimate. Fast motion and quick editing styles can make a candidate seem more dynamic and active. Table 7.5 shows differences in the format used by male and female candidates. Because of the large number of choices and the small n-sizes in some cells, statistical tests are not reported on this category. For the most part, women and men use the same production strategies in their ads (see table 7.5), relying a great deal on the use of computerized graphics and other special effects across the decade. Women were more likely to use slow motion and superimpositions in their spots, and men were more likely to use freeze frames.

Female and male candidates were also similar in the types of ad formats they used, both within election cycles and over the course of the decade. An interesting change, however, can be seen in the use of testimonial ads— that is, ads in which another person appears on camera to attest to the candidate's qualifications for office. In 1990–93, male candidates used testimonials as the format in 20 percent of their spots, compared to only 7 percent for female candidates. However, in 1998, women relied on this strategy for production in 23 percent of their ads, while usage by men dropped to a scant 3 percent. This change may reflect the larger number (four) of women running as incumbents in 1998 as compared to the earlier part of the decade, when only one woman ran as an incumbent in 1990 and 1992, since testimonials are particularly appealing to candidates running for reelection as a way to highlight their accomplishments or record.

Another aspect of video production style is the extent to which candidates use techniques to distort or alter the information that is communicated to voters. Because such techniques have the potential to interfere with the ability of an informed electorate to make rational choices, major concerns about unethical uses of television technology arise. These include editing techniques, special effects, visual imagery/dramatizations, and computerized alteration techniques.[20] Female candidates appeared to resort to such techniques more frequently than male candidates. In 1990–93, for instance, 31 percent of female candidate spots used technological distortions,

TABLE 7.5

Comparison of Production Techniques of Male and Female Candidates, 1990–1998

	1990–93		1994		1996		1998		Totals	
	Male (n = 205)	Female (n = 151)	Male (n = 80)	Female (n = 69)	Male (n = 55)	Female (n = 47)	Male (n = 37)	Female (n = 30)	Male (n = 377)	Female (n = 297)
Production content of ad										
Use of computer effects	99%	98%	99%	96%	99%	99%	86%	83%	98%	99%
Slow motion	8	9	9	19	22	40	32	50	12	21
Freeze-frame	3	5	1	7	2	9	19	30	19	9
Superimposition	17	28	5	4	22	30	22	40	16	25
Format of ad										
Documentary	16	15	4	6	0	0	19	17	11	11
Bandwagon	2	4	19	20	86	64	16	16	19	19
Introspection	26	33	9	9	14	36	22	27	23	28
Testimonials	20	7	5	4	0	0	3	23	12	28
Opposition format	29	7	25	41	0	0	3	7	21	14
Technological distortions	25	31	17	14	NA	NA	51	60	28[1]	34[1]

[1] Excludes 1996 data; not available.

compared to only 25 percent of male candidate spots. Patty Murray used such techniques in a negative ad against her opponent, Rod Chandler, in 1992. Three times the ad shows a head-to-toe picture of Chandler with his hand outstretched as if to shake someone's hand. Instead, a bag of money appears in his hand, while the announcer reads:

> What's Rod Chandler done to help Washington's struggling economy? While the jobs lost rose 38 percent, Rod Chandler was paid 800 grand and passed one bill in 10 years. Family income fell more than 1700 dollars. Chandler voted himself a 51 percent pay raise. Health costs have soared; Rod Chandler grabbed a bundle from health and insurance PACs. How's Rod Chandler done? Good for him, bad for us. Patty Murray for the U.S. Senate. A voice for real change, finally.

In 1998, the percentage of distortions rose dramatically for both sexes, but still female candidates led in the percentage of spots showing potentially troublesome distortions (women 60 percent; men 51 percent).

DISCUSSION

This analysis of studies that have been conducted on the television commercials of female and male candidates competing against each other in U.S. Senate races in the 1990 through 1998 elections reveals ways that women have both transformed the communication content of the campaign as well as adapted to traditional, male-dominated norms.

In the verbal content of their appeals, the increasing use of negative attacks by women—overall and in comparison with their male opponents—defies conventional wisdom, which holds that women should not use such aggressive, unfeminine strategies, and would, in fact, raise the level of civil discourse. While women's usual status as challengers might encourage their increased use of negative attacks, it cannot account totally for the differences in their use of negative ads. For example, of the 47 female U.S. Senate candidates in the years studied, almost half (47 percent) were incumbents or running in open-seat races. In fact, in 1996—the year that women were most negative compared to their male opponents—six of the nine women included in the study were running for open seats. Thus, the increasing use of negative ads by women in the 1990s perhaps indicates the obstacles they face—such as stereotyping by the media and voters that not only limits the expectations of their appropriate role in society but also questions their viability as candidates—and explains the aggressive strategies they tend to use when seeking election. That is, women may be willing to use more negative ads to show they are "tough" enough for politics and as a way to defy stereotypical norms.

Other developments in the use of negative attacks by men and women emerged at the end of the 1990s. Whereas men and, especially, women attacked their opponents on the issues in the 1990 through 1996 elections, men increased their use of personal attacks in the 1998 election. Concurrently, the use of fear appeals by women rose dramatically in 1998. Although this increase in fear appeals in one-third of women's 1998 ads might be related to the overall negativity of their appeals, another explanation can be found in the types of issues they emphasized. For example, in 1998 women tended to focus more than men on such issues as Social Security, health care, and crime, all of which provided opportunities to scare viewers about their opponents' desires to cut benefits or support guns.

The increasing similarities between men and women on the issues they discuss in their ads lends support to Dianne Bystrom's finding that the context of the election year—not the sex of the candidate—determines which issues come to the forefront in their campaigns.[21] That is, both women and men emphasize the issues that appear to be the most salient with voters (and emphasized by the media) in the context of each election. For example, both women and men focused on education, the environment, and senior citizen issues in 1990; the economy, health care, and taxes in 1992–93; taxes and crime in 1994; taxes, senior citizen issues, and education in 1996; and taxes, the economy, and senior citizen issues in 1998.

Overall, the decade shows candidates of both sexes balancing the emphasis between stereotypically "masculine" issues like the economy and taxes with stereotypically "feminine" issues like health care, education, and the elderly. The inclusion of "feminine" issues by male candidates in these races may indicate how female political candidates have changed the communication strategies of campaigns when running for office. That is, when women run for political office, their male opponents are called into a campaign dialogue that includes attention to issues associated with women and their societal concerns.

Interestingly, female and male candidates showed the most significant differences in what issues they discussed in the 1992 and 1998 elections. Perhaps women were trying to set themselves apart from men by emphasizing such traditional, "feminine" issues as education and women's issues in 1992, the so-called Year of the Woman, and the issues of education and health care in 1998.

The differences in the image attributes emphasized by male and female candidates may be related to their background, political experience, status, and gender-related traits. Men were more likely to boast about their performance/success and experience than women in most of the election cycles. Women countered and, perhaps, underscored their "underdog" status by portraying themselves as strong, action-oriented, Washington outsiders. Perhaps more interesting than women's use of "masculine" images to portray themselves is men's increasing use of "feminine" attributes—such as honesty, sensitivity, and trustworthiness—to describe themselves. Again, the inclusion of women in these races may have prompted the men to reveal their feminine as well as masculine side in seeking votes.

Overall, however, both male and female candidates emphasize similar images in their television commercials. They both emphasize mostly "masculine" traits such as strength, aggressiveness, performance, and experience, balanced with such "feminine" attributes as honesty, sensitivity, and understanding. That is, both men and women seem to be presenting themselves as tough but caring—at least when running against each other.

Women and men were consistent throughout the 1990s in the structure of their verbal appeals, both using mostly logical arguments in 1990–93 and shifting toward more emotional appeals in 1998. Only in 1994—when women used mostly ethical proof and men used logical arguments—did they differ in their overall appeal strategies. Again, the context of the 1994 election year—which saw a backlash against many of the gains that women made in 1992—may have prompted female candidates to use ethical proof to defend their qualifications or attack the qualifications of their opponents in a rather hostile campaign environment.

Women and men were equally likely to use inductive reasoning, an element of "feminine" style, rather than deductive reasoning in their television commercials. However, this finding most likely indicates that this style of reasoning works best in a 30-second television spot—for both women and men—rather than points to any effect that women have had on their male opponents.

In the nonverbal content of their appeals, it is interesting to note that women have continued to dress more formally than men do in their television commercials in the 1990s. The choice of attire reflects the gender-based norms that society imposes on women as they face the challenge of portraying themselves as serious and legitimate candidates.

Female candidates also seemed to exhibit another stereotypical "feminine" trait in their commercials throughout the decade—they smiled more than men did. In everyday life, this is regarded as a nonverbal strategy that women use to gain acceptance. Thus, it is interesting that women use this strategy more often than men do in their political commercials and, perhaps, for the same reasons—to gain acceptance from viewers in the traditionally male political environment.

Further evidence of women's ability to transform videostyles, or at least influence changes, are men's increasing use of touch in their political ads over the decade. In 1990–93, there was no significant difference between men and women in their use of touch. But, by 1996 and, especially, 1998, men were significantly more likely to use touch in their ads. However, according to research on nonverbal communication strategies,[22] touch can be used to reinforce status differences (with the person touching being in the position of power) or to show warmth, affection, or affiliation. In keeping with other findings of this analysis, we assume that men are using this nonverbal strategy more often in keeping with their verbal emphasis on such "feminine" attributes as warmth, sensitivity, and understanding.

No other differences in male versus female nonverbal communication strategies were sustained over the course of the 1990s. While women were more likely to use eye contact in 1990–93, 1998, and overall, men used more eye contact in 1994 and 1996. Throughout the decade, women were more likely to appear as the main speaker in their ads, but significantly so only in 1990–93. Both of these differences may have more to do with the production content of the ad, with women appearing more often in their ads and, thus, speaking more and making eye contact more often.

Although not discussed in the results, as the 1994 and 1996 studies did not code for this variable, it is interesting that men appeared more often with their families in their ads than women did in 1990, 1992–93, and, especially, 1998. At the beginning of the decade, men pictured themselves with their families in 12 percent of their ads while women were pictured with their families in 9 percent of their ads. In 1998, 49 percent of male ads show them with family members, whereas only 13 percent of female spots show them with one or more family members. Anecdotally, male candidates—

when describing themselves—began referring more often to themselves as fathers beginning with the 1996 ads, which also may signal the importance of emphasizing family values in recent political campaigns. Women, on the other hand, frequently have referred to themselves as "mothers" in their political ads throughout the decade in describing the variety of roles they play in society.

Differences in production content—which have varied over the election years studied—may reflect changes in advertising styles and strategies. Or, they may reflect the status of the candidate. For example, women's increasing use of testimonials in 1998 may be a sign of their growing legitimacy as candidates with opportunities for such endorsements, or it may reflect their status as incumbents in 4 of the 10 races that year. Differences in production styles also may be related to the verbal and nonverbal content of the ads. For example, women's greater use of slow-motion techniques in 1996 and 1998, techniques that are often used to visually portray an opponent negatively, may be related to the overall negativity of their ads. Women's greater use of technological distortions also may be attributed to the negativity of their appeals. Previous research has shown that these types of distortions are most frequently used in negative ads.[23] The increased use of technological distortions in 1998 by both sexes is in line with trends nationally for higher percentages of abuses with such techniques.[24]

CONCLUSION

Overall, this summary and analysis of the findings of studies that have been conducted on the content of the television commercials of female and male candidates competing against each other in U.S. Senate races in the 1990s reveals some consistencies over time. Throughout the 1990s, women were more likely to use negative attacks, dress formally, and smile more often in their ads. Men used fewer negative attacks, dressed casually, and, at the end of the decade, were much more likely to use touch. In these differences, women seemed to be adapting to stereotypical norms in their dress and facial expressions—both designed, perhaps, to gain acceptance and legitimacy from voters—while defying conventional wisdom in their frequent use of negative attacks. In this regard, rather than raising the level of civility in political advertising, women have adapted to the increasing use of negative appeals by candidates in the 1990s.

However, it also can be argued that the presence of more female U.S. Senate candidates in the decade of the 1990s transformed the behavior of men in these races. That is, men's discussion of such "feminine" issues as health care and elderly issues; their emphasis on such "feminine" traits as honesty, sensitivity, and trustworthiness; and their use of touch in ads may have been prompted by competing against women. The reality of this transformation is also supported by comparing the results of this research to studies that examined male and female candidate advertising in the 1980s, when fewer women (26 in the 1980s compared to 47 in the 1990s) ran for the U.S. Senate. Those earlier studies[25] show that women were more likely to discuss social issues and policy, such as education and health care, and men were more likely to discuss economic issues, such as taxes; that both male and female candidates were more likely to discuss "male" traits, such as competence and leadership, far more often than "female" traits, such as compassion and honesty; and that women were more likely to use touch.

Overall, both female and male candidates in the 1990s appeared to be balancing "feminine" and "masculine" issues, images, and strategies in the verbal, nonverbal, and production content of their appeals. In this regard, they can be seen as impacting each other's communication styles and strategies, both in the context of election years and over the course of the 1990s.

Although these studies considered such influences as political party and candidate status (as challenger, incumbent, or open race), additional analysis of the data beyond the scope of this project would help clarify which differences can be attributed to gender and which are more attributable to the candidate's status or political party affiliation. Studies analyzing the content of political ads in male versus male and female versus female races—of which there are a small but increasing number—also could be compared to the findings of this study to paint a more complete picture of campaign communication strategies.

In addition to studies analyzing the content of television commercials, more experimental research is needed to determine the effects of the styles and strategies employed by female and male political candidates in their television commercials. Although content analysis reveals which strategies candidates and their consultants believe work best in influencing the electorate, experimental research is needed to determine the actual success of the videostyles used by female and male candidates in their television commercials.

NOTES

The authors wish to acknowledge the assistance of Jerry Miller, Ohio University; Terry A. Robertson, Columbia College; and Mary Banwart, University of Oklahoma, for their assistance with coding and data analysis. Lynda Lee Kaid would also like to acknowledge the support of the National Science Foundation under awards #SBR-9729450 and SBR-9412925.

1. Center for American Women and Politics (CAWP), "Women Candidates for Congress 1974–2000."

2. Common Cause, "Critical Role of Television in Political Campaigns."

3. See Geiger and Reeves, "Effects of Visual Structure"; Joslyn, *Mass Media and Elections*; Kern, *30-Second Politics*; Patterson and McClure, *Unseeing Eye*; D. West, *Air Wars*.

4. D. West, *Air Wars*, 1087.

5. See Bystrom, "Candidate Gender."

6. See Kahn, "Does Being Male Help?"; Kahn, "Distorted Mirror"; Kahn, "Does Gender Make a Difference?"; Kahn and Goldenberg, "Women Candidates in the News."

7. See Braden, *Women Politicians and the Media*; Witt, Paget, and Matthews, *Running as a Woman*.

8. Quoted in Witt, Paget, and Matthews, *Running as a Woman*, 181.

9. See Kahn, "Does Being Male Help?"; Kahn, "Distorted Mirror"; Kahn, "Does Gender Make a Difference?"; Kahn and Goldenberg, "Women Candidates in the News."

10. Bystrom, "Candidate Gender"; Bystrom and Kaid, "Videostyle and Technology"; Bystrom, Kaid, and Miller, "Evolution of Videostyle"; Bystrom and Miller, "Gendered Communication Styles"; Bystrom and Kaid, "Videostyles of Women and Men Candidates."

11. Kaid and Davidson, "Elements of Videostyle."

12. See Kaid, "Technology and Political Advertising"; Kaid and Noggle, "Televised Political Advertising."

13. Pearson, Turner, and Todd-Mancillas, *Gender and Communication*.

14. See Benze and Declercq, "Content of Television Political Spot Ads for Female Candidates"; Johnston and Barton White, "Communication Styles and Female Candidates,"; Huddy and Terkildsen, "Consequences of Gender Stereotypes for Women"; Kahn, "Gender Differences in Campaign Messages"; Kahn, "Does Gender Make a Difference?"; Trent and Sabourin, "Sex Still Counts."

15. Bystrom, "Candidate Gender"; Bystrom and Kaid, "Videostyle and Technology"; Bystrom, Kaid, and Miller, "Evolution of Videostyle"; Bystrom and Miller, "Gendered Communication Styles"; Bystrom and Kaid, "Videostyles of Women and Men Candidates."

16. See North et al., *Content Analysis*.

17. Campbell, *Man Cannot Speak for Her*.

18. See Pearson, Turner, and Todd-Mancillas, *Gender and Communication.*

19. See Kaid and Johnston, "Videostyle in Presidential Campaigns."

20. See Kaid, "Ethical Dimensions of Political Advertising."

21. Bystrom, "Candidate Gender."

22. See Pearson, Turner, and Todd-Mancillas, *Gender and Communication,* and Bate, *Communication and the Sexes.*

23. Kaid, "Technology and Political Advertising."

24. See Kaid and Noggle, "Televised Political Advertising."

25. See Benze and Declercq, "Content of Television Political Spot Ads for Female Candidates"; Johnston and Barton White, "Communication Styles and Female Candidates"; Kahn, "Gender Differences in Campaign Messages"; Trent and Sabourin, "Sex Still Counts."

CHAPTER EIGHT

FEMALE LEGISLATORS AND THE WOMEN'S RIGHTS AGENDA

From Feminine Mystique to Feminist Era

CHRISTINA WOLBRECHT

Are women transforming Congress? One way in which both activists and scholars have expected female legislators to transform Congress is by providing substantive representation of the group—women—they descriptively represent. While there are many possible reasons to advocate the election of women, an expectation that women in office will be especially attentive to the interests of women—long ignored, minimized, or unrecognized by political decision makers—has been a central motivation.

In this chapter, I consider whether female legislators have supported and shaped the congressional agenda as it relates to the specific interests of women, what I refer to as women's rights. In addition to determining if women are more likely to support women's rights legislation at the earliest stages, I specifically consider whether female legislators have raised new women's rights concerns and suggested unique public policy solutions over time. To that end, I examine all women's rights bills introduced into the House of Representatives from 1953 to 1992. The expansive historical period examined here encompasses important transformations in the political and social context—from what Betty Friedan called the "feminine mystique" to what Barbara Burrell has labeled the "feminist era"[1]—as well as a relatively large and diverse group of female legislators. Extending the historical period covered here, Michele Swers, in her chapter, explores bill cosponsorship during the subsequent 103rd and 104th Congresses, when the dynamics of party control and discipline warrant special consideration.

This research seeks to build from and improve on the literature on female officeholders in several ways. First, most previous research has examined a somewhat short or recent period of time, usually after the rise of the modern women's movement in the late 1960s, providing a snapshot of the behavior of female legislators in one legislative session or over a period of a few years. This study provides an opportunity to examine women's contributions over four decades, spanning many important changes in the context of women's rights policy making and in the characteristics of women serving in the House.

Second, in contrast to the traditional focus on roll-call voting, this chapter examines the first step of the legislative process, the introduction and cosponsorship of legislation.[2] By the time the House considers legislation on the floor, many of the most interesting and important decisions have already been made: whether a concern will be part of the agenda of decision makers (see the Duerst-Lahti chapter in this volume regarding the importance of agenda control), how a problem will be defined and understood (see the Walsh chapter in this volume on perspectives), and what policy solutions will be considered.[3] Examining the earliest stages of policy making is one way to determine women's effect on the scope and content of the policy agenda for women's rights.

Agenda setting is of particular interest in the case of women's rights. The failure of the political system as a whole to recognize women's unique policy needs impedes women's full and equal participation in American social, political, and economic life. The modern women's movement focused much of its effort on education and consciousness-raising to simply establish the very fact that women have shared interests. Friedan famously identified "the problem that has no name."[4] While she was describing the concerns of one particular group of women (white, educated, middle class), her characterization applies to the interests of all women insofar as they have been long invisible and unacknowledged. Thus, placing women's concerns on the political agenda is a crucial step and an important way in which female legislators may transform Congress.

The identification of public policy solutions is similarly consequential. A multitude of possible policies can address a problem, each reflecting different understandings of its causes or consequences, general preferences for public policy, and views of the success or failure of past policies. Decision makers cannot, and do not, consider every possible solution; thus, the determination of *which* solutions come before the chamber is of considerable consequence. In the case of women's rights, female legislators, because of heightened interest in the issues, better or fuller understandings of the nature of problems faced by women, or unique perspectives gained through gendered experiences, may be a source of original solutions to women's concerns. That is, the presence of women in the legislature may not only increase the attention to and support for women's interests, but shape the types of policies proposed to address their concerns.

Legislators do not identify policy problems and solutions out of thin air, nor do they operate in a vacuum. The sources of issues and policy alternatives are myriad, and beyond the scope of this chapter. This chapter considers one way in which policy issues and proposals enter the congressional agenda: legislation formally introduced into the House. Of course, the political agenda comprises far more than the legislation pending before Congress. The legislature, however, is the primary locus of policy making, and bill proposal is a dominant way in which policy change is initiated. Most introduced bills do not become part of the *active* political agenda, the issues and policy choices occupying the immediate attention of policy makers.[5] Successful policy making requires both further formal action (including committee hearings and passage, floor consideration, and positive votes) and informal conditions (public support, interest group lobbying, party efforts, and so forth). Nonetheless, in many cases, bill introduction is a necessary first step for policy change. Moreover, the bills that members introduce provide one indication of the issues they support and the sorts of public policy solutions they prefer. As a whole, the bills introduced suggest the scope and content of the policies preferred by the members of Congress who introduce them.

This chapter proceeds as follows. I first define women's rights issues as employed in this research. In the following section, I briefly review why we might expect female legislators to be particularly supportive of and active for women's rights, particularly in light of previous research. I then discuss the research design and the hypotheses investigated. Next, I describe the data employed to examine these hypotheses over the 40-year period from 1953 to 1992. I then present the analysis and results. In the final sections, I consider what this research reveals about the influence of gender on congressional policy making and whether women are transforming Congress.

WOMEN'S RIGHTS ISSUES

I define women's rights issues broadly as that set of policies that concern women *as women*. This definition includes questions of women's political, economic, and social rights and opportunities, as well as policies that are otherwise directed specifically toward women. My conception of women's rights issues is consistent with Susan Carroll's oft-used definition: "those issues where policy consequences are likely to have a more immediate and direct impact on significantly larger numbers of women than of men."[6] I have added, or been more purposeful in emphasizing, the presence of intention. *Women's rights issues are those for which women are the intended beneficiary, constituency, or object.*

This definition does not include the numerous policies where women have traditionally been expected to have greater interest, such as those pertaining to the family, children, and other private or domestic sphere concerns.[7] This is not to say that the role of some women as mothers and primary caregivers is not considered in this conception of women's interests. Policies that recognize the particular roles and responsibilities of (many) women, such as motherhood, and seek to provide women greater equality or opportunity, such as by furnishing child care services, are indeed included, as women are the intended and primary beneficiaries of the policy. A bill that funds public schools, on the other hand, is of direct benefit to children, and only indirectly of benefit to women as mothers.

The analysis here focuses on women's rights policies that have as their goal greater equality and opportunity for women.[8] This definition of women's rights support represents a modern liberal feminist conception, meaning that it favors equality for women, but also recognizes women's unique interests, and the need to have those differences addressed in public policy.[9] Within this broad definition, we can further distinguish the general areas of concerns addressed and the specific policy proposals put forward. A range of concerns are subsumed under the rubric of women's rights; they include such areas of interest as employment opportunity, pay inequity, women's health, abortion rights, and education. Moreover, for each area of concern, a myriad of potential policy solutions are possible. For example, policies addressing abortion rights include laws that protect clinic access, create an indigent women's trust fund, and lift the "gag rule" that prohibits physicians from discussing abortion options. Proposals for addressing the problem of domestic violence include programs to educate health care workers regarding identification and assistance of victims and requirements that the courts allow expert testimony regarding battered women's syndrome. Bills designed to address women's employment opportunities include prohibitions against sexual harassment, programs for women-owned businesses, and job training. The analysis in this chapter considers whether female legislators have been more supportive of women's rights overall, as well as whether they have been particularly active in raising new women's rights concerns and proposing unique women's rights policy solutions.

FEMALE LEGISLATORS AND WOMEN'S RIGHTS: EXPECTATIONS AND EVIDENCE

As many have noted, political institutions are by and large the construction of men and have long been organized around the interests of men. Not all interests are sex specific, but it is not difficult to show that women share unique public policy concerns. Yet, until recently, women's interests were generally ignored, minimized, or unrecognized by political decision makers. In particular, the second wave of the women's movement raised awareness of women's unique interests, decried the lack of attention to those concerns by the political system, and (eventually) advocated the election of women as a means to achieve policy representation.

For the most part, previous research on women officeholders has concentrated on the "feminist era,"[10] the period after the emergence of the modern women's movement in the late 1960s. Reasons for this focus include both the impact of feminism on the social sciences (recognition of the importance of questions relating to gender and politics, as well as the increasing numbers of female political scientists) and practical concerns (the comparatively larger numbers of women holding office allow for meaningful analysis). Moreover, although usually unstated, many scholars appear to assume that women who held office before the late 1960s differ substantively from those serving after that time. Women of the earlier generation were socialized in a world that did not recognize women's interests, and thus may not be expected to advocate them. In addition, as Irwin Gertzog (this volume) demonstrates, many early female legislators entered office via widow's succession and are thought to have not pursued an independent legislative agenda.[11]

The reasons female legislators are expected to actively support women's rights and raise women's policy concerns are well articulated in the literature and comprehensively reviewed in the introduction to this volume. A few explanations and findings relevant to this study are highlighted here. The most common rationale is the divergent life experiences and attitudes of men and women. As women themselves, female legislators are expected to be more knowledgeable of and interested in women's concerns. Women in office also may believe they have a special responsibility to represent women in their own district or the country as whole. Even where men and women have the same preferences regarding women's rights, women may give greater priority or effort to women's concerns (see the Carroll chapter in this volume).[12] Previous research finds that women in both state and national legislative office are indeed more supportive of feminist public policy (variously conceived and measured), as indicated by roll-call[13] and bill-introduction behavior.[14] Female legislators also consider bills dealing with women and families to be a greater priority and more important accomplishment[15] and introduce more legislation dealing with women, children, and families than do their male counterparts.[16]

In addition to their general support for women's rights policies, female legislators may propose unique public policy solutions to women's concerns. Research indicates that women approach problem solving and decision making differently than men, which may result in distinct styles of interaction and leadership or shape the types of policy solutions considered by women. For example, evidence from state legislatures suggests women take a broader range of information into account and conceptualize problems in different ways than do men.[17] These differences may lead female legislators to identify previously unrecognized issues or suggest unique public policies to address the concerns of women.

A number of factors may affect the contribution of female legislators to the women's rights agenda, including the passage of time. The emergence of the modern women's movement and other changes in women's experience helped create increased awareness of women's rights among both sexes after the late 1960s, which in turn led to a greatly expanded legislative agenda for women's rights. Perhaps only female legislators of the "feminist era"[18] who had been exposed to the ideas and arguments of the women's movement are particularly supportive of or active for women's rights. Yet even without the benefit of the women's movement and the heightened salience of women's rights, women elected before the late 1960s may still have been more supportive and active for women's rights than their male counterparts for the same reasons—gendered experiences or knowledge, different approaches to problems or decision making, and so on—that lead us to expect different behavior from women in the contemporary era.

Women's routes to political office might also affect the degree to which they represent women's interests. In particular, the pattern of widow's succession described in the Gertzog chapter may influence the behavior of female legislators.[19] Because their political careers may be a function of familial obligation rather than a commitment to nontraditional (i.e., political) roles or to their own ambition, ideals, or interests, congressional widows may not be active for women's rights. On the other hand, a number of congressional widows are accomplished political veterans; some win reelection (sometimes repeatedly) and achieve independent power and influence.[20] Most importantly, congressional widows are of course still women. Like women elected through traditional means, congressional widows may experience gendered lives that lead to support and advocacy of women's rights.

Other factors beyond gender contribute to women's rights support and activity. In particular, different patterns of women's rights advocacy based on members' partisanship are expected, although the direction of that assumption varies over time. In the 1950s and early 1960s, Republicans were generally more supportive of the small women's rights agenda, particularly the ERA, than were Democrats. Since the mid-1970s, however, Democrats have been associated with feminist public policy.[21] Not surprisingly, studies of female legislative behavior since the late 1960s find Democratic party membership to be a powerful predictor of support for women's rights policy.[22]

Ideology also may be an important predictor of a member's support and advocacy of women's rights. In recent years, women's rights support correlates highly with members' positions on the left-right spectrum,[23] and female legislators are often found to be more liberal than their male counterparts.[24] The strong association of women's rights with liberalism is a somewhat contemporary phenomenon, however, clearly characterizing the issue since the early 1970s, but not necessarily before.[25] Thus, as with gender and party differences, time period is an important factor in shaping our expectations regarding the effects of ideology.

RESEARCH DESIGN

Are women transforming Congress? This chapter addresses this question by examining whether female legislators have supported and proposed policies designed to meet women's needs through bill introduction and cosponsorship over the 40-year period from 1953 to 1992. Specifically, I consider two actions surrounding proposed legislation: bill introduction, the individual act of introducing legislation; and bill cosponsorship, the act of adding one's name as an additional sponsor of legislation introduced by another member. I first examine all members—introducers and cosponsors—who attach their names to proposed legislation. (For the sake of brevity, I refer to both acts of adding one's name to legislative proposals, whether first or last, as cosponsorship). As an action over which members have substantial discretion and choice, cosponsorship provides a useful indication of members' interest in, commitment to, and preferences over women's rights. Although bill cosponsorship is not a guarantee of continued advocacy, previous research suggests that issue preferences are a major determinant of bill cosponsorship behavior; that is, members cosponsor legislation with policy outcomes they prefer to the status quo.[26] While rollcall voting requires that members choose between predetermined alternatives they may not have any control over, cosponsorship is at the discretion of the member[27] and thus may reveal more about a member's policy priorities than a roll-call vote. Bill cosponsorship also can serve as an important cue to other members about the nature of the legislation and the level of support it enjoys.[28] Indeed, bill cosponsorship is a consequential act; level of bill cosponsorship appears positively related to bill success.[29] Numerous institutional roles and norms may affect the probability that a member cosponsors any particular piece of legislation; representatives may not cosponsor legislation under the purview of the committees on which they are members, for example. Since I examine the cosponsorship of a large and varied collection of bills, these particular effects are minimized and thus not included in this analysis.

In addition to supporting women's rights legislation, female legislators have been expected to raise new issues and propose unique policies, particularly regarding women's rights. To consider this possibility, I next narrow the focus to bill introduction alone, specifically the initiation of legislation that raises issues not already on the agenda or proposes policy solutions not previously put forward. Such behavior is important because bill introduction is a central way that proposals for public policy enter the congressional agenda. Issues can and do enter the agenda through other means, such as by amendment in committee or on the floor, and the introduction of legislation is no guarantee that the issue or proposal will receive consideration by committee or the chamber as a whole. However, by introducing legislation that addresses previously ignored problems or that suggests unique approaches to women's concerns, members can affect the scope and content of the congressional agenda. Raising new issues or suggesting unique policy solutions through bill introduction may be one way in which female legislators make a distinct imprint on the deliberations of Congress.

The central hypotheses I investigate are that female legislators are more likely than their male counterparts to (1) cosponsor women's rights bills, (2) place new women's rights concerns on the agenda, and (3) suggest unique women's rights public policy solutions. I investigate and control for other factors, including party and ideology, as well as explore changes over time. As awareness of women's rights issues increases, it seems likely that both men and women will cosponsor more women's rights legislation and propose new women's rights issues and policies. Whether women who entered office via widow's succession were less likely than nonwidows to represent women through bill cosponsorship is examined as well.

DATA

I have identified more than 1,700 women's rights bills and almost 13,000 cosponsorships[30] occurring during the 83rd (1953–54) to the 102nd (1991–92) Congresses.[31] A House rules change that slightly complicates data collection merits discussion. Multiple cosponsorship was explicitly banned before 1967 and unlimited cosponsorship was allowed only after 1978.[32] Before

1967, members introduced multiple (sometimes hundreds) of identical bills; this behavior was not cosponsoring per se but, like cosponsorship, was a means for members to register their support for proposed legislation. After 1967, members could and did join together as cosponsors on one or several bills. In the analysis of cosponsorship, I treat all acts of attaching one's name to proposed legislation, both initial introductions and succeeding additions of members as cosponsors, as cosponsorship behavior; thus the multiple introductions before 1967 and the fewer introductions and multiple cosponsorships afterward are considered equivalent. In the later inquiry into the original sources of issues and policy ideas, I focus on the *first* member to introduce the legislation, regardless of whether later members introduce similar legislation or cosponsor that member's bill.

These data can provide a rich picture of one aspect of women's rights activity in the House. The line in figure 8.1 shows that the number of cosponsorships in each Congress grows slowly across the 1970s, with more rapid growth in the 1980s and 1990s. We can also examine the extent of women's rights cosponsorship. The columns in figure 8.1, showing the number of members cosponsoring *any* women's rights legislation in each Congress, reveal generally greater participation in women's rights cosponsorship activity in the 1970s than in the 1950s or 1960s, followed by even greater levels of activity in the 1980s and 1990s. Even in the earlier period, however, women's rights cosponsorship activity extended to considerable portions of the chamber during some Congresses.

Finally, by examining the bills themselves rather than cosponsorships, we can observe the content of the women's rights agenda across this 40-year period. All women's rights bills were coded for the general concern or problem the legislation was designed to address. In table 8.1, an "X" indicates that legislation directed toward the concern was introduced during that Congress.[33] The women's rights agenda in the House, as reflected in proposed legislation, has clearly expanded and diversified significantly over time. Before 1971, bill proposals focused almost entirely on general sex discrimination, employment issues (pay and opportunity), and federal benefits. A few other issues appear briefly, but do not attract more than a single bill introduced by a single member. Beginning in the early 1970s, however, the size and content of the legislation proposed changes dramatically as numerous new concerns were added to the agenda.[34]

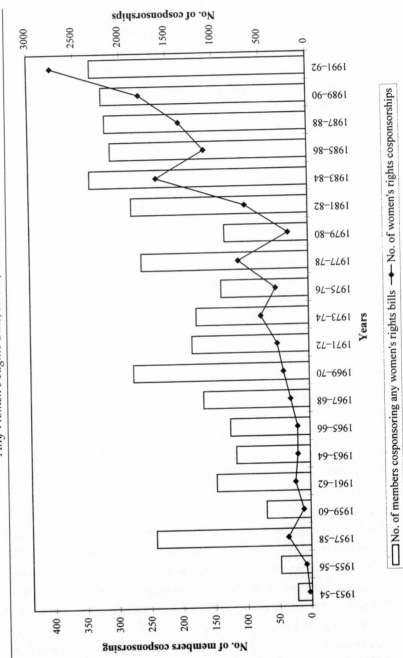

FIGURE 8.1

Total Number of Women's Rights Cosponsorships and Number of Members Cosponsoring
Any Women's Rights Bills, House, 1953–1992

TABLE 8.1
Women's Rights Agenda in the House of Representatives, by Congress, 1953-1992

Concern	1953-54	1955-56	1957-58	1959-60	1961-62	1963-64	1965-66	1967-68	1969-70	1971-72	1973-74	1975-76	1977-78	1979-80	1981-82	1983-84	1085-86	1987-88	1989-90	1991-92
Developing world																		X	X	X
Abortion									X							X	X		X	X
Care of children	X															X	X	X	X	
Domestic violence													X	X	X	X			X	X
Health												X	X	X	X	X	X	X	X	X
Divorce												X	X	X	X	X	X	X	X	
Education											X	X								
Sexual assault				X							X	X	X	X	X	X	X	X	X	
Armed forces						X				X	X	X	X	X		X	X	X	X	X
Employment opportunity				X		X	X	X	X	X	X	X	X	X	X	X	X	X	X	X
Benefits		X	X			X	X	X			X	X	X	X	X	X	X	X	X	X
Pay inequity	X	X	X	X	X	X			X		X	X	X	X	X		X			
Sex discrimination	X	X	X	X	X	X	X	X	X	X	X	X	X	X	X	X	X	X	X	X

NOTE: An "X" indicates that at least one bill designed to address the concern was introduced during that Congress.

The definitions of the concerns categories are as follows:

Developing world: Address the problems of women in developing nations.

Abortion: Address women's access to abortion services.

Care of children: Address the needs of women in their role as primary caregivers for children.

Domestic violence: Address the problem of domestic violence.

Health: Address the health care needs of women.

Divorce: Address the problems faced by women as a result of divorce.

Education: Address women's educational opportunity and experiences.

Sexual assault: Address the problem of sexual assault against women.

Armed forces: Address the experience of and opportunities for women in the U.S. military.

Employment opportunity: Address the opportunities for and conditions of paid work for women.

Benefits: Address women's ability to receive appropriate government benefits (e.g., Social Security, tax deductions, government pensions) because of the particular experiences of women's lives (e.g., widowhood, different patterns of wage work, dependence on spousal income, divorce).

Pay inequity: Address the problems faced by women workers in obtaining fair and equal wages for their work.

Sex discrimination: Address general sex discrimination in social, economic, and political life."

SOURCE: Data collected by the author, *Congressional Record Index.*

ANALYSIS

What role have women played in supporting and constructing the evolving women's rights agenda in the House? I now turn to an analysis of the contribution of female legislators to the women's rights agenda.

Bill Cosponsorship

To determine whether women are more likely than men to cosponsor women's rights legislation, I compare the behavior of women and men over a 40-year period encompassing dramatically changing times and contexts. Two control variables are particularly recommended: party and ideology. If women are more liberal than their male counterparts, differences in ideology might account for observed differences in support for women's rights by female legislators. At the same time, the parties have traded positions on women's rights issues across this 40-year time period, with Republicans slightly more supportive in the 1950s and 1960s and Democrats far more supportive since the 1970s. Perhaps observed gender differences are a function of partisanship rather than gender per se. I also consider women's route to office to determine if congressional widows are less likely to cosponsor women's rights bills than other female legislators.

In order to consider these various effects, as well as to allow for changes in effects over time, I estimate a multivariate model for each of the 20 Congresses in this 40-year period. The dependent variable is a count of women's rights bills cosponsored. The independent variables are member's sex (dummy variable where 1 = female), route to office (dummy variable where 1 = female who entered office via widow's succession),[35] partisanship (dummy variable where 1 = Democrat), and ideology (Poole and Rosenthal's first-dimension NOMINATE scores,[36] positive values indicate greater conservatism). For the sake of space, the individual regressions for each Congress are not reported here.[37] The major findings are easily summarized. The analysis indicates that with the exception of two Congresses in the late 1960s (1967–68 and 1969–70), women cosponsor more women's rights legislation than do men, all other things being equal, in every Congress. Thus, even those women who held office prior to the emergence of the women's movement and the attendant changes in female socialization and consciousness supported more public policy designed to address the interests of women than did their male counterparts.

TABLE 8.2

Predicted Number of Women's Rights Bills Cosponsorships,
Nonwidows, Widows, and Men, Various Congresses

YEARS	NONWIDOW	WIDOWS	MEN
1959–60	1.16	0.32	0.14
1961–62	1.17	0.35	0.31
1963–64	1.25	0.18	0.26
1981–82	2.05	1.04	1.01
1983–84	7.49	3.33	2.65

NOTE: Predicted counts computed from the negative binomial probability density (or the Poisson density when used) with a canonical link using the *predict* command in Stata 6.0. Ideology (NOMINATE score) and party are held at their means.

The analysis suggests that, for the most part, widows do not cosponsor statistically fewer women's rights bills than do other female members of Congress. In only 5 of the 20 Congresses do widows cosponsor fewer bills than do other women. Moreover, these exceptions are not clustered in earlier Congresses, when we might expect to find particularly traditionalistic widows. Women who entered the House via widow's succession cosponsor statistically fewer women's rights bills in three Congresses in the late 1950s and early 1960s (spanning 1959–64) and in two Congresses in the early 1980s (1981–84). To ease interpretation, I report the predicted counts (number of bills cosponsored) generated by the models in order to evaluate the relative impact of route to office. Table 8.2 shows that during the 1959–64 period, nonwidows are predicted to cosponsor at least three times more women's rights bills than are widows. In the 1981–83 period, on the other hand, widows are predicted to cosponsor only about half as many bills as nonwidows. In all but one of these five Congresses, widows are still predicted to cosponsor more bills than men, although the differences are often quite small. Overall, given the insignificance of route to office in three-quarters of the period examined, this analysis provides only limited support for the long-standing assumption that congressional widows are less likely to support women's rights than are women who enter the House via other means.[38]

Interpretation of the results for the party and ideology variables is somewhat complicated by the strong relationship between the two. With one exception (1959–60), liberalism is positively and significantly associated with the number of women's rights bills that members cosponsor in every Congress. On the other hand, while Democrats often cosponsored statistically fewer women's rights bills in the 1950s and 1960s,[39] as expected, they also cosponsored statistically fewer bills in the 1970s, 1980s, and 1990s, contrary to expectations. These counterintuitive findings result from the high levels of correlation between the measures of party and ideology; when ideology is dropped from the model, the party variable behaves as expected, with Democratic party membership associated (generally) with fewer cosponsorships before 1970 and (consistently) with more cosponsorships after. When party is dropped, ideology is a less consistent predictor of cosponsorship before 1971 and a strong predictor after, consistent with previous research.[40]

Predicted counts can again assist interpretation of the model results. Previous scholarship has suggested that women's rights support may be a function not of a commitment to women's rights per se, but of the liberal tendencies of women members of Congress.[41] The first four columns of table 8.3 show the predicted number of cosponsorships for hypothetical conservative and liberal male and female legislators (party is held at its mean value). In every Congress, both conservative and liberal women are predicted to cosponsor more women's rights legislation than their male ideological counterparts, and the degree of the difference generally increases over time. Thus, even when controlling for ideology, women cosponsor more women's rights bills than do men. It is worth noting, however, that differences between liberals and conservatives are larger (in terms of number of predicted cosponsorships) than those between men and women in all but three Congresses (all in the 1950s), although differences between the relative effects of gender and ideology are quite small until the later Congresses.

Some have suggested gender effects are a function of the behavior of Democratic women alone. The last four columns of table 8.3 show the predicted number of cosponsorships for hypothetical Democratic and Republican men and women, with ideology (NOMINATE scores) held at its mean. Women of *both* parties are always predicted to cosponsor more women's rights bills than their male counterparts, and the degree of difference grows over time. Previous analysis has suggested that female legislators tend to be more liberal than the male members of their parties, perhaps causing differences in women's rights support. Here, ideology is

TABLE 8.3

Predicted Number of Women's Rights Bills Cosponsorships, Sex, Ideology, and Party, by Congress, 1953–1992

Years	Conservative		Liberal		Republican		Democratic	
	Men	Women	Men	Women	Men	Women	Men	Women
1953–54	0.01	0.13	0.08	0.73	0.05	0.44	0.02	0.21
1955–56	0.03	0.07	0.28	0.65	0.21	0.49	0.05	0.11
1957–58	0.43	0.72	0.70	1.18	0.82	1.39	0.38	0.65
1959–60	0.14	0.71	0.15	0.72	0.17	0.82	0.13	0.66
1961–62	0.19	0.41	0.51	1.14	0.67	1.48	0.19	0.42
1963–64	0.14	0.30	0.48	1.06	0.50	1.11	0.16	0.35
1965–66	0.18	0.37	0.40	0.80	0.52	1.05	0.20	0.40
1967–68	0.29	0.30	0.68	0.70	0.56	0.57	0.37	0.38
1969–70	0.47	0.69	0.79	1.14	0.78	1.14	0.50	0.73
1971–72	0.24	0.78	1.14	3.67	0.56	1.79	0.51	1.63
1973–74	0.15	0.55	2.47	9.39	1.32	5.03	0.32	1.22
1975–76	0.09	0.38	1.22	4.87	0.76	3.04	0.37	1.08
1977–78	0.52	1.66	2.76	8.87	1.77	5.71	0.98	3.15
1979–80	0.09	0.32	0.91	3.24	0.48	1.71	0.21	0.76
1981–82	0.35	0.62	2.90	5.02	1.46	2.54	0.76	1.32
1983–84	0.82	1.99	8.52	20.67	6.96	16.87	1.46	3.55
1985–86	0.65	1.67	5.17	12.74	3.73	9.19	1.12	2.77
1987–88	0.61	1.61	6.63	17.67	3.48	9.26	1.39	3.70
1989–90	0.61	2.73	8.41	37.63	4.15	18.59	1.51	6.77
1991–92	1.20	4.42	12.54	46.42	6.71	24.83	2.77	10.23

NOTE: Predicted counts computed from the negative binomial probability density (or the Poisson density when used) with a canonical link using the *predict* command in Stata 6.0. Liberal is one standard deviation below the mean; conservative is one standard deviation above the mean. For the liberal and conservative counts, party is held at its mean. For the Democratic and Republican counts, ideology (NOMINATE score) is held at its mean. For all models, in those Congresses where the widow variable is significant, widow is held at its mean for women.

held constant, and gender effects within the parties persist. Turning to differences between, rather than within, the parties, the high correlation between ideology and partisanship, especially in later Congresses, again leads to counterintuitive results regarding party effects, with male and female Republicans predicted to cosponsor more women's rights legislation than male and female Democrats across the 40-year period.

To provide the most accurate representation of the interaction of gender, ideology, and party on women's rights cosponsorship, table 8.4 shows the predicted number of cosponsorships for male and female Democrats and Republicans, with ideology held at the mean value for each hypothetical member type (rather than the global mean). This analysis thus reflects the predicted behavior of hypothetical ideologically average Republican and Democratic men and women. First and most importantly, women of both parties are consistently predicted to cosponsor more women's rights legislation than their male party colleagues, and differences are often considerable. Moreover, with only two exceptions (1967–68 and 1981–82), Republican women are predicted to cosponsor more women's rights legislation than not only their fellow partisans, but Democratic men as well, even during the period (post-1970) when Democrats as a party were stronger supporters of women's rights than Republicans. Likewise, the predicted levels of cosponsorship for Democratic women always exceed those of Republican men, even in the first two decades when Republicans as a party were slightly more supportive of women's rights. Before 1971, Republican women are predicted to cosponsor more women's rights legislation on average than Democratic women in five of nine Congresses, but after that time, Democratic women are always predicted to cosponsor more women's rights legislation on average than women in the GOP. In this analysis, differences between men and women (accounting for both party and ideology) exceed differences between Democrats and Republicans in every Congress except 1967–68 and 1981–82.

The differences between the parties are also more clearly revealed by this analysis. Similar to the pattern among women discussed above, before 1971 the predicted number of cosponsorships for Republican men exceeds that of Democratic men in six of nine Congresses, although differences are not particularly great. After 1971, Democratic men are always predicted to cosponsor more women's rights legislation on average than are Republican men, and differences generally grow over time.

TABLE 8.4

Predicted Number of Women's Rights Bills Cosponsorships, Sex and Party, with Ideology Controlled for Each Group, by Congress, 1953–1992

| | REPUBLICAN | | DEMOCRATIC | |
YEARS	MEN	WOMEN	MEN	WOMEN
1953–54	0.02	0.21	0.05	0.89
1955–56	0.08	0.18	0.10	0.43
1957–58	0.70	1.18	0.46	0.87
1959–60	0.16	0.82	0.13	0.67
1961–62	0.42	0.97	0.25	0.61
1963–64	0.29	0.63	0.23	0.68
1965–66	0.35	0.74	0.24	0.57
1967–68	0.40	0.47	0.47	0.59
1969–70	0.65	1.04	0.58	0.96
1971–72	0.31	2.06	0.76	3.15
1973–74	0.44	2.48	0.72	5.88
1975–76	0.19	1.18	0.50	4.68
1977–78	0.78	3.25	1.44	6.99
1979–80	0.16	0.89	0.39	1.88
1981–82	0.59	1.37	1.52	3.08
1983–84	2.02	7.41	3.03	10.87
1985–86	1.29	4.56	2.31	6.47
1987–88	0.99	4.50	3.17	8.62
1989–90	1.02	7.61	3.83	17.39
1991–92	1.77	9.77	6.21	24.41

NOTE: Predicted counts computed from the negative binomial probability density (or the Poisson density when used) with a canonical link using the *predict* command in Stata 6.0. Ideology (NOMINATE score) is held at its mean for each group. In those Congresses where the widow variable is significant, widow is also held at its mean for women.

Finally, the predicted counts also show that all members have supported increasing numbers of women's rights bills over time, as expected. Yet, again, gender and party differences are also evident in the rates of change. For the House as a whole, the average number of women's rights cosponsorships per member increases at an average rate of 0.32 cosponsorships per Congress. The average increase in predicted cosponsorships for Democratic men (0.32) is the same as the chamber mean, but the average increase for Republican men is only 0.09 per Congress. The predicted counts for women in both parties increase at far greater rates than for men: the number of predicted cosponsorships by Republican women increases at an average rate of 0.50 cosponsorships per Congress, while the average increase for Democrat women is a full 1.24 with each new Congress.

The increasing levels of cosponsorship by all members and the particularly rapid rises in the cosponsorship activity of female legislators are highlighted by a graphical presentation of the predicted counts in figure 8.2. Differences in the earlier period are difficult to discern in this figure because of the large values in the second half of the series, but the figure does demonstrate the general increase in predicted level of cosponsorship behavior among all groups, as well as the relatively steep increase in the predicted level of cosponsorship among female legislators, especially Democrats.

AGENDA SETTING: CONCERNS AND POLICIES

Women in elective office are often expected to raise concerns and offer public policy solutions not currently considered by the political system, particularly with regard to the needs of women. As we have seen, the scope and content of the women's rights concerns before House decision makers have expanded and diversified across this 40-year period. What role have women played in this transformation?

Beginning with the 84th Congress (1955–56),[42] I determined the first time a women's rights concern was raised in a women's rights bill and the member who introduced the legislation. As discussed above (see table 8.1 for a complete list of concerns), I identify 13 distinct categories that delineate the broad concerns related to women's rights that have come before the House. I further code the data to identify each new public policy solution and its original introducer.[43] Thus each bill (and its introducer) is coded for the general area of *concern* (the 13 categories in table 8.1) and then coded more specifically for the *solution* the bill proposes for that concern (more than 100 categories).[44] These data allow me to identify the member who first introduced a bill raising a women's rights concern that had not previously been part of the agenda or proposing a public policy solution that had not been under consideration in the past. We can then determine if female legislators

FIGURE 8.2

Predicted Number of Women's Rights Bill Cosponsorships, by Congress, 1953–1992

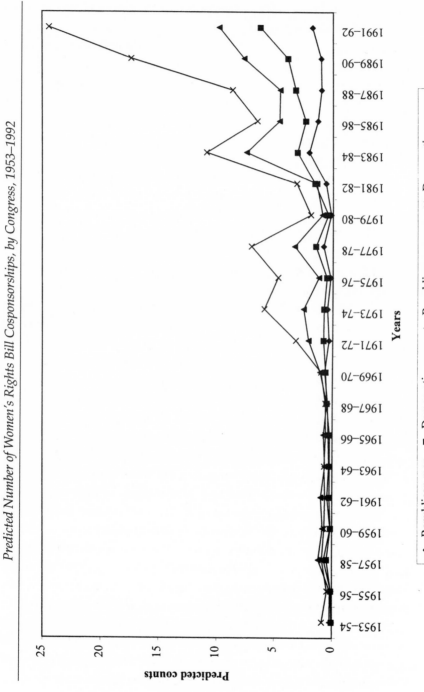

← Republican men ─■─ Democratic men ─▲─ Republican women ─✳─ Democratic women

have in fact been more likely to contribute new concerns and new solutions regarding women's rights.

The first four columns of table 8.5 show the number of *new* women's rights concerns and solutions placed on the House agenda from 1955 to 1992, as well as a breakdown of the sex of the member initiating the legislation. As the table illustrates, during this 40-year period, women constitute, on average, 4 percent of the House membership. At the same time, women place a full 44 percent of new women's rights concerns on the House agenda and propose a full 43 percent of the new policy solutions. The passage of time has some impact on the greater relative propensity of female legislators to raise concerns and suggest solutions: Before 1971, women constitute, on average, 3 percent of the House, raise 25 percent of the concerns, and suggest 37 percent of the solutions. Thus, even in the period characterized by the "feminine mystique,"[45] female legislators were considerably more active for women's rights than their small numbers would predict. This tendency to contribute more than their share is only exacerbated over time. From 1971 on, the "feminist era,"[46] women are, on average, 4.6 percent of the House membership, but responsible for 60 percent of the new concerns identified and 44 percent of the solutions proposed. The effects of growing awareness of women's rights are apparent as well (see also table 8.1). Only 56 percent of new concerns (5 of 9) are first introduced after 1970, but 92 percent (88 of 96) of the different new public policy proposals identified are first introduced after 1970. Again, even though women constitute a tiny percentage of the House membership, they are responsible for introducing more than 40 percent of those new public policy proposals.

Partisanship also influences a member's propensity to add new policy proposals to the women's rights agenda (the small numbers of new concerns discommends a more detailed analysis). As the second four columns of table 8.5 show, before 1971 Democratic women (averaging 2 percent of the House membership) contribute a quarter of the new policies, while Republican women (just 1 percent of all members) provide 13 percent. Women of both parties thus contribute more than their share, but Democratic women are even more active than are Republican women. The pre-1971 party effect is the opposite among men: Republican men (an average of 40 percent of the membership) put forward 38 percent of the new policies, while the more numerous Democratic men (57 percent) are responsible for only 13 percent of novel solutions. Because only a very small number of new women's rights

TABLE 8.5

Sources of New Women's Rights Concerns and Solutions,
by Sex and Party, 1955–1992

	CONCERNS		SOLUTIONS		SOLUTIONS DEMOCRATS		REPUBLICANS	
	MEN	WOMEN	MEN	WOMEN	MEN	WOMEN	MEN	WOMEN
1955–1992								
Percent								
contributed	56	44	57	43	39	40	18	4
	(5)	(4)	(54)	(42)	(37)	(38)	(17)	(4)
Percent of								
membership	96	4	96	4	58	3	38	2
1955–1970								
Percent								
contributed	75	25	63	37	25	25	38	13
	(3)	(1)	(5)	(3)	(2)	(2)	(3)	(1)
Percent of								
membership	97	3	97	3	57	2	40	1
1971–1992								
Percent								
contributed	40	60	46	44	40	41	16	3
	(2)	(3)	(49)	(39)	(35)	(36)	(14)	(3)
Percent of								
membership	95	5	95	5	58	3	37	2

NOTE: n in parenthesis. Data collected by the author.

policy solutions were proposed before 1971, however, inferences should be limited.

During the second half of the period, when the vast majority of new solutions are proposed, Democratic women and Democratic men are responsible for similar portions of the new policy proposals (41 and 40 percent, respectively). However, during this period Democratic women are, on average, a mere 3 percent of the House membership, while Democratic men are, on average, 58 percent; thus Democratic women are responsible for far more original policy regarding women's rights (and Democratic men somewhat less) than we would expect if such behavior was randomly distributed by party and sex. Republican men (averaging 37 percent of all members) introduce just 16 percent of the new policy proposals after 1970; Republican women (2 percent of the membership), only 3 percent. Thus, in the wake of the women's movement and the increasing awareness of women's issues, Democrats, responsible for 81 percent of the new policies, are the main instigators of policy agenda-setting on women's rights, with Democratic women providing far more than their share. Republican women, however, are not particularly responsible for new women's rights policy solutions during this period.

HOW GENDER IS INFLUENCING CONGRESS

Despite their small numbers, female legislators in the House, particularly Democrats, have played a crucial role in bringing about increased attention to women's interests. In the period when general awareness of women's interests was small or nonexistent, female legislators cosponsored more women's rights legislation, on average, than their male counterparts. As the saliency of women's rights increased, all members supported greater numbers of women's rights bills, but the increase in support from female legislators for the expanded and diversified women's rights agenda clearly outpaces that of their male colleagues. When examining the origination of unique public policy proposals, we find a particularly strong role for Democratic female legislators. The number of different policies designed to address women's concerns grew by leaps and bounds after 1970, and Democratic women, only 3 percent of the total membership, were responsible for a full 40 percent of those new policy proposals.

It is possible that the House agenda would have been transformed without the presence of female legislators. As the Anne Costain and Heather Fraizer chapter in this volume illustrates, the advent of modern feminism, the increasing salience of women's issues, the changing social and economic roles of women, and the activism of women's interest organizations coincide with congressional attention to women's unique concerns. Women's interest organizations lobby members of both sexes to sponsor and support women's rights legislative initiatives. Yet, the consistently high levels of cosponsorship among women across this entire period, and their responsibility for so many of the new agenda items and policy proposals, present a strong case for the argument that female legislators, particularly Democrats, deserve considerable credit for much of the growth and diversification of the women's rights agenda in the House.

These findings have important implications for the representation of women's interests. Again, it is clear that male legislators have supported and proposed women's rights issues and policies. At the same time, this research suggests that women's concerns receive greater attention from women who hold public office. Whether it be as a result of their own experiences, role conceptions, or priorities, women in the House have made unique contributions to the creation and expansion of the women's rights agenda. This research also highlights the way in which sex interacts with party. While women of both parties were more active cosponsors than men in both parties, Democratic women tended to outpace Republican women in their levels of cosponsorship, with differences increasing over time. As originators of new public policy solutions to women's concerns, Democratic women emerge in the second half of the period as the source of a large portion of policy proposals. Republican women are not particularly active in this role.

Placing women's rights concerns on the congressional agenda is only the first step, however. Better representation of women's interests necessitates heightened activity at every step, from bill introduction and cosponsorship to passage and implementation. Tracing the torturous process by which proposals becomes policy and identifying the key players who made success possible are difficult tasks, but the importance of the questions justifies the effort. Such an inquiry would surely emphasize that it is not enough to simply elect women who propose women's rights policies; women must obtain positions of power and influence from which they can shape public policy outcomes.[47]

FEMALE LEGISLATORS AND THE WOMEN'S RIGHTS AGENDA: TRANSFORMING OR ADJUSTING?

Are women transforming the congressional agenda? These findings provide a strong affirmative answer. Across the four decades examined here, the scope and content of women's rights bills introduced in the House have expanded and diversified dramatically. Female legislators, especially Democrats, have been at the forefront of that transformation both as cosponsors of women's rights bills and by raising women's concerns and suggesting unique public policy solutions.

The election of women is often viewed as a means of increasing the representation of women's concerns in the political system. This analysis suggests that female legislators do indeed support public policy designed to address women's unique interests—long denied or ignored—but that other considerations, particularly party, are also important. Perhaps more importantly, while bill introduction and cosponsorship are only the first steps toward public policy outcomes that improve the equality and opportunity of women, female legislators have clearly played an important role in shaping the size and content of the women's rights agenda in the House.

NOTES

This chapter benefited from the research assistance of Paul Mueller and from constructive comments and advice from Andrew D. Martin, Layna Mosley, and the editors and reviewers.

1. "Feminine mystique" refers to the famous description of the condition of women in the 1950s by Friedan in *The Feminine Mystique*. "Feminist era" is a term suggested by Barbara Burrell, in *A Woman's Place*, to describe the period following the emergence of the modern women's movement.

2. See Tamerius, "Sex, Gender, and Leadership," for an insightful discussion of why the effects of sex are likely least visible at the roll-call voting stage.

3. Baumgartner and Leech, *Basic Interests*; Cobb and Elder, *Participation in American Politics*; Kingdon, *Agendas, Alternatives, and Public Policies*.

4. Friedan, *Feminine Mystique*.

5. See Kingdon, *Agendas, Alternatives, and Public Policies*.

6. Carroll, *Women as Candidates*, 15.

7. See Sapiro, "Research Frontier Essay."

8. There are, of course, women's rights bills that do not have greater equality and opportunity for women as their goal. Examples include bills that limit abortion rights, that prohibit the participation of women in the military, or that provide exceptions to equal education opportunity. Such bills are not considered in this analysis.

9. The types of policies considered here are comparable to what other scholars have called feminist or women's issues. See Mezey, "Women and Representation"; Mezey, "Support for Women's Rights Policy"; Thomas, "Voting Patterns in the California Assembly"; Leader, "Policy Impact of Women Officials"; Gertzog, *Congressional Women*, rev. ed.

10. Burrell, *Woman's Place*. Important exceptions include Gehlen, "Women Members of Congress"; Frankovic, "Sex and Voting in the U.S. House"; Gertzog, *Congressional Women*; and Poole and Zeigler, *Women, Public Opinion, and Politics*.

11. See Gertzog, *Congressional Women*; Gertzog, "Matrimonial Connection."

12. See Mezey, "Increasing the Number of Women"; Reingold, "Concepts of Representation"; Dodson, "Representing Women's Interests."

13. Burrell, *Woman's Place*; Poole and Zeigler, *Women, Public Opinion, and Politics*; Swers, "Are Women More Likely to Vote for Women's Issue Bills"; Thomas, "Voting Patterns in the California Assembly"; Leader, "Policy Impact of Women Officials."

14. Swers, "Placing Women's Issues on the National Agenda"; Saint-Germain, "Does Their Difference Make a Difference?"

15. Thomas, *How Women Legislate*; Thomas and Welch, "Impact of Gender."

16. Saint-Germain, "Does Their Difference Make a Difference?"; Gehlen, "Women Members of Congress"; Thomas, "Impact of Women on State Legislative Policies."

17. Gilligan, *In a Different Voice*; Whicker and Jewell, "Feminization of Leadership"; C. Rosenthal, *When Women Lead*; C. Rosenthal, "Getting Things Done"; Kathlene, "Power and Influence in State Legislative Policymaking"; Kathlene, "In a Different Voice."

18. Burrell, *Woman's Place*.

19. Gertzog, "Matrimonial Connection"; Gehlen, "Women Members of Congress"; Gehlen, "Legislative Role Performance of Female Legislators"; Werner, "Women in Congress: 1917–1964"; Frankovic, "Sex and Voting in the U.S. House."

20. Gertzog, *Congressional Women*.

21. Gertzog, *Congressional Women*; Wolbrecht, *Politics of Women's Rights*.

22. Cf. Burrell, *Woman's Place*; Swers, "Placing Women's Issues on the National Agenda"; Swers, "Are Women More Likely to Vote for Women's Issue Bills?"; Thomas, "Voting Patterns in the California Assembly"; Leader, "Policy Impact of Women Officials"; David Hill, "Women State Legislators."

23. Thomas, "Voting Patterns in the California Assembly"; Leader, "Policy Impact of Women Officials."

24. Poole and Zeigler, *Women, Public Opinion, and Politics*; Leader, "Policy Impact of Women Officials"; Clark, "Women at the National Level"; Carey, Niemi, and Powell, "Are Women State Legislators Different?"; Welch, "Are Women More Liberal Than Men?"

25. Wolbrecht, *Politics of Women's Rights*.

26. Martin and Wolbrecht, "Partisanship and Pre-floor Behavior"; Kessler and Krehbiel, "Dynamics of Cosponsorship"; Krehbiel, "Cosponsors and Wafflers from A to Z"; Regens, "Congressional Cosponsorship of Acid Rain Controls."

27. Wendy J. Schiller, "Senators as Political Entrepreneurs."

28. Kessler and Krehbiel, "Dynamics of Cosponsorship."

29. William Browne, "Multiple Sponsorship and Bill Success"; R. Wilson and Young, "Cosponsorship in the United States Congress."

30. Recall that the cosponsorship data include both bill introduction (the act of initiating legislation) and cosponsorship (adding one's name as a sponsor to a bill already introduced). By cosponsorship I mean to reference both acts of attaching one's name to proposed legislation. The analysis of unique issues and policy solutions later in the chapter examines introductions specifically.

31. The *Congressional Record Index* was employed to identify potential women's rights bills, using the definition of women's rights outlined here to determine inclusion in the data set. I aggregate bills by Congress, rather than year, because bill-cosponsorship activity is not randomly distributed over time, but tends to be clustered. For further details, see Wolbrecht, *Politics of Women's Rights.*

32. Wilson and Young, "Cosponsorship in the United States Congress." A 1967 rules change allowed as many as 25 cosponsors to proposed legislation.

33. Note that the unit of analysis in figure 8.1 is cosponsorships and members. The unit of analysis in table 8.1 is the bill.

34. Recall that the women's rights bills in table 8.1 are those that have greater equality and opportunity for women as their goal. The issue of abortion was on the House agenda throughout the 1970s via pro-life legislative proposals, but as table 8.1 indicates, pro-choice bills were first found on the House agenda in 1971, but then were not present again until 1983.

35. Lists of female members of the House and of women who entered via widow's succession are derived from the appendix of Gertzog, *Congressional Women.*

36. Poole and H. Rosenthal, *Congress: A Political-Economic History.*

37. For each Congress, I estimate negative binomial regression models via maximum likelihood. This approach controls for overdispersion of the dependent variable. Overdispersion is likely in these data because we might expect that there is learning going on by members of Congress; once one cosponsors, another is more likely to follow. In the cases when no overdispersion is detected (insignificant alpha), the models are estimated via Poisson, which is the limiting case of the negative binomial with equidispersion (see King, *Unifying Political Methodology*). The detailed regression results are available from the author.

38. In the Congresses where the widow variable is insignificant, the models were reestimated without that covariate. Dropping the widow variable does not appreciably change the other coefficients.

39. The coefficient on party is insignificant in 1953–54 and 1959–60.

40. See Wolbrecht, *Politics of Women's Rights.* If the models are estimated with sex and party only, Democrats are statistically more likely to cosponsor women's rights legislation in one Congress (1953–54), and statistically less likely to do so in three Congresses (1957–58, 1961–62, 1965–66), before 1971. Party differences are statistically insignificant in all other pre-1971 Congresses. Democrats are statistically more likely to cosponsor women's rights bills in all Congresses after 1971. If the models are estimated with sex and ideology only, liberalism is associated with women's rights cosponsorship in four Congresses before 1971 (1953–54, 1955–56, 1963–64, and 1967–68); in the other five Congresses before 1971, ideology does not predict level of women's rights cosponsorship. After 1971, liberalism is consistently and strongly associated with women's rights cosponsorship.

41. As indicated by a simple difference of means test, Democratic women are statistically more liberal (first-dimension NOMINATE) than their male counterparts in 7 of 20 Congresses (1953–58, 1973–78, and 1983–84). Republican women are sta-

tistically more liberal than their male counterparts in 6 of 20 Congresses (1971–72 and 1983–92). Generally, and not surprisingly, Democrats are more liberal than are Republicans in every Congress ($p < .000$).

42. Because the data on women's rights bills begins in 1953, it is not possible for me to determine, with this data set, if bills introduced during the 82nd Congress (1953–54) had been introduced in previous Congresses; thus this analysis necessarily begins in 1955.

43. Coding of policy solutions was both specific and broad; specific enough to identify important differences and developments in the solutions being put forward, while broad enough to allow general trends to be identified. Indeed, relatively broad categories were somewhat unavoidable. The brief descriptions employed, while informative, provide only the broadest outlines of the policy being proposed. It is possible, for example, that two bills with the exact same title or abstract contain different provisions for enforcement that substantially change the effect of the law or that represent important new constructions of policy. Even when bill titles differ slightly, a focus on minutiae would obscure the identification of the trends that are of interest.

44. Because some of the concerns and solutions were already on the House agenda at the beginning of the period covered in this analysis (and thus it is not possible to identify the member who first placed them on the House agenda), the number of *new* concerns and solutions analyzed in table 8.5 is smaller than the total number of concern or solution categories.

45. Friedan, *Feminine Mystique*. See Rupp and Taylor, *Survival in the Doldrums*, and Cynthia Harrison, *On Account of Sex*, regarding the relative vibrancy of women's activism during a period conventionally viewed as "the doldrums" for women's rights.

46. Burrell, *Woman's Place*.

47. See Dodson, "Representing Women's Interests."

Early in U.S. history, because they could not vote, some women felt they were not adequately represented in the new nation's governing process. In January 1871, Victoria Woodhull became the first woman to address the U.S. Congress. Calling for women's right to vote, she spoke with "fire and freedom" before the combined House and Senate Judiciary Committees. Courtesy of the Library of Congress.

Not only were women excluded from the legislative process in Congress, but until 1850 no women had even sat in the press gallery. Jane Grey Swisshelm became the first woman to sit with congressional reporters in 1850. She witnessed Senator Thomas Hart Benton (D-MO) threaten Senator Henry S. Foote (D-MS), who subsequently drew a gun in their argument over the Missouri Compromise. Courtesy of the Minnesota Historical Society.

By the end of the 19th century, the Industrial Revolution had brought growing numbers of women together in the urban workplace. A network of more than 3,000 women's clubs and groups formed by 1900. Before women could hope to transform Congress, they marched in major U.S. cities in hopes of transforming politics. Parades such as this one in Washington, D.C., in 1913 thrust the idea of women's suffrage into the public eye. Courtesy of the Library of Congress.

NATIONAL AMERICAN
WOMAN SUFFRAGE ASS'N

The issue of women's suffrage came full force to Congress in 1916 with the election of Jeannette Rankin (R-MT), whose home state granted women the vote in 1914. A strong advocate of women's rights, she campaigned for a constitutional amendment guaranteeing women's suffrage in all states, maternal and infant health care, and an eight-hour workday for women. She claimed Congress lacked a woman to safeguard the interests of the nation's greatest asset: children. An ardent pacifist, Rankin refused to "vote a man's vote" for entry into World War I, which probably cost her reelection. In 1940, Rankin ran for and won a second term in office. When the House voted on U.S. entry into World War II on December 8, 1941, Rankin cast her vote as the sole objector. Courtesy of the Montana Historical Society.

From the beginning, women have not always agreed about women's rights. Ironically, the first woman elected to Congress after the passage of the 19th Amendment and the first woman to preside over a legislative session was Alice Mary Robertson (R-OK), who opposed women's suffrage. Dubbed by the press as Rankin's opposite, she was in the minority that voted against the Sheppard-Towner Maternity Relief Act. She was defeated after a single term in 1922. Courtesy of the Oklahoma Historical Society.

In 1921, representatives from several national women's groups gathered in Washington to celebrate the passage of the Sheppard-Towner Act. The "save the babies" bill was just one of the issues that brought together politically active women of diverse interests and backgrounds. Groups represented here were the National Federation of Business Women's Clubs, the Women's Christian Temperance Union, the National League of Women Voters, the National Consumers League (Jeannette Rankin, fourth from left, bottom row), the General Federation of Women's Clubs, the Association of Collegiate Alumnae, and the Mother-Congress and Parent-Teacher Association. Though the Sheppard-Towner Act represented a giant stride in congressional recognition of women's issues, support fizzled and funding for the act ceased when the number of women who exercised their right to vote was fewer than expected. Courtesy of the Library of Congress.

Though Rebecca Felton (D-GA) served the shortest term (two days) of any senator in history, her career in civic affairs spanned decades—from leading her state's Woman's Christian Temperance Union to managing her husband's service in the House to being the first woman U.S. senator. When Georgia governor Thomas Hardwick gave her a symbolic appointment to the Senate in 1922, Felton took the opportunity to publicly note that her appointment had opened another door for women's political ambitions. Courtesy of the Library of Congress. (Cropped from original.)

Florence Kahn (R-CA), left, and Edith Nourse Rogers (R-MA), right, were both elected in 1925 to an all-male bastion, complete with spittoons and men's rooms only. A cloakroom for women members opened in 1927, providing them a place to receive messages from House pages and make telephone calls. Kahn forced Congress to adapt to women in more substantive ways as well, fighting against the tradition of assigning women to minor panels. She became the first woman to be appointed to the powerful Appropriations committee. "Kahn quips" were legendary. "It's possible to predict how she's going to vote, but only God has the slightest inkling of what she's going to say." Courtesy of the French Collection, Library of Congress.

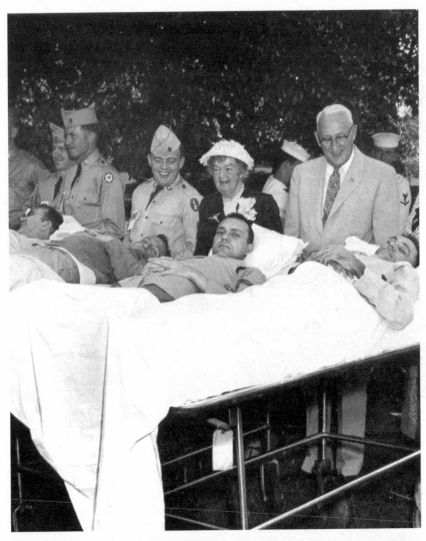

Congressional widow Edith Nourse Rogers (R-MA) went on to win reelection 17 times, making her the longest-serving congresswoman in history. During her career, she was assigned to Veterans Affairs and introduced a bill to establish the Woman's Auxiliary Corps. This forerunner of women's right to wear a military uniform was a landmark concerning public opinion about "woman's place" in society. She died just two days prior to her certain reelection to a 19th term. Here Rogers visits injured vets at Walter Reed Army Hospital. Courtesy Veterans Administration. (Cropped from original.)

Mary Teresa Norton (D-NJ) was the first Democratic woman ever elected to Congress in 1924. During her 13 terms, she was the first woman to serve as state party chair, the first to chair a national platform committee and the first member of Congress to chair three committees. As chair of the Labor Committee, she shepherded the Fair Labor Standards Act of 1938 through Congress. Pictured here at the doorway of the White House. Courtesy of Special Collections and University Archives, Rutgers University.

Ruth Bryan Owen (D-FL), daughter of William Jennings Bryan, was the first woman elected to the House from the Deep South (1929–33). Her defeated opponent challenged her citizenship (and her reelection) because she was married to a British national. She successfully defended her victory, noting that no man had ever lost citizenship through marriage. Pictured here between two aides in 1928 beside her Ford coupe, in which she campaigned throughout Florida's Fourth District. Courtesy of the Florida State Archives.

An outspoken advocate of social policy during the Depression and World War II, Eleanor Roosevelt recast the role of First Lady and became the first to address Congress. This 1940 photo shows her testifying before a House investigating committee on the living conditions of migrant workers. Courtesy of the Franklin D. Roosevelt Library. (Cropped from original.)

Frances Bolton (R-OH) succeeded her husband in the House, then continued on to win 14 reelections. By the end of her career, she had become the ranking Republican on the Foreign Affairs Committee. An expert on international affairs due to extensive travel, she is shown here visiting a market at Kibi, Gold Coast (now Ghana) during a 1955 trip to East Africa. Courtesy of the Western Reserve Historical Society. (Cropped from original.)

Clare Boothe Luce's (R-CT) early membership in the National Women's Party sparked her political interest. Prior to her election to the House in 1942, she traveled extensively as a war correspondent for *Time* and *Life*. In spite of her international experience, Luce was called arrogant by male congressmembers for seeking a first-term appointment to the Foreign Affairs Committee. She won a seat on Military Affairs instead. She became a popular public figure in her party due to her vocal opposition to President's Roosevelt's handling of World War II. Pictured here on the Italian Front in 1945. Courtesy of the U.S. Army Military Institute. (Cropped from original.)

Helen Gahagan Douglas (D-CA) was a famous stage actress and opera singer before running for Congress. Elected to the House in 1944, she garnered a rare freshman appointment to Foreign Affairs. Active in civil rights issues, she was the first white representative to hire black staff members. Here she displays $15 worth of groceries to the House to dramatize the negative impact on poor families of the removal of price controls. Courtesy of the Carl Albert Center Congressional Archives, University of Oklahoma.

Margaret Chase Smith (R-ME) became the first woman to be elected to both the House (1940–49) and the Senate (1949–73), the first woman to be elected to the Senate leadership, and the first woman to have her name placed in a major party nomination for the presidency. While in the House, she achieved the passage of a bill creating the female branch of the Navy. During her first Senate term, she made headlines for her "Declaration of Conscience" speech criticizing Senator Joseph McCarthy's tactics of labeling people Communists. Shown here on the Committee of Expenditures in Executive Departments, which McCarthy, far left, chaired. Courtesy of the Senate Historical Office. (Cropped from original.)

The male members of the 80th Congress (1947–48) saw their female colleagues as accidental, wartime stand-ins and dubbed them the "Petticoat Front." From left to right: Helen Gahagan Douglas (D-CA), Margaret Chase Smith (R-ME), Edith Nourse Rogers (R-MA), Mary Norton (D-NJ), Frances Bolton (R-OH), and Georgia Lusk (D-NM), a successful education activist whose assignment to the Committee on Veterans Affairs was ill-suited to her interests, talents, or reelection. Courtesy of Special Collections and University Archives, Rutgers University.

Coya Knutson (D-MN) won an upset victory against a six-term Republican. When she sought a position on the Agriculture Committee, the chair refused to work with a woman. Speaker Sam Rayburn, pictured here, expressed his admiration for Knutson's unlikely win against an incumbent and declared that Knutson could have her pick of assignments. After two terms, Knutson's career ended when her alcoholic husband wrote the famous "Coya, come home" letter, charging her political life was ruining their family. The widely published letter destroyed her chances for reelection. Courtesy of the Minnesota Historical Society.

"Being a woman in Congress is like being a fragile goldfish among the barracuda,"
Martha W. Griffiths (D-MI), pictured right, once said. These three women proved
up to the test. Edna Flannery Kelly (D-NY), left, labored for more than a decade to
secure passage of legislation calling for equal pay for equal work. Leonor K. Sullivan (D-MO), center, was known as a consumer watchdog who authored legislation
on dangerous food additives, cosmetics, and drugs. She also authored the Food
Stamp Act to replace the dumping of surplus items on the poor. As the first woman
on the Ways and Means Committee, Griffiths cosponsored the Equal Pay Act, led
the fight to include women in the Civil Rights Act of 1964, and brought the proposed Equal Rights Amendment to a vote in 1970. Courtesy of the Leonor K. Sullivan Collection, St. Louis Law Library.

Julia B. Hansen (D-WA) (1960–74) served on several committees in the House, but gave them all up in 1963 to serve on Appropriations. Four years later, she became the first woman in history to chair an Appropriations subcommittee; another thirty years would pass before Barbara Vucanovich (R-NV) would become the second. When the committee chair was asking members if they thought Hansen would be a good chair, Hansen confronted him about his double-standard treatment of her. In her final term, she chaired the committee that reformed House procedures and committee organization for the first time since 1946. Courtesy of the Library of Congress.

Though only one step toward gender equality, the Equal Pay Act of 1963 was a turning point in congressional action concerning social inequalities in both the public and private sector, and marked the start of a number of laws to address civil rights issues. Pictured here are the women of the 88th Congress, including several members who had worked for more than a decade for that moment. Courtesy of the John Fitzgerald Kennedy Library.

Shirley Chisholm (D-NY), elected to Congress in 1968 and known for her liberal, outspoken, and independent views, had to fight discrimination due to both race and sex. She was surprised by "the much greater virulence of the sex discrimination [between] antiblack and antifeminist sentiments." With more than two decades of education experience in New York inner city schools, she was dismayed to be placed on the Agriculture Committee and took her complaint to the House floor. When placed on Veterans Affairs, she quipped, "There are a lot more veterans in my district than trees." In 1971, she helped found the National Women's Political Caucus to promote feminist candidates of both sexes. At a news conference announcing the new organization are, from left, Gloria Steinem, activist Democrat and founder of *Ms. Magazine*; Representative Bella Abzug (D-NY), who is best remembered for her feminist advocacy, flamboyant hats, and sharp tongue in House debate; Chisholm; and Betty Friedan, feminist and author of *The Feminine Mystique*. Courtesy of Associated Press/Wide World Photos.

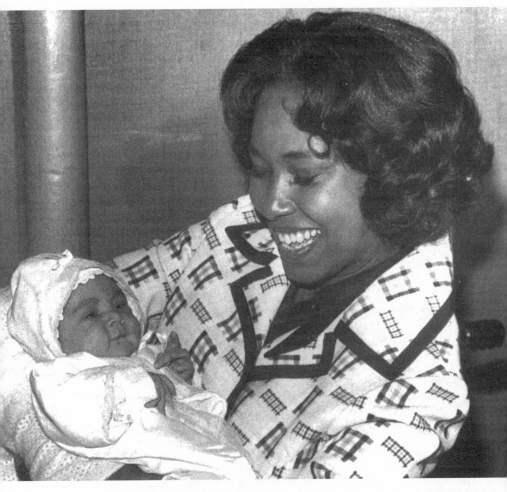

In 1973, Yvonne Burke (D-CA) became the first woman to give birth while serving in Congress. Though serving just three terms, she worked tirelessly to improve life for the poor and needy. After leaving Congress, she won election five times to the Los Angeles County Board of Supervisors. She was the first woman to serve as vice chair of the Democratic National Convention and the first to chair the Congressional Black Caucus. Courtesy of Associated Press/Wide World Photos.

After fifty years, Congress was still not always a welcome place for women, nor for minorities. Patricia Schroeder (D-CO), right, who served 24 years, is shown here with Ron Dellums (D-CA) and his wife, Leola ("Roscoe"). When Schroeder and Dellums were named to the all-male Armed Services Committee in 1973, Chairman F. Edward Hebert (D-LA) declared that women and blacks were only "half" of a "regular" member and thus provided only one chair for the two. Courtesy of Patricia Schroeder.

Barbara Jordan (D-TX) was the first southern black woman elected to the House in 1973. In her first term, her stirring oratory captivated the nation and provided the most compelling defense of the Constitution during President Nixon's impeachment proceedings. An advocate of civil rights and protections for the poor, she fought for bilingual ballots under the Voting Rights Act. In 1976, she became the first black to give the keynote address at the Democratic National Convention. Behind Jordan in this photo is Speaker Carl Albert (D-OK). Courtesy of the Carl Albert Center Congressional Archives, University of Oklahoma.

Millicent Fenwick (R-NJ) was often at philosophical odds with her party, calling for ratification of the ERA. After her election in 1975 at age 64, she served on a variety of committees during her four terms, where she fought for federal funding of abortions, consumer protections, senior citizen credit issues, and ethics reforms. Pictured here at the energy summit in Princeton, New Jersey, in 1979, with her famous pipe. Courtesy Special Collections and University Archives, Rutgers University. (Cropped from original.)

Dubbed "just one of the guys" by her mentor, House Speaker Thomas P. "Tip" O'Neill (D-MA), Geraldine Ferraro (D-NY) became the first woman vice presidential candidate nominated by a major political party in 1984. Although Republicans defeated her and her presidential running mate Walter Mondale, Ferraro believed her campaign opened doors for women in politics. Pictured here during a congressional break at a ranch in Oklahoma. Courtesy of Carl Albert Congressional Archives, University of Oklahoma.

Nancy Kassebaum (R-KS) in 1979 became the first woman elected to the Senate who was not the widow of a member. In 1995, she became the first woman to lead a major full committee. As chair of the Labor Committee, she served as a moderating influence to protect social programs from conservative forces in her own party. Pictured here greeting President Reagan. Courtesy of the Kansas State Historical Society.

Olympia Snowe (R-ME) is middle ground personified. Only the fourth woman to serve in both chambers and a strong supporter of abortion rights, Snowe was the longtime cochair with Representative Pat Schroeder (D-CO) of the Congressional Caucus for Women's Issues. In the Senate, her centrist politics and approachable style have made her a broker of many compromises. Widowed at the age of 26, her own life story has shaped her support for pension reform, child care, family and medical leave, and displaced homemakers. Courtesy of the National Archives.

Lynn Martin (R-IL) served a decade in the House and became the first GOP congresswoman to hold a leadership job, as vice chair of the House Republican Conference. In 1991, after an unsuccessful Senate bid, she became President Bush's
secretary of labor, where she worked to break the "glass ceiling" for corporate
women. Courtesy of Lynn Martin.

In 1983, Barbara Boxer (D-CA), left, became a leading critic of wasteful defense spending and made the Pentagon's purchase of a $7,000 coffeepot infamous. In 1992, she became the third woman to serve in both the House and Senate, and California became the first state ever to elect two women senators. Dianne Feinstein (D-CA), right, was elected to the Senate in the same year, after almost 20 years in elected office in San Francisco. A strong proponent of anticrime legislation, Feinstein has sponsored or cosponsored the Gun Free Schools Act, the Comprehensive Methamphetamine Control Act, the 1997 Juvenile Justice Act, and a bill to ban the manufacture, sale, and possession of military-style assault weapons. Courtesy of Associated Press/Wide World Photos.

The first Latina woman elected to Congress in 1989, Ileana Ros-Lehtinen (R-FL) has become an important figure on the International Relations Committee, chairing subcommittees on economic policy and trade and now on human rights. Cuban-born Ros-Lehtinen has demonstrated her independence on welfare and immigration policy within the GOP. Joining the congresswoman at a news conference on allegations of torture by a Cuban agent are Ed Hubbard, retired Air Force colonel holding the picture, and Lincoln Diaz-Balart (R-FL) at top right. Courtesy of Associated Press/Wide World Photos.

Angered that the Senate Judiciary Committee was not taking seriously the sexual harassment charges against Supreme Court nominee Clarence Thomas, seven congresswomen "marched" on the Senate in October 1991. Although the women were initially thwarted in their attempt to confront Senate Democratic Caucus members, the presence of the press convinced the caucus to meet with them and resulted in allowing University of Oklahoma law professor Anita Hill to testify. From left are an unidentified woman, Louise Slaughter (D-NY), Barbara Boxer (D-CA), Eleanor Holmes Norton (D-DC), Nita Lowey (D-NY), Patricia Schroeder (D-CO), Patsy Mink (D-HI), and Jolene Unsoeld (D-WA). Courtesy of Associated Press/Wide World Photos.

In 1993, Lynn Woolsey (D-CA), with the ball, broke into the lineup of the previously all-male congressional basketball league. More importantly, when welfare reform was debated in 1995, Woolsey brought a new perspective to Congress when she invoked her past experience as the only former welfare mother in the House—"I know it, I lived it." An unidentified woman staff member is pictured guarding Woolsey. Courtesy of *Roll Call*.

Women have influenced Congress not only as members but as lobbyists, members of interest groups, and staff. Sheila Burke became Senator Robert Dole's (R-KS) chief of staff in 1986, and as the majority leader's chief policy advisor during the 1990s she was often called the "101st Senator." Some in the predominantly male Senate criticized Burke, a former Democrat, as too powerful and feminist, while others praised her as capable, professional, and loyal to Dole. Courtesy of Walter P. Calahan.

In 1994, NOW joined forces with women in Congress to rally support to pass the Violence Against Women Act (VAWA). The act appropriates funds to be used to combat crimes against women, to train police officers and prosecutors to identify violent crimes against women, and to develop and enlarge victim services programs and antistalking initiatives. Courtesy of the office of Representative Connie Morella.

Public policy issues often have linked congresswomen in a spirit of bipartisanship, but perhaps none has been as unifying as breast cancer awareness, research, treatment, and funding. Making common cause on this issue, health policy advocates and congresswomen have also transformed discussions about prostate cancer. Witnessing President Bill Clinton signing the Breast Cancer Funding Act of 1994, which provided $325 million for research, are some of the women of the 103rd Congress (1993–94) who helped to engineer its passage. Courtesy of the office of Representative Connie Morella.

Visiting the Dallas construction site of the Women's Museum: An Institute for the Future are two congresswomen who may figure in the GOP's leadership future. From left are Cathy Bonner, president of the museum board; Representative Jennifer Dunn (R-WA); Senator Kay Bailey Hutchison (R-TX); and Lee Durr. Dunn lost her bid for majority leadership in 1998, but retains influence as an ally of President George W. Bush. Hutchison joined the all-male party leadership in 2000 as conference vice chair and chairs an Appropriations subcommittee. Courtesy of Associated Press/Wide World Photos.

Operation Desert Storm advanced equality for women in the military, but new and closer work relationships sometimes provoked charges of sexual misconduct. In 1996, charges of sexual harassment on numerous army bases prompted a group of congresswomen to meet with four generals to ascertain the army's response. Reflecting women's diversity on the Hill, the participants included (left to right) Eleanor Holmes Norton (D), six-term African American delegate representing the District of Columbia; Patsy Mink (D-HI), the first woman of color to be elected to the House (1965) and of Japanese descent; and Susan Molinari (R-NY), a third-generation Italian American politician following in her father's and grandfather's footsteps. Courtesy of Associated Press/Wide World Photos. (Cropped from original.)

Election officials were unprepared for the tremendous voter turnout when Tammy Baldwin (D-WI) ran for Congress in 1998. Polls remained open an additional three hours while more ballots were photocopied. As the first out lesbian elected to Congress, she has been a strong advocate of civil rights. Here she holds a family photo while urging the use of the budget surplus to save Social Security. Courtesy of Associated Press/Wide World Photos.

Perhaps the most visible First Lady since Eleanor Roosevelt, Hillary Rodham Clinton successfully ran for the U.S. Senate from New York in 2000. A skilled attorney and passionate advocate for children's issues, Clinton's first major foray into congressional policy making was as head of the Health Care Task Force during her husband's first term in the White House. Though the health care package was defeated, she now has the opportunity to vote on such issues directly as a member. Courtesy of the Associated Press/Wide World Photos.

Women in Congress cleared another hurdle in October 2001 when Nancy Pelosi (D-CA) was elected by the Democratic Caucus to become minority whip. When she assumed the office in 2002, she became the first woman to hold one of the top three party leadership positions in either chamber or party. As number two in the Democratic leadership lineup, Pelosi could possibly be a future Madame Speaker of the House. She is shown here with colleagues in a preelection strategy session. Photo courtesy of Scott Ferrell and *Congressional Quarterly*.

CHAPTER NINE

The Gendering of Cancer Policy

Media Advocacy and Congressional Policy Attention

KAREN M. KEDROWSKI AND
MARILYN STINE SAROW

I'm a breast cancer survivor. And before I was a breast cancer survivor, I didn't know or really pay much attention to it. I really didn't think it was important. . . . We finally did get legislation to cover mammograms for women age 65 [and over]. . . . What a fight. I think back to Bill Natcher, from Mississippi, one of the most gracious and charming men I ever knew . . . and chairman of the Appropriations Committee. He simply couldn't understand how we could do this. We finally smartened up and included legislation for prostate cancer because we just didn't have a chance. We certainly have made progress on women's health issues.

FORMER REPRESENTATIVE BARBARA VUCANOVICH, R-NV[1]

Representative Vucanovich is indeed right. In the last decade, the federal government has increased funding significantly for prostate cancer and breast cancer. In 1981, the National Cancer Institute (NCI) spent $6.4 million on prostate cancer research. Seven years later, the NCI spent $86.9 million on prostate cancer research, 13.5 times the 1981 amount. Breast cancer research has a similar story. In 1981, the NCI spent

$33.9 million on breast cancer research; in 1998, the amount was $348.2 million—a tenfold increase.[2]

These changes are reflected in the percentage of total NCI funding allocated to prostate cancer and breast cancer. In 1981, prostate cancer received less than 1 percent of all NCI funds, while breast cancer received 3.4 percent. In 1998, prostate cancer's allocation increased to 5.8 percent and breast cancer's allocation increased to 13.6 percent.[3]

How did these increases come about? One might expect federal funding for research into different diseases to correspond to the incidence and mortality rates of the diseases. However, this is not the case. The three leading causes of death—heart disease, stroke, and cancer—have not changed in recent decades. Yet the federal government more generously funds research on diseases with significantly lower mortality and morbidity rates. For example, the federal government spends more money on AIDS research than on any other disease—some $1.4 billion a year.[4] AIDS continues to show a decreasing mortality rate, and by 1998 was no longer ranked in the top 15 causes of death in the United States.[5] Breast cancer receives far more federal research dollars than other prevalent cancers: lung, prostate, and colo-rectal.[6] Moreover, a recent study found no relationship between incidence, prevalence, or length of hospital stays and federal funding for various diseases. The study also found only a weak relationship between mortality and federal funding. These findings appear to indicate that allocating federal research dollars is arbitrary.[7]

This chapter analyzes the increase in funding for both breast cancer and prostate cancer research. First, we show that women's participation transformed the congressional agenda by bringing these two diseases to the attention of members of Congress. Second, we show how women's participation transformed the legislative process by initiating the practice of congressional earmarking of appropriations during the appropriations process. We argue that breast cancer lobbyists used media advocacy techniques to further their cause. We also examine the slightly different case of prostate cancer advocacy, where research funding increased without the organized efforts of lobbying groups. Therefore, a second focus of this chapter is on how the case of prostate cancer mirrors that of breast cancer, and benefited from, or free-rode on, the efforts of breast cancer patient advocacy groups (hereafter "breast cancer advocates").

BREAST CANCER AND PROSTATE CANCER COMPARISONS

In many ways, breast cancer is to women what prostate cancer is to men. First, both breast and prostate cancers involve a private, sexual part of the body, which makes some people reluctant to discuss the disease. Second, the morbidity and mortality rates are similar. According to the American Cancer Society, an estimated 31,900 men died of prostate cancer in 2000, and 180,400 new cases of prostate cancer were diagnosed.[8] In the same year, approximately 41,200 women died of breast cancer, while 182,800 women were diagnosed with the disease. The chance of developing each disease increases with age, and in both cases developing the disease before age 50 is considered more serious. Third, both breast cancer and prostate cancer are highly survivable with early diagnosis. The five-year survival rate for localized prostate cancer is 100 percent; for breast cancer, 96 percent.[9]

Last, common treatment options for both breast and prostate cancers are fraught with unpleasant consequences. Mastectomy and lumpectomy often have painful side effects and are physically disfiguring, which may leave victims uneasy about their physical attractiveness. Another treatment, hormone therapy, can lead to an early onset of menopause or intensify its symptoms. Two common consequences of prostate surgery, impotence and incontinence, are not only embarrassing, but also may call victims' virility into question.

MEDIA ADVOCACY THEORY AND EMERGENT LOBBIES

Media Advocacy Theory

Media advocacy theory stresses the necessity for public health campaigns to refocus media attention from the individual to public policy. Michael Pertschuk, codirector of the Advocacy Institute, defines media advocacy as "the strategic use of mass media for advancing a social or public policy initiative."[10] Basic to the theory is the precept that to develop solutions to public health problems, the media agenda must shift from an emphasis on personal behavior or individual lifestyles to the mobilization of interest groups to pressure policy makers to change the public health environment.

Several groups have successfully used media advocacy efforts at the state and local level, such as Mothers against Drunk Driving (MADD).[11]

Similarly, the history of AIDS activism suggests media advocacy efforts have been powerful forces behind federal policy decisions, though few scholars have examined this theory at the federal level.[12] The AIDS Coalition to Unleash Power (ACT-UP) was successful in securing policy change and increasing media attention at the federal level, and studies have shown a relationship between media coverage of AIDS and federal funding for the disease.[13] The success of AIDS activists attracted attention from other disease advocates. Breast cancer activists sought training by AIDS activists and adapted some of their techniques, such as the use of a ribbon worn on the lapel as a sign of solidarity with victims of the disease.[14]

Emergent Lobbies

A key to successful media advocacy is the development of interest groups whose focus is to change public policy. In the last decade, national lobbying groups organized around breast cancer and prostate cancer. These groups' developments differed in their timing, with breast cancer activist groups forming much earlier. The first notable breast cancer activist was the late Rose Kushner, author of several books on her own experience with the disease. Kushner tried to stimulate public conversation about this topic as early as the 1970s. In her first policy advocacy efforts, she worked with former representative Mary Rose Oakar (D-OH) on increasing basic breast cancer funding.[15]

A long-established breast cancer organization is the Susan G. Komen Foundation. Founded in 1982 by Nancy G. Brinker, who named the foundation for her late sister, a breast cancer victim, the organization is extremely successful at mobilizing both grassroots and corporate support for breast cancer research. Its primary fund-raising event is the Race for the Cure, an event that attracts corporate sponsors and thousands of participants in cities across the country. To date the foundation has raised $240 million for breast cancer research and receives considerable media attention each year, raising awareness of the disease among policy makers, corporate leaders, the media, and the public.[16]

By the late 1980s, various local-level patient support groups coalesced and began to engage in political activity.[17] In 1991, these disparate and generally unorganized local efforts consolidated into a national movement, largely through the efforts of a nationally recognized breast surgeon, Dr. Susan

Love, and advocates such as Fran Visco and Amy Langer. That year, these leaders helped form the National Breast Cancer Coalition (NBCC) and began to shape its agenda.[18]

The timing was fortuitous, as it coincided with a growing awareness of women's health issues—and their neglect—on the part of women members of Congress. Stories about the issue, especially of neglect, are common. For instance, in 1989, the National Institutes of Health (NIH) spent just 13 percent of its budget on women's health issues.[19] Women were overlooked in the NIH-funded Longitudinal Study on Aging for 20 years, meaning that women, who make up a large majority of the elderly in the United States, were excluded in the study that defined the norms of the aging process. Women also were excluded initially from the famous study that documented the benefits of using aspirin for heart attack prevention. In 1990, a General Accounting Office (GAO) study commissioned by the Congressional Caucus for Women's Issues found that the NIH was not following its own guidelines that required women be included as test subjects in NIH-funded proposals, and that findings be analyzed for gender differences.[20]

Breast cancer advocates worked closely with women members of Congress to put forward their agenda. The first priority was lobbying for increased appropriations for research into breast cancer treatments, cures, and prevention. Also, because many women with breast cancer are, in the words of one activist, "daughters of women who died of it—who are getting the same chemo, the same radiation, their mothers got"[21]—treatment and prevention received heightened legislative attention.[22] Since Medicare coverage of mammograms had been eliminated in 1989 when the Medicare Catastrophic Care Act was repealed, reinstatement of the benefit became another priority.[23]

Breast cancer advocates also succeeded in another way that is not clear by simply looking at numbers. Prior to 1992, the NIH received a lump sum appropriation from Congress, who preferred to let scientists at NIH prioritize their research needs. However, that year breast cancer activists persuaded Congress to earmark NIH funds for breast cancer research, a significant change in the legislative process. While some members of Congress did not like to take funding decisions out of the hands of experts, breast cancer and women's health advocates saw earmarking as the only way to ensure that the federal government would address what they considered a long-neglected disease.[24]

It is clear that in the last decade breast cancer has become a cause célèbre on Capitol Hill. For example, former representative Barbara Vucanovich (R-NV) recalls that when Nancy Brinker first approached members of Congress and their staffs about participating in a Washington, D.C., Race for the Cure, various government agencies began to compete to sign up participants.[25] Harold Jaffe, in an article in *Men's Health*, states that members of Congress today use their support of breast cancer funding to demonstrate commitment to women's issues.[26]

On the other hand, prostate cancer patient advocacy groups (hereafter "prostate cancer advocates") were slow to form. In 1991, the first national patient support group, US TOO!, was just forming. Lobbyists for prostate cancer did not appear until 1996 and 1997. It is significant (discussed below) that two women were among the first prostrate cancer lobbyists.[27] In 1996, Michael Milken, after he was diagnosed with and treated for prostate cancer, used some of his considerable personal wealth to found CaP CURE. This private foundation provides funds for research and lobbies for prostate cancer.[28] The Men's Health Network also lobbies on this issue.[29]

If imitation is the sincerest form of flattery, then the NBCC must feel honored indeed. In 1996, the National Prostate Cancer Coalition (NPCC) formed and patterned itself closely after the NBCC by bringing together disparate groups of prostrate cancer advocates.[30] In the words of Rick Atkins, the NPCC legislative director, "Prostate cancer is where breast cancer was 25 years ago. They have done a great job of getting their message out. . . . We have to try to get to communities where there is also activism."[31] Most recently CaP CURE and the NPCC adopted the blue ribbon as a symbol of solidarity with victims of prostate cancer.[32] A primary difference between the two groups is that the prostate cancer advocacy efforts focus not only on men, but on the women in victims' lives.[33]

No one denies that breast cancer advocates have more clout on the Hill than prostate cancer advocates. Some of the difference may be generational. Many women who are diagnosed with breast cancer today are between the ages of 40 and 60. These women are baby boomers who learned political activism in the civil rights and Vietnam War protest movements of the 1960s and are willing to use those tactics to further their cause.[34] By contrast, the typical prostate cancer patient is a man in his 70s whose political socialization is much different. As Senator Ted Stevens (R-AK), a proponent of prostate cancer research, states: "Suppose you walk out of a hearing about funding medical research and there are 150 attractive young women waiting in the hall. And they're buttonholing you about breast cancer research. They'll have an impact. If you had 150 men waiting there . . . they would be older than 50, not as aggressive, not as organized. And they wouldn't want to talk about it anyway."[35]

Gender adds another dynamic. Health, the look of one's body, sexuality, and aging are all sensitive, personal issues—those typically in the "private" sphere. One of the contributions of the feminist movement has been the political empowerment of women to change the agenda and elevate "private" issues into the realm of political discourse. Health is an issue more likely to be discussed when women are elected officials and is cited as an important public issue by women in public opinion polls.[36] Moreover, women are more likely to go to the doctor for routine screening or when they suspect something is amiss. Men, on the other hand, go to the doctor less frequently and often only at the prodding of the women in their lives.[37] Thus men's health activists are as likely to target women in their public health messages as they are the men themselves. This is why it is significant, but not surprising, that two of the first prostate cancer advocates were women who, in their lobbying, asked members of Congress if they knew their own PSA number—a blood test for prostate cancer.[38]

METHODOLOGY

If media advocacy efforts occur, several distinct phenomena should be observable. First, media attention to the disease should increase at about the same time, or shortly after, patient advocacy groups are established. Increased media attention will make it easier to convince policy makers of the urgency of one's cause. Patient advocacy groups may then, in fact, claim credit for increased media attention.[39] In addition, the media should begin using advocacy groups as sources and/or subjects in their news stories. Similarly, the advocacy groups' agenda issues should be reflected in media coverage.

Second, if media advocacy efforts occur, the increase in media attention should be accompanied by an increase in public policy activity and in federal funding of research. Since media advocacy theory expects advocates to court media attention and to use traditional lobbying techniques, whether or not increased policy attention is generated by the increased media attention is irrelevant to this study. The media attention is designed to raise awareness, instill a sense of urgency, and make policy makers more receptive to the advocates' personal appeals. As former representative Susan Molinari (R-NY) states: "If it [a policy problem] didn't make the front page of the newspaper, if we couldn't get it on CNN, it might not have carried the legs to get a lot of our colleagues to say, 'I want to see this issue . . . this is a politically potent issue.'"[40]

To measure media attention, we examined news coverage of these diseases from 1980 to 1998 in five newspapers and the three television networks, omitting obituaries and letters to the editor.[41] The newspapers selected for this study were two national papers, the *New York Times* and *Washington Post*, and three regional papers, the *Los Angeles Times*, *Chicago Tribune*, and *Atlanta Constitution*. The *New York Times* and the *Post* were both selected because of their high credibility with reporters and policy makers alike. The three regional papers are important and respected conduits of information in their areas of the country. The three networks (ABC, NBC, and CBS) still are considered primary television sources for news in spite of shrinking ratings. Appropriate stories were identified through the newspapers' indices, LexisNexis, and the Vanderbilt Television News Abstracts. A total of 4,183 news stories were identified. Of these, 592 stories focused on prostate cancer. The remainder—3,591 stories—focused on breast cancer.

LexisNexis's Congressional Information Service (CIS) was used to search for congressional hearings and legislation introduced on each disease. Federal funding data were collected from the National Cancer Institute, the Congressional Research Service, and the Department of Veteran's Affairs.

Our analysis included appropriate statistical tests, including difference of means tests and a time-series regression model, that mimic previous research studies of AIDS funding and media attention.[42]

FINDINGS

Media coverage of the two diseases shows similar patterns. In both cases, media coverage was minimal in the 1980s, with the number of stories growing rapidly in the 1990s. There are important differences, however. Media coverage of breast cancer always outpaced media coverage of prostate cancer. In the 1980s, there were approximately 30 news stories per year on breast cancer in these eight news outlets. The same outlets carried fewer than 10 news stories on prostate cancer. The total number of news stories is also vastly different, with breast cancer the subject of five times more news stories than prostate cancer (see figure 9.1).

Second, the data illustrate a smoother growth curve in the number of breast cancer stories than in the number of prostate cancer stories. For example, the number of stories on breast cancer doubles from 1986 to 1987, partly due to the diagnoses and treatment of First Lady Nancy Reagan and Supreme Court Justice Sandra Day O'Connor. Media coverage remained steady and then started a steep rise in 1991. Coverage peaked in 1994, when the *Chicago Tribune* broke a story about falsified data in an important federally funded breast cancer study.[43]

Attention to prostate cancer saw a slight spike in media coverage in 1987, with the diagnoses of two Supreme Court justices and former CIA director William Casey. But the increased coverage was not sustained. Media coverage of prostate cancer began a rapid rise beginning in 1991. The number of prostate cancer stories doubled from 1990 to 1991; doubled again from 1991 to 1992; again from 1994 to 1996; and increased one and a half times between 1996 and 1998 (see figure 9.1).

Public Policy Attention

Again, on every measure of public policy attention, breast cancer received more attention from policy makers than prostate cancer. Consider, for example, NCI funding. These two diseases, with relatively similar mortality and morbidity rates, have received quite different amounts of funding. For example, in the 1980s, the NCI spent about $9.5 million on prostate cancer research each year. At the same time, it spent about $53.7 million a year on breast cancer research. Starting in fiscal year (FY) 1992 (with legislation passed in 1991), funding for both prostate cancer and breast cancer started to increase exponentially. By FY 1999, prostate cancer received much more generous funding from the NCI, some $135.7 million, which represents a significant increase over the levels in the 1980s. By contrast, however, NCI spent nearly $400 million on breast cancer research (see figure 9.1).

The same pattern can be seen when looking at NCI funding of these two diseases in comparison to total NCI appropriations. From 1980 to 1998, total NCI appropriations rose from $1 billion to $2.5 billion. The percentage of

FIGURE 9.1
News Coverage and Federal Funding, Breast and Prostate Cancer 1980–1998

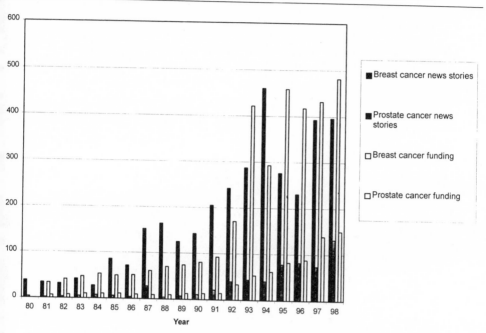

funding dedicated to breast cancer rose from 3.4 percent in 1981 to 13.6 percent in 1998. Again, the rate of increases was most rapid in the 1990s. The same pattern holds for prostate cancer, which received less than 1 percent of NCI funds in 1981 and received about 6 percent in 1998 (see figure 9.2).[44]

The similar results can be seen in the increased policy attention. Consider, for example, legislation introduced dealing with these two cancers. From the 96th Congress (1979–80) through the 100th Congress (1989–90), little attention was paid to either disease. Only four bills introduced mentioned breast cancer; none mentioned prostate cancer. A remarkable change occurred in the 101st Congress (1991–92). Eleven bills were introduced dealing with prostate cancer and 45 bills were introduced dealing with breast cancer, initiating a pattern that continued into the late 1990s. The number of prostate cancer bills continued to rise, peaking at 31 in the 106th Congress (1999–2000). The number of breast cancer bills rose faster, and peaked at 91 in the 105th Congress (1997–98) (see figure 9.3).

FIGURE 9.2

Breast Cancer and Prostate Cancer Funding as a Percentage of NCI Funding

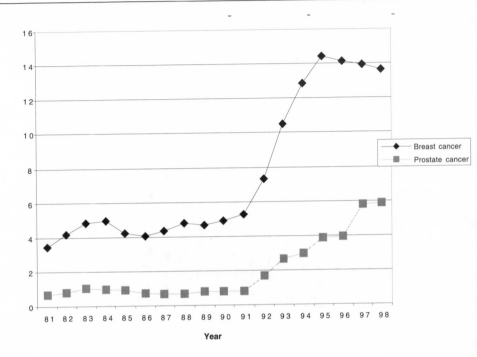

Breast cancer lobbyists are much more likely to appear at congressional hearings, testifying on topics varying from health information to biotechnology. Lobbyists appeared at some 75 hearings during this 19-year period. One-third of these hearings (25) addressed topics directly related to breast cancer, such as the incidence of the disease on Long Island, New York; mammography; and breast cancer appropriations (see figure 9.3). Again, the number of breast cancer activists appearing jumped dramatically in 1991, and remained high through the decade. By contrast, only three congressional hearings in this 19-year period addressed prostate cancer issues. Two were in 1997; one was in 1999.

Media advocacy theory predicts that if organized interests form around a health issue, then both media coverage and public policy attention will increase, and the patterns of their increase will be roughly the same. The

FIGURE 9.3

Congressional Activity, 96th–106th Congresses

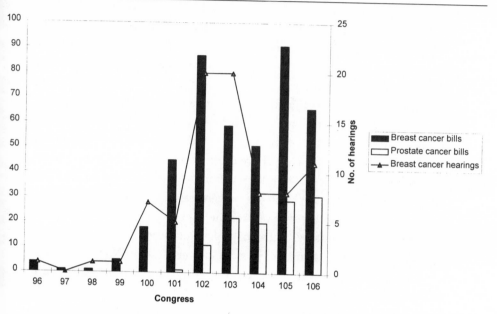

data indicate that both diseases—especially breast cancer—saw a dramatic increase in media and public policy attention starting in 1991. To test if these relationships are linked, we conducted a regression, time series analysis on these data.

First, we explored the degree to which news coverage predicted research funds through the NCI. In the case of breast cancer, the analysis was strongly predictive. The regression model predicts that NCI research funding should increase by $1 million for approximately each additional news story (0.80 stories). This model predicts 75 percent of the observations. Regression analysis is even more predictive in the case of prostate cancer, where even less media coverage (0.70 stories) predicts an additional $1 million in NCI funding on the model. This model predicts 88 percent of the observations.

When total funding (including funds from the Departments of Defense and Veterans Affairs) is used, the analysis remains strongly predictive in both cases. For breast cancer, an additional 1.068 stories yield an additional $1 million in total research funds. This model predicts 67 percent of the observations. For prostate cancer, an additional 1.166 news stories will yield an additional $1 million in total research funds. This model predicts 88 percent of the observations.

Federal funding in most policy areas is incremental, with small changes from year to year. Often the strongest predictor of one year's funding is the previous year's funding. Thus, we also used regression analysis to test annual differences in funding. If news coverage is still a strong predictor, these results will support media advocacy theory, even when controlling for previous years' funding. Using differences in NCI funding only, the analyses were consistent with media advocacy theory, but were much weaker predictors. In the case of breast cancer, each additional 0.13 news stories should produce a $1 million difference in NCI funding, but this model predicts only about half (52 percent) of the observed cases in the breast cancer data. In the case of prostate cancer, the analysis was in the expected direction, but was not statistically significant.

However, when all sources of prostate cancer funding (National Cancer Institute, Department of Defense, and Department of Veterans Affairs) are analyzed, the relationship is stronger. Here, the regression model predicts that each additional 0.19 news stories will result in an additional $1 million difference in federal funding. This model predicts about 30 percent of the observations. These findings suggest media coverage does influence federal funding of research in these two cases. However, media coverage is just one factor in determining funding levels.

The results when regression analysis is used to test annual differences in total funding for breast cancer (from NCI and Department of Defense) are consistent when 1993 is excluded from the model.[45] In 1993, the Department of Defense budget included $210 million for breast cancer research. In 1994, this amount was reduced to $25 million, then stabilized to around $100 million in later years (see figure 9.2).

Media Advocacy Evidence

While these results show a relationship between media coverage and policy attention, they don't prove media advocacy theory per se. To enhance support, we employed difference of means tests (t-tests) to determine if media advocacy is evident for these two diseases. Difference of means tests compare the average number of news stories and funding from two time periods to determine if any observed differences in those average amounts are statistically significant.

The breast cancer data were divided into two groups by date: 1980–90 and 1991–99. This division was selected because the NBCC was formed in 1991. The results of this test support media advocacy theory. The mean number of news stories for 1980–90 is 83.2 articles per year. The mean number news stories for 1991–99 is 311.2 articles per year.[46] Similarly, the average amount of annual total federal research funding for 1980–90 is $58.2 million. The average amount of total federal research funding for 1991–99 is $345.7 million.[47]

Examining prostate cancer data proved more complicated. In this case, media advocacy theory would lead one to expect statistically significant differences in news coverage and funding starting in 1996, with the formation of the NPCC and CaP CURE. Difference of means tests support this prediction. The average number of news stories from 1980–95 is 19 per year; the average number of news stories from 1996–98 is 96.[48] Similarly, average annual total federal research funds from 1980–95 are $22.7 million; the average rose to $124.9 million for 1996– 98.[49]

However, data indicate that the increase in media attention and federal funding began much earlier in 1991 as in the case of breast cancer (see figure 9.1). Dividing the prostate cancer data in the same way as breast cancer data (1980–90 and 1991–98) yields even more interesting results. The mean number of prostate cancer news stories from 1980 to 1990 is 7.27, while the mean number of stories from 1991–98 is 64.0.[50] Similarly, annual total federal research funds for prostate cancer averaged $9.94 million from 1980 to 1991 and $77.0 million from 1992 to 1998.[51]

Further evidence of media advocacy efforts is found in the content of media coverage itself.[52] If media advocacy efforts were used, we would expect that the news coverage would reflect the formation of interest groups and their agendas. Thus we looked for increased coverage of interest groups—as both a source for stories and as a subject of stories—and increased coverage of federal funding, government regulatory activities, and congressional hearings.

The evidence of media advocacy in the case of breast cancer is clear. Again, difference of means tests were used. In the case of breast cancer, all observed phenomena were as expected. Stories about breast cancer interest groups increased from an average of 2.6 stories a year from 1980 to 1990 to an average of 36.1 stories a year from 1991 to 1998.[53] Stories using interest groups as a source increased from an average of 4.6 stories a year prior to 1991 to an average of 45.4 stories a year from 1991 to 1999.[54] The same pattern holds in the case of news stories related to government activity,[55] congressional hearings,[56] and federal funding.[57]

The case of prostate cancer does not provide consistent evidence of media advocacy theory. Difference of means tests were used to test for the same content variables as in the case of breast cancer (interest groups used as story subjects and sources, and stories about government activities, hearings, and funding). First, difference of means tests were used by comparing news coverage from 1980 to 1995 and 1996 to 1998, which corresponds with the 1996 formation of prostate cancer advocacy groups. If these groups used media advocacy theory, there should be an increase in the number of these kinds of stories. Only two tests yielded statistically significant results: the difference of means tests for government activity and interest groups as subject matter.[58] None of the other difference of means tests were statistically significant, including, interestingly, the test for interest groups as a story source.[59] This provides further evidence that media advocacy theory does not hold up as well in the case of prostate cancer.

CONCLUSIONS AND DISCUSSION

Does media advocacy theory explain the changes in media attention and policy outcomes in the cases of breast cancer and prostate cancer? In the case of breast cancer, the answer is yes. When analyzed, all of the expected phenomena occurred, and moreover, the timing was right. Beginning in 1991, the number of news stories in the media, the federal funding allocated, the number of congressional hearings, and the number of bills introduced all increased exponentially, coinciding with the creation of a national advocacy organization.

Prostate cancer is a different story, however, for several reasons. First, while prostate cancer enjoys unprecedented media attention, the total number of news stories dedicated to prostate cancer in these eight media outlets is minute—fewer than 600 stories. Likewise, federal funding for prostate cancer pales in comparison to the level and increases in federal funding dedicated to breast cancer.

Second, prostate cancer begins to command more of policy makers' time and attention, but how much is difficult to determine. While more legislation regarding prostate cancer has been introduced in recent Congresses, the number of bills remains small, with only three hearings on the topic held in the last 19 years.

Third, the timing of the increase in media attention and federal funding in the case of prostate cancer does not occur as media advocacy theory predicts it should. Prostate cancer experienced an exponential increase in media attention starting in 1991, an increase that occurred five years before the first prostate cancer advocacy group even formed.

Piggybacking on Breast Cancer Advocacy

If media advocacy theory fails to explain prostate cancer funding increases, what does? Though we can't answer definitively, our analysis offers some clues. The evidence is that prostate cancer piggybacked on the efforts of breast cancer activists. First, the breast cancer activists set the precedent for earmarking and using Department of Defense funds for medical research. Second, they motivated legislators to think about gender-specific cancers. This link permeates subsequent legislative efforts where "breast and prostate cancer" are linked as one phrase.[60]

While Capitol Hill was not swarming with prostate cancer patients demanding the attention of members of Congress, we know that in 1991 breast cancer advocates were organized, lobbying, and implementing media advocacy efforts.[61]

At the same time, several prominent members of Congress themselves were diagnosed with prostate cancer, including former Senate Republican leader Robert Dole (R-KS), Senator Richard Shelby (R-AL), Senator Jesse Helms (R-NC), and former senator Alan Cranston (D-CA). Former representative Silvio Conte (R-MA) and former senator Spark Matsunaga (D-HI) had recently succumbed to the disease. Senator Ted Stevens (R-AK), a member of the Senate Appropriations Committee, was recovering from prostate cancer. Stevens managed to include in the Senate appropriations bill a provision creating a "Matsunaga-Conte Prostate Cancer Research Center" in 1991. The research center was eventually dropped from the final legislation, but in its place was an earmarked appropriation for prostate cancer research.[62] By 1993, defense appropriations bills carried earmarks for prostate cancer research as well.[63]

However, the increased media attention that prostate cancer advocates enjoyed cannot be ignored. Various celebrities, such as Michael Milken, Norman Schwarzkopf, Timothy Leary, Arnold Palmer, and Stokely Carmichael, to name a few, went public with their diagnoses. Public discussion about something that was once private, personal, and embarrassing no doubt helped members of Congress gain support for their proposals.

In some ways, the piggybacking continues. Since "men aren't invested in their own health," the NPCC continues its efforts to "get to communities where there is already activism."[64] An example is the continuing comparisons between breast cancer and prostate cancer. But free-riding is not enough. Breast cancer has benefited from more media coverage since the early 1980s, and it also has received substantially more federal funding than prostate cancer. The development of breast cancer advocacy groups in the early 1990s increased the amount of media attention and federal funding exponentially, and at a much faster rate than in the case of prostate cancer. The free ride can travel only so far. Today, prostate cancer activists have a long way to go to compete with the level of attention paid to breast cancer.[65]

There is no doubt that women members of Congress and women breast cancer lobbyists brought about dramatic changes in breast cancer policy over the time studied. Additionally, it is important to recognize that women members of Congress were a small minority operating in a male-dominated institution. They had to conform to its norms. As former representative Barbara Vucanovich (R-NV) points out at the beginning of this chapter, women members of Congress engaged in a long-standing congressional tradition, the logroll, to achieve their goals with breast cancer funding. Women members of Congress saw the benefits of adding references to prostate cancer in the legislation in order to gain support for the breast cancer initiatives.

Thus women transformed Congress by bringing not one, but two previously neglected health issues—breast cancer and prostate cancer—onto the agenda. Women also transformed the process for allocation of federal research dollars, at least where NCI and DOD funds are concerned. Women breast cancer lobbyists worked hard with friendly members of Congress (both men and women) to institute earmarking in National Cancer Institute appropriations and to use Department of Defense funds for a domestic, not defense, policy priority. Members of Congress interested in furthering the causes of prostate cancer research copied these tactics long before prostate cancer advocacy organizations formed.

NOTES

1. Barbara Vucanovich, "Women and Reflections on Congressional Life," C-SPAN broadcast, 20 April 2000.
2. National Cancer Institute, "Research Dollars by Various Cancers."
3. National Cancer Institute, "Historical Budget Information."
4. Gross, Anderson, and Powe, "Relation between Funding."
5. National Center for Health Statistics, *National Vital Statistics Report*.
6. Judith Johnson, "Cancer Research: Selected Federal Spending."
7. Gross, Anderson, and Powe, "Relation between Funding."
8. American Cancer Society, "Cancer Statistics."
9. Ibid.
10. Wallack, "Media Advocacy," 376.
11. DeJong, "MADD Massachusetts vs. Senator Burke"; Russell et al., "MADD Rates the States"; Schooler, Sundar, and Flora, "Effects of Stanford Media Advocacy Program"; Treno et al., "Evaluation of Media Advocacy Efforts"; Treno and Holder, "Community Mobilization"; Wallack, "Media Advocacy."
12. Wachter, "AIDS, Activism and Politics of Health."
13. Rogers, Dearing, and Chang. "AIDS in the 1990's"; Dearing and Rogers, "AIDS and the Media Agenda"; Theodoulou, Guevara, and Minnassians, "Myths and Illusions."
14. Wachter, "AIDS, Activism and the Politics of Health," 162.
15. Altman, *Waking Up, Fighting Back*, 324.
16. Komen Foundation, http:www.komen.org.
19. Altman, *Waking Up, Fighting Back*, 19.
17. Boehmer, *Personal and the Political*.
18. Casamayou, "Nice Girls No More"; Langer, "Politics of Breast Cancer."
19. Altman, *Waking Up, Fighting Back*, 19.
20. Schroeder and Snowe, "Politics of Women's Health"; Baylis, Downie, and Sherwin, "Reframing Research Involving Humans."
21. "Politics of Breast Cancer," 616.
22. Stabiner, *To Dance with the Devil*, 5.
23. Schroeder and Snowe, "Politics of Women's Health," 103. See also PL 101–234, Medicare Catastrophic Repeal Act.
24. Rubin, "New Breast Cancer Research Funding."
25. Vucanovich, "Women and Reflections on Congressional Life."
26. Jaffe, "Dying for Dollars."
27. Ibid.
28. James Warren, "Milken's Lobbying Effort a Study in Democracy for Hire," *Chicago Tribune*, 2 June 1997, p. 2.

29. Jaffe, "Dying for Dollars."

30. Men's Health Network, "National Prostate Cancer Coalition."

31. Rick Atkins, telephone interview by Kedrowski, 9 March 2000.

32. CaP CURE, "Getting Involved: Blue Ribbon."

33. Boehmer, "Personal and the Political," 143.

34. Casamayou, "Nice Girls No More."

35. As quoted in Jaffe, "Dying for Dollars."

36. See, for example, Lake and Breglio, "Different Voices: Different Views."

37. Conrad, ed., *Sociology of Health and Illness*, 25.

38. Jaffe, "Dying for Dollars."

39. CaP CURE, "Progress Report: Accelerating a Cure."

40. Molinari, "Women and Reflections on Congressional Life."

41. Obituaries were omitted since they would have artificially inflated the number of stories that focus on personalities. Also, obituaries and letters to the editor are not news stories.

Because the *Atlanta Constitution* was not indexed until 1983, these data do not include stories from this newspaper from 1980 to 1982.

42. Theodoulou, Guevara, and Minnassians, "Myths and Illusions"; Rogers, Dearing, and Chang, "AIDS in the 1990's."

43. These findings are consistent with those found in Corbett and Mori, "Leading and Following."

44. National Cancer Institute, "Historical Budget Information."

45. $R^2 = 0.5233$.

46. $F = 3.02; p \leq .0001$.

47. $F = 94.11; p \leq .0008$.

48. $F = 2.09; p \leq .0449$.

49. $F = 1.94, p \leq .0255$.

50. $F = 22.91; p \leq .0024$.

51. $F = 548.07; p \leq .0051$.

52. Two coders acting independently were used in the content analysis. To measure intercoder reliability, both coders read a sample of 600 news stories. The rate of intercoder reliability was 83 percent.

53. $F = 10.40; p \leq .0000$.

54. $F = 9.52; p \leq .0000$.

55. The number of breast cancer stories relating to government activity rose from an average of 30 stories from 1980 to 1990 to an average of 113 stories per year from 1991 to 1998. $F = 1.34; p \leq .0000$.

56. The number of breast cancer stories on congressional hearings rose from an average of 1.2 stories per year from 1980 to 1990 to an average of 8.9 stories per year from 1991 to 1998. $F = 14.53; p \leq .0022$.

57. From 1980 to 1990, the average number of stories on federal funding for breast cancer was 0.72 stories per year. From 1991 to 1999 the average number was 9.8 stories per year. $F = 28.18; p \leq .0018$.

58. The number of news stories concerning government activity rose from an average of 5.6 stories per year from 1980 to 1995 to an average of 33.0 stories from 1996 to 1998. $F = 4.04$; $p \leq .001$. The number of news stories concerning interest groups (as subject matter) increased from an average of 0.6 stories per year from 1980 to 1995 to an average of 3.0 stories from 1996 to 1998. $F = 1.06$; $p \leq 0.0350$.

59. We conducted difference of means tests with 1991 as a dividing line to reflect the development of breast cancer lobbying groups, which did not yield statistically significant results. This confirms our hypothesis that media advocacy theory does not apply as well in the case of prostate cancer.

60. We noticed the same linkage in media coverage as well. Journalists and medical experts alike frequently compared prostate cancer to breast cancer.

61. Casamayou, "Nice Girls No More"; Schroeder and Snowe, "Politics of Women's Health"; Rubin, "New Breast Cancer Research Funding."

62. Rovner, "Future of Labor-HHS Measure."

63. Towell, "House OKs Defense Spending"; Towell, "$243.7 Billion Compromise."

64. Atkins, interview.

65. For instance, Arizona Senator John McCain included prostate cancer research on his list of "pork barrel spending" in the DOD budget. Breast cancer research apparently did not make the list. Likewise, prostate cancer advocates were unsuccessful in their recent efforts to fund research through the creation of a special "semipostal" stamp modeled after the 40-cent breast cancer stamp. NPCC, "Prostate Cancer Research"; NPCC, "National Semi-postal Bill Re-Authorized."

CHAPTER TEN

TRANSFORMING THE AGENDA

Analyzing Gender Differences in Women's Issue Bill Sponsorship

MICHELE L. SWERS

During the 104th Congress, welfare reform was a cornerstone of the Republican Contract with America. As a senior member of the Ways and Means Committee, which had jurisdiction over major portions of the welfare reform legislation, moderate Republican Nancy Johnson (CT) had the opportunity to influence the direction of welfare policy. Johnson used her institutional clout to attach her bill on child support to the Republican party's reform proposal, thus successfully tying the issue of child support enforcement to welfare reform. Throughout the long months of debate among the parties and the president, Johnson used her political capital to expand child care provisions, buttress child protection programs, and preserve Medicaid benefits for women and children. However, as Johnson sought to moderate the Republican welfare bill, she had to carefully choose her battles. In order to avoid antagonizing party colleagues and key Republican constituencies, including fiscal conservatives who viewed welfare reform as a means of deficit reduction and social conservatives who hoped to guide welfare recipients to a new set of moral standards, Johnson accepted less than her ideal preferences on some issues and hoped for Senate modification of the bill on others.[1]

Nancy Johnson's efforts to pursue policy initiatives for women, children, and families while adjusting her goals to the realities of the institutional

and political contexts raise several important questions about th,
which gender influences the legislative choices of members of C
For example, how do politically significant social identities such as ̨
impact a representative's policy priorities? Does the importance of gι
to a member's decision calculus vary by the policy area? How do changes
in the external political environment and the representative's position
within the institution impact the range of choices open to an individual legislator regardless of his or her abstract policy preferences?

In this chapter, I examine bill sponsorship activity on women's issues
during the 103rd (1993–94) and 104th (1995–96) Congresses, as an initial
step toward determining which members are the most dedicated to placing the concerns of women on the national agenda. Women's issues are
defined as issues that are particularly salient to women because they seek
to achieve equality for women; they address women's special needs, such
as women's health concerns or child care; or they confront issues with
which women have traditionally been concerned in their role as caregivers,
such as education or the protection of children. The analysis demonstrates
how a focus on the influence of politically significant social identities such
as gender expands traditional understandings about the determinants of
congressional behavior.

The comparison of bill-sponsorship activity in the Democratic-controlled
103rd Congress and the Republican-controlled 104th Congress reveals the
tension that congresswomen, particularly Republican women, face as they
try to balance their interest in advancing policies for women with the necessity of designing legislative initiatives that will maintain the support of their
partisan colleagues. The focus on these two Congresses allows me to specify how changes in the political and institutional contexts, including the
identity of the majority party and the external political climate, constrain a
member's willingness to support and advocate women's issue legislation.

UNDERSTANDING THE DETERMINANTS OF
LEGISLATIVE CHOICE

It is a long-standing canon of rational choice congressional research that
the need to secure reelection guarantees that all legislators will adhere to the
demands of the constituency.[2] This premise suggests that social identities
such as gender are largely irrelevant to the shape of policy outcomes. Yet

the overwhelming importance of electoral concerns does not foreclose the possibility that female legislators will have a distinctive policy impact. Research suggests that the same geographical constituency can support many different reelection constituencies.[3] Thus, a female candidate may be more likely to attract supporters who are concerned with women's issues. Additionally, within the wide boundaries of constituency preferences, legislators can choose which policy areas to pursue. While both a liberal Democratic congressman and congresswoman might vote in favor of a specific policy, Congresswoman Johnson's actions suggest that male and female legislators differ in the depth of their commitment to women's issues, and therefore it is women who will spend the time and resources necessary to incorporate women's interests into law.[4]

Indeed, research at the state and national levels indicates that female legislators initiate more bills on gender-related topics, both feminist and social welfare, than do their male colleagues. They are more likely to consider these bills a priority, they are more likely to see their women's issue initiatives passed into law, and they vote more liberally on gender-related legislation.[5] (For a more comprehensive review of the existing literature on women's policy impact, see the chapters by Rosenthal and Wolbrecht in this volume.)

However, much of the state and national research relies on survey data or analyses of single legislative sessions. This reliance on the reported preferences of legislators or cumulated policy activities at a given point in time prevent these studies from determining whether women are more likely to sponsor women's issue bills because they are more likely to be Democrats or because they are more likely to sit on social welfare committees that have jurisdiction over many women's issues. Thus, research on the policy impact of women in legislatures must focus more specifically on how institutional and political context factors facilitate or constrain a member's ability to pursue policy preferences based on gender.

Congressional scholars who examine the influence of institutional position on the legislative decisions of representatives note that where one sits within the institution often determines where one stands on policy. For example, students of political party strength maintain that majority party leaders, with the support of their fellow caucus members, structure the agenda to appeal to core party constituencies and preserve their party's majority status in the next election.[6] Additionally, committee scholars have

found that individuals with seats on key committees exert disproportionate influence over the outcomes of policy at all stages of the legislative
process.[7] Recently, scholars have begun to investigate how institutional and
political context factors, particularly committee position and majority/
minority party status, affect the ability of legislators to achieve gender-related
policy goals.[8] In this chapter, patterns of women's issue bill sponsorship in the
103rd and 104th Congresses are compared in order to evaluate the ways in
which macrolevel factors, particularly the shift from minority to majority status for Republican women (and vice versa for Democratic women) and the
changes in the external political climate, affect a member's willingness to
expend political capital on the pursuit of women's issue legislation.[9]

A THEORY OF WOMEN'S POLICY IMPACT

The approach of each election year finds women's groups raising money to
elect more female candidates under the assumption that electing women
will change the direction of public policy. Through an analysis of the bill
sponsorship patterns of representatives, I hope to more carefully specify
the conditions under which gender influences the legislative choices of representatives. I maintain that congresswomen will be more likely to pursue
women's issue legislation than will their male partisan colleagues. Thus, it
is expected that Democratic women will be more likely to advocate
women's issue bills than will Democratic men, and that Republican women
will be more likely to sponsor these bills than will Republican men. Party
affiliation is one of the most reliable predictors of legislative behavior. Since
the early 1990s, the parties have become even more ideologically polarized,
and party voting remains at historically high levels.[10] If, for example, Democratic women sponsor women's issue bills at a higher rate than Democratic men, this would suggest that social identity does exert an independent
influence on legislative behavior and that women feel a stronger depth of
commitment to pursue polices for women than do their male colleagues.

The prominence of gender considerations as a factor in determining
whether a member supports a particular women's issue bill may vary by
issue area and policy direction. Additionally, institutional incentives such
as membership in the majority or minority party, the member's committee
position, and the views of the district constituency structure the range of
choices available to individual legislators. Thus, it is imperative to identify

as precisely as possible the circumstances in which gender most influences the legislative priorities of members concerning policy initiatives for women. It is equally important to scrutinize the factors that inhibit those decisions in a rational manner.

The Importance of the Policy Area

Within the broad area of women's issue bills, it is possible that the influence of social identity on a member's decision to sponsor a specific bill will vary by the subject of the bill and its policy direction. Thus, I expect that gender will play a more important role in a member's decision to sponsor feminist bills than social welfare bills and that congresswomen will be less likely to sponsor antifeminist bills than congressmen of the same party.

Feminist bills are those bills that seek to achieve role equity or role change for women. In their book *Women and Public Policies: Reassessing Gender Politics*, Joyce Gelb and Marian Lief Palley explain that "role equity issues are those policies that extend rights now enjoyed by other groups (men, minorities) to women. Role change issues appear to produce change in the dependent female role of wife, mother, and homemaker, holding out the potential of greater sexual freedom and independence in a variety of contexts."[11] Examples of feminist legislation include efforts to provide government funding for child care, guarantee reproductive rights, or protect victims of sexual harassment. Conversely, antifeminist legislation seeks to inhibit role change as a threat to the traditional family. Examples of these bills include efforts to inhibit access to abortion or require abstinence-only sex education in schools.

Social welfare legislation encompasses both liberal and conservative proposals concerning such issues as health care, poverty assistance, and education. These issues highlight women's traditional roles as caregiver and have served as women's gateway to political participation throughout history. In election years, both Democratic and Republican candidates emphasize such issues as education and health care in an effort to reach out to women voters.

The idea that the role of gender should be most important in the decision to support feminist legislation seems counterintuitive when one considers the conventional wisdom concerning congressional behavior. For example,

Arnold notes that rational representatives are most concerned with trace-ability.[12] They seek opportunities to promote policies that distribute bene-fits throughout their districts and allow them to claim credit with constitu-ents, such as initiatives to increase funding for education or highway expansion. However, potentially controversial policies such as reproduc-tive rights and affirmative action programs for women, issues that often make up feminist legislation, require members to focus on blame avoid-ance. By restricting themselves to only voting on feminist proposals, not initiating these bills, they do not waste precious political resources pro-moting policies that would expose them to negative attention from grass-roots organizations opposed to feminist causes. This is a rational decision made to enhance their potential for reelection.

The controversial nature of feminist bills means that only legislators with an acute interest in these policies will assume the risks associated with advocating feminist legislation. There are many reasons to believe that female officeholders will display an intense commitment to the pursuit of feminist goals. Gender role socialization and a congresswoman's unique life experiences might make her more sensitive to the importance of these issues.[13] For example, if a member experienced employment discrimina-tion or the difficulty of obtaining child care, she might be more committed to finding a legislative remedy. Additionally, issues like women's health and domestic violence underscore women's status as a minority in Con-gress and encourage congresswomen to view themselves as the represen-tatives of a national constituency of women. Jane Mansbridge refers to this connection with constituents outside one's district, based on a feeling of shared experience, as "surrogate representation."[14] (See Carroll, this vol-ume, for a more extensive analysis of surrogate representation.)

One might expect female legislators, as surrogate representatives of women, to focus on the issues that constitute the gender gap. The gender gap is generally attributed to the fact that women are more likely to favor government spending for the disadvantaged, are less likely to be optimistic about the economy, and are more likely to oppose military intervention than men in general.[15] These attitudes reflect concerns that are better addressed by social welfare legislation than feminist legislation. The close connection between the underlying causes of the gender gap and social welfare legislation offers reason to doubt that the unique policy impact of electing women will be found on feminist issues.

However, female officeholders should not be equated with female voters. As rational legislators, women must build a legislative portfolio that will solidify their reputation both within the institution and at home with constituents. Thus, a representative looks for gaps that need to be filled. Social welfare issues like education or antipoverty programs are firmly entrenched within committee jurisdictions, and these issues have divided the parties since the New Deal. Therefore, members with the most institutional clout, such as committee and subcommittee chairs, exercise great advantages in their efforts to shape social welfare policy. The fact that social welfare issues also tap a wider range of partisan, district, and policy concerns than do feminist issues reduces the significance of gender in a legislator's decision to become active on a bill.

Conversely, feminist issues are more recent additions to the congressional agenda. Some of these issues, such as pay equity, domestic violence, and sexual harassment, only became part of the public discourse as a result of the women's movement in the 1960s and 1970s.[16] These issues provide opportunities for a member to carve out a policy niche. Additionally, since many feminist issues like reproductive rights and domestic violence directly affect women as a societal group, congresswomen will be viewed as having more credibility and expertise on these issues. Credibility and expertise are both highly valued assets in the congressional policy-making process, since these characteristics facilitate access to the bargaining tables of party policy task forces, committee meetings, and conference committees.[17] Female legislators' heightened credibility on feminist issues also advances their ability to build support for their point of view with the public and their congressional colleagues, increasing the likelihood that their efforts will lead to concrete legislative victories they can advertise to their constituents.

The Significance of the Institutional and Political Contexts

Regardless of the abstract policy views that legislators express in their campaigns, members are highly affected by the demands of their party caucus and leaders as well as the external political climate around them. Therefore, the ability of congresswomen to express preferences based on gender is highly dependent on variations in the political and institutional contexts, particularly the identity of the majority party, the relative power of the leadership, and the ideological composition of Congress.

Comparing legislative behavior in the 103rd and 104th Congresses provides an ideal opportunity to assess how the political and institutional environment impacts the decision calculus of members concerning what kind of policies to advocate. Of the two Congresses, the 103rd Congress provided the most favorable environment for the passage of women's issue legislation. The 1992 congressional elections were widely hailed as the "Year of the Woman" and were accompanied by a significant rise in the number of women in the House of Representatives: from 28 in the 102nd Congress to 47 in the 103rd Congress.[18] The election of Bill Clinton brought a president who held liberal views on women's issues and benefited from a gender gap. The fact that women's issues were highlighted in both the congressional and presidential campaigns made the agenda particularly open to women's issue proposals. Additionally, unified government after 12 years of Republican presidential rule offered the prospect, if not the result, of smoother passage of legislation. A member who expended scarce political capital developing and lobbying for a women's issue bill was less concerned about facing a presidential veto at the end of the line.

In contrast, many political commentators described the Republican takeover of Congress in 1994 as the revenge of the angry white male.[19] Agenda control shifted from Democrats, who wanted to expand social welfare programs like national health insurance, to Republicans, particularly the new conservative freshmen, who believed they had an electoral mandate to dismantle the welfare state built up by Democrats during the New Deal and the Great Society.[20] Additionally, core Republican constituencies vigorously opposed liberal positions on women's issues, particularly reproductive rights. With Democrats relegated to the minority, feminist groups lost access to party and committee leaders as groups representing Christian conservatives gained the ear of the new Republican leaders.

Republicans concentrated power in the party leadership, particularly Speaker Newt Gingrich's office, in order to impose party government and reduce the independent influence of committees. These changes strengthened leadership control over the policy agenda. Perhaps the most important institutional change was Gingrich's decision to reward ideological loyalty over seniority in the committee assignment process. He placed new conservative freshmen on prestige committees like Appropriations, Budget, and Commerce and elevated conservative loyalists to committee chairs over more senior members. Gingrich created party task forces to handle important policy matters like Medicare and the effort to eliminate executive departments, further circumventing the committee process. These party task forces excluded Democrats from deliberation and further limited the independence of committee leaders.[21]

Since most women in the House were Democrats, and thus members of the minority party, they had very little opportunity to influence the legislative agenda on women's issues. The Republican leadership further reduced the impact of women as a group by defunding legislative service organizations, including the Congressional Caucus for Women's Issues. Thus, Republicans eliminated the extra staff resources that Democratic and moderate Republican women utilized to develop independent omnibus proposals concerning women's health, violence against women, and other issues. The new women with the potential to gain a seat at the policy-making table included more senior moderate Republican women and a new group of socially conservative Republican freshman women.

Republican Women and the Influence of the Political and Institutional Context

Given the dramatic changes in the institutional and political contexts between the 103rd and 104th Congresses, the behavior of moderate Republican women should most clearly reflect the dual influences of a restricted party agenda and a powerful party leadership on a representative's desire to advocate women's issue bills. As minority party legislators, these moderate women were usually the most willing to defect from their party's standard position to support feminist initiatives on women's issues. However, their party's elevation to the governing majority greatly increased the costs of defection, and altered the rationality of their choices. Majority party membership provides more opportunities to gain leadership positions on committees and to generate action on one's priorities on a range of issues, thus increasing the costs of alienating the party leadership and core party constituencies. To reap the benefits of majority status, Republican women may be willing to downplay their commitment to women's issues in order to make gains on other district and policy priorities that conform more easily to the Republican agenda.

MEASURING COMMITMENT TO WOMEN'S ISSUES

I utilize a database of women's issue bills to examine gender differences in women's issue bill sponsorship for the 103rd and 104th Congresses. The full set of women's issue legislation is divided into subsets of feminist, social welfare, and antifeminist bills to determine whether the impact of gender varies by issue type and policy direction. Specifically, gender is expected to be a more important influence on a member's decision to sponsor feminist legislation than social welfare legislation. In addition, it is expected that congresswomen will be less likely to sponsor antifeminist legislation than will their male colleagues. Throughout the study I pay careful attention to the ways in which the dramatic shifts in party control and institutional power impact the willingness of individual representatives to pursue gender-related policy initiatives.

When studying the bill sponsorship patterns of legislators, one must realize that representatives sponsor bills for a variety of reasons ranging from an interest in promoting good public policy to pure reelection considerations.[22] For example, a member may sponsor a bill on Medicare reform to establish himself/herself as an expert on health issues so he/she will be included in the policy debate when Congress tackles the Medicare crisis. Conversely, members may sponsor a bill for purely electoral reasons. The legislator may want to appeal to a specific group of voters during an election year or immunize himself/herself against criticism from an opponent. For example, Dodson reports that Republican party leaders assigned a popular amendment, which would protect victims of domestic violence from discrimination by insurance companies, to a Republican congressman who was in a difficult reelection fight and needed a women's issue.[23] Despite the fact that bill sponsorship may reflect varying levels of commitment toward women's issues, it is a good first step toward determining which members are working to bring women's issues to the national agenda. Examining bill sponsorship patterns indicates which members are interested in acting as advocates for women's interests and also demonstrates a representative's desire to expend limited political capital, time, and staff resources on the pursuit of women's issue legislation.[24]

To determine which members are bringing women's interests to the national agenda, I measured the number of women's issue bills sponsored by each member of the House of Representatives. Legislators are given credit for initiating legislation only if they are listed as the primary sponsor of the bill. Cosponsors are not included in this analysis.

When identifying which specific bills concern women's issues, one can find reasons to categorize all bills as women's issues or no bills as women's issues. To identify a reasonable sample that can be duplicated, this study relies on the monthly legislative reports of five major liberal and conservative women's groups. Each group claims to represent women's interests and has a legislative department devoted to following women's issues in Congress. The liberal groups include the American Association of University Women and the National Organization for Women. Concerned Women for America and Eagle Forum are conservative groups associated with the religious right. The Congressional Caucus for Women's Issues (whose staff was later reconfigured as Women's Policy, Inc.)[25] is a bipartisan but liberal leaning congressional caucus devoted to the promotion of women's, children's, and family issues.

To ensure that there is no systematic bias in the sample, I reviewed the approximately 5,000 bill synopses per Congress describing the bills proposed by each Republican and Democratic member. Bills matching the subject areas identified by the women's groups were added to the sample. For example, in the 103rd Congress, the women's groups identified 11 bills concerning adoption and foster care. Eight additional bills on this topic were found and included in the sample. The final sample contains 510 bills sponsored by 195 members for the 103rd Congress and 569 bills sponsored by 224 members for the 104th Congress. This sample contains about 10 percent of the bills introduced in the 103rd Congress and 14 percent of the bills offered in the 104th Congress, excluding resolutions.[26]

Table 10.1 provides a general overview of the women's issue bill database. The table lists the number of members sponsoring women's issue bills and each subset of feminist, social welfare, and antifeminist bills, as well as the total number of bills sponsored in each category. Among the feminist bills sponsored during the 103rd and 104th Congresses are bills protecting reproductive rights, expanding family and medical leave, increasing funding for women's health research, protecting victims of domestic violence or sexual harassment, creating programs for women-owned businesses, establishing gender-equity programs in education, enforcing child support laws, and increasing access to child care for welfare recipients.

TABLE 10.1

Women's Issue Bill Sponsorship in the 103rd and 104th Congresses

	103RD CONGRESS (N = 433)		104TH CONGRESS (N = 430)	
ISSUE TYPE	# MEMBERS WHO SPONSOR	# BILLS	# MEMBERS WHO SPONSOR	# BILLS
All women's issue	195	510	224	569
Feminist	99	221	82	175
Social welfare	138	264	176	351
Antifeminist	11	14	29	44

NOTE: In the 103rd Congress, a group of 11 bills concerning the "nanny tax" were included in the full set of women's issues but were not assigned to any of the policy categories. In the 104th Congress, separate sections of an omnibus bill sponsored by Barbara Vucanovich (R-NV) were counted in the feminist and antifeminist category.

The majority of the antifeminist bills introduced in the 103rd and 104th Congresses concern efforts to hinder abortion. Other examples are bills prohibiting funding for international family planning programs, eliminating sex education programs in schools, outlawing gay marriage, prohibiting homosexuals from serving in the military, eliminating affirmative action programs for women and minorities, and requiring welfare recipients to disclose the paternity of the child in order to receive benefits.

The social welfare bills sponsored during the two Congresses span a wide range. Among these proposals are efforts to expand health insurance coverage, reform Medicare, expand coverage of mental health services, increase funding for school lunches, create school choice voucher programs, establish regulations for foster care or adoption, punish crimes against children and the elderly, and reform welfare.

EVALUATING WOMEN'S INFLUENCE ON THE CONGRESSIONAL POLICY AGENDA

Table 10.2 compares women's issue bill sponsorship by gender and party for the 103rd and 104th Congresses. The results clearly demonstrate the importance of institutional position, particularly majority party status, to a

TABLE 10.2

103rd and 104th Congresses: Women's Issue Bill Sponsorship

Issue Type	Democratic Men (103rd n = 222) (104th n = 165)		Democratic Women (103rd n = 36) (104th n = 31)		Republican Men (103rd n = 163) (104th n = 217)		Republican Women (103rd n = 12) (104th n = 17)	
	% Who Sponsor	# Bills	% Who Sponsor	# Bills	% Who Sponsor	# Bills	% Who Sponsor	# Bills
103rd	45	220	72	134	37	111	83	45
104th	54	173	77	111	47	229	59	56

member's level of activity on women's issues. A focus on the absolute number of bills sponsored in each Congress indicates that Democratic and Republican men and women all sponsor more women's issue bills when their party holds power, with Democrats reducing the number of women's issue bills they sponsored from the 103rd to the 104th Congress, while Republicans increased their sponsorship activity from the 103rd to the 104th Congress. Thus, majority party status translates into agenda control, and all members increase their sponsorship rates when they believe they have an opportunity to shape policy outcomes.

Within each party, women are more likely than men to sponsor women's issue bills. Across both Congresses, between 23 percent and 27 percent more Democratic women than Democratic men devoted their scarce political resources to the advancement of women's issue legislation. Among Republicans, 83 percent of Republican women sponsored a women's issue bill in the 103rd Congress compared to just 37 percent of Republican men. However, in the 104th Congress, the percentage of Republican women sponsoring women's issue bills dropped to 59 percent, only 12 percent more than Republican men. This 24 percent drop in the percentage of Republican women sponsoring women's issue bills is largely due to the election of six conservative Republican freshman women, none of whom sponsored any type of women's issue bill: feminist, social welfare, or antifeminist. By contrast, only one of the ten Republican women who served in both the 103rd and 104th Congresses reduced her sponsorship of women's issue bills to zero. The other nine women either sponsored the same number of women's issue bills or increased their sponsorship, with six of these ten women doubling the number of women's issue bills they sponsored.

It is clear that the influence of gender on a member's legislative behavior is highly dependent on his/her overall political ideology. All Democratic women and moderate Republican women are much more open to women's issues than are their male colleagues of the same party and ideology. However, conservative Republican women are not more likely to sponsor women's issue bills than are their conservative Republican male counterparts. When Republican members are divided by ideology into moderates and conservatives, one finds that all of the moderate Republican women serving in the 104th Congress sponsored a women's issue bill, including moderate freshman Congresswoman Sue Kelly of New York.[27] However, only two of the nine conservative Republican women sponsored a women's issue bill. Among these women, Barbara Vucanovich (R-NV), who held a leadership position as House Republican Conference secretary, was the only conservative woman who sponsored more than one bill. Of the five women's issue bills Vucanovich sponsored, four concerned combating breast cancer through expansion of access to preventive measures, such as requiring Medicaid and Medicare to cover mammography screening. Vucanovich's interest in breast cancer reflects her personal experience with the disease.[28] The fifth bill she sponsored, a plank of the Contract with America called the Family Reinforcement Act, was dictated by her membership in the Republican leadership. The bill incorporated several family-friendly proposals such as tax credits for adoption and long-term care expenses, expanded punishments for sex offenses against children, and an antifeminist initiative to prohibit children's participation in surveys without parental consent. It is possible that Republican leaders chose Vucanovich to sponsor this Contract provision because they believed a female sponsor would help portray the Republican party as pro-family.

At this point, it is difficult to determine if conservative women will ignore women's issues or will actively advocate women's issue proposals from an antifeminist point of view. Among the nine conservative women serving in the 104th Congress, six were freshmen. Freshman legislators need to spend time developing their reelection constituencies. Therefore, many freshmen focus their energy on specific district concerns.[29] For example, Barbara Cubin (R-WY) and Helen Chenoweth (R-ID), both from western districts with large amounts of public land, concentrated their efforts on reducing environmental regulations. However, the freshman status of these conservative Republican women does not completely explain their inattention to women's

TABLE 10.3

104th Congress: A Closer Look at Republican Sponsorship of Women's Issue Bills

Representative	Moderate Republican		Conservative Republican	
	Freshman	Nonfreshman	Freshman	Nonfreshman
Men	35%	59%	40%	47%
	(n = 20)	(n = 41)	(n = 45)	(n = 111)
Women	100%	100%	0%	67%
	(n = 1)	(n = 7)	(n = 6)	(n = 3)

Note: Poole and Rosenthal's DW-NOMINATE scores are used to characterize Republican members as moderate or conservative. These scores, which are estimated over all nonunanimous roll-call votes, range from –1, indicating most liberal, to +1, indicating most conservative. Republicans with scores in the lower 30 percent of the Republican party conference are characterized as moderates. The remaining 70 percent of the legislators are characterized as conservatives.

issues. A comparison of women's issue bill sponsorship by conservative Republican men reveals that a similar proportion of conservative male Republican freshmen and nonfreshmen sponsored women's issue bills. Thus, 40 percent of the 45 conservative Republican male freshmen sponsored a women's issue bill, a ratio that is similar to the 47 percent of the 111 nonfreshman conservative Republican men who sponsored women's issue legislation.

Alternatively, the lack of attention to women's issues by conservative Republican women could be a conscious political choice. Given their small numbers in Congress, the conservative women knew that their gender and position on women's issues would gain media attention. Therefore, these women made a point of stating that they did not "claim sisterhood with the so-called 'women's agenda'" and that they viewed themselves as "citizens" rather than as women.[30] Indeed, as Carroll notes in her chapter, this cohort explicitly rejected a role of surrogate representative for women. As these conservative women gain seniority and more conservative women are elected, it is an open question whether they will continue to ignore women's issues and insist that they do not exist or whether they will actively engage these issues from a conservative or antifeminist viewpoint.

TABLE 10.4
103rd and 104th Congresses: Feminist, Social Welfare, and Antifeminist Bill Sponsorship

Issue Type	Democratic Men (103rd n = 222) (104th n = 165)		Democratic Women (103rd n = 36) (104th n = 31)		Republican Men (103rd n = 163) (104th n = 217)		Republican Women (103rd n = 12) (104th n = 17)	
	% Sponsor	# Bills	% Sponsor	# Bills	% Sponsor	# Bills	% Sponsor	# Bills
103rd Congress								
Feminist	23	88	58	72	12	29	75	32
Soc. welf.	33	128	47	59	26	64	42	13
Antifem.	<1	1	0	0	6	13	0	0
104th Congress								
Feminist	19	39	65	70	11	43	35	23
Soc. welf.	44	133	52	41	36	146	59	31
Antifem.	1	1	0	0	12	40	12	3

COMPARING LEGISLATIVE ACTIVITY BY POLICY AREA

When the women's issue database is divided into bills with a feminist or antifeminist policy direction and bills that concern a social welfare issue, the results in table 10.4 indicate that there are important gender differences in the type of legislators who sponsor feminist, social welfare, and antifeminist legislation. Across both the 103rd and 104th Congresses, Democratic and Republican men are more likely to sponsor a social welfare bill than a feminist bill. Since many of the social welfare bills concern issues like health care and education that voters care about and expect their member of Congress to be active on, many legislators responded to constituent concerns about these issues by sponsoring a bill on the subject. For example, to address the health care crisis, members offered a wide array of proposals, including bills to make health insurance costs tax deductible for the self-employed, to expand patients' rights, or to guarantee health insurance portability. As rational choice theories would predict, these bills allowed them to claim credit for taking a position and avoid blame for congressional inaction on health issues.

On the other hand, a smaller percentage of Democratic and Republican men sponsored feminist bills. Unlike the social welfare issues that are routinely ranked as top voter concerns in public opinion surveys, the hot-button social issues that make up feminist legislation such as guaranteeing abortion coverage to Medicaid recipients or providing government funding for child care have the potential to expose cleavages within a member's political party and to mobilize the grassroots forces of important interest groups into opposition in the next election. Thus, it would appear that congressmen are behaving as rational choice theory would predict, by restricting their activity on feminist legislation to casting roll-call votes that reflect the views of their districts instead of actively promoting feminist initiatives.

In contrast to Democratic and Republican men, the behavior of congresswomen does not conform to the picture of the rational legislator who avoids sponsoring controversial feminist legislation and focuses her attention on social welfare proposals. Across both the 103rd and the 104th Congresses, a larger proportion of Democratic women sponsored feminist bills than social welfare bills. In the 103rd Congress, Democratic women sponsored almost as many feminist bills as did their more numerous male colleagues. In the 104th Congress, their commitment to the pursuit of feminist policy initiatives surpassed that of Democratic men, as the smaller group of Democratic women sponsored almost twice as many feminist bills as their male counterparts, and they were the only group of legislators that placed a greater emphasis on feminist rather than social welfare legislation. Thus, it appears that social identity provided the added intensity of interest to encourage Democratic congresswomen to actively pursue feminist policy goals in a political environment that was increasingly antagonistic to these initiatives.

The sponsorship behavior of Republican women is even more intriguing. Moderate Republican women continued to actively sponsor women's issue legislation across both the 103rd and 104th Congresses. However, these women shifted the focus of their proposals from feminist legislation in the 103rd Congress to social welfare bills in the 104th Congress. As shown in table 10.4, in the 103rd Congress more Republican women sponsored feminist bills than social welfare bills. In fact, the small group of 12 Republican women sponsored more feminist bills than their 163 male Republican counterparts did. Conversely, during the 104th Congress, more Republican women sponsored social welfare bills than feminist initiatives.

This shift from feminist to social welfare proposals highlights the impact of changes in the institutional and political contexts on a member's decision calculus concerning what combination of policies to pursue. It is possible that Republican women shifted their resources to the social welfare legislation because, as members of the majority party, they now had more opportunities to shape the final policy outcomes on these issues, which occupy a central place on the congressional agenda. Embracing their majority party advantages, they actively joined the debates on welfare, Medicare, and health insurance reform, knowing that their efforts could lead to the incorporation of their ideas into the ultimate legislative vehicle rather than to a desperate attempt to amend the bill on the floor.

On the other hand, these moderate Republican women may have focused their attention on the social welfare issues rather than the feminist issues because the feminist issues would create conflict with conservative Republican party caucus members and key Republican interest group supporters such as conservative Christians. Members who expose conflicts within the party and antagonize important supporters invite sanctions from party leaders and other party caucus members, which would inhibit their efforts to achieve their other policy and district-oriented goals.[31] Indeed some moderate Republican members assert that it is difficult to advocate for feminist issues like family planning and child care because "you do not want to be perceived as an advocate for Democratic interest groups." Such a perception damages their credibility within the party conference.[32] Thus, when moderate Republican women take on feminist issues, they must work against fellow party members, their natural allies. This situation compounds the inherent difficulty of moving an issue onto the national agenda.

Finally, table 10.4 demonstrates that Republican men sponsor the overwhelming majority of antifeminist bills. Thus, when agenda control shifted to the Republicans in the 104th Congress, the number of antifeminist bills offered by these legislators more than tripled, rising from 13 to 40 bills. The rise in antifeminist proposals reflects both the increasingly conservative Republican membership, with 16 percent of the 45 conservative male Republican freshman sponsoring antifeminist bills, and the status of social conservatives as a key Republican constituency. These groups, including the Christian Coalition, Concerned Women for America, and the Family Research Council, expected the new Republican majority to reverse policies implemented by the Clinton administration and the Democratic majority, which were passed with support from liberal feminist groups. The issue of abortion exemplifies the increasing conservative influence on congressional policy making. During the 104th Congress, party leaders instructed the Appropriations Committee to include in its spending bills numerous legislative policy riders to outlaw fetal tissue research, eliminate rape and incest exceptions for Medicaid coverage of abortions, defund international and domestic family planning programs, and prevent hospitals from losing their accreditation for refusing to teach abortion procedures.[33]

Among Republican women, none of the new conservative freshmen sponsored an antifeminist bill. However, these women demonstrated their support for antifeminist causes by actively signing on as cosponsors of antifeminist legislation. All but one of the six conservative freshman women cosponsored more than the overall Republican party average of five antifeminist bills, and four of these six women cosponsored more than the Republican conservative average of six antifeminist bills.

The two Republican women who sponsored antifeminist bills, Barbara Vucanovich (R-NV) and Jan Meyers (R-KS), both held leadership positions in the 104th Congress. Vucanovich, who served as House Republican Conference secretary, sponsored a plank of the Contract with America that included provisions concerning parental rights that would require parental permission for children to be involved in surveys. This provision was a priority of social conservatives who oppose the practice of surveying students on such subjects as sexual behavior and drug use. As chair of the Small Business Committee, Meyers sponsored a compromise anti-affirmative action bill that Republican leaders promoted after a more comprehensive proposal by Constitution Subcommittee Chair Charles Canady (R-FL) failed.[34] The sponsorship patterns of these two Republican women raise important questions of how women will behave when they reach positions of power in the party leadership and on committees, particularly how they will respond to party goals and whether or not they will make women's issues a priority from either a feminist or antifeminist point of view.

ARE CONGRESSWOMEN TRANSFORMING OR ADJUSTING TO THE INSTITUTION OF CONGRESS?

The analysis of gender differences in bill sponsorship for the 103rd and 104th Congresses provides evidence that women are both transforming and adjusting to the institution of Congress. It is clear that congresswomen are transforming the institution by bringing new issues to the national agenda, particularly feminist issues. They are asking their male colleagues to consider how policy changes will affect women, and they are using their scarce political capital to shine a spotlight on such feminist issues as domestic violence, reproductive rights, and family leave.

Women are also adjusting to institutional norms, since their efforts to pursue preferences based on gender are guided by the limitations of party structures and constituent demands. To gain influence within the institution, women must guard their political capital and professional reputation with party and committee colleagues. Therefore, like all legislators, female representatives must choose their policy priorities with an eye toward what both the district constituency and fellow party members will support. The fact that moderate Republican women shifted their sponsorship patterns across the two Congresses, from an emphasis on sponsoring feminist bills in the 103rd Congress to social welfare bills in the 104th Congress, suggests that these women recognized that majority party status provides them with a better opportunity to influence the direction of policy on social welfare issues. As majority party members, these women also found that they had to tread carefully when they pursued feminist policy objectives because they risked losing opportunities to see action on other policy priorities if they antagonized party leaders, fellow Republican caucus members, and key social conservative interest groups.

The experience of Jennifer Dunn (R-WA) in the leadership elections for the 106th Congress illustrates the cross pressures faced by Republican women. In 1998, both Dunn and the socially conservative former football star Steve Largent (R-OK) launched campaigns to unseat Dick Armey (R-TX) as majority leader. A legislator with leadership ambitions, Dunn had shifted her voting record to the right after moral-issue conservatives fought to deny her a seat as a delegate to the 1996 GOP convention. Between 1996 and 1998, her rating from the Christian Coalition rose from 77 percent to 100 percent, and the National Abortion and Reproductive Rights Action League (NARAL) correspondingly dropped her vote score from 60 percent in 1995 to 17 percent in 1998.[35] Additionally, Dunn served as House Republican Conference vice chair in the 105th Congress, and she had become a prominent spokesperson for the Republican leadership agenda. Despite her leadership credentials and her efforts to allay the fears of social conservatives, Dunn was eliminated in the early rounds of balloting.[36] Thus, Dunn's inability to gain the support of conservative party members concerned about her abortion record contributed to her defeat and cost her access to the rewards of party leadership. After Armey announced his plans to retire in 2002, Dunn responded to questions about her future leadership ambitions by stating that "I've always said there should be a woman in the top leadership. Someone with a different set of experiences. . . . We'll see what develops."[37]

In the final analysis, my research demonstrates that careful attention to the influence of politically significant social identities such as gender on representatives' policy choices can improve traditional understandings of the factors guiding legislative behavior.[38] While rational choice theory highlights the overwhelming importance of electoral concerns, a focus on gender can help explain why a moderate Republican would utilize her scarce political capital in the pursuit of tax credits for child care expenses rather than estate tax reform when both policies would be supported by the district constituency. Similarly, attention to gender considerations can help explain why a member would push the envelope and possibly antagonize party colleagues and interested groups to defend reproductive rights, when the more rational course would be to avoid engaging the issue beyond a roll-call vote.

Additionally, my research highlights the ways in which the political and institutional contexts both facilitate and constrain the ability of members to pursue their policy goals. Those who expect elected women to always champion women's interests and to reform the policy-making process itself must recognize that majority/minority party status, committee position, and the need to garner the support of one's partisan colleagues alter an individual's calculus concerning the desirability of pursuing a particular policy agenda. A legislator who breaks with institutional norms risks damaging her reputation within the party as an effective legislator, and she jeopardizes the future support of colleagues on a wide range of priorities that could benefit her district. Thus, the process of developing an individual legislative agenda is a complex balancing act in which gender clearly does matter, but the influence of identity is conditioned by the member's position within the institution and changes in the political environment.

NOTES

1. Casey and Carroll, "Wyoming Wolves and Dead-Beat Dads"; Norton, this volume; Katz, "House Passes Welfare Bill."

2. Mayhew, *Congress: The Electoral Connection*; Arnold, *Logic of Congressional Action*.

3. Fenno, *Home Style*; Fiorina, *Representatives, Roll Calls, and Constituencies*; Fox, *Gender Dynamics in Congressional Elections*; Reingold, "Concepts of Representation" and *Representing Women*.

4. In his book *Participation in Congress* (1996), Hall discusses the importance of the intensity of a representative's preferences in determining which members will participate in committee deliberations on a bill.

5. Dodson and Carroll, *Reshaping the Agenda*; Thomas, *How Women Legislate*; Saint-Germain, "Does Their Difference Make a Difference?"; Welch, "Are Women More Liberal Than Men?"; Burrell, *Woman's Place*, see ch. 8; Tatalovich and Schier, "Persistence of Ideological Cleavage"; Dolan, "Support for Women's Interests"; Swers, "Are Women More Likely to Vote for Women's Issue Bills?"; Tamerius, "Sex, Gender, and Leadership"; Dodson et al., *Voices, Views, Votes*; Gertzog, *Congressional Women*, 2nd ed.; Foerstel and Foerstel, *Climbing the Hill*.

6. Cox and McCubbins, *Legislative Leviathan*; Aldrich, *Why Parties?*; Rohde, *Parties and Leaders*; Aldrich and Rohde, "Transition to Republican Rule"; Sinclair, *Legislators, Leaders, and Lawmaking*.

7. Hall, *Participation in Congress*; Shepsle and Weingast, "Institutional Foundations of Committee Power"; Krehbiel, *Information and Legislative Organization*; Maltzman, *Competing Principals*.

8. Debra Dodson et al., *Voices, Views, Votes*; Dodson, "What a Difference an Election Makes"; Dodson, "Women Transforming Congress" conference; Norton, "Committee Influence over Controversial Policy"; Norton, "Women, It's Not Enough to be Elected"; Norton, "Congressional Committee Power"; Norton, this volume; C. Rosenthal, *When Women Lead*; C. Rosenthal, "View of Their Own"; Swers, *Difference Women Make*.

9. For an analysis of the impact on bill sponsorship of microlevel factors that are internal to the institution, including member's committee position, subcommittee position, and leadership roles, see Swers, *Difference Women Make*.

10. Aldrich and Rohde, "Transition to Republican Rule"; Poole and Rosenthal, *Congress: A Political-Economic History*; Burden and Clausen, "Unfolding Drama."

11. Gelb and Palley, *Women and Public Policies: Reassessing Gender Politics*, 6.

12. D. Arnold, *Logic of Congressional Action*.

13. Gilligan, *In a Different Voice*; Tong, *Feminist Thought*.

14. Mansbridge, "Should Blacks Represent Blacks and Women Represent Women?"

15. Seltzer, Newman, and Voorhees Leighton, *Sex as a Political Variable*; Shapiro and Mahajan, "Gender Differences in Policy Preferences"; Kaufmann and Petrocik, "Changing Politics of American Men."

16. Costain, *Inviting Women's Rebellion*; Wolbrecht, *Politics of Women's Rights*; Sanbonmatsu, *Gender Equality, Political Parties, and the Politics of Women's Place*.

17. See Krehbiel, *Information and Legislative Organization*, for a discussion of the importance of expertise in congressional committees.

18. Wilcox, "Why Was 1992 the 'Year of the Woman'?" This number excludes the delegate from Washington, D.C., Eleanor Holmes Norton, who is included in my analysis of bill sponsorship. Center for American Women and Politics, "Women in Elective Office 1994."

19. Peter Brown and Howard Scripps, "White Male Voters Receptive to GOP Message," *Cleveland Plain Dealer*, 27 November 1994, p. 8A; Patricia Edmonds and Richard Benedetto, "Angry White Men: Their Votes Turn the Tide for GOP," *USA Today*, 11 November 1994, p. 1A.

20. Gimpel, *Fulfilling the Contract*; Killian, *Freshmen: What Happened?*

21. Aldrich and Rohde, "Transition to Republican Rule"; Aldrich and Rohde, "Balance of Power"; Aldrich and Rohde, "Republican Revolution and the House Appropriations Committee"; Oleszek, *Congressional Procedures*.

22. Schiller, "Senators as Political Entrepreneurs."

23. Dodson, "What a Difference an Election Makes."

24. Hall, *Participation in Congress*, highlights the importance of the allocation of time and limited resources by members as a key step in the policy process.

25. In the 104th Congress, the House Republican Conference defunded legislative service organizations like the Congressional Caucus for Women's Issues (CCWI). The staff of CCWI then formed Women's Policy, Inc., a think tank dedicated to providing nonpartisan research and information on legislative actions affecting women and families. In the analysis of the 104th Congress, Women's Policy, Inc. replaces the CCWI.

26. No significance should be attached to the fact that there are more women's issue bills in the 104th Congress than in the 103rd. If the sample for the 103rd Congress included all the health reform bills proposed in response to the Clinton health care plan, the sample size would reach over 750 bills. However, such a sample would be skewed toward health bills and would not provide a good measure of general interest in women's issues.

27. To characterize Republican members as moderate or conservative, I use Poole and Rosenthal's DW-NOMINATE scores for the 104th Congress. These scores are estimated over all nonunanimous roll-call votes. The scores range from −1, indicating most liberal, to +1, indicating most conservative. Given the increasing ideological polarization of the parties throughout the 1990s, Republicans with DW-NOMINATE scores in the lower 30 percent of the Republican party conference are characterized as moderates. The remaining 70 percent of the legislators are characterized as conservatives.

28. Dodson et al., *Voices, Views, Votes*.

29. Fenno, *Home Style*.

30. Miller, "Will These Women Clean House?"

31. Regression analyses of feminist and social welfare bill sponsorship support the trends displayed in table 10.4. Even after controlling for party, ideology, con-

stituency characteristics, and members' committee positions, gender is a significant predictor of which members support feminist legislation. Regarding social welfare bills, being a female legislator is a significant predictor of sponsorship only when the woman is a member of the majority party, Democratic women in the 103rd Congress and Republican women in the 104th Congress. This finding indicates that congresswomen are more active on social welfare bills only when their party controls the congressional agenda and they therefore have more opportunity to influence the direction of national policy on these issues. See Swers, *Difference Women Make*.

32. Personal interviews, Washington, D.C., 30 July and 18 August 1999.

33. Clemmitt, Primmer, and Simms, *Record*.

34. Ibid.

35. Ota, "Well-Choreographed Campaign by Dunn," 3048.

36. Katz and Doherty, "New GOP Leaders' Watchword."

37. Foerstel, "Delay Wants Blunt to Succeed Him."

38. In this volume, Duerst-Lahti suggests that the institutional structures and norms that guide congressional behavior reflect a masculinist culture that needs to be challenged.

CHAPTER ELEVEN

WOMEN, COMMITTEES, AND INSTITUTIONAL CHANGE IN THE SENATE

LAURA W. ARNOLD AND BARBARA M. KING

The 1992 class of senators took their seats in an environment that might be definitively called the "Year of the Woman" in the Senate. This class included freshmen Senators Carol Moseley-Braun (D-IL), Dianne Feinstein (D-CA), Barbara Boxer (D-CA), and Patty Murray (D-WA). The four new women exceeded the number of female senators previously elected to the Senate without spousal ties.[1] In 1993, Kay Bailey Hutchison (R-TX) joined the Senate after a special election.

This unprecedented electoral result was followed by two kinds of press coverage. First, the male domination of the Senate was discussed. For instance, *Congressional Quarterly Weekly Report* opened a story on leadership elections and committee assignments with the following: "A few more women have joined the old boys' club, but little else about the Senate will change when the 103rd Congress convenes in January."[2] Much of the discussion of the underrepresentation of women in the Senate was prompted by the conflict surrounding the confirmation of Clarence Thomas to the Supreme Court. The Senate's approach to law professor Anita Hill's allegations of sexual harassment against Thomas raised an outcry from the press and the public that motivated the candidacy of several women in 1992. As *U.S. News and World Report* put it, "One year later, the questions of the

Thomas-Hill affair remain unanswered, yet the political impact could not be more certain: A record number of women are running for Congress."[3]

The second major theme of the press coverage was change. The press speculated on the potential of these women to transform the character of the Senate itself rather than following their predecessors by molding their own personalities to institutional traditions and norms. For example, note the following from the *San Francisco Chronicle*: "Underlying the numbers is the popular expectation, fueled by political pundits and media commentators, that these women will shake up Congress, perhaps even transform it."[4] The women in the class of 1992 often fueled this expectation themselves. In Barbara Boxer's notable words, "We will crack open the closed doors of the Senate, open them wide and start running a country, not a country club."[5] Moseley-Braun was even more direct, saying, "By my very presence, the U.S. Senate will change."[6]

Using committee assignments as a prism, this study looks at the impact the women of 1992 had on the Senate, in both the short and long term. In light of the furor surrounding the Senate's handling of the Thomas confirmation hearings, Senate leaders had an incentive to showcase their newly elected female members. Clearly, the visible presence of women could go a long way in repairing the esteem of the institution, especially in women's eyes. Thus, this chapter seeks to evaluate whether the women of the class of 1992 received out-of-the-ordinary committee assignments. As we shall see, the assignments of at least some of these women were better than the average first-year senator should expect. Therefore, we need to discern whether this was a single accommodation of an extraordinary event or a change in assignment behavior on the part of the leadership. In other words, did their assignments have implications for future senators? While the class of 1992 has done quite well in establishing themselves in the committee system, there is little evidence to suggest that systematic change in committee assignments occurred as a result.

The experience of the class of 1992 becomes even more instructive as the number of women continues to increase. As noted, in 1993 Hutchison joined the group elected in 1992. Four more women were elected in the next three elections: Olympia Snowe (R-ME) in 1994, Susan Collins (R-ME) and Mary Landrieu (D-LA) in 1996, and Blanche Lambert Lincoln (D-AR) in 1998. In 2000, four more women won Senate seats, although with less focus on the candidate's gender than had been true in 1992. This class included possibly the best known first-term senator ever, former First Lady of the United States Hillary Rodham Clinton. The three other women in the class of 2000 were prominent in their own right, although Clinton dominated the national spotlight. Former First Lady of Missouri Jean Carnahan was elected after her husband died tragically during his campaign against incumbent Senator John Ashcroft. Debbie Stabenow (D-MI) and Maria Cantwell (D-WA) also defeated incumbents in their electoral contests. The experience of the class of 1992 provides valuable insight into how the Senate as an institution reacts to the changing composition of its membership.

Beyond possible changes in the committee assignment process lies another component of institutional change, namely representation. How has the increasing number of women senators affected the Senate as a representational institution, especially in regard to representing women? This chapter also uses the distribution of committee assignments to explore the ramifications of assignments for representation. Specifically, analysis and discussion will focus on descriptive representation, the idea of "standing for" someone in the legislative process, as well as substantive representation, the idea of "acting for" a group or constituency.[7]

The Thomas-Hill affair invited scrutiny of not only the Senate Judiciary Committee, but of the Senate as a whole. Press accounts called the Senate "an institution under siege" and described it as "insensitive to women and out of touch with America."[8] Dewar reported that senators believed "their handling of the issue had damaged the legislative body's reputation, especially among women."[9] U.S. News and World Report referred to the confirmation process as "a dirty circus" and identified a public that was "angry with the Senate."[10]

Consequently, the Senate needed to present itself as more representative and took measures to do so. Judiciary Chair Joseph Biden (D-DE) insisted that at least one woman be seated on the Judiciary Committee, reportedly commenting that, "Come hell or high water, there will be women on that committee."[11] In an unusual move, the party leadership gave Biden permission to expand the size of the committee in order to provide room for women since no Democratic vacancies existed.[12] To make sure women served, Biden actively recruited potential committee members, sending Barbara Boxer flowers after her primary victory, symbolically inviting her to seek appointment to the committee.[13] He also recruited Dianne Feinstein, who had expressed the most initial interest in a seat on Judiciary.[14] In addition, he flew to Chicago and called Carol Moseley-Braun. Biden insisted that she see him, in spite of her reluctance to discuss committee service. Though she was packing for her move to Washington and had not expected his visit, she relented and saw him.[15] Ultimately, Feinstein and Moseley-Braun were named to the panel.

In addition to seeking to make women more visible, leaders may have recognized a real need for female voices in decision making given the scrutiny the institution was under at the time. One poll taken a year after Thomas's confirmation asked respondents what they had learned from the confrontation between Thomas and Hill. In that poll, 14 percent of respondents said "the single most important lesson learned from the Hill/Thomas controversy" was that "more women should be elected to the Senate."[16] Aware of diminishing institutional esteem among the public, Senate leaders had incentive to place these women in prominent committee positions for political as well as policy reasons.

Newspaper accounts detail the extraordinarily good committee assignments received by the class of 1992. For example, reports in the *San Francisco Chronicle* and the *Washington Post* referred to the "high-profile assignments."[17] However, there has been no systematic examination of these women's committee assignments. If all, or even some, of the women elected in 1992 received extraordinarily good assignments, the nature of the committee assignment process might be expected to have been changed. Future senators could possibly claim the behavior as a precedent to be followed. The expectation that change in assignment behavior for one class would have an impact on future classes is only partially confirmed by the historical evidence.

Perhaps the best analogy to the class of 1992 is the influx of liberal Democrats following the 1958 election. Assuming office in the 86th Congress, these senators were elected largely from competitive states in the Northeast. Their large numbers, 14 in all, and their need to expand their electoral base in competitive states put pressure on the leadership to grant these senators better committee assignments than traditionally had been given to freshmen senators. The leadership responded immediately. Some suggest that this class, with the help of those elected in 1960 and 1962, provided the impetus for transforming the Senate from a closed, almost aristocratic body dominated by senior Southern conservatives to a more open, individualistic, and democratic institution.[18] However, by the 90th Congress in 1967, the value of assignments given to freshmen had fallen significantly and was actually lower than the value of assignments during the height of the "inner club" days.[19] Thus, the class of 1958, while accommodated as an extraordinary group, failed to change the institutional structure of the committee assignment process.

Barbara Sinclair has argued that changes in the Washington environment provided the primary impetus for transforming the Senate into a more open institution.[20] The growing number of interest groups, the enhanced role of the media, and the widening issue agenda significantly altered the environment in which senators worked. The Senate was forced to transform itself to meet the evolving demands placed on its members.

Thus, external pressure through the election of a prominent class of senators or through an altered political environment can cause either momentary or lasting change. The election of 1992 provides elements of both scenarios. Like liberal Democrats of the 1958 class, the 1992 women arrived with a high level of media attention and strong expectations about their policy-making role. Because many observers chose to see the 1992 election outcomes as a message to the Senate that it needed to diversify its membership in the aftermath of the Thomas-Hill affair, the Senate's political environment also was changed. Thus, we might anticipate a momentary accommodation of these women or a more fundamental change in the Senate's assignment patterns. As we will explain, our evidence lends support to the theory that it was only a momentary accommodation.

COMMITTEE ASSIGNMENTS AND REPRESENTATION

Although the assignment of some women to high-profile committees appears to have been a momentary accommodation, more lasting change possibly is found in the level of representation found in committee assignments. Committee assignments should be considered in the context of both descriptive and substantive representation. Descriptive representation is often referred to as "standing for" someone in the legislative process. As such, the focus of this type of representation is on the composition of the legislature. Is the legislature reflective of those it represents in terms of the characteristics of its members?[21]

After the Thomas-Hill controversy, those familiar with the hearings believed having women in the Senate was a necessity. For example, Phil Kuntz speculated before committee assignments were made for the 103rd Congress that "it seems likely the women will end up on at least some powerful committees to mitigate the Senate's reputation as a male stronghold. At least one of the new women senators will probably join the Senate Judiciary Committee, given the battering the all-male committee took last year over its handling of sexual harassment allegations against Supreme Court nominee Clarence Thomas."[22] Additionally, leaders from both parties actively sought to recruit women to serve on the Ethics committee, which was about to embark on an inquiry into allegations of sexual harassment by Senator Robert Packwood (R-OR). Thus, the assignments made to the 1992 class of women have been, in part, a function of the need for descriptive representation on certain committees, most notably the Judiciary Committee. Senator Biden's aforementioned pursuit of women to serve on the committee illustrates his commitment to achieving some descriptive representation.

As Hannah Pitkin notes, the idea of representation as merely descriptive is incomplete, as this conceptualization of the term does not necessitate action.[23] Pitkin asserts that a complete concept of representation must incorporate the idea of "acting for" a particular group or constituency, what she calls substantive representation. This kind of representation is purposive action designed to further the interests of someone.[24] Thus, beyond providing visible evidence of a female presence on Senate committees lies the goal of substantive representation. Although substantive representation does not necessarily require a threshold of descriptive representation, there is evidence that some descriptive representation is necessary. For instance, Jane Mansbridge argues that descriptive representation enhances substantive representation.[25] Minority representatives are able to foster trust and facilitate communication between themselves and their constituents that lends legitimacy to governing institutions. Further, descriptive representation allows for the crystallization of interests, a necessary requisite of substantive representation.[26]

While women naturally remain concerned with constituent representation, they also tend to have a broader legislative focus because they see themselves representing women generally, what Susan Carroll describes as surrogate representation in her chapter in this volume.[27] Therefore, so-called women's issues, those pertaining to women, children, and family, place high on the list of legislative priorities.[28] Female representatives share the experience of being female, a mutual experience that allows women representatives the capacity for a broader sense of the female perspective than male counterparts without such an experience. In turn, women representatives differ from their male colleagues in terms of their awareness of, support of, and commitment to feminine issues.[29] Thus, they are in a unique position to articulate and be responsive to "women's" interests in a way unavailable to their male counterparts. In effect, their descriptive similarities have substantive implications. So, did the women in the class of 1992 find themselves in a position to act for women on their issues, or on issues more generally, as a result of their committee assignments?

COMMITTEE ASSIGNMENTS IN THE SENATE

Committees are the "central structural components" of the U.S. Congress.[30] As Sinclair argues, "the distribution of valued committee positions provides the single best observable indicator of the distribution of influence in Congress."[31] Committee assignments are an indication of the institutional power base from which a senator operates and are crucial to a senator's daily life and prospects for playing a significant role in policy making. The positions held by a member of Congress are critical in defining the career of a legislator.[32] Senators are themselves well aware of the importance of committee assignments and the implications they have on a career. As Senator Robert C. Byrd (D-WV) has stated, "As all new senators realize, their careers in this institution will largely be determined by the committee assignments they receive."[33]

Not all committees are equally powerful or attractive to senators. Service on the more prestigious Senate committees provides certain benefits to senators. For example, Senator George McGovern (D-SD) remarked, "Service [on an important committee] increases your prestige in the Senate. It gives you more press attention."[34] Being on the "right" committees can significantly influence a senator's ability to participate in politics and influence policy. Thus, who gets seats on the most preferred committees is a significant aspect to consider.

Norms and rules play a significant role in the allocation of Senate committee assignments. While the parties make assignments, these assignments are governed largely by seniority and are subject to what is known as the "Johnson Rule." According to the Johnson Rule, no senator should receive a second assignment to one of the Senate's four most prestigious committees until all other senators have received one assignment to one of these committees. Known as the "Big Four," these prestige committees are Appropriations, Armed Services, Finance, and Foreign Relations. Senators view the Armed Services and Foreign Relations Committees as prestigious and powerful because they provide a platform for national recognition and an opportunity for important international policy making. The Appropriations and Finance Committees derive their power from their position as the key holders of the "power of the purse." Appropriations and Finance control spending and taxing, respectively. Through this duty, both committees reach deep into national and international policy making.

Historically, senior senators hold more valuable committee assignments than junior senators, although the gap has narrowed substantially.[35] This narrowing of the gap between junior and senior senators in committee assignments made the prospect for further transforming the committee assignment process though the influx of women more difficult since junior senators were doing much better in the 1980s and 1990s than they had in the past. While there was a time when first-term senators consistently received the crumbs from the committee assignment table, that time passed with the 1977 committee system reorganization.

This reorganization was designed to increase the efficiency of the Senate in light of increasingly unmanageable time demands, provide more opportunities for junior senators, and increase the visibility of the Senate in policy making.[36] According to Laura Arnold, the reorganization did result in improved assignments for junior senators.[37] While previous membership change had provided momentary accommodation for new members, it was not until 1977 that junior senators consistently received valuable committee assignments. Thus, the expectation that the influx of women in the 1990s would bring about long-term change in the committee system without some accompanying institutional reform, like the committee reorganization of 1977, ultimately lacks precedence.

Another crucial factor in the assignment process is the availability of seats on powerful committees. Two issues come into play. First, do vacancies exist as a result of either retirement or adjustments in the party ratios? Since a property right norm remains in place, incumbent senators are routinely returned to their committee assignments from the previous Congress. Thus, only voluntary departure, electoral defeat, or changes in partisan composition lead to openings on committees. In some cases, a senator may choose to leave a committee for a more powerful committee, thereby creating an opening. However, senators rarely leave the most powerful Senate committees voluntarily.

The second factor is the degree of competition a senator faces when placing a request for a particular committee. As Christopher Deering and Steven Smith note, this is the single greatest factor in determining whether a request for assignment will be granted.[38] Competition for an assignment clearly comes from other new senators, but it also comes from incumbent senators seeking to improve their assignments. Thus, many of the openings in a Congress to the most prestigious committees are given to incumbent rather than new senators. For example, there were six openings on the Finance Committee as the parties began work on assignments for the 105th Congress. Returning rather than new senators filled all of these openings.

Thus, the expectation that the women of 1992 would transform the Senate, especially the committee assignment process, is quite ambitious. The assignment process is firmly rooted in institutional tradition and subject to somewhat unpredictable changes in membership as well as the supervision of the party leadership.

INSTITUTIONAL POSITIONS IN THE SENATE: DATA

The analysis includes all senators serving from 1949 (81st Congress) to 2001 (107th Congress).[39] For each senator, information was collected on his or her standing committee assignments from Congressional Quarterly's *Committees in the U.S. Congress* and various issues of *Congressional Quarterly Weekly Report*. Using Charles Stewart and Timothy Groseclose's Grosewart committee attractiveness scores, the Committee Power Index (CPI) was created to measure the value of a senator's committee assignment package. Grosewart scores measure the attractiveness of committees based on senators' decisions to give up one or more committee seats to attain alternative assignments. (For more on Grosewart scores and alternative scoring methods, see www.ou.edu/special/albertctr.wtc.) They rely on the assumption that senators seek to move from less to more prestigious committees. Thus, high scores indicate committees on which senators seek to serve. Committees with negative Grosewart scores, referred to as "burden committees," are so unattractive that senators seek to leave these committees even without a compensating assignment.[40]

The CPI is the sum of the Grosewart committee scores for each member's committee assignments. The CPI makes possible a clear differentiation between the relative prestige of committees and provides a mechanism to examine the full complement of committee positions held by a senator in a given Congress, what Groseclose and Stewart refer to as the committee portfolio. Further, the CPI, and Grosewart scores more generally, is a measure of the institutional value of committee assignments. Some senators may have particular constituency or personal policy interests that make less institutionally valuable committees more attractive for service. In fact, senators may sometimes have to choose between pursuing institutional power and constituency or policy interests in their committee assignments. Neither the CPI nor the Grosewart scores from which it is derived can measure constituency value for a senator. However, constituency-based committees do not afford the same institutional power as other committees. Thus, in looking at the institutional positioning in the Senate, the CPI is an appropriate measure.

Since committee assignments are greatly influenced by a senator's level of seniority, another variable used in the analysis is tenure in office defined as the number of years served. For most of the analysis, senators are grouped to approximate the six-year term in office. Thus, senators serving 1 to 6 years are considered first-term senators, while senators serving 7 to 12 years are considered second-term senators, and so forth.

THE VALUE OF SENATE COMMITTEE ASSIGNMENTS FOR THE 103RD CONGRESS

There is mixed evidence at best for the proposition that the women in the class of 1992 received extraordinarily good committee assignments and virtually no evidence that assignment behavior was transformed by this class. As table 11.1 demonstrates, there is clear variability in the quality of assignments given to the Democratic class of 1992, including its women. Feinstein and Murray did quite well, both receiving assignments on the Appropriations Committee, which is arguably the most constituency-service friendly of the "Big Four" committees. Feinstein's assignments, the highest in terms

TABLE 11.1

Committee Assignments for Freshman Senators, 103rd Congress, 1993

Senator	Committee Assignments			CPI
Democrats				
Boxer	Banking	Environment	Budget	–.29
Campbell	Banking	Energy	Veterans	–.21
Feingold	*For. Relations*	Agriculture		1.78
Feinstein	*Appropriations*	Judiciary	Rules	3.08
Moseley-Braun	Judiciary	Banking	Sm. Business	.43
Murray	*Appropriations*	Budget	Banking	2.20
Republicans				
Bennet	Banking	Energy	Sm. Business	–.56
Coverdell	*For. Relations*	Agriculture	Sm. Business	1.48
Faircloth	*Armed Services*	Banking	Environment	.42
Gregg	Budget	Commerce	Labor	.71
Hutchison	*Armed Services*	Commerce	Sm. Business	1.03
Kempthorne	*Armed Services*	Environment	Sm. Business	.17

NOTE: Italics indicated "Big Four" committee.

of the CPI, closely reflected her requests as she actively lobbied for both Appropriations and Judiciary.[41] Feinstein's CPI of 3.08 far exceeded what a first-term senator might expect, much less a first-year senator. Since the committee reorganization of 1977, first-year senators have an average portfolio value of 0.56, while first-term senators average 1.19.[42] Feinstein's CPI was 1.89 points higher than the average first-term member, which represents the equivalent of a seat on Appropriations, the second highest rated committee. Perhaps even more startling, the value of Feinstein's assignments is greater than that of the average senator serving three or more terms.

Patty Murray also fared remarkably well, exceeding the average portfolio value of second- and third-term senators. Murray's CPI value of 2.2 was 1.1 points above the first-term average for senators since 1977, the equivalent of an additional seat on the Judiciary Committee. Murray's placement on Appropriations provided an excellent opportunity for constituency service. She also benefited from her assignment to Budget, a valuable committee in and of itself. Russell Feingold (D-WI), another Democrat elected in 1992, also did quite well, suggesting that he may have benefited from the assignment environment as well. He was assigned to the prestigious Foreign Relations committee and to Agriculture, giving him the opportunity to demonstrate influence in a policy area very important to Wisconsin. His CPI of 1.78 puts him near the mean CPI for second-term senators in the 103rd Congress.

Thus, the assignments of Feinstein, Murray, and Feingold considered alone support the argument that the women in the class of 1992 got extraordinarily valuable assignments and that Feingold was a beneficiary as well. However, these three senators make up only half of the Democratic class of 1992. The other three Democrats, Carol Moseley-Braun, Barbara Boxer, and Ben Nighthorse Campbell, (CO) were less fortunate than their peers. None of the three received a "Big Four" assignment, and all had CPI's well below the mean for first-term senators (1.19) and even for first-year senators in the period since the 1977 committee reorganization (0.56).

As noted, availability is an issue in how valuable initial committee assignments are likely to be. There were no open Democratic slots on Finance, all the open Armed Services slots were given to incumbent senators, and two of the three Appropriations openings were given to their first-year classmates, Feinstein and Murray. The availability argument does not hold up well under closer scrutiny, however, since Democrats were violating the Johnson Rule. Senators Byrd (Appropriations and Armed Services) and Moynihan (Finance and Foreign Relations) violated the Johnson Rule in the 102nd Congress and continued to do so in the 103rd. More troubling for the new senators of the 103rd Congress was that Chuck Robb (D-VA) became a new violator of the Johnson Rule when he was given an additional assignment to the Armed Services Committee, even though he already served on Foreign Relations. Thus, the leadership not only tolerated old violations of the Johnson Rule, but also helped create a new violation while excluding Moseley-Braun, Boxer, and Campbell from prestige assignments.

Moseley-Braun did receive her sought-after assignment to Banking, although it ranks low in prestige. She reluctantly accepted the Judiciary slot, but was quick to abandon it for a seat on Finance in the following Congress. Boxer and Campbell fared least well. Both had negative ratings on the CPI, indicating significant service on the burden committees. While their assignments do represent some breadth in terms of issue areas, little prestige or institutional power is associated with them. Boxer apparently sought the assignment to Environment and Public Works, despite its low ranking. Her "best" assignment was to Budget, a fairly prestigious committee but one with a clearly prescribed role. Campbell's only assignment that was not on a burden committee was to Banking, the lowest rated of the non-burden committees.

Thus, one cannot conclude that the Democratic women elected in 1992 were universally successful in gaining access to powerful committees or that they somehow lifted the tide for other senators during that assignment cycle. However, Democrats were not the only ones assigned to committees in 1993. What kind of assignments Republicans received also is important to note, especially the assignments given to Kay Bailey Hutchison.

A good deal of variation is found in the Republicans who entered the Senate in 1993. As table 11.1 indicates, Kay Bailey Hutchison, the only Republican woman entering the Senate in 1993, fared significantly better than most of her Republican counterparts. Hutchison may have benefited not only as a woman in a high-profile year, but also as the product of a special election. She was assigned to her committees in a noncompetitive atmosphere when the Republican balance in the Senate favorably shifted. She received an assignment to the Armed Services Committee, valuable as a "Big Four" committee and an asset for a senator from Texas, which has a strong defense-related economic base. Her CPI of 1.03 places her well above the mean for first-year senators since the 1977 committee reorganization (0.56). Note, however, that the value of her assignments pales in comparison to the value of Feinstein's and Murray's assignments.

On average, Republican senators in their first year did not fare as well as their Democratic counterparts. The mean CPI for first-year Democrats was twice that of first-term Republicans (1.17 versus 0.54). As the minority party, Republicans had fewer openings with which to work. Even Republicans who received "Big Four" assignments did not fare as well as their Democratic counterparts. In fact, the average CPI for first-year Republicans with seats on the "Big Four" was only 0.78 compared to an average CPI of 2.35 for the three similarly situated Democrats.

Even if there was a desire on the part of the leadership to use the entrance of the 1992 women as a vehicle for altering the committee assignment process or simply giving preferential treatment to these highly visible first-term members, fulfilling that desire might take some time. The constraints placed on assignments by the norms and rules of the Senate

FIGURE 11.1

Committee Power Index for Women Who Entered the Senate in the 103rd Congress, 1993–2001

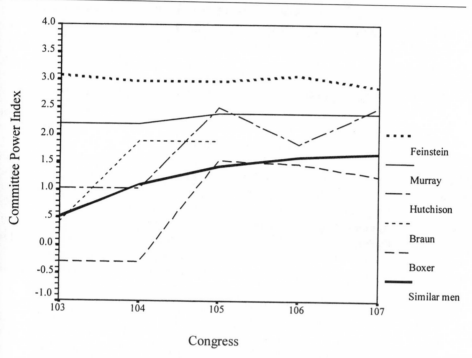

Congress

as well as the availability of committee positions pose a significant barrier to immediately rewarding these members. As a result, the subsequent assignments of those who entered the Senate during the 103rd Congress as well as the assignments of those who entered after 1993 are analytically important.

Figure 11.1 shows the value of the subsequent assignments made to the women who entered the Senate in 1993. Of immediate note is the fact that those senators who received initially fewer valuable assignments did close the gap with their peers rather quickly. Moseley-Braun's move to the Finance Committee in the 104th Congress greatly enhanced the value of her assignments. Both Boxer and Hutchison enhanced their assignments greatly from the 104th to 105th Congresses when each was awarded a seat on the Appropriations Committee.[43] In addition, both Feinstein and Murray maintained quite attractive committee portfolios. Remarkably, Feinstein was able to do so in spite of being forced off of the Appropriations Committee when the party ratios were adjusted after the 1995 Republican takeover of Congress.

When comparing the assignments of these women with the assignments of other senators during the 103rd–107th Congresses, there is evidence that

TABLE 11.2

Committee Assignment Data for Women Senators, 104th to 107th Congresses

SENATOR	COMMITTEE ASSIGNMENTS				CP
104TH CONGRESS (1995–1996)					
Boxer	Banking	Budget	Environment		−0.2
Feinstein	For. Relations	Judiciary	Rules		2.9
Hutchison	Appropriations	Commerce	Sm. Business		1.0
Kassebaum	For. Relations	Labor	Indian Affairs		1.8
Mikulski	Appropriations	Labor			1.9
Moseley-Braun	Banking	Finance			1.9
Murray	Appropriations	Budget	Banking		2.2
Snowe	For. Relations	Budget	Commerce	Sm. Business	2.0
105TH CONGRESS (1997–1998)					
Boxer	Appropriations	Banking	Budget	Environment	1.5
Collins	Labor	Govt. Affairs			−0.3
Feinstein	For. Relations	Judiciary	Rules		2.9
Hutchison	Appropriations	Commerce	Rules		2.5
Landrieu	Agriculture	Energy	Sm. Business		−0.4
Mikulski	Appropriations	Labor			1.9
Moseley-Braun	Banking	Finance			1.9
Murray	Appropriations	Budget	Labor	Veterans	2.3
Snowe	For. Relations	Budget	Commerce	Sm. Business	2.0
106TH CONGRESS (1999–2000)					
Boxer	For. Relations	Budget	Environment		1.4
Collins	Health (Labor)	Govt. Affairs			−0.3
Feinstein	Appropriations	Judiciary	Rules		3.0
Hutchison	Appropriations	Commerce	Rules	Environment	1.8
Landrieu	Armed Services	Energy	Sm. Business		0.6
Lincoln	Agriculture	Energy			−0.
Mikulski	Appropriations	Health			1.9
Murray	Appropriations	Budget	Health	Veterans	2.
Snowe	Armed Services	Budget	Commerce	Sm. Business	1.4

107TH CONGRESS (2001–2002)

Boxer	For. Relations	Environment	Commerce			1.26
Cantwell	Judiciary	Energy	Sm. Business			0.27
Carnahan	Armed Services	Commerce	Govt. Affairs			0.91
Clinton	Budget	Health	Environment			–0.15
Collins	Armed Services	Health	Govt. Affairs			0.80
Feinstein	Appropriations	Judiciary	Rules	Energy		2.87
Hutchison	Appropriations	Commerce	Rules			1.84
Landrieu	Appropriations	Armed Services	Energy	Sm. Business		2.45
Lincoln	Finance	Agriculture				2.01
Mikulski	Appropriations	Health				1.92
Murray	Appropriations	Budget	Health	Veterans		2.39
Snowe	Finance	Budget	Commerce	Sm. Business		2.27
Stabenow	Budget	Agriculture	Banking			0.43

as a group these women achieved more than their peers in obtaining quality committee assignments. By the 105th Congress, all of the women except for Boxer had a CPI higher than the average for male senators at similar levels of seniority. In Boxer's case, her personal policy commitments clearly mitigate her CPI score, since she asked for and received placement on the Environment and Public Works Committee, a burden committee with a negative Grosewart score. Thus, she sought service on it despite the few institutional rewards for doing so.

By the end of their first term, these five women of the Senate fared better than similarly situated male colleagues. All were seated on one of the "Big Four" committees. In addition, all of these senators except for Moseley-Braun had at least one other seat on a committee of relatively high value. For example, Boxer and Murray sat on the Budget Committee (ranked seventh), while Feinstein and Hutchison sat on the Rules Committee (ranked sixth). Thus, even those women who started with relatively weak assignment portfolios now had highly valuable committee portfolios. While the leadership may not have been willing or able to provide a high profile for each of these women upon their entrance into the Senate, the Democratic leadership did work to increase the value of assignments for those initially left out.

LOOKING BEYOND THE 103RD CONGRESS

There is little evidence that the women entering the Senate after 1993 were the beneficiaries of enhanced committee assignments, even the class of

2000 that included four additional women. Of the eight women elected after 1993, only Olympia Snowe (R-ME), Blanche Lambert Lincoln (D-AR), and Jean Carnahan (D-MO) fared better than the men in their respective classes. Furthermore, with the exception of Snowe and Carnahan, no women entering the Senate from 1995 to 2001 received initial "Big Four" committee assignments (see table 11.3). Susan Collins, Mary Landrieu (D-LA), Blanche Lambert Lincoln, and Hillary Rodham Clinton (D-NY) initially had negative CPI scores, indicating that their service on the burden committees outweighed their service on more valuable committees.

Collins, Landrieu, and Lincoln suffered from constraints on the availability of prestigious assignments. When Collins and Landrieu were assigned to committees in 1997, only two of eight first-year Republicans and one of five first-year Democrats were assigned to a "Big Four" committee. In fact, no first-year senators were assigned to either Finance or Appropriations in 1997. Lincoln's assignment circumstance proved to be even worse. No first-year senator was appointed to any of the "Big Four" committees in 1999 even though there were eight new senators. This is partly the result of fewer available seats on the "Big Four" committees. While the average number of vacancies for these committees had been just above 11 for the 103rd through 105th Congresses, there were only seven vacancies on "Big Four" committees when the parties began to consider assignments for the 106th Congress. Subsequent assignments did place all three of these women on "Big Four" committees. By the 107th Congress, Collins sat on Armed Services, Landrieu had moved to Appropriations, and Lincoln attained a highly coveted spot on Finance.

The appointment environment at least partially explains the extraordinarily valuable assignments garnered by Olympia Snowe. Snowe seems to have benefited not only from the institutional context of 1995, but also from the showcasing of female senators during the 103rd Congress. Elected as a member of the 1994 class that regained the Republican party control of the Senate, Snowe was assigned to committees in conjunction with drastic changes in the party ratios on committees. Because the elections had dramatically shifted the partisan complexion of the Senate and increased the supply of Republican seats on committees, Republican leaders had an enhanced opportunity to both reward currently serving senators and to give valuable seats to new senators.

TABLE 11.3

Initial Committee Assignments for Women Elected after 1993

	REPUBLICANS		DEMOCRATS					
	OLYMPIA SNOWE (1994)	SUSAN COLLINS (1996)	MARY LANDRIEU (1996)	BLANCHE LAMBERT LINCOLN (1998)	MARIA CANTWELL (2000)	JEAN CARNAHAN (2000)	HILLARY CLINTON (2000)	DEBBIE STABENOW (2000)
	Foreign Relations Budget Commerce Small Business	Health, Ed., Labor Government Affairs	Agriculture Energy Small Business	Agriculture Energy	Judiciary Energy Small Business	Armed Services Commerce Government Affairs	Budget Health, Ed., Labor Environment	Budget Agriculture Banking
Committee Power Index for first portfolio of committee assignments								
	2.04	−0.33	−0.45	−0.15	0.27	0.91	−0.15	0.43

Mean Committee Power Index for first-year senators: Republicans = 0.65 (n = 30) and Democrats = 0.41 (n = 19)

NOTE: Italics indicates "Big Four" committee.

Evidence suggests that leaders tried to accomplish both goals. While incumbent senators took all the new seats on the Appropriations and Finance Committees, five first-year senators were placed on the Foreign Relations or Armed Services Committees. Snowe was among those assigned to Foreign Relations, although she later moved to Armed Services and then on to Finance in the 107th Congress. When looking at the average value of assignment portfolios for first-year senators, those assigned in the 104th Congress (1995) fared far better than did those in other recent Congresses. In the 104th Congress the mean CPI for first-year senators was 1.19 compared to 0.83 in the 103rd or 0.39 in the 105th.

The class of 2000 also deserves a closer look. One startling detail is that perhaps the most visible first-term senator ever, Hillary Rodham Clinton, received such poor assignments. During the course of her campaign, Clinton indicated an interest in a wide range of committees, including Finance and Appropriations.[44] With six openings on these two committees, an unusually high number, one might have thought Clinton had a good chance of getting one of the coveted assignments. However, no newly elected senator was assigned to either of these panels in 2001. Thus, Clinton was shut out of her most preferred committees. However, her appointment to Health, Education, Labor, and Pensions, another committee she sought, does provide her an opportunity to demonstrate her recognized expertise on health care issues.

Another very visible new senator was Jean Carnahan, who was thrust into the spotlight when her husband, Governor Mel Carnahan, was killed in a plane crash during his Senate campaign. Under Missouri law, no process existed for removing Mel Carnahan from the ballot with the election less than a month away. On October 25, less than two weeks before the election, newly appointed Governor Roger Wilson announced that he would appoint Jean Carnahan to fill the Senate seat if her husband won the majority of the vote on election day. After five days of deliberation and an active effort to encourage her acceptance by Democrats statewide, Carnahan agreed to accept the appointment should it come and began a muted campaign for the Senate.[45] Carnahan was elected in a close contest against the incumbent Senator John Ashcroft.

Arriving in the Senate, Carnahan received better than average assignments for a first-year senator and better assignments than any of her incoming female colleagues. Her CPI score of 0.91 was the fourth highest in the class of nine Democrats newly sworn in 2001.[46] She was placed on the Armed Services Committee, one of four newly elected Democrats and the only woman placed on the Committee. In fact, she was the only woman elected in 2000 to receive appointment to a prestige committee.

Why did Carnahan fare well in the assignment process? The answer probably lies less in her position as grieving widow and more in her position as senator approaching a special election in two years. Because of the nature of her appointment, the term served would consist of only two years rather than the customary six. Thus, in a Senate equally divided, the leadership probably sought to position Carnahan for reelection. A similar situation following the 1992 election helped net Diane Feinstein extraordinarily good committee assignments.

The remaining two women elected in 2000, Maria Cantwell and Debbie Stabenow, fell near the middle of the pack of assignments for new Democrats. While neither received a prestige assignment, Cantwell's placement on Judiciary, the fifth-ranked committee, mitigated the damage to the value of her committee portfolio caused by serving on two burden committees. Stabenow's moderate CPI score was the result of avoiding service on the most onerous committees.

Notably, the women elected in 2000 did not fare particularly well in their assignments when compared to some of their male colleagues. Even Carnahan's assignments were eclipsed by three first-year male senators, Ben Nelson (D-NE), Mark Dayton (D-MN), and Bill Nelson (D-FL). Bill Nelson was head and shoulders above the rest of the class with a CPI score of 3.27, which was largely the result of his appointments to both Foreign Relations and Armed Services, a clear violation of the Johnson Rule.

In order to put these various classes in context and draw conclusions about the fate of women in the committee assignment process since the 1992 election, figure 11.2 plots the mean CPI score for senators at various levels of seniority since 1949. In historical context, it is clear that, on average, the women entering the Senate in 1993 (the 103rd Congress) did receive quite valuable committee assignments. By their third year in office (104th Congress), the value of these women's assignments was nearly that of the average second-term senator. As was previously noted, this provides good evidence of some accommodation for the members of this group. However, the accommodation has not translated into any long-term change for first-term men or women. By the 106th Congress, once the women of 1992 had

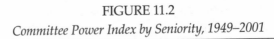

FIGURE 11.2

Committee Power Index by Seniority, 1949–2001

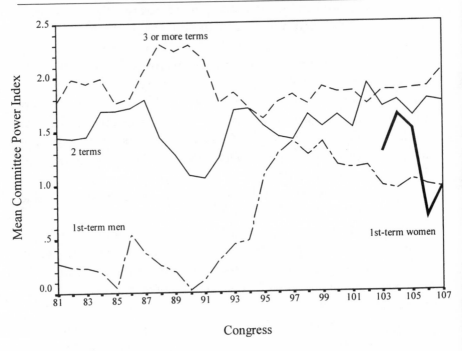

Congress

moved into the second-term class, men and especially women were receiving less valuable assignments. While men and women share the same mean CPI in the 107th Congress, its value for first-term senators continues to gradually decline.

THE BREADTH OF COMMITTEE ASSIGNMENTS

Beyond analysis of the institutional value of the committee assignments lies consideration of the breadth of interests covered by the women of the Senate after the 1992 election. As Noelle Norton and Debra Dodson have demonstrated, in order to have a voice in policy making, sitting on a committee with jurisdiction over an issue is very important.[47] This fact suggests an additional question for examination. Did the addition of these women result in a greater breadth of representation across all issues, or did it lead to greater representation of women on the committees most closely associated with the issues commonly classified as "women's issues"?

On the one hand, increasing the number of women in the Senate should by definition increase the representativeness of all of the Senate. However, one possibility is that the issue areas covered by the committee assignments of women are more closely associated with women's issues, leading to a greater level of representation on these particular issues, but inhibiting representation on a broader range of issues. If women are concentrated in particular areas based on beliefs about their expertise, or because they are given typical freshmen assignments on less valuable committees, then enhanced representation across all issues may not be achieved at the committee level.

Literature focusing on women in elective office suggests that the presence of women is important for the incorporation of women's issues into legislation. For instance, Arturo Vega and Juanita Firestone found that bill introductions and voting behavior of women legislators led to an increase in the representation of women's issues.[48] Other studies also indicate that the presence of female legislators is likely to increase the introduction of legislation pertaining to women's issues.[49] However, the addition of new women does not enhance female representation on committees that address these "women's issues" as straightforwardly as might be thought. The diverse jurisdictions of many Senate committees mean that these issues may fall under the purview of more than one committee. Furthermore, many committees have large and diverse jurisdictions where "women's issues" make up a small fraction of the agenda. Nevertheless, an initial examination is warranted.

Women's issues have an important place on the agenda of two committees: the Health, Education, Labor, and Pensions Committee (Health) and the Environment and Public Works Committee (Environment). The jurisdiction of Health includes health care, education, and substance abuse treatment among many other things. Although the Energy Committee deals with some environmental policy, environmental issues are largely the purview of the Environment Committee. Interestingly, neither committee is noteworthy as a source of institutional power.

Referring to table 11.4, note that the Health Committee (formerly known as Labor and Human Resources) has had consistent female membership throughout the 1990s, continuing in the 107th Congress. This is consistent with the committee's recent history. In the 1980s, both Paula Hawkins (R-FL) and Nancy Landon Kassebaum (R-KS) served sequentially on the committee. During the 102nd and 103rd Congresses, Barbara Mikulski (D-MD) and

TABLE 11.4
Representation on Senate Committees, 1991–2001

CONGRESS (TOTAL # OF WOMEN)

Committees with women senators (# of women on the committee/% of committee membership)

102ND (2)	103RD (7)	104TH (8)	105TH (9)	106TH (9)	107TH (13)
*Appropriations	*Appropriations (3/10)	*Appropriations (2/7)	Agriculture (1/6)	Agriculture (1/6)	*Agriculture (2/10)
*Banking	Armed Services	*Armed Services (1/5)	*Appropriations (4/14)	*Appropriations (4/14)	*Appropriations (5/18)
*Foreign Relations	*Banking (3/16)	*Banking (3/18)	Armed Services (1/6)	*Armed Services (2/10)	*Armed Services (3/13)
*Labor (2/12)	*Budget (2/10)	*Budget (3/14)	*Banking (2/11)	*Budget (3/14)	Banking (1/5)
*Small Business	*Environment (1/5)	*Commerce (2/10)	*Budget (3/14)	*Commerce (2/10)	*Budget (4/18)
	*Foreign Relations (1/5)	*Environment (1/6)	*Commerce (2/10)	*Energy (2/10)	*Commerce (4/18)
	*Judiciary (2/11)	Finance (1/5)	Energy (1/5)	*Environment (2/11)	*Energy (3/14)
	*Labor (2/12)	*Foreign Relations (3/18)	*Environment (1/6)	Foreign Relations (1/6)	*Environment (2/11)
	*Rules (1/6)	*Judiciary (1/6)	Finance (1/5)	*Govt. Affairs (1/6)	*Finance (2/10)
	*Small Business (2/9)	*Labor (1/6)	Foreign Relations (1/6)	*Health (3/17)	Foreign Relations (1/6)
		*Rules (1/6)	*Govt. Affairs (1/6)	(formerly Labor)	*Govt. Affairs (2/13)
		Small Business (1/5)	Judiciary (1/6)	Judiciary (1/6)	Judiciary (2/11)
			*Labor (3/17)	*Rules (2/13)	*Health (4/20)
			*Rules (2/13)	*Small Business (2/11)	*Rules (2/11)
			*Small Business (2/11)	*Veteran's Affairs (1/8)	*Small Business (3/17)
			*Veteran's Affairs (1/8)		Veteran's Affairs (1/7)

Committees without women senators

Agriculture	Agriculture	Agriculture	Banking
Armed Services	Commerce	Energy	*Finance*
Budget	Energy	Govt. Affairs	
Commerce	*Finance*	Veterans Affairs	
Energy	Govt. Affairs		
Environment	Veterans Affairs		
Finance			
Govt. Affairs			
Judiciary			
Rules			
Veterans Affairs			

* Female membership on committee proportionate to female membership in Senate.

NOTE: Italics indicates "Big Four" committee.

Kassebaum sat on the committee. Notice that while there is representation on this committee, it was not enhanced by the elections of 1992. This may have been a function of seat availability. There were no Democratic openings on the committee in 1993. No women were added to Health until 1997 when Patty Murray and Susan Collins joined Barbara Mikulski on the committee. Hillary Clinton joined the Health committee in 2001, when the number of women in the Senate increased from 9 to 13.

Turning to the Environment Committee, Barbara Boxer was assigned to this committee immediately on entering the Senate and has maintained that assignment ever since. In 1999, Kay Bailey Hutchison joined her on the committee. Although Hutchison subsequently left the committee in the 107th Congress, Clinton joined the committee, sustaining the female presence. Thus, the two committees most directly concerned with "women's issues" do include women senators. However, in the case of the Health Committee, the representation was not due directly to the 1992 elections. Enhanced representation on this committee only came as the critical mass of women in the Senate was beginning to build. Referring to table 11.4, note that membership on either committee has not greatly exceeded the proportion of women expected to serve on the committee given the total number of female senators. Thus, the representation seems to be a matter of breadth, rather than the concentration of women on particular committees associated with women's issues.

Another approach evaluates whether women are left off of committees stereotypically associated with male strengths. Two committees stand out as clearly associated with this stereotype: Armed Services and Foreign Relations, both "Big Four" committees. Are women excluded from service on these committees? The answer appears to be no. Since 1992, there has been steady representation of women on Armed Services, beginning with Hutchison's appointment in 1993. Although no women were initially appointed to Foreign Relations in 1993, Nancy Landon Kassebaum's presence on the committee meant it already had some female representation. Feinstein's, Boxer's, and Snowe's subsequent service on the Foreign Relations committee only enhanced that representation. Once again, women are not concentrated on particular committees concerned with "women's issues" or excluded from others associated with male expertise, a pattern that could undermine a female senator's opportunity to attain the institutional power and prestige advantageous for the substantive representation of women. But then, how much breadth of representation have women senators achieved?

Table 11.4 shows the number of women senators on each of the standing committees in the Senate from 1991 to 2001. The entry of the class of 1992 and Kay Bailey Hutchison later in 1993 doubled the number of committees on which a female senator sat from 5 (102nd Congress) to 10 (103rd Congress). By the 105th Congress, women sat on all standing committees, 9 of which had female membership proportionate to their membership in the entire body. In the 107th Congress, 13 standing committees have female membership commensurate to overall female Senate membership.

Since the entry of the 1992 class, a woman's voice has been heard across a much larger portion of the legislative agenda. Such representation has the substantive benefit of representing women in the agenda-setting stage, as well as the possibility of incorporating a female viewpoint into a wide range of issues, even those not traditionally categorized as "women's issues." Substantive representation was potentially further enhanced by the collective membership on "Big Four" committees, roughly approximating the numbers expected given the percentage of women in any particular Congress. Women have been particularly well represented—consistently somewhat higher than their proportion for the entire body—on Appropriations, which is the second highest ranking committee on the Grosewart scale. The institutional power of such committee assignments may have afforded the respective senators some leverage to further women's interests.

Although the number of standing committees having proportionate female membership increased slightly in the 106th Congress, overall breadth of representation decreased. Two committees, Banking and Finance, that formerly had women members were without them. This occurred even though the number of women in the Senate remained steady. The absence of women's voices was most noticeable on the Finance Committee. This was especially problematic because of its status as the most powerful committee in the Senate. According to Senator John Danforth (R-MO), Finance is in a "class by itself" based on its wide jurisdictional reach.[50] Thus, the absence of women from this committee meant that a woman's voice was not heard at the committee level on issues such as Social Security, taxation, trade, and tax-related health care proposals. Of further concern was that no women senators were able to use the institutional power benefit of serving on Finance to achieve other policy or constituency goals.[51]

This situation was rectified in the 107th Congress with the assignment of Olympia Snowe and Blanche Lambert Lincoln to the Finance Committee. Their presence on this committee represents the first time in history that two women have served simultaneously on Finance. In 2001 each party has a woman whose institutional power and prestige is enhanced by her position on Finance, a position that provides leverage beneficial to the attainment of policy or constituency goals. Notably, their position on Finance means that female representation on this committee is commensurate to female representation in the Senate as a whole, despite the seniority disadvantage of female senators. With Banking also gaining a female member, Debbie Stabenow, representational breadth also has been enhanced, reflecting the level of the 105th Congress.

Women serve on a wide variety of committees in the Senate. They are not concentrated in areas associated with women's issues, although they are clearly represented on these committees. The achievement of breadth in committee assignments has substantive implications for representation. Women senators are represented on all major Senate committees, including five on Appropriations and two on Finance, the highest-ranking committees on the Grosewart scale. Such wide representation is a substantive feat, especially from an institutional perspective that understands a senator's effectiveness as influenced by the power he or she holds within the institution. Representational breadth also provides all women senators an opportunity to introduce a female viewpoint into a variety of policy debates, an opportunity only bolstered by the influx of new women and the increasing seniority of those previously elected.

CONCLUSIONS

The commentators and pundits who expected an immediate revolution in the Senate after the elections of 1992 have been somewhat disappointed, since these women have not dramatically transformed the committee system. Some, however, like Feinstein and Murray, have used the existing system along with impetus provided by external shocks to carve out prominent platforms for their work. However, the expectation of an immediate impact may have been too great, given that committee assignments are a function of membership and leadership preferences as well as because of institutional constraints. For membership changes to successfully challenge existing traditions and norms, they must be accompanied by changes in the institutional structure or rules.

After the Hill-Thomas spectacle, many people clearly believed that the Senate needed to diversify its membership. Leaders in the Senate recognized that the public perception of the Senate as an institution had been harmed. After the election in 1992, there was a strong push to reflect the Senate's growing diversification in some committee assignments, most notably to Judiciary and Ethics, and to provide visibility for some of the new women. Now that more women serve in the Senate, the consciousness of a need to provide a prominent role for women entering the Senate seems to have faded.

Nonetheless, a noticeable difference in the Senate is the changed level of representation across its committees. Women now sit on almost all Senate committees and have leadership roles on some subcommittees. As stated previously, 13 of the 16 standing committees in the 107th Congress have female membership commensurate with overall female institutional numbers. Further, three of the "Big Four" committees have proportionate membership and all have at least one female member. As Mansbridge and Karin Tamerius assert, substantive representation is linked to the descriptive presence of women.[52] The institutional power that comes with more prestigious committee assignments further supplements the substantive representation already achieved through the representational breadth found in Senate committees.

However, assignments on "Big Four" committees, though roughly commensurate with the overall number of women, fall slightly below the expected number in every Congress examined in this study, with the exception of the 104th. Further, focusing on proportional institutional power can be misleading, as such power is measured in terms of assignment distribution, therefore neglecting that women are underrepresented in the Senate in the first place. Evidence does not suggest any effort, at least in the more recent Congresses, to give assignment packages to women that may compensate for their lacking numbers in the institution as a whole. Although representation breadth is notable, as is the institutional power of some women senators, no institutional practices have been set into place to compensate for the lacking descriptive presence needed to secure the substantive representation of women. In all but a few cases, the representation of women's interests comes by way of only a few women per committee. Such representation provides the possibility for woman's voice to be heard in the agenda-setting stage, but greater numbers likely are needed to achieve the requisite power to sustain that voice throughout the process.

In conclusion, we should note that other areas of inquiry ought to be explored to see how (or if) the increasing number of women is changing the character of the Senate and its agenda in a way that achieves more substantive representation for women. Further investigation of the legislative impact of these women is clearly warranted. Is the breadth of issues on which these women have been active as wide as the breadth of their committee assignments? In what ways have these women worked together to enhance their voice within the Senate or within their respective parties? These women are a diverse group, themselves distributed across the two political parties. As Kay Bailey Hutchison put it, "I am not philosophically in touch with the women that won in '92. But on some issues we will come together."[53] Assessing the value and distribution of committee assignments is only a first step in evaluating the institutional impact of increasing the number of women in the Senate.

NOTES

Previous versions of this chapter were presented at the Carl Albert Center conference "Women Transforming Congress: Gender Analyses of Institutional Life," University of Oklahoma, Norman, April 2000, and at the annual conference of the American Political Science Association, Washington, D.C., August 2000. The authors would like to thank Rosalee Clawson, Zoe Oxley, and Rebecca Deen for helpful advice as well as David Kimball, Randall Strahan, and Georgia Duerst-Lahti for comments on the manuscript.

1. Nancy Landon Kassebaum (R-KS), Paula Hawkins (R-FL), and Barbara Mikulski (D-MD) were the other female senators elected without previous congressional service by their spouse.

2. Kuntz, "Organization of the New Senate," 3565.

3. Borger and Gest, "Untold Story," 28.

4. Lyric Wallwork Winik, "Crashing the Ultimate Men's Club," *San Francisco Chronicle,* 7 January 1993, p. 8/Z1.

5. Susan Yoachum and Jerry Roberts, "Historic Night for 6 Women Candidates," ibid., p. A:1.

6. Steve Daley, "Sen. Braun Takes Her Oath of Office," ibid.

7. Pitkin, *Concept of Representation.*

8. *Congressional Quarterly Almanac,* 1991, 280.

9. Helen Dewar, "Feinstein and Braun End Male Rule on the Senate Judiciary Committee," *Washington Post*, 7 January 1993, p. A:8.

10. Borger, "Judging Thomas," 32; Borger and Gest, "Untold Story," 28.

11. Idelson, "Wanted: A Few Good Women," 64.

12. Donovan and Kuntz, "House Panels Recarve Turf," 63.

13. Kuntz, "Organization of the New Senate," 3565.

14. C. Lochhead, "Feinstein, Boxer Get Plum Assignments," *San Francisco Chronicle*, 7 January 1993, p. A:3.

15. Moseley-Braun, interview by Laura Arnold, 1 December 1999.

16. Borger and Gest, "Untold Story," 11.

17. Lochhead, "Feinstein, Boxer Get Plum Assignments"; Dewar, "Feinstein and Braun End Male Rule on the Senate Judiciary Committee."

18. Ripley, *Power in the Senate*; Foley, *New Senate*.

19. Arnold, "Distribution of Senate Committee Positions."

20. Sinclair, *Transformation of the U.S. Senate*.

21. Pitkin, *Concept of Representation*; Duerst-Lahti and Verstegen, "Making Something of Absence."

22. Kuntz, "Organization of the New Senate," 3565.

23. Pitkin, *Concept of Representation*.

24. Pitkin, *Concept of Representation*; Duerst-Lahti and Verstegen, "Making Something of Absence."

25. Mansbridge, "Should Blacks Represent Blacks and Women Represent Women?"

26. Ibid. According to Pitkin the idea of interests is necessary to the act of representing.

27. Bratton and Haynie, "Agenda Setting and Legislative Success"; Dodson, "Representing Women's Interests"; Barrett, "Gender and Race in the State House"; Carroll, "Representing Women."

28. Bratton and Haynie, "Agenda Setting and Legislative Success"; Dodson, "Representing Women's Interests"; Dolan and Ford, "Women in State Legislatures"; Thomas, *How Women Legislate*.

29. Tamerius, "Sex, Gender, and Leadership."

30. Smith and Deering, *Committees in Congress*, 1.

31. Sinclair, "Distribution of Committee Positions in the Senate," 277.

32. Hibbing, *Congressional Careers*.

33. Byrd, *Senate 1789–1986*, 651.

34. Senator George McGovern, interview by Laura Arnold, 17 September 1996.

35. Sinclair, "Distribution of Committee Positions in the Senate"; Arnold, "Distribution of Senate Committee Positions."

36. Parris, "Senate Reorganizes Its Committees."

37. Arnold, "Distribution of Senate Committee Positions."

38. Deering and Smith, *Committees in Congress*.

39. There is nothing magical about starting with the 81st Congress. Doing so simply provides a sufficient time line for comparisons within the modern Senate. Committee assignments for the 107th are as reported at the opening and do not include subsequent modifications due to changes in party control.

40. For a fuller discussion on Grosewart scores, see Groseclose and Stewart, "Value of Committee Seats in the House."

41. Glen Bunting, "Feinstein to Join Senate Judiciary Committee," *Los Angeles Times*, 7 January 1993, p. A:3; Idelson, "Wanted: A Few Good Women."

42. Since the value of assignments made to freshmen senators greatly increased after the committee reorganization (see Laura Arnold, forthcoming), we compare CPI scores with those of other first-term and first-year senators since that time only.

43. Boxer's placement on the Appropriations Committee is an interesting tale of state delegation cooperation. When the Republicans took over the Senate in 1995, the number of Democratic slots on Appropriations was reduced. As the most junior member of the committee, Feinstein lost her seat. When an opening occurred in the 105th Congress, Feinstein was eligible to claim it. Rather than do so, Feinstein made a deal with Boxer to allow Boxer to take the Appropriations seat until her reelection. Feinstein and Boxer agreed to trade prestige assignments in the 106th Congress. The arrangement helped shore up Boxer's electoral chances and demonstrates an inordinate amount of cooperation between senators, even those from the same state.

44. McCaffrey, "Hillary Clinton and Charles Schumer Get Committee Assignments," AP wire, 11 January 2001.

45. Terry Ganey, "It's Jean Carnahan vs. John Ashcroft," *St. Louis Post Dispatch*, 31 October 2000, p. A:1.

46. Zell Miller (D-GA) was first elected in 2000, but had been previously appointed to fill a vacancy created by the death of Paul Coverdell. Thus, he is not counted as a new senator.

47. Norton, "Women, It's Not Enough to Be Elected"; Dodson, "Representing Women's Interests."

48. Vega and Firestone, "Effects of Gender."

49. Bratton and Haynie, "Agenda Setting and Legislative Success"; Thomas, "Impact of Women on State Legislative Policies"; Thomas, *How Women Legislate*.

50. Senator John Danforth, interview by Laura Arnold, 27 September 1996.

51. The absence of women on Finance was quite possibly not a conscious decision of the party leadership. Traditionally, service on Finance is earned with accumulated seniority. Junior members are very rarely seated on the committee. Since few women have accumulated much seniority in the Senate, the norm of seniority encumbers their appointment to the position. In fact, until Carol Moseley-Braun cracked open the door in the 104th and 105th Congresses, no woman had served on Finance except Senator Hazel Abel (R-NE), who was appointed to the committee for less than a month in 1954. During an interview with Laura Arnold, Moseley-Braun

asserted that in order to gain the Finance seat, she had to provide the decisive vote in Tom Daschle's bid for Democratic leader. Once she lost her seat in 1998, however, no woman was appointed immediately to replace her.

52. Tamerius, "Sex, Gender, and Leadership"; Mansbridge, "Should Blacks Represent Blacks and Women Represent Women?"

53. *CQ Almanac*, 1993, 8-A.

CHAPTER TWELVE

Transforming Policy from the Inside

Participation in Committee

NOELLE H. NORTON

In the 103rd Congress (1993–94), a group of women in coalition lost their bid to vote on the floor of the House of Representatives for the removal of federal restrictions on Medicaid-funded abortions because of the parliamentary maneuvering by Appropriations Committee Chair William Natcher (D-KY). In contrast, during the 104th Congress (1995–96), Nancy Pelosi (D-CA), the ranking minority member of the Appropriations Committee's subcommittee on Foreign Operations, skillfully used a series of parliamentary procedures and the aid of a coalition of congresswomen to ensure that a subcommittee-designed substitute amendment was offered on the House floor to determine funding for international family planning.[1]

These contrasting examples suggest how strategic participation by women members in committee deliberations and on the floor can alter policy outcomes on legislation important to women. Before 1992, women legislators rarely held the critical institutional positions to make a significant difference in drafting legislation. Although they participated in individual and coalition efforts to sponsor legislation of interest to women, they were underrepresented on key committees and thus did not always have access to the information and resources to participate fully. In this chapter, I present evidence that shows how women legislators are now much more likely than they were in the past to use their seats on committees and subcommittees to participate in making reproductive policy and welfare reform policy—both policies of interest to women. Further, I show that women legislators are now more likely to affect the outcomes of legislation important to women through their increased access to the bicameral conference committees as members of subcommittees with jurisdiction over women's policy issues.

The evidence presented here suggests that women have become strategic actors within the institutional power structure of Congress and can more readily influence policy outcomes on women's issues. Not only are congresswomen realizing increased descriptive representation on committees and subcommittees, as shown by Laura Arnold and Barbara King (this volume), but they can now act on a strong sense of surrogate responsibility as described by Susan Carroll (this volume). In his work on congressional participation, Richard Hall briefly noted that both gender and subcommittee membership have "notable effects" on a Congress member's degree of participation in crafting legislation.[2] We will see how a congresswoman's sex indeed affects her ability to provide substantive representation through increased participation at the early stages of the legislative process.

RESEARCH ON WOMEN LEGISLATORS
AND COMMITTEE POWER

Previous research indicates that women legislators are more interested in working on and voting for legislation concerning women, children, child welfare, and the family than are their male counterparts.[3] Moreover, reproductive rights legislation has been identified as especially important to women legislators.[4] Recent voting studies of the 103rd Congress show that women members were more likely to vote together, regardless of party, on issues that more directly affect women like abortion and women's health,[5] and a report by the Center for American Women and Politics (1995) similarly shows that women members from both parties were involved in supporting women's issues through several steps of the legislative process, including bill sponsorship, collective action, and participation in floor debate.[6] As the numbers of women legislative leaders have increased, research on the connection between representation of women's interests and institutional power has also grown. For example, research on women state legislators in the 1990s shows that women are more likely to serve on prestige committees than they have in the past,[7] and research on women and black state legislators shows that when members of either group serve on a committee with jurisdiction over women's interests they are more likely than their white male colleagues to introduce and work on women's interests.[8]

Still, research on the opportunity for congresswomen to participate as surrogate representatives for women is scarce. Research efforts have naturally been limited because congresswomen have rarely held the institutional positions enabling them to gain access to participate in drafting the legislation important to them. My earlier analysis of reproductive policy crafted between 1969 and 1992 revealed how congresswomen had minimal opportunities to participate because they were rarely assigned to committees with reproductive policy jurisdiction: only one woman sat on each of the key committees; only three women held key subcommittee positions; only four women offered reproductive policy amendments on the floor of the House; and women participated in only 5 out of a sample of 90 conference committees dealing with reproductive policy legislation.[9] The question that motivates this research, then, is whether women members of the U.S. Congress have been able to gain access to the critical positions that permit them to work more on legislation important to women.

In his book *Participation in Congress*, Hall develops and tests a general theory of legislative participation that can help us gain a better understanding of how important committee assignments are for congresswomen. He argues that members must make hard choices on how much of their time, effort, and resources they can commit to any given issue. In a study of a sample of bills considered by three committees in the 97th, 98th, and 103rd Congresses, Hall finds that the coalition building, strategizing, and bargaining necessary to create legislation forces members to limit their participation. Subcommittee and committee membership provide members with informational and resource advantages that allow them to work on the policies they identify as important. Although constituency interests are critical in the decision to seek committee assignment, Hall contends that personal policy interests determine how actively members will participate on an issue once seated on the appropriate committees.[10] Further, Hall finds that the "members and leaders of reporting subcommittees are far more likely to voice their views and take action on them than are other committee members."[11] It is the subcommittee members most interested in a piece of legislation who are willing to pay the information and transaction costs to work on that legislation. Hence, Hall's theory suggests that congresswomen who do not sit on the subcommittees with jurisdiction over women's interests will not be able to pay the costs necessary to participate actively in legislative decision making important to achieving their goals.

Despite recent claims that committee power has eroded in relation to the parent chamber or in relation to the party,[12] Hall develops a strong argument. He notes, however, that the importance of committee position might depend on the salience of the policy issue under consideration. When issues are salient, he surmises, most "members of Congress may well get into the deliberative mix."[13] This possibility requires us to consider whether committee and subcommittee positions are even important for those interested in participating in high-salience policies of interest to women, such as abortion, family planning, and welfare reform. Thus, this chapter starts by examining committee participation on a sample of controversial reproductive policies in order to assess whether these high-salience policies are handled by committee participants or by a larger "deliberative mix."

In the second part of the chapter, I extend the analysis of committee participation to show that there is a strong connection between gender, committee membership, and the representation of women's interests. Here I show that congresswomen have been able to participate actively in making reproductive policy more often than in the past because they are now seated on committees and subcommittees that provide them with important informational and procedural advantages. I conclude by evaluating how congresswomen might be transforming the product of legislation. My evaluation considers whether they are able to change reproductive and welfare reform legislative outcomes from their newfound positions of power. This analysis provides a direct test of women acting for women.

DATA AND METHODOLOGY

In this three-part study, I use a sample of reproductive policy bills and a case study of welfare reform legislation passed in 1996 to analyze how important it is for women Congress members to hold key committee seats. As noted, reproductive and welfare policies have been identified by other scholars as important to women legislators; thus, they provide excellent examples for analysis of the influence women hold over policy that affects the lives of women. Hall's tentative conclusion that subcommittee membership and gender affect the representation of women's interests was made by analyzing a broad range of nongendered bills considered in three committees—Agriculture, Energy and Commerce, and Education and Labor. The use of two policies of interest to women will allow more concrete conclusions.

A sample of reproductive policy legislation considered in the House of Representatives between 1969 and 1998 constitutes the first part of the analysis, where I consider whether committee members held the positions that enabled them to participate in constructing this controversial national policy.[14] Reproductive policies provide a good example of high-salience policy because debates over them have been characterized as the most volatile and emotionally charged that members have faced in Congress. For example, in the debate over the Defense Authorization bill for fiscal year (FY) 1997–98 (H.R. 3230), Pat Schroeder (D-CO) argued that 8 out of 12 hours during committee debate were spent on abortion disputes rather than on defense issues. In her "supplemental views" to the committee report, Schroeder wrote "perhaps we should rename the committee the House committee on morals in the military."[15]

The reproductive policy sample includes 173 bills identified as those containing significant pieces of reproductive policy legislation that originated in the House of Representatives between 1969 and 1998. Bills used in the sample were identified as those containing some form of reproductive policy by *Congressional Quarterly Almanac* (1969–98) and five national-interest groups dedicated to reproductive policy issues.[16] Use of six sources ensures that the sample represents a comprehensive list of reproductive policy legislation given serious consideration on the House floor or by a committee for three decades.[17]

In the second part of the analysis, I evaluate the social demography of committees and subcommittees with jurisdiction over the sample of 173 reproductive policies. The involvement of women legislators in reproductive policy making at subcommittee, committee, floor debate, and conference committee meetings between 1969 and 1992 is compared to the involvement of women committee members between 1993 and 1998. This allows me to determine if women have become increasingly involved in reproductive policy decisions since their numbers in the House increased dramatically in 1992.

In the final part of the analysis, I demonstrate how women use their institutional positions to transform policy outcomes. In the case of reproductive policy, the analysis shows that congresswomen exercised influence most effectively while seated on the bicameral conference committees charged with brokering deals between the House, Senate, and president. The case study of the House and Senate deliberation over the Personal Responsibility and Work Opportunity Reconciliation Act (1996), which includes a step-by-step analysis of the two key welfare reform bills, H.R. 4 (1995) and H.R. 3734 (1996), provides corroborating evidence of the importance of participation by congresswomen in subcommittee and committee markup meetings.

THE LOCUS OF INFLUENCE OVER REPRODUCTIVE POLICY IN THE 1990s

Political practitioners, journalists, and academics alike suspect that controversial policies such as abortion and family planning encourage participation by Congress members on the House floor where visibility is high, in contrast to work in committee where participation is hard to trace.[18] In the case of reproductive policy, the new Republican majority in the 104th Congress appeared to have the opportunity and motivation to shift the locus of policy debate away from committee control and to the floor where it might benefit more of its pro-life conservatives. The Republican party leadership marked abortion and family planning for increased attention as part of its Contract with America, and the GOP had in fact broadened its traditional fight against Medicaid-funded abortions to include opposition to partial-birth abortions and further funding of international family planning programs.[19] Journalists reported that members of the freshman class of the 104th Congress also were much more likely to demand floor votes on these contentious issues than they had in the past.[20] By the 105th Congress, Republican leaders had identified several reproductive policy-related "hot-button GOP riders" that would help provide the congressional party faithful with ways to gain higher profiles.[21] Further, there are examples of the party leadership pulling committee-designed reproductive policy measures from consideration in the 105th Congress. For example, just prior to a Rules Committee meeting to establish the procedure to consider the FY 1997–98 State Department Authorization bill, the Republican leadership replaced the committee-designed bill (H.R. 1486) with a party-designed bill (H.R. 1757). This last-minute juggling allowed a series of restrictive international family planning amendments to be offered on the floor, even though these same amendments were originally rejected by a committee majority during the markup meeting.[22] Although these amendments passed on the House floor, the original committee-designed bill was approved and the floor amendments were discarded by the conference committee. Still, this example demonstrates that the party took an active interest in reproductive policy design.

A closer review of the origins of reproductive policy brings the importance of committee participation back into focus. By identifying the policy origins and the names of the floor activists, I discovered that most reproductive policy from 1969 through 1998 was written by "interested" members who were affiliated with a subcommittee that had jurisdiction over this policy type. In fact, subcommittee activists had more access to reproductive policy legislation in the 103rd, 104th, and 105th Congresses than in past years. From 1969 through 1992, 83.3 percent of all reproductive legislation (i.e., 105 out of 126 bills and amendments) in the House was crafted, amended, or originated in subcommittee and committee meetings and negotiations. Only 11.9 percent of all House reproductive legislation (15 out of 126 bills and amendments) originated on the floor and eventually became law. Between the 103rd and 105th Congresses, however, none of the reproductive policies originated on the House floor. One hundred percent (47 out of 47) of the policies debated between 1993 and 1998 were structured by committees at some point in the legislative process, whether it was in subcommittee markup, committee markup, or in conference committee meetings, which are filled with the original subcommittee members with jurisdiction.[23]

It is important to note that over 27 percent of the successful policies considered between 1993 and 1998 were designed in conference committee negotiations, while in previous years only 11 percent of these policies were influenced by the conference committees. For example, Ernest Istook (R-OK) was successful in attaching an amendment requiring parental consent for family planning services to the FY 1999 Labor, Health, and Human Services Appropriations bill (H.R. 4274); and Chris Smith (R-NJ) was successful in reinstituting Reagan-era restrictions on international family planning funds in the FY 1996 Foreign Operations Appropriations bill (H.R. 1868).

Both of these amendments had been defeated during committee markup and were only attached during the open-floor debate. They were both removed, however, by the conference committee before they could become part of our national reproductive policy legislation.

A close inspection of the names of floor amendment authors further shows that committee members were responsible for a majority of the reproductive policy legislation considered on the House floor. Floor amendments were coded to determine if they were authored by members on the committee or subcommittee with original jurisdiction over the bill, by members on subcommittees with jurisdictions related to reproductive policy, or by rank-and-file members without any committee or subcommittee connection to reproductive policy. This analysis uncovers a decline in rank-and-file or noncommittee amendment attempts. Table 12.1 shows that a decline in "rank-and-file" amending activity started in the 97th Congress (1981–82). By the 103rd through the 105th Congresses, noncommittee members offered only five of all floor amendments, while the rest were authored by members on the committee with original jurisdiction over the bill (56.5 percent of floor amendments) or by members on subcommittees with related jurisdictions (36.3 percent of floor amendments). One of these noncommittee amendments was offered by Connie Morella (R-MD), who wanted to add a "rape and incest" exception to the family-planning restrictions attached to the FY 1996 Foreign Aid Authorization bill (H.R. 1561), while another three were offered by members of the Republican party leadership. Both of these examples show that even the few noncommittee amendments were offered by members who had strong interests in reproductive policy legislation.

Despite this evidence, some legislative scholars might still argue that the source of committee strength over reproductive policy lies with the party leadership. They might suggest that the party majority upholds and protects committee positions on the floor simply out of loyalty to the party majority on committee.[24] Further, they would argue that parties use their committee assignment decisions to control membership and to structure future decisions.[25]

While true in part, these observations should not lead to an underestimation of the importance committee participation holds for those who are motivated to work intensely on a specific policy issue. Leadership dominance clearly cannot explain situations in which the committee and party

TABLE 12.1

Authors of Reproductive Policy Floor Amendments, 93rd–105th Congresses[a]

Congresses	Committee[b]	Related Panel[c]	Rank and File[d]
93rd and 94th (1973–76)	8.3% (1)	58.3% (7)	33.3% (4)
95th and 96th (1977–80)	45.0% (18)	20.0% (8)	35.0% (14)
97th and 98th (1981–84)	35.7% (5)	14.3% (2)	50.0% (7)
99th and 100th (1985–88)	57.9% (11)	15.8% (3)	26.3% (5)
101st and 102nd (1989–92)	55.6% (15)	37.0% (10)	7.4% (2)
103rd–105th (1993–98)	56.5% (39)	36.3% (25)	7.2% (5)

NOTE: Number of amendments in parentheses (N = 181.) No amendments were made on policies passed between 1969 and 1973.

a The authors of reproductive policy amendments are identified by type for Congresses displayed in four- and five-year increments.

b Includes amendments made by standing committee members.

c Includes amendments made by members of subcommittees with related reproductive policy jurisdiction.

d Includes actions by noncommittee members and members without reproductive policy jurisdiction on another committee.

SOURCE: *Congressional Record*, 1969–98.

leadership differ and the committee ultimately wins. In two instances where the Republican party leadership exerted external control over committee reproductive policy decisions, the committee position was passed into law. For example, the international family planning struggle, FY 1997–98 State Department Authorization cited earlier, was concluded in favor of the committee. Though the party-authored bill prevailed on the House floor, the committee-designed bill was reinstated during the conference committee deliberations and the provision allowing continued support for the United Nations Family Planning Agency was approved.[26] Similarly, during House floor consideration of the FY 1999 Treasury, Postal Service, and General Government Appropriations bill (H.R. 4104), the Republican leadership refused to support a committee-approved provision requiring health plans to cover contraceptives for federal employees. Even when the contraceptive provision was supported during floor debate by a majority of House members, the GOP leadership instructed the conference committee to remove the provision from the final measure. In the end, the conference committee, filled with members of the subcommittee who supported the requirement to cover contraceptives, insisted on including that coverage in the final bill.[27]

In summary, consideration of influence over reproductive policy must take into account the continuing importance of committees with jurisdiction. Floor debate is a far less important locus of activity, and party leadership influence clearly does not always trump committees with jurisdiction. Committee membership is important for those interested in influencing policy important to women.

WOMEN IN COMMITTEE AND SUBCOMMITTEE

Prior to the 103rd Congress, congresswomen rarely held committee positions with reproductive policy jurisdiction. They expressed their commitment to reproductive policy legislation through passionate floor debates, the sponsorship of legislation, and participation in coalitional efforts coordinated with the bipartisan Congressional Caucus for Women's Issues. By the 103rd Congress, however, the numbers of women sitting on the committees with reproductive policy jurisdiction had sharply increased.

The election of more women to Congress in 1992 along with the increased seniority of veteran congresswomen led to the assignment and promotion of many more women on important committees. At the end of the 104th Congress, congresswomen feared that the impending retirement of several senior women would jeopardize recent gains of institutional and procedural power. The announcement of the first five retirees in 1995 included Barbara Vucanovich (R-NV), the first female Appropriations subcommittee chair in 26 years, Pat Schroeder, the second-ranking Democrat on the Judiciary Committee, and Cardiss Collins (D-IL), the ranking member on the Government Reform and Oversight Committee. At the announcement of even more departures among the ranks of senior members, Connie Morella and Barbara Vucanovich both called for bipartisan meetings with the Republican leadership to request that more women be placed on top committees in the 105th Congress. At the time, Schroeder was quoted as saying "others will now have to try to hold up the sky for us."[28]

Congresswomen are clearly aware that committee assignment and committee leadership roles significantly enhance their ability to participate on a given policy. In the interviews conducted by the Center for American Women and Politics (CAWP) during the 103rd and 104th Congresses, a majority of the congresswomen mentioned that committee work was a central feature of their congressional life.[29] Responding to a question about the difference the increased presence of women in Congress made, Nancy Johnson (R-CT) said, "Frankly, it isn't the increased presence of women, it's the increased number of women in power."[30] Similarly, Marcy Kaptur (D-OH) contends that her committee position allowed her to participate as an active player:

> You can decide to be an inside player or an outside player. And, depending on what you choose, it governs how you behave. I'm an inside player in the sense I'm on Appropriations, which took me four tries and I finally made it and I'm now the senior Democratic woman on Appropriations. I'm very proud of that. I had to fight every step of the way to get it. I had no godfather, I had no rich uncle, I had nobody and I'm not 62 years old. I got there at a young enough age.[31]

In an effort to keep more women playing the game at the top levels, Barbara Kennelly (D-CT) says she traded everything she had to get Karen Thurman (D-FL) on the Ways and Means Committee in the 104th Congress.[32]

Assignments on top committees are important placements for those interested in working closely on reproductive policies because these policies are typically handled by the Appropriations, Commerce, International Relations, and Judiciary Committees. When Morella's, Vucanovich's, and Kennelly's requests to place women on "top" committees were honored, the number of women dealing with reproductive policy increased. Table 12.2 outlines the number of reproductive policies in the jurisdiction of these committees, the average number of committee members, and the number of women committee members for the Congresses between 1969 and 1992 and between 1993 and 1998, respectively. The data show that the number of women members sitting on committees with reproductive policy jurisdiction has increased from an average of one woman per committee to an average of four women per committee. By the 105th Congress, there were at least three women sitting on every committee with reproductive policy jurisdiction and as many as six women sat on the Appropriations Committee, which makes decisions about funding for Medicaid abortions, contraceptives, and domestic and international family planning.

As women gained seats on committees with reproductive policy jurisdiction, they also gained seats on like subcommittees. Before the 103rd

TABLE 12.2

Committee Jurisdiction over Reproductive Policies, 1969–1998

| Committee | % Reproductive Policy Under Jurisdiction | | Average # on Committee[a] | Average # of Women, 91st–102nd[b] | Average # on Committee | Average # of Women, 103rd–105th |
	1969–92	1993–98	1969–92	1969–92	1993–98	1993–98
Appropriations	49.2 (62)	59.6 (28)	56	2.1 (3.7%)	60	5.0 (8.3%)
Commerce	23.0 (29)	4.3 (3)	42	1.1 (2.6%)	42	4.5 (10.7%)
Judiciary	10.3 (13)	12.8 (6)	33	1.3 (3.9%)	35	3.5 (10.0%)
Education and the Work Force	7.1 (9)	4.3 (2)	34	1.2 (3.5%)	43	4.5 (10.5%)
National Security and International Relations	6.3 (8)	14.9 (7)	50	1.0 (2.0%)	54	3.5 (6.5%)
Government Operations[c]	4.0 (5)	0.0 (0)				
Ways and Means	0.0 (0)	2.1 (1)				

NOTE: Number of policies in parentheses. (N = 173).

a Average number of committee members only recorded for 4 committees with most important reproductive policy jurisdiction.

b Average number of women sitting on each committee, only recorded for the 5 committees with most important reproductive policy jurisdiction. In parentheses is the percentage of women legislators sitting on each of the 4 committees.

c Government Operations had jurisdiction over Nixon's National Commission on Population Growth; Ways and Means had jurisdiction over welfare reform.

SOURCE: *Congressional Quarterly Almanac, 1969–98; Congressional Quarterly Weekly Report, 1995, 1996, 1997; CQ Weekly, 1997, 1998; Congressional Record, 1969–98.*

Congress, only three women had been assigned to subcommittees with specific reproductive policy jurisdiction. Subcommittee membership confers valuable procedural advantages to those motivated enough to want to participate on a piece of legislation through all steps of the legislative process.[33] This meant that the opportunities granted to subcommittee members such as managing a reproductive policy bill on the House floor, participation in the design of the restrictive floor rules, speaking and offering amendments on the House floor first, and sitting on the conference committees have rarely been available to congresswomen.

In the 104th Congress, however, congresswomen sat on 11 out of the 12 subcommittees with specific reproductive policy jurisdiction between 1995 and 1996; and by the 105th Congress congresswomen sat on all but one of the eight subcommittees with jurisdiction between 1997 and 1998. Moreover, women have slowly started to gain some seniority on these subcommittees. In the 105th Congress, Nancy Pelosi served as the ranking minority member on the Appropriation's subcommittee on Foreign Operations, giving her the opportunity to manage all of the debates about international family planning for the Democrats on the House floor between 1997 and 1998; and Marcy Kaptur (D-OH) served as the ranking minority member on the Appropriation's subcommittee on Agriculture, Rural Development, FDA, and Related Agencies, giving her the opportunity to manage debate over RU-486 research in 1998. In her CAWP interview during the 103rd Congress, Pelosi describes her assignment to another subcommittee with jurisdiction over appropriations for reproductive policy as her most important legislative accomplishment: "Well, first of all, I consider my service on the Appropriations Committee and the Labor, Health and Human Services subcommittee as sort of the heartbeat of my activity in Congress, and the center and focus, because it's the basic priorities of our country, jobs, health, human services, and education."[34] In the same interview, Pelosi notes that the presence of other women on the subcommittee makes a "formidable phalanx" when dealing with reproductive policy.

We cannot assume that the numbers of women who actively participate in reproductive policy making at all steps of the legislative process increase simply because the numbers of women with reproductive policy committee and subcommittee assignments increased. Although subcommittee members hold a central place in a policy network, Hall found that only about 50 percent of the members on the reporting subcommittee were active players on a given bill for each of the three committees he studied.[35] He indicates that the intensity subcommittee members reveal for an issue is a function of their policy interests, reelection goals, group identification, and subcommittee leadership roles. In other words, even subcommittee members choose to participate in designing the few policies for which they have interest, time, and resources.

Table 12.3 shows that congresswomen revealed their intense interest in reproductive policy by actively participating in subcommittee markup, committee markup, floor amending, and conference committee deliberation on more reproductive policy legislation than they had prior to the 103rd Congress. The first and second rows of table 12.3 compare the numbers of reproductive policy bills on which congresswomen were actively involved at the subcommittee and committee levels before and after the 103rd Congress. A reproductive policy was counted as having active congresswomen present if one or more women participated beyond showing up for meetings and voting for amendments. If a congresswoman was present at the subcommittee or committee markup meeting, but inactive, the bill was not counted as having active women present. Only bills where women actively participated in debate or offered amendments during the markup meetings were counted as bills with active women participants. The data on table 12.3 show that it was rare to have active women participants on reproductive legislation in subcommittee and committee markups prior to the 103rd Congress. This means that women were rarely debating or amending these policies from their seats inside the committee or subcommittee. Between the 103rd and 105th Congresses women were not only present in greater numbers, but they were actively involved in debating and amending reproductive policy in 49 percent (23 out of 47) of the subcommittee meetings and in 70 percent (33 out of 47) of the committee meetings.

The third row in table 12.3 shows that women lawmakers were also more actively involved in crafting reproductive policy on the House floor during the 103rd to the 105th Congresses. Forty-four percent (20 out of 46) of the reproductive policy bills considered between 1993 and 1998 included debates on amendments written and offered by women. Prior to 1993 only 4 percent (4 out of 104) of the reproductive policy bills considered on the House floor included debates on woman-authored amendments. More important, however, is that most of the amendments offered after 1993 were authored by women who were using their prerogatives as committee

TABLE 12.3

Percentage of Reproductive Policy Legislation with Active Women Participants, at Four Steps of the Legislative Process, before and after the 103rd Congress

BILLS AT STEPS IN LEGISLATIVE PROCESS	90TH–102ND CONGRESSES (1969–92) % OF BILLS ♀ ACTIVE PARTICIPANTS	103RD–105TH CONGRESSES (1993–98) % OF BILLS ♀ ACTIVE PARTICIPANTS
1. Subcommittee markup	4.8 (6/126)[a]	48.9 (23/47)
2. Committee markup	6.3 (8/126)	70.2 (33/47)
3. Floor amending	3.8 (4/104)	43.5 (20/46)
4. Conference committee	5.5 (5/90)	83.7 (31/37)

NOTES: ♀ = Women.

    a The number in parentheses indicates the number of reproductive policies on which congresswomen were active participants over the total number of bills in the sample at each step of the legislative process (n of bills with women participating/total N in the sample). There are 126 bills in the 1969–92 portion of the sample; 104 of those bills were debated on the House floor; 90 had conference committees. There are 47 bills in the 1993–98 portion of the sample; 45 of those bills were debated on the House floor; 37 had conference committees.

SOURCES: *Congressional Record* 1969–98; *Congressional Quarterly Almanac,* 1969–98; *Congressional Quarterly Weekly Report,* 1995, 1996, 1997; *CQ Weekly* 1997, 1998; Committee Meeting Minutes from Appropriations, Commerce, Judiciary, and Economic and Educational Opportunities Committees, 1975–96; Rules Committee Reports 1969–98; Conference Committee Reports, 1973–98.

members with reproductive policy jurisdiction. Sixty-five percent of these woman-authored amendments were made by congresswomen with committee and subcommittee assignments with reproductive policy jurisdiction over the bill under consideration; another 35 percent were offered by women with assignments to related subcommittees with reproductive policy jurisdiction; and only one of these amendments was offered by a noncommittee woman. In fact, a small group of highly motivated women activists on key subcommittees offered a majority of all reproductive-policy amendments offered. Rosa DeLauro (D-CT), Nita Lowey (D-NY), Eleanor Holmes Norton (D-DC), and Pat Schroeder offered 65 percent of all amendments that were offered by women between the 103rd and 105th Congresses.

Finally, the fourth row on table 12.3 shows the number of the conference committee negotiations on reproductive policy that included one or more women conferees. Out of the 90 conferences held on 126 bills considered between 1969 and 1992, women were included in only 5.5 percent. However, by the 103rd Congress, women were sitting on almost all of the conference committees that dealt with reproductive policy issues. Out of the 31 conferences held on 37 bills considered between 1993 and 1998, women were included in 84 percent. Several of the conference committees held after the 103rd Congress actually included three or more women. For example, reproductive policy issues on the Defense Authorization bill in 1996 (H.R. 3230) and 1998 (H.R. 3616) had five women conferees at work; and the FY 1996, FY 1997, and FY 1998 Labor, Health and Human Services Appropriations bills (H.R. 3019, H.R. 3755, and H.R. 2264) had six women conferees at work.

Table 12.3 does not identify individual participation rates or distinguish between the participation rates of conservative and liberal congresswomen, which leads to questions about the ideological emphasis of the activists for each bill. A review of the committee assignments for conservative women shows that they rarely held seats on committees with jurisdiction over reproductive policy. For example, in the 104th Congress only two Republican women held seats on committees handling this issue, and only one of these two played an active role as a participant on a subcommittee. Jan Meyers (R-KS) held a seat on the International Relations subcommittee that considers international family planning legislation, and she typically supported increased reproductive rights. In her interview with CAWP, Meyers reports that she used her subcommittee position on International Operations and Human Rights to consistently oppose cutbacks in international family planning. By the 105th Congress, two more conservative women had been assigned to key subcommittees, but there is no evidence that they were active participants in drafting reproductive policy. Anne Northup (R-KY), a pro-life advocate, held a subcommittee seat on the Appropriation's Labor, Health and Human Services subcommittee. But, the reproductive policy activists on that panel were three Democratic women—Rosa DeLauro, Nita Lowey, and Nancy Pelosi. Further, Ileana Ros-Lehtinen (R-FL), who moved to the International Operations and Human Rights subcommittee in the 105th Congress, told CAWP that she was strongly pro-life, but "because of time restrictions and other issues" she did not become actively involved in this issue.[36]

On the whole, the committee assignment data and CAWP interviews suggest that Republican congresswomen fall into two distinct categories when dealing with reproductive policy: moderate activists and conservative non-activists. The moderates tend to be active proponents of reproductive rights, while the conservatives generally chose to limit their pro-life activity to voting and minor support roles. Moderate Republicans like Connie Morella, Olympia Snowe (R-ME), and Jan Meyers actively participated as members of key subcommittees, whereas more conservative women like Helen Chenoweth (R-WY), Jennifer Dunn (R-WA), and Barbara Vucanovich indicate that they were more interested in spending time on other issues. In her CAWP interview, Dunn summarizes the sentiment of the conservative nonactivists: "It is not a primary issue for me, and if I were to list for you the top ten issues of importance for me, that would probably be right around number ten."[37] Hence, the evidence indicates that reproductive policy activists were both Republican and Democratic congresswomen who were interested enough to participate through committees to design this policy.

In summary, subcommittee assignments have allowed women interested in reproductive policy to participate in the legislative process at a stage that was previously unavailable to them. In addition to sponsorship and voting, congresswomen now have the ability to write a policy in subcommittee, amend a policy at a full committee meeting, manage a bill on the floor as a key member of the subcommittee, offer amendments on the floor without facing a series of restrictive amending rules designed to benefit committee members, and exercise influence inside conference committees.

FROM OPPORTUNITY TO INFLUENCE IN COMMITTEE

The increased numbers of women in Congress and on the committees and subcommittees improve the chances for influencing policy outcomes. But assignment to a committee and active participation does not always guarantee influence over policy outcomes. Those who study gendered communication in legislative organizations note that women legislators can have difficulty adjusting to the institutional norms and procedures expected in a traditionally male-dominated legislative institution.[38] In fact, success on a committee or subcommittee may be elusive for women legislators because of gendered communication patterns and differences in the leadership styles found acceptable for men and women.[39]

In spite of these disadvantages, women legislators have been able to use their newfound positions as subcommittee and committee members to transform opportunity into influence over gender-related policy outcomes. In this final section, I will show how women were able to influence specific reproductive policy between the 103rd and 105th Congresses as members of the bicameral conference committees and how women inside subcommittee and committee markup meetings influenced gender-related welfare reform policy.

Reproductive Policy

An inspection of the success and failure rates of the reproductive policy legislation reveals that there is a correlation between the number of women committee participants and the likelihood that these women will succeed in achieving their legislative goals. The 37 reproductive policies that made it to a conference committee and were passed into law between the 103rd and 105th Congresses were used for this part of the analysis. Reproductive policy outcomes that were fully supported by a majority of women on the committee of jurisdiction were counted as successes; outcomes that included some, but not all, of the positions supported by a majority of women on the committee were counted as partial successes; and outcomes that were not supported by a majority of the women on the committee were counted as failures. This measure of success avoids an implied preference for one ideological position by using the position supported by a majority of committee women, both Democratic and Republican.

Analysis of the data indicates no correlation between the number of bills with active women participants on committees and subcommittees or between the number of floor amendments offered by women and their likelihood of success. However, there is a strong correlation between the number of bills with women on the conference committee and the likelihood of success. When women held two or fewer seats on the conference committee, the position supported by committee women was likely to fail. Sixty-one percent of the conferences with two or fewer women could be counted as reproductive policy failures for women committee members. On the other hand, when women held three or more seats on the conference committee, 72 percent could be counted as partial or complete successes for committee women. There is one notable exception to this explanation for gender-related success. When Henry Hyde (R-IL) and/or Chris Smith, two avid pro-life congressional leaders, were also sitting on the conference committee, the number of women on the conference committee no longer served as a predictor for policy success rates. When either Hyde or Smith sat on a conference committee dealing with reproductive policy, women committee members lost 60 percent of the time regardless of how many women were assigned to the conference committee. The presence of highly motivated pro-life policy activists like Hyde and Smith, who both held committee and subcommittee leadership positions, may have worked as a counterforce to the increased number of women conferees. Hyde and Smith have both accrued the resources and are willing to invest their time in these kinds of issues. Further, both come from Catholic districts and receive 100 percent voting scores from the National Right to Life Committee; both have sought and won assignment to subcommittees with jurisdiction over these policies; and both have ascended to key committee and subcommittee leadership positions in more than two decades of House service. In fact, both of these men are significantly more active within a reproductive policy inner circle than are their Republican women colleagues.

Examples of how the increased numbers of women in conference committee appear to have contributed to changes in reproductive policy outcomes explain the observed relationship. First, an amendment by Smith to cut or severely restrict funding on the annual international family planning funds included in the Foreign Operations Appropriations bills has passed on the House floor since 1995. Smith, however, is not on the Appropriations Committee and was not invited to sit in as a conferee in 1996 or 1997. Instead, four women were asked to join the conference committee as representatives of their subcommittees. Nancy Pelosi and Nita Lowey, from the House, and Patty Murray (D-WA) and Barbara Mikulski (D-MD), from the Senate, worked with the rest of the conferees to successfully remove the Smith amendments from both of these Appropriations bills (H.R. 3540, 1996; H.R. 2159, 1997). Similarly, six women sat on the 1995 and 1997 Labor, Health and Human Service Appropriations conference committees (H.R. 3019, 1995; H.R. 2264, 1997). Although an Istook (R-OK) amendment in 1995 to remove the "rape and incest" exception for Medicaid-funded abortions and another amendment in 1996 to require parental notification for use of family planning services successfully passed on the House floor, they were removed by the conference committee before final passage of these bills.

One might argue that the relationship between the number of women on a conference committee and the success of women's policy positions is spurious and that women do not transform legislation through positions as conferees. The efforts of the Senate negotiators and the president could be more significant influences on reproductive policy success or failure than the numbers of women in conference. Several academic studies, however, indicate the hypothesis about women in conference should be investigated further. For example, several legislative scholars contend that conference committees and motivated committee members are the foundation of committee power.[40] In addition, several gender scholars report that women are more likely to influence the decision-making process when their numbers increase over a certain threshold[41] and when they are especially interested in gender-related policy outcomes.[42] Taken together, both avenues of research suggest that conference committee seats are important positions for congresswomen to seek if they are interested in transforming legislation.

Welfare Reform

The case of welfare reform further illustrates how congresswomen can make a difference from inside committee rooms. Welfare reform (H.R. 4) was first introduced in the House by Clay Shaw (R-FL), chair of the Ways and Means subcommittee on Health. As originally designed, H.R. 4 would give states more control over welfare, restrain federal spending, and curtail welfare eligibility by imposing work requirements. The bill also would have denied benefits to teenage mothers and required a "family-cap" limiting the number of children covered. As originally introduced, the bill included no provisions for funding child care programs and child support enforcement.

Although generally supportive of welfare reform, both Republican and Democratic women began to modify this initial reform proposal in subcommittee and committee meetings to include provisions that might aid female welfare recipients. For example, in the Ways and Means subcommittee on Health, Barbara Kennelly offered four amendments that would improve child care funding, enforce child support, and limit paternity-reporting requirements. Although none of her amendments were accepted by the subcommittee, these same proposals were offered by Republican women during the full committee meeting and were adopted in part.

In the Ways and Means Committee markup meetings, three female committee members offered 33 percent of all amendments. Although the amendments offered by the Democratic women failed, Republican committeewomen were quick to reword the amendments designed to aid women welfare recipients. For example, Kennelly again attempted to cut the paternity-reporting requirement as she had in the subcommittee. Her concern was for women who might be abused if paternity was established or who simply might not be able to comply with the requirements. Her amendment failed, but Nancy Johnson and Jennifer Dunn offered an alternative proposal that would stop women from being penalized if they were able to establish paternity at some point in the future.[43] Johnson also worked to increase funding for child welfare. She offered an amendment that would guarantee funding at 1994 levels for child welfare that was accepted by the committee. Although these alterations did not substantially change the basic reform proposal, it shows that women committee members were willing to work together to aid women recipients.

Not only did women legislators in the House work together to make subtle changes, but they counted on collaboration with women on key committees in the Senate. During the House Ways and Means committee meetings, Kennelly and Johnson supported an amendment that would have required states to make child care available. Although this amendment failed, Johnson and Kennelly knew that Nancy Landon Kassebaum (R-KS), chair of the Senate Labor and Human Resources Committee, would support a similar proposal.[44]

Senate committees are not as critical for agenda setting as are House committees.[45] Nevertheless, women senators did hold key committee positions during the welfare reform design and were able in some instances to make a difference. Barbara Mikulski and Carol Moseley-Braun (D-IL) both held seats on the Finance Committee that handled eligibility and work requirements, while Kassebaum, as chair of the Labor and Human Resources Committee, handled child care and job training. The bill that emerged from the Senate Finance Committee was not significantly different from the bill passed by the House.[46] However, Kassebaum's committee significantly improved the child care funding by reauthorizing the Child Care and Development Block Grant of 1990 rather than collapsing this program into the welfare reform package.[47]

Women inside the House and Senate committees carried out the commitment of Republican and Democratic women to child care and child support enforcement. These women were able to modify the bill before the full

House and Senate vote. When the bill was heard on the House and Senate floors, women committee members offered a total of eight gender-related amendments that successfully passed in both houses. By the time the bill reached the conference committee, the family-cap and restriction of benefits to teenage mothers had been removed; while funding for child care and child support had been added by congresswomen with welfare reform committee jurisdictions. The five women who sat on the final conference committee succeeded in ensuring these provisions were not dropped from the conference committee report. Although President Clinton vetoed H.R. 4, the welfare reform package that eventually passed (H.R. 3734) in 1996 still included all of the provisions supplied by the perseverance of a handful of women from their committee positions.

CONCLUSION

Critics of our national reproductive and welfare policies would argue that there has been no real transformation in the kind of gender-related policy produced in Congress since women began to participate in their design. Reproductive policy in the U.S. Congress remains fragmented in several committee jurisdictions and narrowly focused on abortion, unlike similar policy in other Western democratic nations. Additionally, feminist scholars have argued that congresswomen have not done enough to ensure that national welfare reform policy adequately addresses the long-term effects of reform on women or on motherhood.[48]

Nevertheless, the evidence presented here suggests that the increased number of women participating on key subcommittees and committees enhances their ability to influence reproductive policy. Further, the analysis of welfare reform demonstrates how the congresswomen working in coalition from inside House and Senate committees and subcommittees altered welfare reform provisions. Given the small numbers of women in Congress, their recent appointment to important committees, and the absence of committee leadership positions for women, it is notable that congresswomen were able to transform both reproductive and welfare policies to the extent that they did in the 104th and 105th Congresses.

The steady increase in the numbers of women representing reproductive and welfare policy interests, however, has not been sustained through the 107th Congress. Although there are more congresswomen on House committees and subcommittees than ever before, there has been little change in the numbers of women representing women on these issues. In the 107th Congress, 17 of all House subcommittees have more than 20 percent female membership, including two Appropriations subcommittees dealing with funding for Medicaid abortions and international family planning. But the other 12 subcommittees that might handle reproductive and welfare policy have less than 15 percent female membership. Moreover, there appear to be fewer female reproductive policy activists on the subcommittees with jurisdiction. For example, the Judiciary's subcommittee on the Constitution, which deals with the constitutionality of abortion and abortion restrictions, has lost activists like Pat Schroeder and Maxine Waters (D-CA). Only one woman freshman, conservative nonactivist woman Melissa Hart (R-PA), sits on the Constitution subcommittee. Further, the International Relations Committee, which authorizes international family planning legislation, is now led by two activist male members—Hyde and Smith—while the moderate activist Jan Meyers has retired.

If congresswomen perceive themselves as surrogate representatives for women and intend to work on legislation of interest to women, they must continue to find ways to enhance participation at all steps of the legislative process. Regardless of policy preference, congresswomen must seek assignment to panels that provide them with the information and resources to actually participate in representing women beyond the bounds of their district.

NOTES

1. See "Abortion Funding Rebuff Shows House Divided," *Congressional Quarterly Weekly Report* 51 (3 July 1993): 1735; and "Special Report: International Family Planning," *Congressional Quarterly Weekly Report* 55 (20 December 1997): 3116.

2. See Hall, *Participation in Congress*, 209.

3. See Barrett, "Policy Priorities of African American Women"; Dodson, *Gender and Policymaking*; Saint-Germain, "Does Their Difference Make a Difference?"; Thomas, *How Women Legislate*.

4. See Berkman and O'Connor, "Do Women Legislators Matter?"; Thomas and Welch, "Impact of Gender"; Thomas, *How Women Legislate*.

5. See J. Dolan, "Support for Women's Interests"; Swers, "Are Women More Likely to Vote for Women's Issue Bills?"

6. Dodson et al., *Voices, Views, and Votes*.

7. Dolan and Ford, "Change and Continuity among Women."

8. Bratton and Haynie, "Agenda Setting and Legislative Success."

9. Norton, "Women, It's Not Enough to be Elected," 124–28.

10. Also see Fenno, *Congressmen in Committees*. Hall develops Fenno's argument that representatives are alike neither in the interests they adopt nor in the issues on which they choose to spend time.

11. Hall, *Participation in Congress*, 174.

12. See Krehbiel, "Why Are Congressional Committees Powerful?"; Krehbiel, *Information and Legislative Organization*; Cox and McCubbins, *Legislative Leviathan*; and Kiewiet and McCubbins, *Logic of Delegation*.

13. Hall, *Participation in Congress*, 252; and Hall and Grofman, "Committee Assignment Process."

14. See Norton, "Analyzing Roll-Call Voting Tools," for analysis of the controversy over reproductive policy.

15. See H.R. 104–563, "Supplemental Views of Pat Schroeder."

16. Interest groups include National Abortion Action Rights League, National Right to Life Committee, National Women's Political Caucus, National Organization for Women, and Planned Parenthood Federation of America.

17. Approximately 70 percent of the reproductive policies in this sample were considered as riders or amendments to other legislation and 30 percent as full bills, like family planning authorization bills and late-term abortion bills.

18. See Bach and Smith, *Managing Uncertainty in the House*; Davidson, "Procedures and Politics in Congress"; Norton, "Committee Influence over Controversial Policy"; and Steiner, *Futility of Family Policy*.

19. Langdon, "Debate Shifted from Roe."

20. Koszczuk, "House G.O.P. Freshmen Soften Their Edges."

21. Taylor, "Hot Button GOP Riders."

22. Doherty, "GOP Leaders Scuttle Bipartisan Bill Nod."

23. For details on the method used to code reproductive policy origins, see Norton, "Committee Influence over Controversial Policy."

24. Maltzman, "Maintaining Congressional Committees."

25. Cox and McCubbins, *Legislative Leviathan*; Peterson and Wrighton, "Continuing Puzzle of Committee Outliers."

26. See "Issue: State Department Authorization," *CQ Weekly* 56: 3128.

27. See "Issue: Treasury, Postal," *CQ Weekly* 56: 3089.

28. K. Foerstel, "Number of Female Departures," 3760.

29. The interviews with women who served in the 103rd and 104th Congresses were conducted by Center for American Women and Politics (CAWP). The interviewing method is described by Sue Carroll, this volume.

30. Nancy Johnson, CAWP interview, 3 December 1997.

31. Marcy Kaptur, CAWP interview, 19 July 1995.

32. Barbara Kennelly presentation at the "Women Transforming Congress" conference, Norman, Okla., 14 April 2000.

33. Hall, *Participation in Congress*; Hall and Evans, "Power of Subcommittees."

34. Nancy Pelosi, CAWP interview, 19 September 1995.

35. Hall, *Participation in Congress*, 119.

36. Ileana Ros-Lehtinen, CAWP interview, 18 July 1995.

37. Jennifer Dunn, CAWP interview, 15 June 1998.

38. C. Rosenthal, *When Women Lead*.

39. Kathlene, "Power and Influence in State Legislative Policymaking."

40. Hall, *Participation in Congress*; Shepsle and Weingast, "Institutional Foundations"; Shepsle and Weingast, "Why Are Congressional Committees Powerful?"

41. See Kanter, *Men and Women of the Corporation*, and Saint-Germain, "Does Their Difference Make a Difference?"

42. Berkman and O'Connor, "Do Women Legislators Matter?"

43. Katz and Rubin, "House Panel Poised to Approve GOP Welfare Overhaul Bill."

44. Ibid., 690.

45. See Deering and Smith, *Committees in Congress*; Binder and Smith, *Politics or Principle*; Sinclair, *Transformation of the U.S. Senate*.

46. Katz, "House Passes Welfare Bill."

47. Freedman, "With Child Care Bill."

48. See Borris, "When Work Is Slavery."

CHAPTER THIRTEEN

INVISIBLE POWER

*Congressional Staff and Representation
behind the Scenes*

CINDY SIMON ROSENTHAL AND
LAUREN COHEN BELL

B oth praised and criticized in her role as chief of staff for Senate majority leader Robert Dole, Sheila Burke was something of a rarity during her 17-year congressional staff career—a very powerful woman
staffer. Burke's combination of policy knowledge and Senate procedure was
augmented by Dole's unquestioned trust in her. According to one account,
"her ability to speak for him is the mainstay of her power."[1] During most
of her professional life, gender was never an issue to Burke, but in 1994 and
1995 she found herself the target of right-wing activists who vilified her as
"Hillary Lite," a proponent of militant feminism, and as a "feminist Sven-
gali" who manipulated her old-fashioned boss.[2] Her critics were offended
not only by her moderate policy positions and pro-choice views, but also
her influence as a woman and a powerful staffer. Criticism of Burke's rapport and influence with Senator Dole illuminates the discomfort some feel
about the increasing presence of professional women in the workforce and
the behind-the-scenes role of faceless unelected congressional staff.

Congress has become a "representative bureaucracy" in which staffers
play crucially important roles that are hard to neglect. To date, however,
most legislative explorations of representation have assumed the relationship between the representative and the represented to be unmediated and
have attached little importance to staff contributions.[3] It is certain that few

American founders imagined a legislature where staffers outnumber their elected overseers by margins of 45 to 1.[4] But the reality of the modern institutionalized legislature includes legions of staffers. Some achieve powerful policy roles and professional leadership stature, like Burke, while others handle day-to-day operations of the legislature, engaging in routine acts of representation such as contact with interest groups, citizens, the media, and the executive branch. The advent of women in these positions leads us to ask how congressional staff power and gender intersect.

In this chapter, we examine the extent to which congressional committee staffs reflect the demographic composition of society and identify the institutional determinants that predict female employment levels. In the second half of our analysis, we explore and elaborate on the connection between passive and active representation. Has an increased presence of female congressional staffers contributed significantly to policy favorable to women? Does the position of professional women on congressional committee staff enhance representation of women in Congress? Our analysis seeks to answer these questions by identifying the different committee staff dynamics that can transform passive roles into active representation.[5]

GENDER, REPRESENTATION, AND CONGRESSIONAL STAFF

Scholars Robert Salisbury and Kenneth Shepsle treat congressional staff and each member as a single unit of analysis, one of 535 autonomous "enterprises" in Congress.[6] Numbers alone argue for considering the more than 24,000 congressional staffers as part of the demography of the representative body. There is little that members do in the modern legislature that is not impacted by their staffs.[7] Staffers serve as extensions of the members, and in many ways "walk in the shadows" of representatives and senators.[8]

The dimensions of gender representation are particularly important in the case of the U.S. Congress. Female members of Congress—13 in the Senate and 60 in the House—constitute just 13.6 percent of the 107th Congress's 535 voting members. The proportion of women is greater among powerful and influential congressional staffers than among Congress members. In 1998, women made up 24.5 percent of the congressional staffers who earned $100,000 or more.[9] In 1999, the Capitol Hill newspaper Roll Call named 10 women (20 percent) among its "fabulous 50 staffers" who derive their power from "access, expertise or clout."[10] According to the 1999 *Congressional Staff Directory,* 11 women direct the majority or minority staffs of the 35 standing committees (15.7 percent of top committee posts), and 50 women head subcommittee staffs (21.6 percent of the subcommittees that clearly identify majority and minority staff directors).[11] At present 153 women serve as chiefs of staff in members' offices (28.6 percent).

Women staffers who work on Capitol Hill necessarily engage in the myriad of legislative tasks and representational functions. As personal staff, women are called on to "stand in" for their bosses (mostly men), and thus are a crucial part of the descriptive representation of the institution. When women as committee experts are intimately involved in policy deliberations, they are also essential to substantive representation. For these reasons, we turn our focus on the intersection of gender and representation in congressional staffs.

THE CASE FOR THEORIES OF REPRESENTATIVE BUREAUCRACY

We employ the concept and terminology of representative bureaucracy for insight into the representational roles of congressional staffers. Research on public bureaucracies by public administrationists suggests there are important empirical and normative reasons to examine the ranks of unelected professionals. Congressional staffers are engaged in representation that is both *passive* (a synonym for Pitkin's *descriptive* representation, emphasizing the shared demographic characteristics that allow the representative to stand for others) and *active* (what Pitkin calls *substantive* representation, focusing on the representative's ability to act on behalf of others).[12]

The literature on representative bureaucracy draws attention to the social demography of organizations, which, as Georgia Duerst-Lahti argues in this volume, reveals much about an institution's history, clientele, purposes, and key actors. Three factors draw attention to this literature. First, scholars of representative bureaucracy grapple with central concepts of accountability and democratic control of nonelected professionals by their elected bosses, a relationship that applies as much to legislative staff as to executive agency personnel. Scholars argue that bureaucrats, who are two or three steps removed from electoral accountability, maintain a degree of democratic responsibility if they reflect characteristics of race, sex, ethnicity, and social class of the public served.[13]

Though congressional staffers are closely identified with elected members, they still are "unelected representatives" who often have extraordinary policy discretion and power delegated to them.[14] Congressional staffers may have policy interests, expertise and resources independent of those of their employer and, therefore, are "[not] immune to the temptation to substitute their own judgment for those of their employer-members."[15] As members of Congress come and go, staffers become an important source of institutional memory and expertise. Michael Malbin, author of *The Unelected Representatives*, describes congressional staffers as "experts without constituencies,"[16] who might be tempted to represent interest group concerns.[17] Political scientist Christine DeGregorio, in a study of policy networks in the U.S. House, acknowledges that a certain amount of staff power is derivative—a spillover from the boss's influence—but she notes that congressional aides possess independent leadership resources from their institutional position, expertise, personal talent, and affability and accessibility.[18] She finds that congressional staffers constitute a significant proportion (35.5 percent) of "recognized leaders" or "champions" operating fairly autonomously in various policy domains.

Second, scholars of representative bureaucracy are concerned about relationships of responsiveness. Responsive to whom? is the question. The literature provides two answers: one asserts that administrative personnel should be responsive to elected officials, while the other argues that bureaucrats should be responsive to the public.[19] In other words, staff assignments may express what the member wants to communicate to various constituencies, or staff assignments may depend on various interest groups' and constituencies' expectations.

Public administrationists Barbara Romzek and Jennifer Utter find that congressional staff work has attributes and norms of a profession. Congressional staffers must balance professional norms derived from their expertise, status, commitment to public service, and autonomy with deference to superiors on policy.[20]

Finally, the representative bureaucracy literature provides a model to understand how passive representation leads to active representation. Essentially the model posits that minority or female bureaucrats differ in attitudes from majority white male public servants and thus act on behalf of client populations in a variety of settings. Public administration scholar

Sally Selden outlines the model that drives most studies of representative bureaucracy:[21]

Passive Representation
→Potential for Active Representation (Values and Attitudes)
→Active Representation

Congress, with its extensive network of staff, provides a unique setting in which to examine the connection between passive and active representation. The first part of our analysis examines passive representation, while the second turns to the dynamics of active representation by congressional committee professionals.

Committee staffers are particularly suited for offering insight concerning the dynamics of representation, for two main reasons. First, committee staffers who work in specific policy areas develop substantive policy expertise. As DeGregorio notes, committee staffers exercise pivotal policy expertise, in contrast with personal legislative aides who are often policy generalists and in contrast with leadership staffers who enter the final stages of policy deliberations and whose expertise is mostly procedural.[22]

Second, committee staffers confront divided expectations of accountability and responsiveness and have multiple professional obligations—to the institution, to different members, to party, and to their policy areas. Committee staffers often have personal connections to members who may see the staffers as extensions of their own work, while they also serve other committee members and can become deeply immersed in the policy issues of the committee. These competing interests and relationships place committee staffers in a dynamic and multidimensional policy and representational environment.

HYPOTHESES, VARIABLES, METHODS, AND DATA

Using data gathered from volumes of *Congressional Staff Directory* and the *Almanac of the Unelected*, we examine the gender, age, and position of 2,707 committee staff members working for 22 House and Senate committees between 1980 and 1999. For the 103rd and 106th Congresses only, due to the availability of greater biographical detail, we compare professional background, memberships, professional training, and education to assess characteristics in congressional committee staff structure that predict where we are most likely to find female staffers working. In addition, we draw on in-depth interviews to examine different staff representational roles and the dynamics leading to active representation by staffers.

Several hypotheses drive our inquiry of representation on congressional committee staffs. First, we hypothesize that women are employed as professional committee staffers to roughly the same extent as in similar occupations in the public and private sectors. Second, just as women legislators have been assigned or drawn to the policy domain of "women's issues,"[23] we expect that women policy professionals will also be more heavily represented on these committees. We define women's issues as those dealing with women specifically—women's health, gender equity, sexual harassment—or those pertaining to policies of general interest to women in their traditional occupational and family roles—education, social welfare, and health care.

Third, we anticipate that certain factors will be associated with higher percentages of women professionals on congressional committees. Most importantly, we hypothesize that the presence of female committee staff directors will be a significant predictor of employment of female staff.[24] In turn, we expect that members of Congress who are younger, who come from states in which women hold greater economic and political power, and who vote for gender economic equity legislation will be more likely to employ women as committee staff directors. Other control variables include party and region (e.g., South and non-South states.)

The data on committee staff demographics come from six Congresses between 1980 and 1999. To capture shifts in staffing that might be associated with important changes in partisan or gender representation, the datapoints include years when party control shifted (e.g., 1982, 1986, and 1994) and before and after the "Year of the Woman" (1992). In addition, the chosen period follows the rapid buildup of committee staff resources during the early 1970s and thus represents a relatively flat period of staff growth.[25] We focus on 22 committees (12 House and 10 Senate), using Fenno's classification to select a mix of policy, prestige, and constituency committees, including at least one committee in each chamber that is considered undesirable by members.[26] These 22 committees account for 64.7 percent of all standing committee staff. The selected policy committees handle the bulk of legislative policy making[27] and include committees and subcommittees handling the bulk of women's issues and feminist legislation.[28] Finally, the sample is composed of roughly parallel committees in the House and Senate to facilitate comparisons between the chambers.

Biographical data on committee staffers include variables regarding age, sex, and years of professional and congressional service. In addition, dummy variables capture different types of professional experiences, professional memberships, specialized training and education, married or not, and children or not.[29] We exclude clerical and administrative support staff because the high proportion of women in such positions tends to overstate the potential influence of women and because these staffers do not have equivalent opportunities to influence substantive policy.

For the 103rd and 106th Congresses, we also analyze the circumstances in which we are most likely to find women working as professional committee staffers. In this second data set, we examine 318 majority or minority committee or subcommittee offices.[30] In all, 1,092 committee professionals work in those 318 organizational units. For each office, we include variables about the hiring chair or ranking member: the member's votes on three gender-equity issues,[31] a dummy variable for districts in the South where more traditional attitudes toward women's roles might be expected, average pay of women in the workforce in the member's state, and the member's age and party. Other variables related to the organizational unit include a dummy variable for women's issue committee or subcommittee, the sex of the staff director, and the number of professional staffers on the committee or subcommittee. In our sample, women hold 78 (24.5 percent) director positions, which compares favorably to the percentage (22.6 percent) of female staff directors in all committees and subcommittees.

One shortcoming in the data is that not all congressional committee staffers have biographies in the two directories consulted. Generally, our sample includes more senior committee professionals (and thus possibly more men). However, these data may also overstate the presence of female committee staffers since we have included all of the women's issue committees and subcommittees.[32] Comparison of the gender composition of our selected 22 committees with other committees not included in the study reveals no significant differences in the percentage of women staff professionals. We conclude that our sample offers a representative picture of committee professionals working on congressional committees.

FIGURE 13.1
Women in Various Sectors
Managerial and Professional Positions

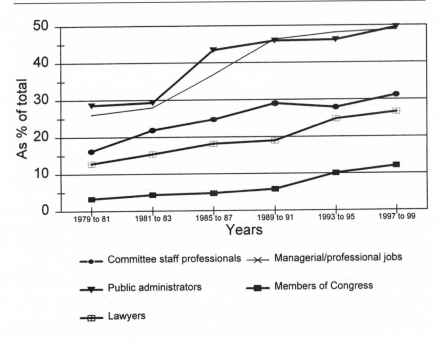

—•— Committee staff professionals —×— Managerial/professional jobs

—▼— Public administrators   —■— Members of Congress

—⊞— Lawyers

THE PICTURE OF PASSIVE REPRESENTATION: WHO WORKS FOR CONGRESSIONAL COMMITTEES?

Women as a percentage of congressional committee staffers doubled between 1980 and 1999. This tracked increases found in other occupations, specifically the U.S. Census Bureau's occupational category of "managerial and professional specialty," and subcategories of "officials and administrators, public" and "lawyers and judges." The upward trend in the percentage of women committee professionals stalls only between the 101st and 103rd Congresses. Figure 13.1 shows the percentage of women in each occupation and as members of Congress.

Women committee professionals clearly are more numerous than female members of Congress, but figure 13.1 illustrates that Congress falls short of the percentage of women in managerial and professional jobs broadly or public administration specifically. The percentage of women working in committee staff positions slightly outpaces the percentage of women work-

TABLE 13.1

Comparison of Characteristics of Committee Staff in 103rd and 106th Congresses

CHARACTERISTIC	103RD CONGRESS		106TH CONGRESS	
	WOMEN	MEN	WOMEN	MEN
Average age (yrs.)	39.3	42.3 *	39.5	42.2*
Committee experience (yrs.)	4.7	5.3	5.4	5.5
Other cong. experience (yrs.)	4.6	5.0	4.3	4.1
Total prof. experience (yrs.)	15.0	17.4**	16.1	17.5
% married	23.2	39.3***	26.0	37.6**
% with children	20.1	33.6***	14.5	28.3***
	N = 606		N = 486	

NOTE: Significant levels are computed based on t-tests for independent samples for the first four variables and cross-tabulations for the last two variables.
$* p < .05$
$** p < .01$
$*** p < .001$

ing in the field of law, which is a significant comparison group given the number of counsels employed by congressional committees. Though not shown in figure 13.1, the occupational subcategories of economists, accountants, and auditors include women at percentages quite similar to that found in the broader managerial-professional category.

Second, women committee staffers differ in significant ways from their male colleagues but are similar in other aspects. Table 13.1 reports characteristics of committee professionals.[33]

In terms of differences, women committee professionals on average are younger than their male colleagues. The data show women have fewer years of overall professional experience, but comparable years of legislative experience on the Hill. On average, women are also less likely than their male colleagues to report being married and having children. As one staffer commented: "The challenges of balancing family and work are very great. You might have a conference committee that starts at 5 o'clock and runs until midnight. It's tough for a woman to make it in some offices. . . . You have to really sacrifice if you want to move up."

The backgrounds of congressional staffers stand in contrast with the backgrounds of members of Congress. As Sue Thomas and coauthors demonstrate in their chapter in this book, female members are likely to have significant marital and caregiving responsibilities that intrude upon or postpone their congressional ambitions, while male members tend to have traditional families that include a female stay-at-home caregiver. Female staffers are more likely to be members of the growing population of single young professional women or childless two-career families. This means that the life experiences of women staffers differ not only from their male colleagues but from those of their male or female bosses as well.

Men and women come to their committee staff jobs from similar professional backgrounds. Most common are prior legislative work (59.8 percent), a stint in a federal agency (35.5 percent), private legal practice (30.7 percent), or private sector experience (30.6 percent). No significant sex differences emerge in the types of precommittee work experiences.

In sum, we find no surprising differences between men and women working as congressional committee staffers. Female staffers come to their committee jobs at an earlier age but have similar tenure on the Hill. There is some evidence that staff careers unfold in slightly different ways, however, as women and men negotiate their different demands associated with family and marriage. In terms of professional preparation for the role of committee professional, we find no significant differences between the men and the women. The data contain no evidence to suggest that women will be more likely than their male coworkers to pursue "active representation" because of differences in previous professional work.

Where Are the Women Committee Staffers?

Table 13.2 reports the percentage of women committee staffers in different organizational settings in six Congresses since 1979. In line with our expectations, the difference in percentage of women working for women's issues committees compared with other committees is statistically significant in every Congress, except the 101st. The difference in the percentage of females on Republican and Democrat committee staffs is not significant in any of the six Congresses. However, it is worth noting that the decline in the percentage of women between the 101st and 103rd Congresses appears to be confined to Republican staffs, House committees, and nonwomen's

TABLE 13.2

Percentage of Women among Senior Committee Staff Positions, 1979–1999

	96TH CONGRESS (1979–80) % FEMALE	97TH CONGRESS (1981–82) % FEMALE	99TH CONGRESS (1985–86) % FEMALE	101ST CONGRESS (1989–90) % FEMALE	103RD CONGRESS (1993–94) % FEMALE	106TH CONGRESS (1999) % FEMALE
BY COMMITTEE:						
Women's issues	*	*	**		*	*
Other issues	18.9	25.1	29.2	30.6	30.9	34.1
	11.5	16.9	16.2	26.8	22.0	25.6
BY PARTY:						
Republican staffs	NA	20.5	28.5	31.1	26.7	29.7
Democrat Staffs	NA	23.4	21.3	28.5	29.5	34.2
BY CHAMBER:						**
Senate Committees	17.5	22.1	28.1	28.0	28.3	38.3
House Committees	14.8	21.8	22.2	29.8	27.6	25.9
Overall	16.2	21.9	24.7	29.0	27.9	31.2
	N = 382	N = 455	N = 396	N = 484	N = 606	N = 486

Notes: Significance levels are based on the chi-square statistic calculating cross-tabulations within each cell.
* $p < .10$
** $p < .05$
*** $p < .01$
**** $p < .001$

issues committees. The difference between House and Senate staffs is significant only in the 106th Congress. We note the 10-point jump in the percentage of female staffers on Senate committees in the 106th and speculate that it may be an aftereffect of the Senate's characterization as a "male bastion" during the Clarence Thomas hearings or the result of membership turnover.

Because of the access to more detailed data on the 103rd and 106th Congresses, we can analyze the circumstances under which women constitute a higher percentage of committee staffers. Shifting from individual staff as the unit of analysis to the organizational unit, we use the percentage of females on a committee or subcommittee's professional staff as the dependent variable. Table 13.3 reports the mean percentage of female congressional professionals among different committees and subcommittees and under male and female staff directors. So few of the chairs or ranking members are female (17 of 318) that we do not report the percentage of female staffers by the sex of the member.

Table 13.3 clearly demonstrates that certain conditions are more likely to be associated with higher percentages of women professionals working for committees. Women professionals are significantly more likely to be found on key congressional subcommittees that handle the bulk of women's issues. The association between female staffers and women's issue committees more broadly is not statistically significant, however. This apparent paradox can be illustrated by the House Commerce Committee, which at the full committee level handles one of the largest volumes of women's issue bills. Almost all of the women's legislation comes through the Subcommittee on Health and Environment, while the other four subcommittees focus on issues such as telecommunications, trade, energy, finance, and hazardous materials.

The presence of a female staff director is strongly and significantly associated with a greater percentage of female committee professionals. Female staff directors are three times more likely to hire other women for committee staff roles than are their male colleagues. When a man is a committee or subcommittee staff director, on average only one in five of the committee professionals is a woman; but when a woman is a committee or subcommittee staff director, on average three out of five of the senior professionals are women. This general pattern of results was borne out in OLS multiple regression analysis, which controls for the effect of a host of other variables.[34]

TABLE 13.3
Mean Percentage of Women as Senior Committee Staff in
Various Organizational Settings (103rd and 106th Congresses)

| | Type of Committee | | Type of Subcommittee | | Staff Director[1] | |
| | Women's Issues | Other | Women's Issues | Other | Female | Male |
	x̄%	x̄%	x̄%	x̄%	x̄%	x̄%
Republican committee staffs	32.5	23.3	33.3	27.9	69.2	20.7***
Democrat committee staffs	29.1	23.9	42.0	20.5***	56.5	18.8***
House committees	26.5	24.6	33.5	23.0*	60.5	16.6***
Senate committees	34.8	19.3*	40.6	26.5**	62.8	24.0***
Overall	30.8	23.6*	37.4	24.2***	61.5	19.8***
	N = 318		N = 318		N = 244	

NOTE: Means for the compared groups are computed using independent sample t-tests. Significance levels are for one-tailed tests.
* p < .05
** p < .01
*** p < .001
[1] In many subcommittees, only one professional may be employed. To fairly assess the impact of women staff directors on the employment of other women, we include only those cases in which the total number of committee professionals is greater than one.

This confirms other research, showing that women in managerial ranks improve the opportunities for more equitable treatment of women, while men favor men in hiring and advancement.[35]

Surprisingly, the characteristics of the chairs or ranking members offer no clue as to who is most likely to hire a female staff director. Analyzing which members are most likely to have a female staff director, we control for the age of the member, women's issue committee or subcommittee, southern state, party, staff size, the member's support for gender-equity legislation, and women's average pay in the member's state. Using logistic regression with a dichotomous dependent variable coded 1 for female and 0 for male staff director, none of the variables in the model proves significant. Stated differently, none of the members' personal traits or district characteristics significantly predicts an increased likelihood of women being hired as staff directors.

We speculate that Hill-oriented hiring networks and experience outweigh district influences, member policy preferences, or personal characteristics in the hiring process. Salisbury and Shepsle find that committee staffers frequently survive chairperson turnover.[36] The career pathways of congressional staffers often include many shifts. For example, after Senators John Ashcroft (R-MO) and Charles S. Robb (D-VA) lost their 2000 reelection bids, their senior staff members landed in at least five different Senate offices and as many interest groups and trade associations.[37]

FROM PASSIVE TO ACTIVE REPRESENTATION

The findings above illustrate that women professionals are most numerous on subcommittees where women's issues are dealt with and that female staff directors are engaging in one form of active representation of women's interests, that is, creating employment equity for other women. Two questions remain. First, does passive representation on congressional committee staffs translate into active policy representation by congressional aides? Second, what factors increase the likelihood of active representation by women staff on behalf of women's issues? To understand the dynamics that lead from passive to active representation by staff members, we explore two pieces of legislation that were introduced during the 105th Congress—the Consumer Bankruptcy Reform Act (CBRA) and the Violence Against Women Act (VAWA). These are two very different types of legislation in the same committee—the Committee on the Judiciary—in both the House and in the Senate. We conducted 17 in-depth, confidential interviews in August 1999 with key Congressional staffers and interest group leaders who were actively involved with one or both of these pieces of legislation.[38] A hierarchy of active representation roles emerges. The hierarchy illustrates that active representation depends on the convergence of several factors: the degree to which gender representation is salient to the issue, the demands of interest groups, and whether the resources and opportunity for staff activism align.

Most issues are gendered, meaning they have varying degrees of gender impact and differential import for men and women.[39] Under current consumer bankruptcy law, alimony and child support payments are nondischargeable debts, to be paid by debtors first and in full. During the debate, banks and lender-advocacy groups suggested treating credit card and other unsecured debts the same as nondischargeable debts. These proposed CBRA changes would disproportionately burden women whose husbands or former husbands seek bankruptcy protection. This aspect of CBRA mobilized women's groups and consumer-advocacy groups, since alimony and child support are owed primarily by men to women. The salience of this gender impact, however, seemed to get little mention in press reports compared with industry concerns about escalating consumer bankruptcy filings and delinquent debt.

By contrast, VAWA programs and funding are designed to protect women and children exclusively, making the gender dimensions of VAWA straightforward. First proposed in 1990 and enacted in 1994 in the Violent Crime Control and Law Enforcement Act,[40] Title IV of VAWA authorized an office within the Department of Justice to administer grants to states and localities to assist with education, law enforcement training, and enforcement mechanisms to combat violence against women and children, especially domestic violence.

For passive representation to become active representation, we posit the following:

Passive representation + Demand + Resources + Opportunity = Active representation

Contributing to the policy mix and environment are interest groups that generate *demand* for active representation, thus heightening member motivations and attaching a premium to staff policy expertise. Congressional staffers must also possess the *resources* for policy influence and the *opportunity* to act for women's interests.

Congressional staffers fit into one of several categories that more fully suggest their ability to engage in active representation. In figure 13.2, we identify an initial iteration of staff representational roles along with factors generating demand, resources, and opportunity.

We conclude that passive representation of women on congressional committee staffs translates into the active representation of women's interests only when a number of conditions are met. Three of the most important are (1) when interest groups *demand* or expect a level of passive representation on an issue; (2) when a staff member possesses the necessary *resources* of interest, expertise, and status; and (3) when the *opportunity* structure of member-staff relations, staff autonomy, and political salience coincide. When these conditions are less than optimal, active representation will not occur.

FIGURE 13.2

A Hierarchy of Passive-Active Representational Roles of Congressional Staff

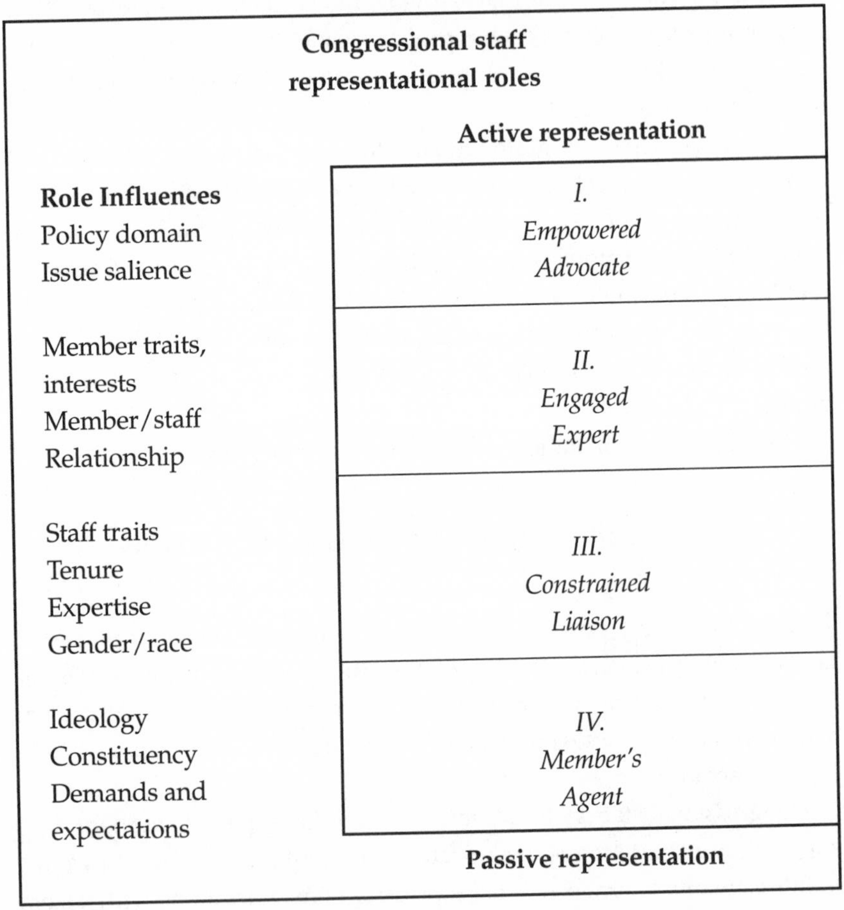

Congressional staff representational roles	
	Active representation
Role Influences Policy domain Issue salience	*I.* *Empowered* *Advocate*
Member traits, interests Member/staff Relationship	*II.* *Engaged* *Expert*
Staff traits Tenure Expertise Gender/race	*III.* *Constrained* *Liaison*
Ideology Constituency Demands and expectations	*IV.* *Member's* *Agent*
	Passive representation

Our hierarchy envisions four different roles, including:

- *empowered advocates*—committee staffers who have the ability, seniority, expertise, autonomy, access to the member, and trust to be independent advocates on an issue and whose advocacy may have a strong effect on their member's voting behaviors.
- *engaged experts*—committee staffers who have substantial levels of autonomy and expertise but who work in situations where they

are less able to strike out on their own or where their role requires dispassionate participation in the process.

- *constrained liaisons*—committee staffers whose lack of status, relationship to the member, or the nature of the issue limit their role to providing information and advice but rarely engaging in independent advocacy outside of one-on-one conversations with their bosses.

- *member agent*—committee staffers who possess extremely limited autonomy, lesser status and seniority, and little access to the member and whose primary representational contribution is in situations where passive representation matters to interest groups.

Key aspects of resources and opportunity include the member's motivations and policy interests and the staffers' interests, expertise, and status. For active representation to take place, the member must desire or condone empowered advocates and the staffer must possess the resources to move from mere member agent to engaged expert or empowered advocate. In other words, members and staffers must both have the interest and motivation to act. While we discuss demand, resources, and opportunities separately, they clearly interact with one another in the dynamics of staff representation. How these dynamics interact on VAWA and CBRA are described below.

Demand for Active Representation

Members who are not otherwise engaged in an issue nonetheless often respond to interest group intensity by designating a staffer to present the right "face" to the interest groups. On VAWA, virtually every member from both parties sought a degree of staff visibility on the issue. As former congresswoman Susan Molinari noted, "One of the least controversial pieces of legislation that came out of the House of Representatives was the Violence Against Women Act. It was so popular that in fact if you look on any one of the 435 members of Congress's campaign literature, they were the chief sponsor of [VAWA]."[41] The visibility of the issue reflects in no small part the activism of women's interest groups. As one former female House Judiciary staffer said, "What member wants to risk being characterized by one of the women's groups as being *for* violence against women?"

The demands of VAWA produce a largely female congressional staff that extends substantially beyond committee staff to include personal office staff. According to an internal House working group document, 74 House staffers (only three of whom were men), were working on VAWA during the summer of 1999.[42] Similarly, an August 5, 1999, contact list provided by the National Task Force on Violence Against Women identified 35 female Senate staffers, 11 male Senate staffers, 35 female House staffers, and 4 male House staffers as actively working on VAWA.

The bankruptcy interest group environment produces very different demands shaping the congressional staff network. First, the dominant interest groups come from the competing sectors of the financial services industry, and consumer groups and women's groups are somewhat less visible and less effective in heightening awareness about the gender dimensions. As one female Senate staffer noted, "It is a highly technical issue and it is enormously unpalatable to take a position that looks like protecting deadbeats. . . . You've got to have resources to tell a persuasive story and the public interest groups simply don't have the resources to get up to speed on the issue."

In 1998 and 1999, principal staffers working on CBRA came from the Judiciary Committee in both the House and the Senate, although the Banking Committee in the House retained control over the credit card provisions in the legislation for that chamber. On this intensely partisan issue, both Republican staff and Democrat staff from the committees are overseen by male members of Congress, and the staffers are led by a male staff director on four of the six principal staffs. In all, eight men and seven women compose the core of the highly technical staff network of the CBRA.

One male staffer who works for a House Democrat emphasized the requirement for technical expertise: "It's really nitty-gritty. There have been cases where the courts have decided cases based on where we stuck a comma." Another male staff member, who works for the Republicans, concurred: "Both bankruptcy and perhaps immigration are areas of the law that are practiced by people who concentrate in that field. The level of congressional involvement in the technicalities is limited." Bankruptcy reform interest groups demand technical expertise in a highly specialized area of law in which relatively few attorneys specialize, which limits opportunity for staff advocacy on behalf of women. An African American lobbyist with a banking coalition noted that the bankruptcy lobbyists talk about congressional staff all the time and are very attentive to party philosophy and the staffer's background in bankruptcy, but "on this issue, sex, race, and religion [of the staff member] have little significance."

If the bankruptcy reform groups expect technical expertise irrespective of gender, the interest groups attentive to VAWA see expertise and sex as essentially linked. Male staffers are not often assigned to the issues that women's groups care about, simply because those groups are less likely to take male staffers seriously. A female staffer noted: "I think both parties believe very strongly that women deliver the message better [on women's issues]. They all feel very sensitive that it looks bad to not be able to find a woman to talk about women's issues. They don't like to publicize that. It's contrived, but they don't want to appear not to have women to handle the women's issues. Look at a roundtable on these issues—it's all women." Another female staffer concurred: "Some of the women's groups, particularly the strident ones, feel that if a woman's not handling the issue, then it's not being properly handled." A female political director of a prominent women's organization confirmed the same point: "We just prefer to have a feminist. . . . Bad women are worse than a good man. We'd rather have a good man, don't kid yourself. But I love feminists, and feminists tend to be 9-1 women."

This demand for passive representation can affect both a member's response to interest groups and internal staffing decisions. A male staff member said: "It's not that it's a set of 'women's issues,' it's about being most effective for your boss. You have a certain credibility problem [as a male staffer on 'women's issues']. The credibility is not always there. The core element is being as effective as you can and representing your boss as well as you can. And if the comfort level can be improved [by having a woman handle 'women's issues'] then that makes a difference." A female staffer agreed: "With domestic violence meetings, a couple of the male staffers were like 'do you want to go to the meetings?, 'cause the groups don't seem too thrilled when I walk in the room.' It might be institutionalized within the groups, especially the ones who are victims' advocates." With both CBRA and VAWA, the interest groups generated expectations and demands for certain staff qualifications—substantive and demographic. These demands can either be ignored or integrated into the system of staffing. How then do staff assignments confront these demands given the available resources?

Resources for Active Representation

A staff member brings to the representational equation his or her substantive expertise, personal interests, and professional status. Clearly both VAWA and CBRA involve a few key staffers who possess high levels of experience, knowledge, and clout. The much larger network of female staff on VAWA, however, is not peopled by those who hold the necessary resources to engage in active representation. In the view of some experienced Capitol Hill professionals, women's issues tend to draw interested female staffers with expertise but often lacking in seniority or positional status. The female political director of a prominent women's organization described the typical staffer assigned to handle women's issues as a woman who has a background in women's studies and is "just dying" to handle the women's issues portfolio. She added: "Women's issues usually get a fellow or a summer intern or someone who's doing 16 other issues, god bless you . . . usually an entry-level woman." A woman judiciary counsel described how her initial assignments reflected a lot of "chick issues," including VAWA. Her more senior male colleagues shuffled assignments that they no longer wanted or that were no longer high profile. With expertise and experience, she moved beyond her initial portfolio of issues. A female chief counsel concurred: "There are a whole lot of women who work on the Hill, but there are fewer women in senior positions, so as the working groups get smaller and smaller, there are fewer women." Thus with VAWA, the picture of passive representation appears robust; nonetheless, relatively few empowered advocates work on the issue, and opportunities for active representation are limited.

Another woman, who served as administrative assistant to the House Judiciary Committee, acknowledged the interplay of interest, expertise, and status in her assignment as the lead staff person on VAWA. After another female staff member left the committee, she "volunteered to handle it," but she was quick to point out that in the event that VAWA came to the top of the agenda, her chief of staff, an attorney, would take over primary responsibility. "It will definitely go into new hands," she said, acknowledging her lack of a crucial resource—status.

Status, when combined with interest and expertise, is essential to active representation. Professional standing also becomes part of the calculus of the policy opportunity structure, the third ingredient for active representation.

The Opportunity for Active Representation

Several factors contribute to the opportunity structure within which staff act. Resources condition the circumstances of staff opportunities, but a staff member must be in the right place at the right time. Member-staff relationship, the degree of autonomy that a staff member enjoys, and the member's own interest, expertise, and policy preferences on an issue are significant for creating opportunity.

Seniority affords greater opportunity. Staffers with established reputations and longer tenure have earned the trust of members of Congress. With that trust comes autonomy and access that allow a staffer to advocate on behalf of particular issues or interests with the member. Senior staffers also are known by the interest groups that court their members, and can act as the conduit between the groups and the members. As one House committee staff member noted, "The former chief counsel here tended to pursue his own ideas. As a junior counsel, I've never had that kind of access to the chairman."

Staff influence on the member's voting behavior clearly varies, however. A female Senate staffer who worked on VAWA explained: "I feel personally interested in this issue. My boss has a very good record on women's issues—almost perfect. But I know . . . that he's not very engaged in it." Because of his detachment, she is able to direct his thinking: "In our office, [the chain of command] starts with the staff level, then it goes to [the legislative director], and then to [the senator] himself. Within our office, things don't really come down from him. He basically trusts us."

By contrast, the member-staff relationship may be controlled from the top down. A House committee staffer explained: "From the very first step, [my job is] putting together a portfolio for the chairman—'this is what the industry says, this is what the consumers say, this is what the leadership says, this is where the momentum is, what do you want to do?' He reads our reports, he makes his determination, then we carry out his determination. I just like to tell the member or the staffer the very neutral facts. How they package it or wrap it, that's their job." Another female committee staffer finds her role constrained by the structure of staff assignments. She works directly for the full committee chairman, while the lead subcommittee chairman relies most on his personal staff rather than the committee staff. She concluded, "I'm under-involved in strategizing—that comes from the personal staff. My job is looking at technical issues."

Finally, politics may limit staff opportunity. One female staffer who was very active on the CBRA had the necessary interest, commitment, and standing within her office to engage in active representation on gender aspects of the bill but was unable to do so because the member and his constituents lacked interest in the CBRA more generally. She attempted to engage in advocacy—"I called up [a Harvard researcher] and said: 'now talk me through this. I want to know how this issue affects [women's] groups, core constituencies"—but found that her opportunities were limited. "This bill is highly technical, but no one wants to defend deadbeats."

Subsequent action on CBRA and VAWA in the 106th and 107th Congresses confirms the importance of interest group demands in shaping the conditions under which descriptive representation can be transformed into substantive representation. The actions (and inaction) on these two issues illustrate that neither a handful of well-placed staffers operating as empowered advocates nor an extensive network of members' agents can deliver substantive policy clout in the face of unfavorable interest group demand.

Neither bill—reauthorization of VAWA or a bankruptcy reform bill—had received final action through the first few months of the 107th Congress when the transfer of Senate majority power to the Democrats threw all policy deliberations into turmoil. Nonetheless, both issues were arguably ripe for some kind of resolution. The financial services industry continued to press Congress in the 106th for a reform bill as individual bankruptcy filings soared to more than 1.2 million in 2000. The need for reauthorization of VAWA was heightened when the U.S. Supreme Court on January 11, 2000, agreed with a lower court decision on *Brzonkala v. Morrison et al.*, nullifying the law's provisions that gave women a federal civil redress in cases involving gender-motivated violence.

Despite the fact that both bills were on the agenda, only bankruptcy reform moved forward. VAWA saw very little attention in the 106th and 107th, even though minority Democrats in both houses introduced legislation to reauthorize the law. When the 106th Congress's first session began in January 1999, new versions of the Consumer Bankruptcy Reform Act (CBRA) were introduced both in the House, by Representative George Gekas (R-PA) and 106 cosponsors, and in the Senate, by Senator Charles Grassley (R-IA) and 10 cosponsors.

The 1999 version of the 1998 bankruptcy bill addressed several of the concerns voiced by women's interest groups. Child support and alimony claims were placed at the "first priority" level, which would allow judges to order bankruptcy filers to pay any child support and alimony claims before paying other, unsecured debts. The bill also removed exemptions that in the past had permitted some debtors under certain circumstances to have their child and spousal support obligations waived through the bankruptcy process. Finally, the 1999 version of the legislation gave bankruptcy judges the power to reduce creditors' claims by up to 20 percent when the debtor was able to show that he or she had been the victim of unfair credit-granting practices.

These changes, however, did not go far enough to satisfy advocates for women and children such as the National Women's Law Center, whose executive director provided lengthy testimony before the House Subcommittee on Commercial and Administrative Law on March 18, 1999.[43] A year later, the NWLC and 12 women's groups continued to raise concerns about the proposed reform bill, arguing that the "first priority" status would be "virtually meaningless" in protecting children in families owed support.[44]

Though women's advocates were not satisfied, the concessions on child support were sufficient to win the votes of House Democrats as legislation moved through the 106th. In the Senate, women's groups won further concessions when an amendment, authored by Senator Charles Schumer (D-NY), was attached to the bill, making debts related to abortion clinic violence nondischargeable in bankruptcy.[45] In the waning days of the 106th, after complicated parliamentary maneuvers, a bankruptcy reform bill was ultimately passed and sent to President Clinton who pocket vetoed the bill in part because the clinic violence debt provision had been dropped. At the beginning of the 107th Congress, Senator Grassley introduced S. 420, which was essentially the same legislation that Clinton pocket vetoed only a few weeks earlier. Despite pleas from 19 women's groups that the bill would "inflict greater pain on the hundreds of thousands of economically vulnerable women and families who are affected by the bankruptcy system each year,"[46] the Senate approved the bill March 15, but its fate was put in doubt when the partisan balance in the Senate shifted.

The demands of the relevant interest groups and their abilities to generate attention both contributed to the difference in interest and attention to these two issues in the 106th and the first part of the 107th. The financial services industry poured more than $37 million in political contributions, most of it to Republicans, into the 2000 congressional elections.[47] The majority Republicans made some concessions to the concerns of women's groups on bankruptcy reform to win some bipartisan support, but no evidence suggests that key women staff acting as empowered advocates influenced the concessions. Indeed, the bill remained largely unpalatable to activist feminist groups. At the same time, the demands of women's groups for action on VAWA fell largely on deaf ears, despite the seemingly large network of congressional staff assigned to work on the issue.

While the outcome of both issues remains unclear, the ultimate fate of CBRA and VAWA will likely depend on the balance of partisan power in the Congress and the degree to which the controlling majority will heed the demands of the respective interest groups. Interest group demand, in turn, will condition the opportunities for activist women congressional staffers to advocate for substantive policy changes.

DISCUSSION

The number of women who work on Capitol Hill has clearly increased over the past two decades, and significantly higher proportions work on committees or subcommittees where women's issues are considered. Nonetheless, as the brief case studies show, many lack sufficient autonomy or seniority to engage in high levels of active representation.

The salience of gender to a particular issue clearly matters in each of these roles. With the CBRA, only a handful of members of Congress, mostly members of the committees of jurisdiction, invested staff resources in the legislation, as evidenced by the narrow staff network that emerged on the issue. Even fewer members were drawn to the issue because of its potential gender impact. Further, women's interest groups, though they were somewhat engaged, had only a limited involvement and were not highly mobilized. Not surprisingly, therefore, we found none of the CBRA staffers operating as empowered advocates. Even within the committees of jurisdiction, staff with high levels of autonomy found it difficult to act at any representational level above engaged expert. The CBRA staffers neither engage in active representation on behalf of women nor affect the representational behavior of the members for whom they work, as they likely would on issues with greater gender salience.

By contrast, gender is highly salient in the case of the Violence Against Women Act. The full range of staff representational roles—from empowered advocate to member agent—is evident within the extended and largely female staff network. For members who were only tangentially focused on the issue, the level of interest group participation generated the necessary demand for passive representation. For members with bottom-up staff systems or senior female staffers on board, the opportunities for active representation also existed. The significant difference between VAWA and the CBRA, then, is that some women staff members were able to engage in the highest levels of active representation on VAWA and to affect the behavior of the member of Congress for whom they worked. However, on the whole, the large number of women staff members on VAWA did not have the resources and opportunity needed to facilitate action on VAWA in the 107th.

While other scholars, including Susan Carroll in this volume, have focused on the practice and the normative implications of descriptive and substantive representation by African Americans and women legislators, we have explored the role of congressional staff in representation. We find that women are passively represented on congressional committee staffs in slightly fewer numbers than are found in similar occupational groups. However, women are represented in greater percentages on committee staffs where the opportunities for active representation of women's interests are greatest.

Do congressional staffs engage in active representation of women's interests? To the extent that female staffers hire more women staff, the answer must be "Yes." In terms of substantive policy interests, the answer is "It depends." Congressional staffers find themselves in various situations with different opportunities to act for women's policy concerns. Not all lead to active representation due to constraints on resources and the realities of constituency demands.

NOTES

1. Jason Deparle, "Sheila Burke Is the Militant, Feminist, Commie Peacenik Who's Telling Bob Dole What to Think," *New York Times Sunday Magazine*, 12 November 1995, 34.

2. Ibid., 32–38.

3. Much of the literature on staff is dated or largely descriptive, focusing on the work responsibilities of staffers (e.g., Kofmehl *Professional Staffs of Congress*, 3rd ed., 1977; H. Fox and Hammond, *Congressional Staffs*, 1977; Malbin, *Unelected Representatives*, 1980; and Rundquist, Schneider, and Pauls, "Congressional Staff," 1992) or

describes staff management (e.g., two Congressional Management Foundation publications, *Setting the Course* and *Working in Congress: The Staff Perspective*).

4. According to Ornstein, Mann, and Malbin's *Vital Statistics on Congress, 1997–1998*, the Congress employed 24,091 staffers in 1997, down from 28,031 in 1987, which is still far more than the handful of clerks who were the first authorized, full-time employees of congressional appropriations committees in 1856.

5. Like Coleman, Brudney, and Kellough in "Bureaucracy as a Representative Institution," we attempt to elaborate on the complex of factors linking passive to active representation. The only two studies focusing specifically on women as congressional staffers have looked at issues other than the links between passive and active representation. Specifically, Friedman and Nakamura, "Representation of Women on U.S. Senate Committee Staffs," explore turnover in women's staff careers, while Johannes, "Women as Congressional Staffers," looks at the predominance of women working on congressional casework.

6. Salisbury and Shepsle, "U.S. Congressman as Enterprise."

7. Rundquist, Schneider, and Pauls, "Congressional Staff."

8. Bisnow, *In the Shadow of the Dome*, 23.

9. Abigail Reese, "Six Figure Staffers See Their Ranks Grow by 3 percent," *Roll Call*, 14 September 1998.

10. *Roll Call*, "Roll Call's Fabulous Fifty Staffers," 13 September 1999, http://www.rollcall.com/rcfiles/fab50staff99.html.

11. *Congressional Staff Directory*, 54th ed.

12. Pitkin, *Concept of Representation*.

13. Donald Kingsley coined the term "representative bureaucracy" in his study of the British civil service of that title. However, the notion that administrative power might be democratically controlled through a socially integrated executive branch staff has a long tradition in the American context. For more about representative bureaucracy literature, see Mosher, *Democracy and the Public Service*; Waldo, "Development of a Theory of Democratic Administration"; Krislov, *Representative Bureaucracy*; and Krislov and Rosenbloom, *Representative Bureaucracy and the American Political System*.

14. Malbin, *Unelected Representatives*.

15. Romzek and Utter, "Congressional Legislative Staff," 1275.

16. Malbin, Unelected Representatives, 247–48.

17. Ibid., passim.

18. DeGregorio, *Networks of Champions*, 31–32. See also DeGregorio's discussion of entrepreneurship as a form of staff working styles in "Professionals in the U.S. Congress: An Analysis of Working Styles," *Legislative Studies Quarterly* 13: 459–76.

19. For a review of this literature, see Selden, *Promise of Representative Bureaucracy*.

20. Romzek and Utter, "Congressional Legislative Staff," 1275. See also Romzek and Utter, "Career Dynamics of Congressional Legislative Staff."

21. Selden, *Promise of Representative Bureaucracy*, 8.

22. DeGregorio, *Networks of Champions*.

23. See, for example, Tamerius, "Sex, Gender, and Leadership"; Thomas, "Impact of Women on State Legislative Policies"; Thomas, *How Women Legislate*; Norton, "Women, It's Not Enough to Be Elected"; and the chapters in this volume by Swers, Wolbrecht, Carroll, and Norton.

24. Prior research on women in management bears this out. See for example, Huffman, "Who's in Charge?"; Baron, Mittman, and Newman, "Targets of Opportunity"; and Blum, Fields, and Goodman, "Organization-Level Determinants of Women in Management."

25. See figure 5.1 in Ornstein, Mann, and Malbin, *Vital Statistics on Congress 1997–1998*, 136.

26. Fenno, *Congressmen in Committee*, first pointed out that members bring different political goals to their committees: institutional prestige, policy making, or constituency reelection goals. Bullock, "Motivations for Congressional Committee Preferences," added the insight that members avoid some committees. The committee names varied at times during the period analyzed and some committees were eliminated or merged with others. Applying names used during the 106th Congress, the House committees included Education and the Workforce, Commerce, Judiciary, Ways and Means, Appropriations, National Security (formerly Armed Services), Banking and Financial Services, Small Business Government Reform and Oversight, Agriculture, Post Office and Civil Service (disbanded in the 104th), and Transportation and Infrastructure (formerly Public Works). The Senate committees included Labor and Human Resources, Commerce, Science and Transportation, Judiciary, Appropriations, Finance, Agriculture, Nutrition and Forestry, Armed Services, Governmental Affairs, Veterans Affairs, and Environment and Public Works.

27. Deering and Smith, *Committees in Congress*.

28. Swers, "Placing Women's Issues on the National Agenda," identified House committees most involved with women's issue legislation or feminist legislation in the 103rd and 104th Congresses. In addition, we use Swers identification of key subcommittees involved in women's issue legislation when we analyze the 103rd and 106th Congresses separately. To identify key women's issue committees for the decade of the 1980s, we rely on Hardin's "An In-depth Look at Congressional Committee Jurisdictions," and on Norton's "Women, It's Not Enough to Be Elected." Hardin identifies House and Senate committees handling 4,843 health bills between 1979 and 1993. Norton identifies House committees handling a sample of 105 reproductive rights bills between 1969 and 1992. From these three sources, we identify the women's issue committees as Education and the Workforce, Energy and Commerce, Judiciary, Ways and Means, Government Operations, Appropriations, and the House Post Office and Civil Service committees.

29. The *Congressional Staff Directory* list of all committee staff includes biographical entries only on more senior professional staff. Piacente and Eigen's *Almanac of the Unelected*, 12th ed., supplemented our data, but includes information on only the more influential staff. Also, biographical entries varied in detail over the 20-year

period. We also recognize that not all staff provide detailed information. For example, in many cases, staff do not report such information as marital status and children.

30. The 318 organizational units include all majority and minority committee or subcommittee staff offices from the 22 committees studied. When members chair more than one committee or subcommittee, each committee staff office is counted as a separate organizational unit.

31. We used three gender-equity votes in the 103rd and 106th Congresses drawn from the American Association of University Women's key vote scorecard.

32. To compensate for the potential imbalance of women's issue committees, we also included committees with masculine domains (e.g., Armed Services, Veterans Affairs, and Public Works).

33. Because of changes in the detail used in the staff directories utilized for this project, the comparisons in the 1980s cohorts are less detailed.

34. Using multiple regression, we test a model to explain which committee settings are most associated with higher percentages of women. Chairs or ranking members of women's issue subcommittees and female staff directors remain significant predictors ($p < .001$) of higher percentages of women committee staffers. Variables controlling for party, women's issue committees, gender-equity votes by the chair or ranking member, and overall staff size were not significantly associated with higher percentages of women. As expected, younger members were significantly more likely to have a higher percentage of women on their committee staffs ($p < .05$), and as expected, congressional members from southern states were less likely to have a higher percentage of women on their committee staffs ($p < .05$). Contrary to expectations, the average pay of women in a member's state was negatively and significantly associated with the percentage of women on the committee staff. Overall the model had an R^2 of .370, and F statistic of 15.251, $p < .001$.

35. Huffman, "Who's in Charge?"; Baron, Mittman, and Newman, "Targets of Opportunity"; and Blum, Fields, and Goodman, "Organization-Level Determinants of Women in Management."

36. Salisbury and Shepsle, "Staff Turnover and Ties-That-Bind."

37. "Hill People," National Journal, 23 December 2000, 3988–89.

38. Our interviews were guided by the methods advocated by Fenno in Home Style. In each interview, questions focused on the staffer's role with regard to the legislation, relationships with the member, interest groups concerned with the bills, the composition of the network of staff involved in the policy area, and career information.

39. Kenney, "Field Essay: New Research."

40. Leslie Gladstone, "Women's Issues: Selected Current Legislation," CRS Report for Congress, 12 July 1999, 5.

41. Susan Molinari, speech at the "Women Transforming Congress" conference, Norman, Okla., 13 April 2000.

42. Based on a list obtained from the National Organization for Women's Legal Defense and Education Fund. NOW LDEF obtained this list from a female

staffer working for a female member of the House of Representatives and had not altered it.

43. Testimony of Joan Entmacher, vice president and director of Family Economic Security, National Women's Law Center, on H.R. 833, "Bankruptcy Reform Act of 1999," http://www.nwlc.org/details.cfm?id=30&section=childpercent20.

44. Correspondence to U.S. Representative Robert Menendez, 7 June 2000, http://www.nwlc.org/details.cfm?id=207&section=child percent20and percent20 family percent20support.

45. This issue was important to the feminist women's groups because two highly visible bankruptcy cases involved Randall Terry and Reverend Robert Behn and Bonnie Behn, who refused to pay court-related fines and fees associated with their anti-abortion protests against clinics.

46. Letter to members of the U.S. Senate, "Women and Children's Groups Oppose S. 420," http://www.nwlc.org/details.cfm?id=617&section=child percent 20and percent20family percent20support, March 2, 2000.

47. Greg Miller, "Bill Making Bankruptcy Filings Harder for Individuals Nears OK," *Los Angeles Times*, 15 March 2001, p. A:1.

CHAPTER FOURTEEN

ENLARGING REPRESENTATION

Women Bringing Marginalized Perspectives to Floor Debate in the House of Representatives

KATHERINE CRAMER WALSH

This issue is not about party and politics. It is about people. It is about sound bodies, strong minds and sturdy spirits. This issue is about moving forward in the future. It is not about wallowing backward to the past.

REPRESENTATIVE EVA M. CLAYTON (D-NC)[1]

House of Representatives member Eva Clayton said these words in 1995 in the midst of a floor debate on welfare reform. She was explicitly trying to do what many members do in a more subtle fashion: frame the debate to favor her point of view. The "issue" could have been about many things: taxation, the minimum wage, or states rights, to name just a few. But Representative Clayton chose to emphasize "the issue's" impact on people. In just a few words, she represented a perspective.

One common argument in favor of increasing the number of women in Congress is that women bring not only distinct policy goals, but also distinct ways of understanding policy to the legislative process. This chapter tests that assumption. I investigate the way women debate on the floor of the House to ask whether women are transforming Congress by contributing perspectives that their male colleagues do not. The premise underlying this research is that the quality of representation is an issue of perspectives, as well as preferences. If policy preferences or goals were the only input to governing, representation would be a mere matter of aggregating votes. But Congress is designed to do more.

In particular, Congress has the capacity, along with the mandate, to deliberate.[2] Granted, the nature of this deliberation varies between the Senate and the House of Representatives. Among the important differences is the fact that Senate deliberation at times resembles a careful consideration of information in an attempt to reach the best possible public policy,[3] while the House rarely meets this ideal.[4] Instead, most deliberation in the House takes place within committees,[5] if it takes place at all.[6] Moreover, some researchers even argue that it is useful to conceptualize House floor debate as talk that is redundant, with information revealed in other portions of the legislative process.[7]

Given these characteristics, House floor debate may not alter votes on a bill currently under consideration. However, House floor debate gives legislators the opportunity to perform for their colleagues as well as their constituents. Through debate members can communicate to colleagues that they can "hold their own," and are worthy of a seat in the chamber. This is particularly significant to women, whose presence in Congress is still relatively new. As one woman member of the 104th Congress said, "I think that the difference between men and women [in Congress] is not always quantitative, it's qualitative. . . . In floor debate, there are jungle rules: You have to establish yourself early on that you can hold your own, that you know what you're talking about and are able to stand up for yourself. If you don't, you'll become a perpetual victim, people will interrupt you, bully you."[8] Moreover, even if the perspectives that members use do not sway their colleagues' roll-call votes, they may influence how other legislators interpret a bill or how they understand future bills. If legislators make convincing arguments through the use of perspectives, they increase the legitimacy of such points of view in subsequent deliberation.

Perhaps more importantly, floor behavior matters because it is a public demonstration of the quality of representation. Since the advent of C-SPAN in 1979, legislators are potentially communicating to the public whenever they speak on the floor, through both live coverage and excerpts broadcast on the nightly news.[9] In this way, floor debate exposes whether the perspectives of certain social groups are included or excluded in the legislative process. This matters because if members of certain social groups do not feel represented, they may exhibit less trust in government. Similarly, floor behavior has the potential to improve orientations toward government among historically disfranchised constituencies.[10] According to Mansbridge, when a subordinate group in society has historically been represented by a dominant group, inattention and distrust are likely to result. In such a context, the visible representation of perspectives—such as through floor debate—can signal shared experience that "facilitates vertical communication between representatives and constituents."[11] Thus floor behavior has implications not just for discrete effects on policy outputs but also for citizens' orientations toward government.

Debate represents the perspectives in three primary ways. First, during deliberation, legislators "frame" their arguments. A frame is the central core of the packaging of an argument, which indicates what is at stake in a given piece of legislation.[12] Frames are at once cognitive tools and social resources. They influence individual psychology by tapping into widely shared understandings, or "frames of reference," that suggest which considerations are relevant for making sense of the message.[13] Such claims reflect broader worldviews. For example, Luker shows how the worldviews of activists on different sides of the abortion debate result in claims about what the issue is about: a woman's right to autonomy over their bodies vs. obeying God's plan for the world.[14] Framing shows up in debate in two ways. First, frames appear implicitly in the way legislators emphasize certain aspects of an issue. Second, frames appear explicitly when legislators state, "This issue is about . . . , " as Representative Clayton did when debating welfare reform. Both approaches have the potential to induce constituents and colleagues to think about legislation from a different point of view.

Debate represents perspectives in a second way when legislators make claims about whom the bill will impact. Occasionally, members of Congress talk about the effect of legislation on a population group (e.g., "African Americans" or the "the working poor") and stress the importance of considering the group's needs. Whom legislators announce that they are considering, whom they claim that they are acting on behalf of, or whom they claim that the legislation helps or harms are dimensions of their perspectives that are not always conveyed by the frame. For example, two legislators can debate welfare reform legislation through the frame of its effect on taxes. One can claim to represent the concerns of single mothers in need of day care (advocating an increase in taxes), while the other can speak on behalf of Americans wanting lower taxes. Therefore, making explicit claims about which constituencies the legislation affects is part of a legislator's declaration about whose views should be represented.

The representation of perspectives happens during debate in a third way as well. Legislators offer testimony, or speak *as* a member of a social group.[15] When a legislator speaks as a member of a group that holds relatively less political power in society, this is an act of increasing the range of views represented. Therefore, women can expand representation by testifying about their own personal experiences, since currently men and women have divergent life experiences in American society. Likewise, any legislator may talk about the effect of welfare reform on mothers, but only a woman who has herself been a mother on welfare can represent that point of view directly.

Perspectives can be represented during floor debate in each of these ways, and therefore debate is worthy of attention when considering whether and how women are transforming Congress. In this chapter I ask, Do women bring perspectives to debate that men do not represent as readily? I focus on the presence of this difference,[16] and suspend analysis concerning debate's influence on policy content and public trust.[17] I investigate perspectives through a content analysis of floor debate on five pieces of major legislation within the 104th Congress, since this Congress had one of the highest female to male ratios to date at the time I conducted the study: 47 women to 388 men.[18] I analyze frames, mention of constituencies, and reference to personal experience to demonstrate that women members of Congress contribute otherwise marginalized perspectives to floor debate. In this way, women are transforming Congress by broadening the range of public interests that the institution considers.

EXPECTING *GENDERED* PERSPECTIVES

The expectation examined in this chapter is that women in Congress represent perspectives that differ from those represented by men. To justify this expectation, it is useful to acknowledge that congressional norms might suggest the opposite expectation—that women would *not* represent different perspectives than men. For many years, research on Congress has suggested that new members try to adapt to the norms of the institution, rather than import novel ones.[19] In order to be taken seriously by other members, new women representatives might try to emulate the behavior of men in the chamber. Indeed, some research has suggested that in order to get along, women do exactly this. That is, they adjust to male norms of the institution by using male language,[20] or male decision-making styles.[21] In addition, we might expect that reelection concerns cause members of Congress to present themselves as masculine, since, for national-level office, voters tend to prefer candidates with masculine traits.[22]

However, the influence of social norms is hard to ignore. On balance, cultural expectations and constraints produce systematic differences in the life experiences of men and women. Men and women tend to fill roles that bridge the public and private spheres in different ways.[23] Pervasive segregation along the lines of sex in the workplace[24] and in voluntary associations[25] produces divergent life experiences that men and women reference when making sense of the world.

These patterns are accompanied by expectations about suitable female behavior. Acting contrary to the way "most" women act (by appropriating male behavior, for example) might not win respect for a woman in the House, but rather result in a backlash. Women in Congress are a visible minority. Like women who have gained access to other predominantly male organizations, they are likely to be judged not only by their ability to perform the duties of the job, but also by how well they measure up "to images of womanhood."[26] They face the danger of being discounted by "fellow" members and/or constituents for straying too far from accepted female behavior.[27] Part of fitting in involves working within the cultural confines of what it means to be female. Research on women candidates for Congress has found that women face a tension between appearing both sufficiently feminine and "professional" that is often manifest in dilemmas over what to wear when campaigning.[28] To illustrate, Rosenthal reports that when Donna Sytek became Speaker of the New Hampshire House, she "found herself subtly changing her wardrobe from conservatively tailored business suits to create a style that would be perceived by her male colleagues as a bit softer but still authoritative."[29] Such predicaments concerning how to dress illustrate that women in Congress might behave in traditionally feminine ways to avoid being ostracized for testing norms of womanhood.

We might also expect women to act within the constraints of widespread notions of womanhood to increase their perceived credibility. Just as there are expectations about how women ought to dress and behave, there are socially based ideas of women's areas of interest and expertise in the political realm.[30] Evidence obtained through experiments shows that women candidates are assumed to be more adept at dealing with education, government integrity, health care,[31] problems of disabled and also elderly people, and civil rights.[32] Survey studies give similar results: the public perceives women politicians as more competent on issues related to children and families, health, education, the environment, and civil rights. Men are expected to be more competent in foreign affairs and directing the military.[33]

These expectations do not stop at the Capitol steps. As within the public, socialized notions of sex roles and gender stereotypes among politicians and bureaucrats influence "how women and men define their areas of expertise, how they will interact with others, and whom they will respect as leaders."[34] For example, men within state legislatures perceived that women were more expert on the Equal Rights Amendment.[35] The notion that men are more expert with public (as opposed to private) matters has also reared its head in state legislative and congressional committee meetings, where women witnesses have been treated as less credible than men.[36] Just as women in legislatures on the state level confront stereotypes that they are inherently less competent by virtue of their sex,[37] women in national-level politics surely face this challenge as well.

Finally, women likely represent perspectives that differ from those represented by their male colleagues out of a sense of duty. Women as a social group are often onlookers rather than participants in the legislative process. When women become members of Congress, they likely have special insight into the way policy will affect, or ought to affect, populations that have not been considered regularly by men. Thus they may feel a duty to represent women and also to act as "surrogate representatives," or advocates for women outside of their own district,[38] as many women in the 103rd and 104th Congresses professed to do.[39] This sense of duty to represent women may extend to other marginalized constituencies, constituencies traditionally given less attention in the legislative process. This is especially likely among women legislators of color, who know firsthand the burden of discrimination based on gender as well as race.

I define a marginalized constituency as a social group that holds relatively little power in the legislative process. This is an intentionally broad definition and differs from related concepts used by other scholars. For example, in researching policy outputs, Anne Larason Schneider and Helen Ingram distinguish "target populations," or "persons or groups whose behavior and well-being are affected by public policy," by how much power these populations have in society as well as by whether the group is viewed positively or negatively.[40] Likewise, Melissa Williams defines "marginalized groups" as social groups that suffer systematic inequalities, are viewed negatively, and in which membership is involuntarily achieved based on unchosen characteristics.[41] I define marginalized constituencies solely on the basis of exclusion from formal channels of political decision making.[43] While social stigmatization is related to exclusion from legislating, I make the strong claim that women are more likely than men to represent politically less powerful groups, whether or not these groups are widely disliked. The breadth of this definition provides a more rigorous test of the claim that women, more than men, speak on behalf of such ignored populations. The more groups included, the more likely that men, as well as women, are representing these constituencies.

Summary of Expectations for the Three Components of Perspectives

To recap, women in Congress should be expected to represent women's perspectives and the perspectives of constituencies commonly ignored in the legislative process because of divergent life experience, social expectations about appropriate behavior, strategic concerns, and/or a sense of duty.[43]

Representing the views of women and other marginalized constituencies is likely to show up in each of the three aspects of perspectives identified earlier. First, with respect to the frame, or the overall packaging of a point of view, women are more likely than men to frame floor statements by emphasizing aspects of legislation related to children, families, women, health, education, the poor, the environment, and minorities. Second, with respect to claims about which constituencies ought to be target populations of a given bill, women are more likely to speak on behalf of social groups typically peripheral to the political process, such as women, racial minorities, the unemployed, and children. Third, with respect to testimony about personal experience, women are likely to enlarge representation during debate by talking about their lives as women and mothers.

Methods

To study whether women bring a distinct set of perspectives to the floor, I restricted my analysis to debate of major legislation. Prominent bills are more likely to generate enough speeches from a diverse array of members to enable detection of existing gendered differences. I sampled five such bills considered on the floor in the 104th Congress. Of the women, 35 were Democrats and 12 were Republicans. I purposively sampled two bills directly relevant to children, families, and motherhood, because these topics provided the opportunity for women members of Congress to invoke perceptions of female expertise in contrast to male colleagues. The sample included a welfare reform bill popularly known as the "Personal Responsibility Act" (H.R. 4) and a "Partial Birth Abortion Ban Act" (H.R. 1833). To investigate whether women bring unique perspectives to consideration of policy more generally, that is, not just during debate over bills traditionally considered "women's interest" legislation, I randomly sampled three additional bills considered on the floor during the 104th Congress.[44] These included H.R. 2126, a defense appropriations bill; H.R. 3322, a bill regulating and appropriating money for civilian science research, such as research conducted through the National Science Foundation and the National Aeronautics and Space Administration; and H.R. 1170, a bill that emerged from controversy over California's Proposition 187, which denied many public services to illegal immigrants. The bill required a three-judge court, rather than a single federal judge, to rule future referendums unconstitutional.[45]

The sampling frame from which I chose speeches to code was composed of every speech made on the floor during consideration of these bills within the 104th Congress on each day that the bill was considered in the House. This included floor consideration of all amendments to the bills and news articles or letters that were quoted by a member in the midst of a speech. It did not include extensions of remarks, introductions, or short clarifications. I coded the first statement made by each participant in the debate, as well as an additional systematic sample of speeches.[46] The sampling of speeches used to analyze mentions of typically disregarded constituencies and references to experience in private roles included every speech made during consideration of the five bills. Of the constituencies mentioned across the bills, I classified the following as "marginalized": children, mothers, low-income people, cancer patients, poor people, handicapped kids, teen mothers, residents of public housing, sick people, welfare recipients, legal immigrants, homeless people, students, poor families, and disaster victims.[47] Recall that this code was intended to capture politically less powerful populations. Though these groups obviously vary in the degree to which they are ignored in mainstream politics, each of them is among the politically disfranchised.

To code references to personal experiences, I recorded whether the speaker called up experience in a particular role or job, other than experience in Congress, to support his or her statement.

Coding for frames proceeded as follows: To allow for the possibility that women and men do not use different perspectives on the floor of the House, I created the coding categories by reading through portions of the debate while blind to the identity of the speakers. Thus the list of code categories was developed in a way that minimized my knowledge of the sex of the debators.[48]

To increase the reliability of this coding procedure, an assistant helped develop the coding frame on the welfare reform bill (the first bill analyzed). Independently, we each read every third page of the first day of deliberations, recording the frames used. The frames we independently derived were reliably similar, differing not in content but in scope.[49] The final coding frame for the welfare reform debate was a synthesis of the two.

To code for constituencies mentioned, I recorded whether the representative explicitly mentioned that a group (e.g., "children," "the American people," or "middle-class people") would benefit from the legislation, or ought to be taken into consideration when voting on the legislation.

Reliability checks were used to test the coding on all five of the bills. Four assistants who were blind to the hypotheses of the study and the identities of the speakers coded between 10 and 50 speeches chosen at random from debate on two of the bills. Percentage agreement was calculated for the number of speeches coded identically. For frames, the average rate of agreement across raters was 73 percent. Agreement on coding constituencies was 93 percent, and was 100 percent on coding for mention of experiences.

While the debate on the five bills was coded speech by speech, the unit of analysis was the participation of a member. That is, I investigated the perspectives that each participant in the debate brought to the floor on a given piece of legislation.

RESULTS

Women Framing in Ways Similar to Men

The perspectives that women voice on the floor of the House suggest that women do not limit themselves to traditionally feminine domains; however, they represent perspectives that men seem less likely to contribute. In this way, they are enlarging the range of perspectives represented during debate. I use the term "enlarging" because women are framing debates in ways similar to their male colleagues, yet they speak on behalf of marginalized constituencies more than men, and talk about their experience in roles that only women can represent. Thus their participation enhances debate by broadening, or enlarging, the array of people and viewpoints present. This expansion of perspectives stands out most clearly during debate on welfare reform and "partial birth" abortion.[50]

To see the way women are enlarging representation through framing, consider the debate on welfare reform. Women tended to represent the same perspectives that men do, in addition to perspectives that emphasize children and the need for programs such as day care and job training that enable people to work. During debate on the bill, 155 men and 33 women

TABLE 14.1

Percentage of Women Participants in Each Debate

BILL NO.	BILL CONTENT	TOTAL PARTICIPANTS	WOMEN PARTICIPANTS
H.R. 4	Welfare reform	155	33 (18% of total)
H.R. 1833	"Partial birth" abortion ban	21	14 (40% of total)
H.R. 3322	Civilian science research	49	7 (14% of total)
H.R.1170	3-Judge court for certain injunctions	20	3 (15% of total)
H.R. 2126	Defense appropriations	62	8 (13% of total)

TABLE 14.2
Welfare Reform Debate Frames

FRAME	EMPHASIS
Patterns of reliance on welfare system	Cycle of dependency on welfare benefits, number of "deadbeat parents," willingness to work for benefits, self-esteem
Tax relief	Change welfare expenditures, consideration of legislation's effect on budget deficit, tax levels
States' rights	Issues of delegating welfare authority to the states, size of federal bureaucracy, flexibility in implementation
Children	Health of children, children's future
Fraud	Waste and fraud in implementation
Enabling work	Preparing people for employment, including issues of training, child care, the minimum wage
Safety net	Welfare as a mechanism to help those in need

participated, speaking a total of 510 statements. These were categorized into seven different frames, as catalogued in table 14.2. Both men and women used each of these frames. However, 19 percent more women than men used the "children" frame, while men did not use any of these frames significantly more than women.[51]

This difference is not simply an artifact of the high correlation between gender and political party. (Recall that 35 of the 49 women in the 104th Congress were Democrats.) In other words, it is not the case that women more commonly emphasize children simply because Democrats tend to emphasize children. Democrats, in general, did focus on the welfare reform bill's reductions of federal school lunch programs, and thus did often frame their arguments in terms of its effects on children. But even among Democrats, women were more likely to emphasize children. Fifty-two percent of the 21 Democratic women taking part in the debate framed their statements in

TABLE 14.3

Use of Frames by Gender

	Women	Men	Difference
H.R. 4: Welfare Reform	N = 33	N = 155	
Effects on children	42%	23%	+19%*
Enabling work	41%	21%	+20%*
H.R. 1833: "Partial birth" abortion ban	N = 14	N = 21	
Repulsiveness, inhumanity of the procedure	21%	48%	–27%***
H.R. 3322: Civilian science research	N = 7	N = 42	
Protecting current and future citizens	71%	24%	+47%*
New technology/global competition	71%	14%	+57%**
Job creation; economic growth	57%	12%	+45%*
H.R. 2126: Defense appropriations	N = 8	N = 54	
National safety/strength of the nation	0%	22%	–22%***
H.R. 1170: 3-Judge courts for injunctions	N = 3	N = 17	
Judicial power	100%	82%	+18%*
Workload of judiciary	100%	41%	+59%***

*** $p < .001$
** $p < .01$
*$p < .05$

terms of children, while only 27 percent of the 56 Democratic men participants did so.[52] Moreover, Republican women also used the children frame, albeit to a lesser extent than the Democrats. Twenty-five percent of the 12 Republican women participants framed their debate to focus on children.[53]

The tendency of women to expand the range of frames used during debate extended to other legislation as well. Table 14.3 shows that analysis of debate on the other four bills revealed that men used two frames more often than women, but women used five frames more often than men.[54] The frames that women emphasized were not universally reflective of a woman's perspective. One frame used more often by women did convey a traditionally feminine perspective, that of caregiver. This packaging was used during debate over civilian science research, and emphasized the need to protect current and future citizens. However, the other four frames used more often by women than men are more consistent with a traditionally masculine perspective.[55] These include talking about the need to develop technology, to stay competitive on the global market, to create jobs, and to sustain growth.

Although the frames women used were not solely feminine, the emphases or frames that men used more often than women are consistent with stereotypically masculine views. First, men were the only members to talk about the importance of maintaining national safety when discussing defense appropriations.[56] When debating "partial birth" abortion, they talked more often in terms of the "heinous"[57] or "inhumane"[58] nature of the procedure. In short, when men showed a specialization in use of frames, it resonated with a stereotypical male point of view, while women represented both traditionally female and traditionally male frames. It appears that women can speak in the terms their male colleagues use as well as contribute previously overlooked perspectives.

Speaking on Behalf of Marginalized Constituencies

When we move beyond frames to consider the constituencies that members spoke on behalf of during debate, the work women are doing to broaden the representation of perspectives is even more clear. As expected, women were more likely than men to mention marginalized constituencies, or members of social groups typically ignored in the legislative process (i.e., those with little political power). Recall that "marginalized constituencies" was defined broadly. Even so, more women represented these commonly disregarded populations than did men. Over three-quarters (77 percent) of the 39 women participating in the debates on these bills discussed the effect of the legislation on one or more of these constituencies, while only 56 percent of the 209 men participating did so.[59] Table 14.4 displays gender differences in the mentioning of these groups, calculated for each constituency as well as for politically marginalized constituencies in general. Men were more likely to speak on behalf of several of the groups, but this was only statistically significant with respect to disaster victims. Considering debate across all five bills collectively, women more actively represented constituencies typically peripheral to the political process.

One might argue that it is not gender that matters for the content of floor remarks but ideology or partisanship. As long as a legislator's politics incorporate concern for the disfranchised, such an argument might claim,

TABLE 11.1

Mention of Marginalized Constituencies by Gender

Constituency	Civilian Science	Defense Funding	"Partial Birth" Abortion	3-Judge Court	Welfare Reform	Base N Women[1]	Base N Men	% Women Who Named This Group	% Men Who Named This Group	Difference
Children	x	x	x	x	x	38	209	74	47	+27%***
Mothers, pregnant women		x	x	x		37	186	32	12	+20%**
Low income	x					7	42	14	3	+11%
Cancer patients	x					7	42	4	0	+4%
The poor or the needy		x	x	x		33	187	21	18	+3%
"Handicapped kids"					x	33	155	6	3	+3%
Teenage mothers unwed mothers			x		x	33	155	6	4	+2%
Public housing residents					x	29	140	6	6	0%
Sick, disabled, or people with AIDS		x		x		33	180	3	4	−1%
Welfare recipients					x	29	140	9	11	−2%
Legal immigrants					x	33	155	6	8	−2%
Homeless	x				x	34	170	3	6	−3%
Students		x				8	54	0	4	−4%
Poor families		x				8	54	0	4	−4%
Disaster victims	x					7	42	0	7	−7%
All marginalized constituencies						39	209	77	56	+21%

[1] Base Ns are the denominators used for calculating the percentages. They refer to the number of men or women who participated in debate during which the given constituency was mentioned.

*** $p < .001$

** $p < .01$

* $p < .05$

it makes little difference whether the speaker is male or female, black or white. Considering the Democrats, there is indeed little difference (just 11 percentage points) in the extent to which male and female Democrats mention marginalized constituencies.[60] However, there is a distinct gender difference among Republicans. While only half of the Republican men talked about the effect of policy on dependent groups, 77 percent of the Republican women did so.[61] In sum, women are speaking for the politically less powerful in circumstances in which men are reluctant to do so.

Several examples help illustrate the way men and women speak differently on behalf of constituencies. When debating welfare reform, Nick Smith (R-MI) said, "H.R. 4 helps promote families. Too often, welfare discourages traditional families. Benefit formulas have discouraged marriage and encouraged women to have illegitimate children. . . . This bill, H.R. 4, also makes needed changes in our food and nutrition programs. . . . If hard-working Americans are going to pay taxes for this program, it should be for nutritious food for individuals who might otherwise go hungry."[62] Although Smith mentioned unwed mothers and welfare recipients, he was not speaking on their behalf. Instead, this speech represented American taxpayers in general.

Compare his remarks to those of a Republican woman. The next day, while debating an amendment to the same bill, Barbara Vucanovich (R-NV), addressed the implications for several marginalized constituencies. "Although it is imperative that we discourage out of wedlock pregnancies, increasing the financial pressure on women faced with a crisis pregnancy lacks compassion and will undoubtedly cost the lives of many innocent unborn children. . . . Once the choice is made to have a child we should ensure that children raised by welfare mothers are not unfairly penalized and suffer further the dire consequences of poverty."[63] Here, Vucanovich was speaking on behalf of two marginalized constituencies: women "faced with a crisis pregnancy" and children "raised by welfare mothers."

Women's representation of often overlooked constituencies such as children was also evident during debate on legislation not commonly associated with "women's interests." When debating civilian science legislation, a woman, Nydia Velazquez (D-NY), interjected the interests of homeless people into the debate. "Mr. Chairman, I rise today in strong support of the Roemer amendment to eliminate funding for the space station. . . . How can we tell millions of homeless people that there isn't enough money to put a safe roof over their head, and then, continue to fund the space station?"[64]

In addition, only a woman, Sheila Jackson-Lee (D-TX), addressed the needs of the poor, children, and/or the elderly when talking about the three-judge court proposed in response to Proposition 187. "We now find ourselves here in this legislative body disturbing that sacred process by suggesting that a few disgruntled citizens did not get their way in California, partly to put poor people out in the street, denying educational rights to children and health benefits to the elderly that are in this country, a whole other story, a whole other issue. But because that was not a decision that some in this body appreciated, we now want to alter the Constitution of the United States."[65]

It is no coincidence that Jackson-Lee and Velazquez, the people who are notable for their mention of marginalized constituencies in the debates over civilian science research and the three-judge court, are women of color. If the perspectives that representatives bring to the floor reflect their experience as members of American society, we ought to expect racial minorities to be especially empathetic to politically disfranchised groups while legislating. When "racial minority" is defined as African Americans, Latino/as, and Asian Americans, the data support this assertion. Considering both men and women, 71 percent of the 34 people of color who took part in these debates mentioned constituencies peripheral to the political process, while only 57 percent of the 214 white participants in the debate did so. This 14 percent difference is only marginally statistically significant, but by restricting the focus to the difference between whites and African Americans, the significance increases. Seventy-seven percent of the 21 African Americans participating in these debates mentioned marginalized constituencies, a 20 percent increase over the proportion of whites performing such representation.[66]

Narrowing the analysis further to just women, there is a suggestion of a difference by race, albeit slight. While 76 percent of the 29 white women debating these bills spoke on behalf of marginalized constituencies, 80 percent of the 10 women of color did, and 85 percent of the 7 African American women did so.[67] Though the differences between white women and women of color are not statistically significant, the direction of the gap supports the idea that representation is broadened when carried out by people who can personally identify with members of groups with less political power.

Enlarging Representation through Testimony

Women's ability to expand the scope of representation is most clear with respect to the third aspect of perspectives: whether and how legislators invoke personal experiences to make their arguments. Women give voice to experiences closely tied to private roles, such as motherhood, which their male colleagues do not as readily represent. For example, during debate over welfare reform, Lynn Woolsey (D-CA), invoked her past experience as the self-proclaimed only former welfare mother in the House:

> As the only Member of Congress who has actually been a single, working mother on welfare, my ideas about welfare do not come from theory or books. I know it, I lived it. . . . I will never forget what it was like to lie awake at night worried that one of my children would get sick, or trying to decide what was more important: new shoes for my children or next week's groceries. . . . So my colleagues see I know about the importance of a safety net, and I also know about the importance of work.[68]

The tendency for women to talk about experience in private roles emerges most clearly during debate on the legislation associated with women's issues (welfare reform and "partial birth" abortion). Debates of the other legislation (defense appropriations, the three-judge court legislation, and civilian science appropriations) produced fewer mentions of personal experiences of any kind.[69]

During the debate on welfare reform and "partial birth" abortion, women distinctly referred to experiences in private roles more often than men. Only 5 percent of the men participating in these debates (8 of 149) invoked their experience in private roles. However, 33 percent of the women (11 of the 33 women participating in these debates) talked about personal experience, and each of them spoke of their firsthand knowledge of motherhood. Although some male members of Congress did talk about private experience (as fathers, sons of immigrants, or sons of low-income parents), they more often talked about their occupational and political experiences as doctors, sheriffs, mayors, and state legislators. Of the 20 men mentioning personal experience, 12 talked exclusively about professional roles.

Even when Democratic and Republican women took opposing stands on legislation, such as in debate over "partial birth" abortion, members of both parties appealed to their experience as mothers to emphasize the credibility or sincerity of their statements. Half of the 14 women taking part in the debate referred to their experience with motherhood. For example,

Andrea Seastrand (R-CA): "As a mother of two adopted children, I clearly understand the importance and significance of this legislation."[70]

Nancy Johnson (R-CT): "As a mother who lost a child, I can tell my colleagues that the tragedy of death is miraculously assuaged by the miracle of birth."[71]

Ileana Ros-Lehtinen (R-FL): "As a mother of two children, I do not comprehend how we can allow any baby to be subjected to such inhumane treatment."[72]

Nita Lowey (D-NY): "As the mother of three grown children, I thank God every day that my children were born healthy and strong. However, not everyone is so lucky."[73]

Carolyn Maloney (D-NY): "As the mother of two children, I know firsthand the joy and excitement that a pregnant woman has when she awaits the birth of a very much wanted child."[74]

Lynn Rivers (D-MI): "Many people have talked here today about their own experiences as parents and the joy and the happiness that they went through holding the baby for the first time, counting the fingers, counting the toes. You are right."[75]

Men, on the other hand, invoked their experience as physicians:

David Weldon (R-FL): "Mr. Chairman, prior to coming to the House of Representatives, I was practicing medicine and indeed, I was sitting at my desk and reading a copy of the American Medical News where this procedure was first described back in 1993. . . . It is purely an elective procedure."[76]

Tom Coburn (R-OK): "Having been involved in obstetrical care, delivering over 3,000 children, caring for women with complicated pregnancies . . . this procedure is an unneeded, gruesome attack on life."[77]

Pat Schroeder (D-CO), taking the floor after Coburn, summed up the difference: "Mr. Chairman, I am not a doctor. But I am a lawyer. I am a mother. I have been married 33 years. I think I belong in the Marriage Hall of Fame, and I will put my family values against anyone. I must say, as a woman today standing in this Chamber, I feel like I am in the Chamber of Horrors, because no one really talks about the mother."[78]

Although men did not talk about a mother's point of view, women did. And the perspective of motherhood was not limited to debate over abortion or welfare reform. Jane Harman (D-CA) offered this perspective during debate over defense appropriations: "As a mother of two draft-age children, my first question about any defense acquisition is, "Will it save lives?"[79] And Zoe Lofgren (D-CA) used a similar perspective to debate funding for a global climate change program during consideration of the civilian science research bill. "My children are 11 and 14. I do not want them to be adults and live in a world where climate change is too late to impact. . . ."[80]

Sometimes women invoke their experience with motherhood without adding the phrase "as a mother." For example, when Marge Roukema (R-NJ) rose in support of the welfare reform bill, she countered Democratic criticism that the bill excessively cut school lunch programs by saying, "Members of the committee have heard me say this before and I will say it again: Children will not go hungry and homeless. Not on my watch."[81] As a woman, Roukema could credibly make this claim because of the widespread belief that taking care of children is a female domain.

Likewise, Carrie Meek (D-FL) used the authority derived from shared notions of women's expertise to chastise her male colleagues for implying they could sympathize with mothers on welfare. In the following remarks, she claimed that the perspective she brings to the job enables her to legislate better than many of her colleagues.

> Mr. Chairman, the debate on this floor regarding welfare reform has been in my opinion, as far from what is real in the world as anything I have ever seen. . . . Many of you would not know a welfare mother if you saw her. Not only would you not know her, but you do not know how they live. You do not know what it takes to feed their children. You do not know what it takes to find a job. . . . I stand here today to say to you that all of this is a bunch of baloney. It does not lead down to the neighborhoods where the people are poor and need help. All this about wearing second-hand clothes, where have you heard of such a mess before? Wearing second-hand clothes? It goes to show you where the mindset is. How can you make an amendment if you do not have the right mindset?[82]

Meek's ability to publicly question whether privileged members of society can adequately understand life as welfare recipients came from her capacity as a woman to empathize with mothers. From this standpoint, she could question the "mindset" of her male colleagues, and give voice to this troubling aspect of the quality of representation: that those who act on our behalf may have no familiarity with the lives they are regulating and legislating. Because women on average have experiences that men do not, their testimony on behalf of women's lives and experiences can remedy this disconnect.

THE PLACE OF GENDER IN
CONGRESSIONAL FLOOR DEBATE

The growing numbers of women in Congress have the potential to not only transform the institution and national-level legislation but to change the study of legislative behavior. Changes in the gender balance in Congress have forced empirical consideration of the effect of heterogeneity in a representative body. When the people composing a legislature represent a diversity of life experiences as well as a diversity of policy preferences, students of the legislative process have good reason to investigate representation in ways that extend beyond measuring congruence between members' and constituents' issue positions.

Recognizing the distinction between preferences and perspectives also develops our understanding of the difference between Hannah Pitkin's concepts of substantive and descriptive representation.[83] Typically, substantive representation is defined as the representation of preferences or policy goals, while descriptive representation is conceptualized as reflecting the demographics of a constituency.[84] However, since demographics are often shorthand for shared social experience as members of a given social group, descriptive representation is partly about representing perspectives.[85] Thus, the concept of descriptive representation is not obviously less important for policy outputs, and may, in actuality, speak to a more intimate link between the representative and the represented.

Some argue that descriptive representation is not a necessary condition for competent representation, for example, with respect to the interests of African Americans.[86] But representation does not just occur during roll-call votes,[87] or just in the way legislators spend their time. Instead, authentic "standing for" representation involves giving voice, with genuine empathy, to the concerns and experiences of society's members who are not present during debate.

TRANSFORMING BY ENLARGING

This study provides evidence that women enlarge the scope of representation in Congress by bringing perspectives to House floor debate that are not as readily or as authentically presented by their male colleagues. Analysis of the frames women use, the constituents that they speak on behalf of, and the personal experience they refer to while debating show that women make their arguments in ways that draw attention to the perspectives and interests of politically less powerful constituencies. Women more often than men mention the effect of legislation on underrepresented constituencies, and they bring to the floor firsthand experience of the difficulties mothers face. Since women act as empathetic delegates of underrepresented concerns, they are transforming Congress into an institution that considers more closely the thoughts and fears of the whole population. Thus, women's perspectives incorporated into debate enlarge the representative nature of the legislative process.

This is not to say, however, that women in Congress only use stereotypically female perspectives. To the contrary, in the analyses conducted here, women were more likely than men to use several stereotypically male as well as several stereotypically female frames. Moreover, they tended to mention a broader array of constituencies than men, not just different constituencies.[88] Floor debate is an arena in which women demonstrate their competence on a wide range of topics, which increases the possibility that the public and other members will not discount female candidates or representatives by virtue of their sex. By continuing to represent a variety of perspectives, women in Congress can expand perceptions of women, rather than perpetuate existing stereotypes.

Enlarging the perspectives presented within Congress may also transform the public's understanding of various issues. In so far as elite discourse influences popular opinion,[89] changes in congressional debate may cause the public to think about issues in terms not previously considered.

For example, would the issue of day care be as relevant to welfare reform if women were not part of the debate?[90] Public demand undoubtedly encourages attention to day care. But would that need be as readily represented if some of the legislators did not speak of it themselves, firsthand? Thus in the relationship between constituents and representatives, the legitimization of the place of a woman's point of view in public affairs will continually evolve.

In time, men may feel pressure to represent the views of women in debate to reply to increasing numbers of women in Congress.[91] However, having women in Congress simply allows women to do it themselves. Women are transforming Congress because they choose to debate legislation by representing the perspectives of women and marginalized constituencies, offering viewpoints that have developed from personal experience. Although men can speak about parenthood, they cannot speak with authenticity about what it is like to be a mother. And although men can talk about the effect of legislation on children, constituents and colleagues are possibly more likely to listen to women's perspectives on this topic. Therefore, while women may be adjusting to an institution that has been established and developed from a man's point of view, they are, at the same time, transforming it into a body that gives consideration to a broader array of perspectives, and does so with sincerity.

NOTES

1. *Congressional Record*, no. 52, 21 March 1995, H3392.
2. Bessette, *Mild Voice of Reason*.
3. Fenno, "Senate through a Looking Glass."
4. Granstaff, *Losing Our Democratic Spirit*.
5. Smith, *Call to Order*.
6. Connor and Oppenheimer, "Deliberation: An Untimed Value."
7. Austen-Smith, "Information Transmission in Debate."
8. Personal interview, 21 February 2000.
9. T. Cook, *Making Laws and Making News*; Frantzich and Sullivan, *C-SPAN Revolution*.
10. Williams, *Voice, Trust, and Memory*, 45–50, 137.
11. Mansbridge, "Should Blacks Represent Blacks and Women Represent Women?" 64.
12. Gamson and Lasch, "Political Culture of Social Welfare Policy."

13. Zaller, *Nature and Origins of Mass Opinion*. There is a vast and growing literature on political information framing. For more on framing effects, see Nelson and Kinder, "Issue Frames and Group-Centrism"; Dennis Chong, "How People Think, Reason and Feel."

14. Luker, *Abortion and the Politics of Motherhood*.

15. On the merits of testimony during deliberation, see Sanders, "Against Deliberation."

16. Because my intent is to investigate whether or not women are transforming Congress (a predominantly male institution), I use the perspectives used by men as the norm against which I compare those used by women.

17. Levy, Tien, and Aved, "Do Differences Matter?" show evidence that the presence of women's perspectives in debate does indeed influence the content of policy.

18. There were 48 women in the 103rd Congress, an increase from 29 in the previous two sessions. Clark, "Women at the National Level."

19. Matthews, "Folkways of the U.S. Senate." But see Hall, *Participation in Congress*, ch. 4.

20. Winsky-Mattei, "Gender and Power."

21. C. King, "Sex-Role Identity and Decision Styles."

22. Huddy and Terkildsen, "Consequences of Stereotypes," show with evidence from experiments that women tend to favor candidates with masculine personality traits, while men tend to disadvantage candidates with feminine traits.

23. Sapiro, *Political Integration of Women*.

24. Reskin, "Sex Segregation in the Workplace"; Blau and Ferber, *Economics of Women, Men, and Work*; Bielby and Baron, "Woman's Place."

25. McPherson and Smith-Lovin, "Sex Segregation in Voluntary Associations."

26. Kanter, "Some Effect of Proportion."

27. See Duerst-Lahti, "But Women Play the Game Too," for evidence of this constraint within state administrative decision-making arenas. See also Jamieson, *Beyond the Double Bind*.

28. R. Fox, *Gender Dynamics in Congressional Elections*, 36–40.

29. C. Rosenthal, *When Women Lead*, 4.

30. Sapiro, *Political Integration of Women*, ch. 7.

31. Sapiro, "If Senator Baker Were a Woman."

32. Like Sapiro, Rosenwasser et al., "Attitudes Toward Women and Men in Politics," find support for the idea that women are perceived to be more competent with respect to education.

33. Burrell, *Woman's Place*, ch. 2; Alexander and Andersen, "Gender as a Factor."

34. Duerst-Lahti and Kelly, "Study of Gender Power," 60.

35. Hill, "Female State Senators as Cue Givers."

36. With respect to state legislatures, see Kathlene, "Power and Influence in State Legislative Policymaking," and Kathlene, "Position Power vs. Gender Power." With respect to Congress, see Mattei, "Gender and Power."

37. Githens, "Women and State Politics."

38. Mansbridge, "Should Blacks Represent Blacks and Women Represent Women?" 641–43.

39. Carroll, "Representing Women: Congresswomen's Perceptions."

40. Schneider and Ingram, "Social Construction of Target Populations," 334; Schneider and Ingram, *Policy Design for Democracy*.

41. Williams, *Voice, Trust, and Memory*, 15–16.

42. Across debate on all five bills, no legislator spoke on behalf of a group that Schneider and Ingram specifically name as politically weak and negatively constructed ("deviants"), which includes criminals, drug addicts, communists, flag burners, and gangs.

43. For a similar argument about the combined effects of strategic concerns and socialized behavior, see Kahn, "Gender Differences in Campaign Messages," 483–85, on how female candidates emphasize areas of concern on which women are expected to have expertise.

44. To sample the bills, I used a list of major legislation from http://www.thomas.loc.gov. I randomly chose a legislation topic (such as "hazardous substances"), and then randomly chose bills within that topic until I sampled one that had been considered on the floor of the House.

45. The House approved each of these bills. The welfare reform bill was eventually signed into law as a House-Senate compromise bill, after President Bill Clinton vetoed a previous version. The ban on "partial birth" abortion was passed in the Senate, but vetoed by President Clinton. Although the veto was overridden by the House, it failed passage in the Senate over the veto. The defense appropriations bill became law after a slight reduction in the Senate. It provided $243.1 billion to the DOD for fiscal year 1996. Both the three-judge court and civilian science research legislation were referred to Senate committees.

46. Specifically, for H.R. 4 (welfare reform) and H.R. 1833 ("partial birth" abortion ban) every speech was coded for frame, constituency, and experience. For H.R. 2126 (defense appropriations) and H.R. 3322 (civilian science), every speech was coded for constituency and experience. Every speaker's first speech, every speech made by a woman, and every fifth speech were coded for frames. For H.R. 1170 (3-judge court), every speech was coded for constituency and experience. Every speaker's first speech, every speech made by a woman, and every second speech were coded for frames.

47. Examples of nonmarginal constituencies according to this classification are federal workers, doctors, small business owners, the scientific community, and "high tech" workers.

48. When coding the debate on the welfare reform bill and the "partial birth" abortion bill, an additional frame category was used to code short speeches that did not clearly convey a frame.

49. More specifically, we arrived at the same list of frames although our labels differed slightly. The main difference was that one of us included a cate-

gory to capture statements that claimed that the debate was about the definition of "welfare."

50. The prominence of this difference may be due to the fact that more women participated in these debates than in deliberation on the other bills analyzed (as shown in table 14.1). However, previous research has shown that gender is particularly prominent in contemporary debates over welfare reform, and therefore the size of the difference is not likely a statistical artifact. Duerst-Lahti, "Making Good Citizens."

51. Throughout this chapter, analysis of difference in mean scores is analyzed via one-tailed t-tests for independent samples, not assuming equal variance. A t-test of the difference in proportion of men and women using each frame showed that men did not use any frames more than women such that $p < .05$. A t-test of the difference in proportion of women and men using the children frame revealed $t = 2.119, p = .020$.

52. A one-tailed t-test of the difference in proportions of male and female Democrats showed $t = 2.069, p = .024$.

53. A one-tailed t-test of the difference in proportions of Democratic and Republican women showed $t = 1.594, p = .062$.

54. When investigating the use of frames on the defense appropriation bill, debate during consideration of the Dornan amendment was excluded from the analysis. This amendment prohibited abortions at defense facilities. I focused only on the other portions of debate in order to analyze floor behavior that was not about a clearly gendered issue.

55. Gilligan, *In a Different Voice*; Kathlene, "Alternative Views of Crime."

56. Instead of using this frame, women packaged their remarks to emphasize either the priorities of the federal government more generally, pork barreling and/or corporate welfare, the need for a ready defense, the safety of the troops, or the need for deterrence.

57. Charles Canady (R-FL), *Congressional Record*, no. 171, 1 November 1995, H11605.

58. Bob Goodlatte (R-VA), *Congressional Record*, no. 171, 1 November 1995, H11608.

59. A one-tailed t-test of the difference in proportions of men versus women speaking on behalf of marginalized constituencies, not assuming equal variances, shows $t = 2.737, p < .004$.

60. Among the 87 Democratic men, 66 percent mentioned marginalized constituencies, while 77 percent of the 26 Democratic women did so ($t = 1.156, p = .127$).

61. Among the 114 Republican men, 51 percent talked about the effect of policy on dependent groups, while 77 percent of the 13 Republican women did so ($t = 1.997, p = .032$).

62. *Congressional Record*, no. 52, 21 March 1995, H3396.

63. *Congressional Record*, no. 53, 22 March 1995, H3519.

64. *Congressional Record,* no. 179, 30 May 1996, H5692.

65. *Congressional Record,* no. 153, 28 September 1995, H9621.

66. For the difference between members of color and white members, $t = 1.520$, $p = .078$. For the difference between black members and white members, $t = 1.851$, $p = .038$.

67. For the difference between women of color and white women, $t = .265$, $p = .397$. For the difference between black women and white women, $t = .600$, $p = .281$. An analysis of the difference between Republican women and Democratic women is not possible here since no Republican women of color took part in these debates.

68. *Congressional Record,* no. 52, 21 March 1995, H3377.

69. Only 10 of the 98 participants (10 percent) talked about any kind of personal experience during consideration of defense appropriations, civilian science research, and the three-judge court. However, 31 of the 182 participants (17 percent) in debate over welfare reform and "partial birth" abortion invoked personal experience. Although only two women talked about their experiences outside of Congress during debate on this latter type of bill, they relied exclusively on experience in private roles. At the same time, eight men argued with the aid of personal experience, but only one referred to a private role. During debate over civilian science, Harold Volkmer (D-MO) said, "I can remember back when I was a youngster, and things have changed dramatically up to the present time" (*Congressional Record,* no. 178, 29 May 1996, H5612).

70. *Congressional Record,* no. 171, 1 November 1995, H11608.

71. *Congressional Record,* no. 171, 1 November 1995, H11609.

72. *Congressional Record,* no. 171, 1 November 1995, H11610.

73. *Congressional Record,* no. 171, 1 November 1995, H11613.

74. *Congressional Record,* no. 171, 1 November 1995, H11615.

75. *Congressional Record,* no. 171, 1 November 1995, H11614.

76. *Congressional Record,* no. 171, 1 November 1995, H11614.

77. *Congressional Record,* no. 171, 1 November 1995, H11616.

78. *Congressional Record,* no. 171, 1 November 1995, H11616.

79. *Congressional Record,* no. 138, 7 September 1995, H8616.

80. *Congressional Record,* no. 179, 30 May 1996, H5708.

81. *Congressional Record,* no. 52, 21 March 1995, H3375.

82. *Congressional Record,* no. 54, 23 March 1995, H3625.

83. Pitkin, *Concept of Representation.*

84. For example, see Swain, *Black Faces, Black Interests.*

85. Mansbridge, "Should Blacks Represent Blacks and Women Represent Women?"

86. Swain, *Black Faces, Black Interests.*

87. Tamerius, "Sex, Gender, and Leadership."

88. Women mentioned an average of 2.90 total constituencies across debate on all five bills, while the average among men was 1.85 ($t = 2.607$, $p = .006$).

89. Zaller, *Nature and Origins of Mass Opinion.*

90. Casey and Carroll, "Wyoming Wolves and Dead-Beat Dads."

91. Levy, Tien, and Aved, "Do Differences Matter?" See also C. Rosenthal, *When Women Lead,* for a similar argument that the presence of women in state legislatures may encourage men to adopt leadership styles more commonly found among women.

CHAPTER FIFTEEN

LEGISLATIVE CAREERS

The Personal and the Political

SUE THOMAS, REBEKAH HERRICK, AND MATTHEW BRAUNSTEIN

It comes to the point I have to make a decision. The choice is to run for majority leader or leave. I have taken a lot of time and I have realized something has changed, and this is my family. My decision is to put family first. I have decided not to run for re-election. . . . Twenty years from now, my daughter won't give a hoot if I was speaker or majority leader or on a highway crew. She wants to know if her daddy's there."[1]

BILL PAXON,
RETIRED MEMBER OF THE U.S. CONGRESS

During the budget stalemate of 1990, the House met for endless hours trying to override a presidential veto in order to keep the government running. It was the same day [Ron] Dellums' son Brandy was getting married, and all the years of guilt over not being there for his children were weighing heavily on the congressman. "Let's override this veto and let me love my son." Later Dellums got mail from all over the country thanking him for reminding them that congressmen are human, that they have families and lives beyond Capitol Hill "and this business can crush the dreams" of spouses and children.[2]

Decisions to retire by U.S. Representatives Ron Dellums (D-CA) and Bill Paxon (R-NY) caused a media stir not only because the decisions were surprises and because Paxon was considered by many to be the Republican heir apparent to then Speaker Newt Gingrich (R-GA), but also because both focused on the deprivation faced by families of professional politicians. Indeed, Paxon said his decision was based solely on his need to be available to his two-year-old daughter. We do not question whether or how much political calculation was involved in these decisions or whether this publicly stated reason was his sole motivation to retire. Instead, we use the events as a springboard for asking questions about the extent to which our culture has absorbed the need for women and men to contribute to both private and public lives.

Women in politics have long been making decisions, including decisions to run,[3] to seek higher office, and to retire from office, based on family concerns. Similarly, studies in fields other than politics show that women bear a double duty when they add public sphere responsibilities to the private sphere ones that are considered their province.[4] Little public attention has focused on these decisions, in part because women have been expected to put family first and career second, and in part because elite political involvement was seen as primarily the province of men. Women's participation was expected to be affected by family needs. While men were expected to be concerned about their families, they were not expected to put those concerns before career.

Times have changed, however. Women's involvement in work outside the home has increased dramatically, and they run for and win political office in record numbers.[5] Because men are becoming increasingly involved in family care, debates swirl about what responsibilities women and men should share in both public and private spheres. That men's decisions to forgo public sphere opportunities for their families make the news while similar decisions by women go unnoticed attests to the rarity of this choice in our culture. Opportunities abound for convergence and revisioning of these gender-based divisions of labor and the notions of what career demands ought to be for both sexes.

This chapter focuses on the careers of women and men in legislative office, with special attention given to gender-based comparisons of public and private sphere responsibilities, how children and family affect career decisions and perceptions, and how the entrance of significant numbers of women into legislatures might be transforming both men's and women's perception of public obligation and private duties. The findings inspire reflection on what is necessary to realign public and private life for the benefit of both sexes.

POLITICAL SCIENTISTS: THE INVISIBILITY OF HOME LIVES

Traditional political science literature on legislative careers falls into three general categories: political recruitment, ambition and its consequences, and retirement. While the literature has, in recent times, included the political careers and family concerns of women, none of the studies do so in more than a most limited fashion. Each of these three areas of investigation focuses on a different set of questions. For example, recruitment studies focus on the social circumstances associated with candidates who are recruited to run, on their backgrounds, and what political opportunities and barriers they encounter.[6] Ambition literature has focused on the importance of personal and progressive ambition (i.e., the desire to move up in the political ranks once a career is launched). Finally, the retirement literature asks why political officeholders relinquish office when they do. The three topics are related, but each places a different emphasis on personal characteristics, social circumstances, and institutional factors as explanations for outcomes. Most importantly, however, all these studies relegate family considerations to a secondary concern.

Recruitment theory has typically focused on how social background, including socialization, psychological and personality proclivities, and political structure or opportunities affect decisions to enter politics. Sometimes issues of marital status, family considerations, or sex of the potential candidate are used as independent variables in models dominated by political variables, but the design of the research follows the assumptions of the researchers—that private sphere considerations are of secondary importance in decisions to run for office. An example from state legislatures is Wayne L. Francis's 1989 study of lifestyles and career patterns of state representatives. Among the chief findings of the study are that satisfaction with career is linked to the number of workdays in legislatures and individual success rates on legislation. Francis attributes the effect of the number of workdays solely to the need to integrate legislative life with outside employment in states that don't offer full-time compensation. Francis does

not consider the possibility that the satisfaction with the number of legislative workdays might be related to time spent away from family—or
even that women and men might have different reasons for shorter legislative work schedules.[7]

Women and politics scholars have begun to examine men's and women's
paths to office and the factors that affect them differently. Most of this literature focuses on women's candidacies and how they compare to men's
on a host of variables from fund-raising to vote shares.[8] There is still much
territory to explore about women's paths to office, especially how their private sphere roles affect those paths.

The study of careers in progress and political ambition has a large and
rich literature. Beginning with Joseph Schlesinger (1966),[9] examination of
ambition focused, as with recruitment theory, on social background variables, political affinity, and the opportunity structure. Gender never entered
the picture, in part because at that time few women ran for or won office.[10]
Modern literature on ambition, career conduct, and decision making examines how ambition correlates with other legislative activity. General findings suggest that progressively ambitious legislators who face opportune
political openings also possess risk-taking personality traits.[11] These individuals are also often highly legislatively productive.[12]

Women's political ambition is also explored in the literature. In the 1970s,
women's ambition was found to be significantly lower than men's.[13] More
recently, studies find no differences between the sexes or very small differences.[14] But motivations for political ambition seem to differ between the
sexes. Timothy Bledsoe and Mary Herring (1990) report that women are
more influenced by the strength of their current positions, while men are
more self-motivated and more single-minded.

Few studies explore differences in ambition levels among women, but
one that does finds differences in ambition related to whether or not the
women held previous office, whether or not they had intentional political
careers, their age, and whether or not they have minor children during
office.[15] Together, these studies suggest that ambition alone does not account
for women's presence and continuity in office, or lack thereof. The culprits
are the unbalanced nature of family responsibility allocation and socialization effects, especially those presupposing how women should conduct
themselves in the public sphere.

Some research focuses on how public/private issues in political careers play out for women and men. Susan J. Carroll (1989) reports that family situations affect both men's and women's careers, but more so for women. Delayed entry and the presence of a supportive spouse are much more indicative of women's career path than men's.[16] Virginia Sapiro (1982) found that women and men delegates to national party conventions were just as likely to feel public/private conflict, but women tended to forgo political pursuits in the face of that conflict whereas men pursued politics regardless of its presence.[17]

A sizable portion of the literature concerning retirement decisions focuses on public sphere variables such as electoral vulnerability, organization of the governmental body, presence or absence of redistricting, and salary. When personal factors are explored, studies center on individual propensity to take risks and the incumbent's age. Family considerations are rarely raised, and then only in tangential ways.[18]

Only in the women and politics literature is there some discussion of private life's effects on retirement decisions. For example, Diane Blair and Ann Henry (1981) find that, in Arkansas, family factors affect more retirement decisions for both men and women than financial considerations. Traditional assumptions about careers dictated the questions formulated in research on legislative careers. If family considerations are considered exogenous, little information about familial impact will emerge.

Beyond examining the differences between women's and men's careers, studies suggest there are ways to reconfigure underlying assumptions and cultural values about public/private sphere responsibility. It is this thread that needs to be explored empirically and normatively, and it is the focus of the remainder of this chapter.[19]

DATA SOURCES AND EXPECTATIONS

The data used for this project are in four parts and include both state- and national-level respondents. The first analyses stem from a mail survey of women and men in state legislatures across the nation. State legislative service is the most common prior political office for members of Congress, and if gender differences exist in this population, they are likely to be reflected in Congresses of the future.

Because it was not possible to survey people in all 50 states, 15 states were targeted for attention—Arizona, California, Colorado, Illinois, Kentucky, Maryland, Massachusetts, Mississippi, New York, Ohio, Oklahoma, Pennsylvania, Vermont, Virginia, and Washington. These states were chosen to ensure as much diversity as possible in terms of region of the country, political culture, professionalization of legislature, and, especially, proportion of women in state legislatures.[20] All women of the lower chambers in each state were surveyed, along with a sample of men—the men outnumbering women in all legislatures, sometimes by as much as 90 percent. We surveyed about equal numbers of men and women in each instance. In all, 399 women were surveyed and 584 men. The response rate stood at 44 percent overall; for women it was 49 percent and for men 40 percent. Women's response rates exceeded men's in all but four states: Washington, Vermont, Ohio, and Colorado.

The survey instrument posed 140 questions in six categories, including career influences, perceptions of governing body, sustenance of career, achieving personal satisfaction, integrating home and profession, and background information. Two portions of the survey are used in this chapter—the sections on background information and career influences. Background information included year elected, committees, prior offices, leadership positions, plans for other offices, ideology, party, education, age, religion, marital status, race, numbers of children, ages of children when running for office, whether or not the spouse works outside the home, and whether or not the officeholder raises or raised children alone, especially while in office. The section on career influences contained questions about reasons for getting involved in politics. We also asked the respondent's age when she or he first dreamed of a political career, when she/he first ran, and the primary reason for running when she/he did.

A second data source comes from a survey of former members of Congress conducted in the fall of 1999. The survey was sponsored by the Dirksen Congressional Center and the Caterpillar Foundation for a project designed to examine gender differences in job satisfaction, home life, and relationships on the Hill. The former members surveyed entered after 1970. Addresses were found for 401 former members, 39 of whom were women. A modified Total Design Method[21] was used in conducting the survey.[22] Two hundred twenty-two former members (19 of whom were women) responded, for a response rate of 56 percent. The women who responded were similar to congresswomen generally in their party makeup and age of entry, but served longer than the average congresswoman. Many of the questions used in the survey were based on questions used by Lascher to measure the job satisfaction of California county supervisors.[23]

The third source of data for this chapter are statements from interviews with a half-dozen current members of Congress that reflect the same survey questions administered to state legislators and members of Congress. Because soliciting survey responses from current members of Congress is a much more difficult undertaking than it is on the state level, many fewer members are included. Hence, we make no claims about the diversity or representativeness of the answers. However, the responses from members of Congress mirrored those of the broader, more representative data gathering on the state level and, for that reason, we include quotes from members throughout the chapter.

Members of Congress often are quoted speaking about, or write directly about, their lives as legislators. For example, Representative Pat Schroeder (D-CO) recently wrote of her life as a female member of Congress with small children. We include this type of anecdotal evidence as our final data source.

The expectations for the study derive from both the career literature on Congress and state legislatures and the literature on women officeholders. Specifically, we predict that the following will hold true:

H1: Women and men are likely to differ with respect to family duties and their sense of how their political careers affect their families. Women in office, more than men, are expected to bear the responsibility for home chores and maintain primary care of the children.

H2: We anticipate that motivations for political roles will differ for women and men, with women likely to cite different reasons for involvement. We expect that community activities and issue activity will be bigger spurs to women's political entry and that men will be more likely to get involved because of a long-held dream or a planned step in a career trajectory. Because women officeholders hold different life experiences than men, it stands to reason that they have been motivated to pursue political involvement in slightly different ways.

H3: The women and politics literature is replete with evidence that family responsibilities affect female and male politicians differently. Studies to date do not address differences between male and female officeholders who have children and those who do not. Given that changing societal mores make it more likely and necessary than in the past for men to consider the effects of political careers on their spouses and children, we predict that legislators with children (women and men alike) will perceive career motivation differently than those without children.

WHETHER MARS OR VENUS, WOMEN ARE THE CARETAKERS FOR BOTH PLANETS

Anecdotally, women in office frequently note a discrepancy in family responsibilities. The most amusing among these stories is offered by former member of Congress Pat Schroeder. In her autobiography, she says of her husband,

> Jim is a loving and concerned father, but soon after I was elected, I was reading an interview in which Jim was asked how my election had changed his life. His answer was, "I spend more time involved in things like taking the children to the pediatrician." I immediately ran to the House cloakroom and called him. "For five hundred dollars," I asked him, "what is the name of the children's pediatrician?" Knowing he was busted, he coughed and said, "Oh, I was misquoted. I meant I *would* take them to the pediatrician if need be.[24]

Our analysis of survey responses from state legislators offers statistical verification of the anecdotal perceptions of legislators typified by Representative Schroeder. Hypothesis 1 concerns the breakdown of family responsibilities for officeholders. It is possible that the need for frequent campaigning and busy legislative days impels those with dreams of holding office to seek partners with minimum commitments outside the home. For men, this appears to be true. For example, 73 percent of male officeholders in our state survey indicated their spouses have not worked during at least some of their time in office, but only 27 percent of the women responded this way. The results from the U.S. House of Representatives were similar, as all of the former congresswomen who were married had working spouses, while only 33 percent of the former congressmen's spouses worked outside the home. These results suggest that women often wait to start their political careers until their spouses have retired or plan to retire.

Because it is not as acceptable for men to confine their work to the private sphere, it is less likely that women officeholders will be afforded the opportunity to pursue politics in a single-minded way. These data suggest this to be the case. Women state legislators and congresswomen are less likely to have children or more likely to have fewer children than male counterparts. Women are also more likely to be single or divorced. For example, 42 percent of the congresswomen had children living at home while in office compared to 77 percent of the congressmen. Political analysts note that it is almost imperative for men to appear as responsible family men to be perceived as high-quality candidates. For women in office or running for office, however, the presence of small children may be perceived negatively, as it suggests the woman's neglect of family responsibilities. That means that to join the political elite, women must limit private sphere family opportunities that are available to men with nonworking spouses.

What about women, like Schroeder, who do both? In the public sphere generally, "the gap between men's and women's work responsibilities may be shrinking, but mom still is usually the one who stays home when a child gets sick. A recent survey by the Families and Work Institute found that working fathers took only a third as much time off as working mothers in such cases."[25] Is the same true for political women? The above social science finding is supported by anecdotal evidence: Judy Martz, Montana's first female lieutenant governor says, "A woman has to juggle a little more than a man. When I come home, I'll have to buy the milk and the dog food, vacuum the floor, and clean the bathroom. I don't expect my husband to do these things."[26] And, in 1996, U.S. Senator Kay Bailey Hutchinson commented, "This job is all-consuming, 20 hours a day. I never feel caught up or that I have enough time. Some of us joke that what we really need are wives, because it is very difficult to do what you have to do as a senator and also take care of your family. We need to address family life and the pace of work here."[27]

Another flagrant example of the ways in which family needs have a differential impact on women and men is evident in the story of Republican Jane Swift, acting governor of Massachusetts. Approximately a week before Governor Swift was scheduled to give birth to a set of twins, her doctor

TABLE 15.1
Bivariate Data on Background Variables+

State Legislators	Men	Women++
Children		
None	13%	18%
Two	34%	30%
Primary responsibility for:		
Clean	16%	62%***
Cook	18%	66%***
Shop	24%	67%***
Dishes	22%	54%***
Laundry	20%	70%***
Primary care of children while in office:		
Spouse	57%	33%***
Officeholder	12%	22%***
Primary care of ill children while in office:		
Spouse	61%	33%
Officeholder	11%	18%*
Child alone while in office	8%	25%***
Spouse does not work	24%	11%***
Spouse worked during time in office	16%	6%
Benefits to family:		
Status	7%	6%*
Pride	9%	18%*
Role Model	2%	5%*

Former Members of Congress Dependent variables:	Men	Women
Children living at home while in the House:		
Yes	77%	42%***
No	23%	58%***
Benefits to family (based on 5-point scale with 5 = strongly disagree and 1 = strongly agree)		
My family benefitted from:		
My service	3.05	2.83
My duties interfered with:		
My time with family	1.77	1.89
Primary caregiver (based on difference of means)		
Spouse was primary caregiver	59%	0%
Spouse caregiver but member played		
significant role	29%	0%
Pretty equal	8%	29%

Member caregiver but spouse played a significant role	1%	15%
Member primary caregiver	2%	57%
Member married*		
Yes	95%	68%
No	5%	32%
Spouse Worked*		
Yes	33%	100%

+ The questions put to state legislators asked them the number of children they have; which of the following tasks in the home they have primary responsibility for doing or supervising: cleaning, cooking, shopping for food, dishes, laundry, and paying the bills; an open-ended question asking what the chief benefits the legislator's spouse, partner, or children derive from their legislative career; if officeholder has children living at home, who is their primary source of care (the choices for these tasks were "you, your partner, relative, friend, nanny, day care, or n/a"); who is the primary source of children's care when they are ill (with the same set of choices); a question asking whether or not there were any years in office in which the officeholder raised a child alone; whether the officeholder's spouse or partner works outside the home; whether or not there have been years when the spouse or partner did not work outside the home and whether or not any of those years overlapped with time in office.

++ In all, 399 women were surveyed and 584 men. The response rate stood at 44% overall; for women it was 49% and for men it was 40%.

*** Significant at the .01 level

** Significant at the .05 level

* Significant at the .10 level

hospitalized her to prevent early delivery. A group of male legislators (Democrats) attempted to get her declared temporarily incapacitated so that Democratic Secretary of State William Galvin, who had plans to run against Swift in the next election, could take over. While doing official business over a phone, by e-mail, or a fax machine, and with the help of aides was acceptable when President Ronald Reagan suffered his near fatal shooting, questions were raised about a woman who was giving birth. Trying to declare a pregnant governor unable to govern highlights the ways in which reproductive and family duties are used to hamper women's assent in the public sphere.

Systematically, as table 15.1 shows, a much greater proportion of women state legislators than men are primarily responsible for cleaning, cooking, shopping, dishes, and laundry. They have primary care of children and are more often than not the ones to stay home when the children are ill.

Although not shown, each of these findings withstands multivariate controls and remains strong and highly statistically significant. Similarly, 57 percent of the former congresswomen with children report being the primary caregiver compared to only 2 percent of the congressmen. These are important findings because they show that private sphere expectations of women and men are not changing despite women's entry into the realm of politics as well as other public roles.

These findings in part reflect the likelihood that men have stay-at-home partners, but the pattern holds even in situations where that is not true. As has been the case in the wider professional realm, women, regardless of public sphere responsibilities, are primarily responsible for running the family.[28]

Perhaps double duty leads women and men to view the benefits of their political careers differently with respect to families. When asked what the primary benefits of officeholding were to their families, a greater proportion of women state legislators than men noted that their families were proud of them; men were more likely to cite status considerations and the fact that their families were able to work together on officeseeking and holding. They made the pursuit a family enterprise.

The exact same questions were not asked of U.S. Congress members, but available data reveal interesting patterns that parallel our state findings. When asked the degree to which "My family benefited from my service," and "My duties interfered with my time with my family," U.S. congresswomen had a slight, though not statistically significant, tendency to indicate a favorable view of the impact of their careers on their families. When responses from congresswomen with children were compared to those of congressmen with children, a significant pattern emerged. Women with children were less likely to see their duties interfering with their family time, which may suggest that women feel better able to balance family obligations than men (2.13 for women and 1.56 for men on a 5-point scale with 5 representing "strongly agree"; $p = .06$).[29]

Of course, the demands of political careers create difficulties for the families of politicians. Almost all respondents to the state legislative survey, for example, spoke of the time crunch. When women's comments differed from men's, they were stark. A few female state legislators mentioned "spousal disapproval" and "objections of husband" or "proud of me, but would prefer my being home" as hurdles to overcome in constructing a public and private life. The comments of men emphasized the price paid by them and their families for a political career, such as: "Being in public life was one of the largest factors leading to my divorce," and "Gone too much; too busy to spend time with wife," and "No TIME together—we just broke up." In response to the question about what the chief benefits to family were of the officeholder's career, one man wrote: "None—they sacrifice a lot—they don't gain *anything.*" Male members of Congress spoke in similar refrains: "I would like for all of us to go out to eat and make it all the way through our meal and be on the way out the door before we are interrupted," and "Can't walk down a grocery store aisle with your child without keeping an eye open for a constituent who at least wants a friendly hello, perhaps a recognition by name, or even a lengthy chat about Constitutional protection for the flag (or fill in the blank)—all at the expense of your child."

The differences in the comments of women and men may reflect the tendency for women who are married to enter political life only in the case of a very supportive spouse, whereas men in either situation run for office. As Susan Carroll (1989) has noted, for women in politics, a supportive spouse is a necessity; for men it is preferable, but optional. Indeed, Pat Schroeder, a member of the House of Representatives for 24 years, concluded that, "Clearly, being treasured at home freed me to be strong and brave in public."[30]

These results suggest that while societal expectations have changed with respect to women's presence in the public sphere and the political world in particular, adjustments in attitudes and behaviors about the private sphere have not occurred at the same pace. Society now accepts women in political office at much greater levels than in the past, but hasn't made the same kind of adjustment for men's role in the private sphere. Adequate leeway is not given for men to give equal attention to work and home. What that means is that all the parts of the family equation suffer. Women can join the public sphere, but it usually requires them to perform double duty. Men can do more at home, but usually not at the expense of going full tilt at work. Children have the benefit of seeing two fully engaged parents, but they lose the opportunity to spend the kind of time with parents that is so deeply needed. In short, public sphere expectations remain consonant with the norm developed when careers or jobs in the public sphere needed two people—one at home and one on the job. They have not adjusted to the needs or desires for two parents, married or not, to participate in both realms.

TABLE 15.2

Bivariate Data on Career Influences

DEPENDENT VARIABLES:	MEN	WOMEN
Reasons Respondents got Involved in Politics (1–7 scale; 1 = agree) % of respondents choosing 1		
Issues	15%	36%***
Social change	28%	42%***
Governmental mandate	26%	20%
Personal fulfillment	12%	15%
Community activities	24%	47%***
Was asked	23%	12%*
Always wanted to	69%	30%***
Age first dreamed of political career		
4 - 18 years old	24%	14%***
22 - 29 years old	19%	6%***
30 - 40 years old	21%	29%***
Age first ran for office		
40 - 49 years old	20%	37%***
Reason respondent got involved when he/she did:		
Stating issue motivation	8%	18%***

*** Significant at the .01 level
** Significant at the .05 level
* Significant at the .10 level

Hypotheses 2 and 3 examine career influences on officeholders, both past and present. The state level data, written statements by members of Congress, and the survey of former members of Congress illuminate the reasons officeholders pursued political careers and what inspired their decisions. When asked about levels of agreement or disagreement with seven reasons that might have influenced the respondents' motivation, women and men state legislators answered in different ways.[31] Table 15.2 shows bivariate differences contrasting men and women's experiences.

On the bivariate level, consistent with the hypothesis, a higher proportion of women than men said that a particular issue or set of issues helped fuel their political pursuits. Similarly, women were more likely than men to agree that community activities spurred their involvement. A poignant and dramatic example on the congressional level was offered by U.S. Representative Carolyn McCarthy (D-NY):

> My Irish temper and a terrible tragedy got me into politics. As I am sure you are aware, my husband was killed and my son was critically wounded when a gunman opened fire on the Long Island Rail Road on December 7, 1993. From that moment on getting my son better was my only concern. But as miracles took place and Kevin got better, I needed to make sense of it all. I was asked to talk about my tragedy all over New York State and the easy access to guns. Congress was debating the repeal of the Assault Weapons Ban. I began lobbying on behalf of victims everywhere to stop this unthinkable repeal. When my own Congressman voted to repeal the ban, I was outraged. As luck would have it—a reporter caught me just after the vote. The reporter asked, "Mrs. McCarthy are you mad enough to run against Dan Frisa (my congressman). That's when my Irish temper kicked in and I replied yes. I wasn't serious at the time—although the next day every newspaper said I was. I kept thinking who am I to run for Congress—I am a nurse and mother from Long Island. I am not a politician. But people began calling and voicing their strong support. One of the callers reminded me that I would have a vote—a real voice in the gun debate. That's when I decided to run for office.[32]

Women legislators' motivations to serve stemmed partly from a desire for social change, especially changes in women's status in society and politics. Women state legislators frequently commented on the absence of women in their representative bodies, as in the following:

1. "There was an open seat and I wanted to see more women in the legislature."
2. "Laws impacted my life without my (woman's) participation."
3. "A need for a woman and a younger person on our school board."
4. "I wanted a woman in office."
5. "The opportunity to break the gender barrier."

A greater proportion of men, on the other hand, highlighted the desire to influence the breadth of the governmental mandate or to gain personal fulfillment. One male state legislator responded, "Political office has been a wonderful personal growth experience." Also notable is that men were more than twice as likely as women to indicate that they ran, in part, because they were asked to do so.[33]

The findings comport with previous literature on officeholders in that, as noted earlier, women have long been motivated by issue-related concerns and community activities.[34] Additionally, Edmond Costantini and Kenneth Craik (1977) found that gender-based differences in career outlooks for officeholders included the view that politics is for men at least partially a function of personal and career enhancement, whereas for women it was at least partially a labor of love.

We also asked state-level respondents to reveal the age they first dreamed of a political career, the age they first ran for office, and why they got involved when they did. A smaller proportion of women than men identified early dreams of a political career, and a smaller slice ran for office at early ages (see table 15.2). When men and women answered why they got involved when they did, gender-based differences were apparent. Consistent with earlier findings of this study, women were likely to state an issue motivation and men were likely to cite personal fulfillment. In individual comments, women state legislators tended more often to talk about timing in terms of age of children or marital status, although a few men in state legislatures did comment that young families and political office are hard to mix. "I did not, nor would I consider public office with children at home."

Table 15.3 explores these relationships by controlling for a host of variables, including sex, education level, age, party, religion, number of children, whether or not a prior office was held, presence or absence of a mentor, and the state the officeholder represents. The first half of the table shows those variables on which sex of the officeholder was statistically significant; the second half shows those variables on which the number of children was significant. As with the bivariate data, all else being equal, a higher proportion of women in state legislatures got involved in politically elite activity because of an issue motivation or as a result of community involvement. Men were likely to get involved because they had always wanted to. Even with control variables, a higher proportion of men than women were likely to have dreamed of political office at an early age and to have fulfilled those dreams by running. A specific example is that controlling for education, party, religion, prior office, and so on, women dream of running for office more than 3.3 years later than men and run for office almost 1.8 years later.

TABLE 15.3
Multivariate Analysis: Career Influences

Dependent Variable	b COEFF (SEX)	BETA WEIGHT	STANDARD ERROR	R^2
Issue	-.361***	-.150	.119	.107***
Community Activity	-.216**	-.095	.112	.113***
Always Wanted	.355***	.132	.134	.095***
AgeDream	3.318***	.136	1.148	.138***
AgeRun	1.783**	.102	.806	.169***

Dependent Variable	b COEFF (CHILDREN)	BETA WEIGHT	STANDARD ERROR	R^2
Social Change	.163***	.133	.061	.131***
Growth	.114*	.093	.062	.107***
AgeRun	.897**	.098	.444	.169***

*** Significant at the .01 level
** Significant at the .05 level
* Significant at the .10 level

NOTES: Coding: AgeDream and AgeRun in years; other dependent variables are a 1–7 scale with 1 = strongly agree and 7 = strongly disagree; sex 0 = male, 1 = female; children 0–5+ depending on number of children per respondent.

Each equation contained the following independent variables: sex, PID (party identification), educational level, presence or absence of a mentor, whether or not a prior office was held, number of children, religion, year born, and all but one of the states surveyed to allow an omitted category.

The b coefficients for each dependent variable were the only significant and meaningful predictors in the equations except for the following: In the "community activity" equation, PID was significant and negative (meaning that Republicans were more likely to get involved because of community activity) and Catholicism was significant and positive (Catholics more likely than others to get involved because of community activities); in the "always wanted to" equation, year born was significant and negative; in the "agerun" equation, education was significant and positive, and children was significant and positive; in the "change" equation, PID was significant and negative (meaning that Republicans agreed that wanting political change motivated them); in the "growth" equation, year born was negative.

Since gender is correlated with motivations to seek office, it should also be associated with motivations to leave. The replies from former members of Congress support this conclusion. Congresswomen were more likely than men to leave because of the effects of the job on the family. We correlated House career length and agreement with the following statements: "My family benefited from my service" and "My duties interfered with my time with my family." For women, the correlations were −.66 ($p = .00$) and .36 ($p = .13$), respectively. For men, the correlations were weak and statistically insignificant: −.05 ($p = .48$) and .04 ($p = .61$).

In addition, congresswomen were more likely than men to leave the legislature based on their perceived ability (or inability) to affect policy. Women's agreement with the statement, "Many of the things I did seemed trivial" and their career length were strongly related and significantly correlated (.48, $p = .04$), while men's correlation for the same was very weakly negative and not significant (−.05, $p = .50$) for men. Similarly, the correlation between women's career length and agreement with "I had little ability to influence important public policy issues" was .50 ($p = .03$), but only .16 ($p = .02$) for men.[35] This is quite consistent with gender differences in the motivations of state legislators to seek office in the first place. The correlations support the suggestions that women's interest in political careers is more greatly affected than men's by their perceived ability to have an impact on policy.

The second half of table 15.3 speaks to Hypothesis 3—that the presence or absence of children and the number of children affects the pursuit of political careers and motivations for them. Multivariate analysis of state legislative respondents indicates that the fewer the number of children, the more likely the respondent was to have gotten involved for social change or personal growth. Additionally, higher numbers of children meant running at a later age. For example, each additional child in the household delays the decision to run for office by almost a year.

These findings were consistent with the closest comparable data from the survey of former members of Congress. While members of Congress were not asked about the presence or absence of children in their life, they were asked a question about having children while in Congress. The average age of entry into the House for members with children while in office was 50, but it was 42 for those without children while in office ($p = .00$). Little needs to be said by way of explanation for these findings, as they simply support our expectation that family responsibility impedes or delays women's entry into political careers.

The remaining data on former members of Congress are not comparable to the state legislative survey findings. They are, however, interesting. The presence of children while in office has no clear effect on reasons for leaving the House of Representatives. Members with children differed only modestly from members without children with respect to job effects on career length. For members with children, career length and agreement with the statement "My family benefited from my service" were negatively correlated, but this was not statistically significant ($-.11$, $p = .15$); for members without children, a similar pattern emerged ($-.13$ ($p = .34$). Similarly, the correlation between parent's career length and agreement with "My duties interfered with my time with my family" was .02 ($p = .78$) and .16 ($p = .22$) for nonparents. In other words, parents or nonparents did not differ in their assessment of the pluses and minuses of longer congressional careers on their families.

There also was not much difference between parents and nonparents in the effects of their perceptions of their policy impact and career length. The correlation between parent's career length and agreement with the statement "Many of the things I did seemed trivial" was weak and not statistically significant ($-.06$, $p = .53$), and was .17 ($p = .18$) for nonparents. Conversely, the correlation between parent's career length and agreement with "I had little ability to influence important public policy issues" was .23 ($p = .00$), and was .11 ($p = .40$) for nonparents. For these former members of the House of Representatives, gender appears to be a more important influence on retirement than the presence of children in the home.

Taken together, the comparisons between parents and nonparents in legislatures suggest that much more work is needed on the effect of children on the career perceptions and decisions of officeholders. Parental status has an effect on motivation to enter politics, although it may not have a systematic and consistent effect on decisions to leave or perceptions of level of policy impact. At the same time, it is imperative to note that local, state, and national officeholders may differ on these variables. In any case, the exploration of hypotheses about the presence or absence of children and the number of children of respondents is of concern precisely because family status affects who runs for office, when, how they perceive their role in office, and the time commitment to public life, and has implications for how ideas about family participation affect the structure of public sphere careers.

Overall, the findings offered in this chapter suggest that men and women sometimes bring quite different backgrounds to political office, have different family experiences and duties in and out of office, face somewhat different hurdles, and have different sorts of visions about the pursuit of political life. Coupled with previous research in women in politics, the findings make clear that women officeholders, even if they have different burdens than men, have similar success levels in their pursuit of office, retention, and legislation while in office.[36] It seems that women have learned to adapt to both the private and public worlds and to succeed in both. The larger questions may be what these differences signal about the price for success and the structure of the public sphere more generally. That is the focus of the next section.

IMPLICATIONS: TOWARD VISIONS OF THE FUTURE

The two quotes that open the chapter, from men choosing family responsibilities over elected political office, suggest two points. The first is that the world of work and family and the division of labor by sex is changing, albeit slowly. Second, men suffer from excluding themselves from the lives of their families and may also want change. Certainly, this trend is larger than the political realm; it cuts across occupational categories. In *He Works/ She Works*, Rosalind Barnett and Caryl Rivers found that work was just as important to women as men and that men are much more concerned about family life and desirous of flexible work situations to accommodate family concerns than is often assumed. Similarly, Cary Cooper and Suzan Lewis note that "careers remain a major source of identity for most people, but members of the new work force are seeking a balanced life with involvement in both paid employment and family, where neither takes over completely."[37]

There is also ample evidence that men in politics wish to see the creation of different expectations of their work lives. Several state legislative respondents commented that providing child care in the statehouse, altering legislative scheduling around family time, providing child care reimbursement as one of the daily expenses for which legislators are compensated, and aligning the legislative calendar with children's academic calendars is important to creating a political work world in which families and careers can both be pursued.

Members of the U.S. Congress also think about these issues. "Democratic Representative Tim Roemer of Indiana, with his children ages one and two, wants the House to set 'a good example for the rest of the country' by organizing its work so that members can be a steady presence in their children's lives. '[Y]ou don't just talk about family values and vote on family values in Congress. You need to also practice family values.'"[38]

Six years later, Representative Roemer felt that being a congressional representative and a parent don't always mix easily. Roemer, who at 44 and with four young children, announced in January 2001 that he would not seek reelection in 2002. Roemer said, "It is no longer possible for me to meet the many demands of serving in Congress, and to completely fulfill my responsibility as a husband and father."[39]

This theme resonates with other members of Congress. Phil Duncan, in the *Congressional Quarterly Weekly Report*, noted, "At the outset of the 104th Congress, House Speaker Newt Gingrich, R-GA., promised to make the chamber more 'family friendly.' . . . To advise him on family concerns Gingrich created a House Family Quality of Life Advisory Committee."[40]

The opening quotes to the chapter also suggest that the imbalance in family and work life may very well be more seriously addressed as men become clearer and more vocal about what they are losing in the time bind. It certainly is not unprecedented for women to benefit when men challenge differential treatment based on sex. (See, for example, the U.S. Supreme Court case *Craig v. Boren*, dealing with beer drinking ages in Ohio, which were higher for men than women, or debates about unisex rates for auto insurance.)

Whatever the motivation, the imbalance needs addressing. Children need the debate to be furthered so that they can have the access to both their parents necessary for solid development. Another benefit of resolution is enhanced sex-role socialization. Cooper and Lewis (1994) note that studies of adolescent girls in two-worker families show that the extent to which girls hold nonstereotypical views of gender roles depends on the extent to which their fathers were involved in family life rather than whether or not their mothers had paid employment.

Men and women need the debate furthered so they can lead lives that accommodate both public and private needs. If accomplished, men will benefit from a larger role in their families. Women can pursue their ambitions for political life on all levels. Indeed, that will likely be limited until some balance is found. Shirley Williams says: "Until those happen [the real revolution in shared family responsibilities] you will not see more than a very small number of women, in my view, opting for a job as demanding as politics."[41] Given that women make up only 22.5 percent of state legislatures and 12.1 percent of the U.S. Congress, she may very well be right. Democracy needs the debate to be resolved so that all the voices in society are well represented in the halls of governance and all available talent is used.

That change is possible is argued by many authors on this subject. Christina Nippert-Eng maintains that "through the aggregation of these personal boundary negotiations, culture is preserved and changed as conceptual frameworks are shored up, bent, or restructured to accommodate more private realities and visions."[42] Cultural norms about workplace and family can prove as difficult to penetrate and as impervious to change as the cultural boundaries identified by Gelb in her chapter in this volume. Even the most "successful" legislators can find their status diminished or their effectiveness constrained by societal understanding about family duties and responsibilities.

Other authors discuss not just the possibility but the practicalities of such change. In *The Overworked American*, Juliet Schor (1992) argues that change in the way we allocate time to our professional lives and the demands on that time will not happen unless we organize and demand it. She further notes that "the growth of worktime did not occur as a result of public debate. There has been little attention from government, academia, or civic organizations. For the most part, the issue has been off the agenda, a non-choice, a hidden trade off."[43] Similarly, Arlie Hochschild in *The Time Bind* (1997) argues for a "new time movement" such as has been the case before in our history related to an eight-hour workday.

And government is perhaps the best place to lead the revolution of which Williams, Schor, and Hochschild speak. If we think of our government as a representative branch reflecting and mirroring our values, then it is also the place we can influence the grand experiments of values change.

NOTES

Sue Thomas wishes to express deep appreciation to Beth Stark, Kerry Mulvihill, Alba Rojo, and Emma Craswell for their help in performing survey mailings, data coding, and other tasks, Mary Bendyna for her SPSS expertise, Wesley Joe for translating datafiles into usable form, Michael Moore for sharing his knowledge about legislative careers, and the Georgetown Summer Grant Program, the Faculty Deans Grant Fund, the Publication Fund, and the Competitive Grant-in-Aid Fund for the resources to perform survey analysis. Rebekah Herrick acknowledges the Dirksen Congressional Center and the Caterpillar Foundation for sponsoring and funding the survey of former members of Congress.

1. Peter Perl, "Bill Paxon's Awe in the Family," *Washington Post*, 26 February 1998, p. B:1.

2. Megan Rosenfeld, "21-Gun Send-Off," *Washington Post*, 7 February 1998, p. B:1.

3. Carroll, "Personal Is Political"; Blair and Stanley, "Personal Relationships and Power."

4. Hochschild and Machung, *Second Shift*; Holtzman and Williams, "Women in the Political World."

5. Burrell, "Campaign Finance"; Duerst-Lahti, "Bottleneck"; Darcy, Welch, and Clark, *Women, Elections, and Representation*; Carroll, *Women as Candidates*.

6. Frantzich, "De-Recruitment"; Prinz, "Career Paths."

7. For a congressional-level example, see Maisel and Stone, "Determinants of Candidate Emergence."

8. Carroll, "Political Careers of Women Officials"; Carroll, *Women as Candidates*; Darcy, Welch, and Clark, *Women, Elections, and Representation*; Carroll and Strimling, *Women's Routes to Office*; Burrell, "Campaign Finance"; Duerst-Lahti, "Bottleneck"; Fox, *Gender Dynamics*; Herrick, "Reappraisal of the Quality of Women Candidates"; Rosenthal, "Divided Lives."

9. Schlesinger, *Ambition and Politics*.

10. Ibid.; Wilson, *Amateur Democrat*; Matthews, *Social Background*; Black, "Theory of Professionalization."

11. Abramson, Aldrich, and Rohde, "Progressive Ambition"; Maisel and Stone, "Determinants of Candidate Emergence."

12. Rohde, "Risk-Bearing and Progressive Ambition"; Brace, "Progressive Ambition"; Squire, "State Legislative Careers"; Herrick and Moore, "Political Ambition's Effect"; Hibbing, *Congressional Careers*; Canon, *Actors, Athletes, and Astronauts*.

13. Costantini and Craik, "Women as Politicians"; Stoper, "Wife and Politician;" Sapiro and Farah, "New Pride and Old Prejudice"; Githens, "Spectators, Agitators or Lawmakers"; Gertzog, *Congressional Women*.

14. Carroll, *Women as Candidates*; Costantini, "Political Women and Political Ambition"; Carey, Niemi, and Powell, "Are Women State Legislators Different?"

15. Dolan and Ford, "Changing Times, Changing Styles."

16. See also Dodson, "Change and Continuity." For similar patterns among state-level public administrators, see Johnson and Duerst-Lahti, "Public Work, Private Lives."

17. See also Stoper, "Wife and Politician."

18. Frantzich, "De-Recruitment"; Hibbing, *Choosing to Leave*; Prinz, "Career Paths."

19. Carroll, *Women as Candidates*; Dodson, "Gender Difference"; Sapiro, "Private Costs of Public Commitments."

20. Diversity in political culture was a major criterion for selection because those in different traditions might develop different views of the political world. Elazar, *American Federalism*, identifies three major cultures: the traditionalistic, the moralistic, and the individualistic. Washington, Colorado, Vermont, California, and Ohio represent the moralistic political culture; Maryland, Pennsylvania, Illinois, New York, and Massachusetts the individualistic culture; and Arizona, Kentucky, Oklahoma, Virginia, and Mississippi the traditionalistic culture. The highly professionalized legislatures in this sample are California, New York, and Massachusetts. The middle range includes Illinois, Ohio, Pennsylvania, and Colorado. A. Rosenthal, "State Legislative Development."

21. Dillman, *Mail and Telephone Surveys*; Salant and Dillman, *How to Conduct Your Own Survey*.

22. We conducted four mailings to each former member. The first let respondents know a survey was coming. The second included the survey, a cover letter, and a return self-addressed stamped envelope. The third mailing was a postcard to remind the respondents to return the survey. And a final mailing was sent to those who had not responded and included the same items as the second mailing.

24. Lascher, "Impact of Job Satisfaction."

24. Schroeder, *24 Years of House Work*, 144.

25. Jacqueline Salmon, "Fever Pitch," *Washington Post*, 1 February 1998, p. A:1

26. "On the Road," *Ms. Magazine*, May/June 1997, 29.

27. D'Antonio, "If I'd Only Known Then," *Redbook*, September 1996, 97–100.

28. Hocshchild, *Time Bind*; Cooper and Lewis, *Managing the New Work Force*.

29. One indicates strong agreement and 5 indicates strong disagreement.

30. C. Rosenthal, "Divided Lines"; Schroeder, *24 Years of House Work*, 133.

31. Diamond, *Sex Roles in the State House*; Kirkpatrick, *Political Woman*; Carroll and Strimling, *Women's Routes to Office*; Gertzog, *Congressional Women*; Assendelft and O'Connor, "Backgrounds, Motivations, and Interests."

32. Carolyn McCarthy, interview by author, 3 March 2000.

33. Each of these findings was statistically significant at the .05 level or below.

34. Assendelft and O'Connor, "Backgrounds, Motivations, and Interests."

35. Each of these findings was statistically significant at the .05 level or below.

36. Thomas, "Voting Patterns"; Thomas, "Impact of Women"; Thomas, "Effects of Race and Gender"; Thomas, *How Women Legislate*; Thomas, "Women in State Leg-

islatures"; Dodson and Carroll, *Reshaping the Agenda*; Tamerius, "Sex, Gender, and Leadership."

37. Cooper and Lewis, *Managing the New Work Force*, x.

38. Duncan, "Routines in the House."

39. Gregory Giroux, "Roemer Says He Won't Run for 7th Term," *CQ Weekly*, 27 January 2001, 234.

40. The House failed to even remotely accomplish its goal, though the need or desire for it is apparent. Duncan, "Routines in the House," also notes that "since January 4 the House had adjourned at 9 p.m. 54 percent of the time."

41. Shirley Williams, introduction, 30.

42. Nippert-Eng, *Home and Work*, xiii.

43. Schor, *Overworked American*.

CHAPTER SIXTEEN

REPRESENTING WOMEN IN BRITAIN AND THE UNITED STATES

The Quest for Numbers and Power

JOYCE GELB

The 1997 election of Labourite Tony Blair in England and the accompanying landslide election brought with it an unprecedented number of new women MPs to the British House of Commons. In this chapter, the experience of that dramatic increase at Westminster will be evaluated and the future prospects for women's increased representation will be explored. More important, I ask: To what extent have the gains of Labour women borne fruit in the New Labour government under Blair, in a system of centralized strong party leadership?

The article will examine (1) the reasons for the dramatic doubling of British women in Parliament in 1997, (2) the importance of changing opportunity structures in order to increase women's representation, (3) the extent to which increased numbers have produced gains in leadership and power, and (4) the extent to which increased numbers have led to institutional changes in terms of party culture and future electoral gains for women. Finally, the analysis will look at the similarities and differences between the British experience and the American one in the U.S. Congress.

In the case of Britain, the chapter will suggest the following:

1. Changes in women's representation in Britain were the result of changes in political culture and rules, or the "political opportunity

structure." These in turn were predicated on women's mobilization within the Labour party and supportive male leadership.

2. Increased representation by gender does not guarantee increased power or leadership impact, particularly in a strong, centralized party system in which the political agenda is articulated by cabinet members.

3. While the dramatic increase in numbers has produced some gains for women, these appear at the present to be largely incremental rather than radical in nature. In addition to the strong party system, the traditional politics of the House of Commons have proven difficult to alter substantially to date.

Comparison with the U.S. case will suggest that the likelihood of fundamental institutional change like that witnessed in Britain is remote. Though the so-called Year of the Woman in 1992 and the less dramatic but important numerical increases in the 2000 U.S. election have steadily increased women in Congress, slow growth will likely continue in the future absent some unforeseen change in the political opportunity structure. However, the lack of dramatic transformation in numbers of women in Congress does not preclude incremental increases in representation, policy impact, and leadership roles for women in the U.S. legislature, as other authors in this volume have demonstrated.

CHANGING THE RULES AND OPPORTUNITY STRUCTURE

The concept of political opportunity structure refers to institutions, values, and political alignments that shape the goals and strategies available to advocates of social change.[1] These may include processes of candidate selection, access to money and networks of political support, and different national electoral systems. Political opportunity structures also include party culture or type of organizational structure, which in the case of the British Labour party is highly bureaucratic and centralized. Does altering the rules change the internal party structure and dynamics?

In Britain, a strong tradition of socialist feminism led women to gravitate toward left parties and labor unions in order to further their political goals once the second wave of feminism had begun in the 1960s and 1970s. Despite concern about participating in male-dominated structures, women were active in the Labour party throughout the 1980s. Through their increased presence at party conferences, they sought to influence the policy-making structure of the party to ensure more attention to women's concerns. The increased representation of women as candidates and party officials led one observer to suggest that after 1987 "a quiet revolution" was taking place in the Labour party.[2] During the 18 years of Conservative rule, 1979–97, the opportunity structure was, in general, inhospitable to women's interests. However, during this period, women's activism made the party more receptive to integrating the demands of the women's movement and helped lay the groundwork for the Labour party's electoral victory in 1997.[3]

Changing Party Opportunity Structures in Britain

What accounts for the dramatic increase of British women MPs? The explanation rests with the Labour party since female representation declined in the Conservative and Liberal Democratic parties during the same period. Clearly, a combination of factors including women's mobilization, changes in the predominant culture of the Labour party, and the process of internal organizational reform produced a new opportunity structure for women that enabled them to utilize positive discrimination in the Labour nomination process. Labour altered party practices to permit women to contest winnable seats, which contributed to the success of Labour women in a year of electoral momentum.

The 1997 election produced 101 women Labour MPs—or 24 percent of the parliamentary representation—up from 4 percent before 1983 and 9 percent in 1992.[4] At the same time as the Labour party's special measures produced impressive gains, female MPs in the Conservative Party declined to 13, or 7.8 percent (the same number as in 1931), despite the large numbers of women who are party members and occupy party positions. While the Liberal Democrats doubled their parliamentary representation in 1997, the number of women MPs elected through that party fell from 4 to 3 (compared to 43 men), or 6.5 percent of the party total.[5]

Among the 101 women Labour MPs were 65 first-time elected women MPs. This increase in women's representation may be attributed to three factors: women's activism within the Labour party, which had pressed for increased representation in nominees and party posts for almost two decades; the policy of positive action implemented by the Labour party beginning in 1988; and the landslide victory for Labour.[6]

Several forces unleashed in the Labour party contributed to women's successful mobilization for more candidacies and power during the 1980s. While Margaret Thatcher's Tories dominated the British political agenda, women mobilized within the Labour party, which began to modernize party procedures. First, the Labour Women's Action Committee emerged to press for more female candidates and more attention to such issues as child care. EMILY's List, U.K., developed within the Labour party (utilizing the example of its American progenitor) and began to raise money specifically for women candidates.[7] Second, as the party sought to reorganize to mount a more effective opposition to Tory rule, the prior power of the union bloc vote that had dominated Labour party politics was reduced, resulting in a more positive climate for women's mobilization. Finally, women activists were able to take advantage of the process of party modernization, initiated by the party leadership, and advance their concerns onto the mainstream agenda.[8]

At a succession of party conferences beginning with 1988, Labour delegates approved resolutions stipulating that every constituency nominating slate—or shortlist selected by local members from whom the final candidate would be drawn—should include at least one woman candidate if a woman was nominated in that constituency. They resolved that women should constitute at least 40 percent of all party committees and delegations and suggested that local constituency associations voluntarily adopt all-women shortlists and that all-women shortlists would operate in half of all vacant and targeted Labour seats.[9] Additional rules stipulated that the names of at least three women be on any valid ballot (raised to four in 1993). Under pressure from women activists, Labour committed to policies supporting improvement of child care and equal opportunity in the workplace.

Strategies for Positive Action Implemented by Labour

Lovenduski contrasts three types of party strategies for increasing the number of women in decision making and candidacies: (1) rhetorical—accepting women's claims in party platforms and agendas; (2) positive action—providing training, financial assistance, and some targets to increase women's participation; and (3) positive discrimination—setting aside places on decision bodies, candidate slates, shortlists.[10] Gradually the Labour party moved from one stage to the next during the 1980s and 1990s.

Under the social democratic style leadership of party leaders Michael Foot, Neal Kinnock, and John Smith, the Labour party accepted a move toward "positive (or affirmative) action," altering the party's culture and political opportunity structure.[11]

The first effort to increase positive action to increase women's candidacies was in 1988, when the Labour party adopted the objective of increasing women's representation at all levels of the party.[12] Gradually, voluntary efforts to increase the number of women became mandatory, and the logic of utilizing quotas was extended to parliamentary candidacies.[13] In 1989, the party accepted the concept of quotas to increase women's representation at every level of the party. Specifically, the party conference called for these efforts: (1) for women to be half the statutory branch officers and branch delegates to the constituency party, (2) for constituency parties to select a woman delegate at least every other year, (3) for trade unions to include women as conference delegates, and (4) for quotas to ensure women's election to the party's ruling body, the National Executive Committee (NEC). By 1990, rules changes supported by the party conference led to quotas of 40 percent women for every party-related position.[14]

The fall 1993 annual party conference went further than its predecessors by agreeing to introduce all-women shortlists in half of the "inheritor" seats—or open seats where a Labour MP retired—and half the "strong challenger" seats, defined as most winnable. Although controversial, positive actions/quotas were adopted on a vote of two-thirds of party members and three-quarters of all elected politicians.[15] John Smith, then party leader, supported such efforts to improve women's political prospects and endorsed them heartily. From 1994 to 1996, the NEC was given the power to intervene where regional targets were not achieved, and new women constituency officers (at least three of seven local party officers designated in each constituency had to be women under the new rules) were usually sympathetic to increasing women's candidacies.[16]

In Britain, two disgruntled male applicants challenged the policy of all-women shortlists in 1996. In the case *Jepson and Dyas Elliott v. the Labour Party* (1996, IRLR 116 ET) decided by an industrial tribunal, the court concluded that the party selection procedure facilitates access to employment and is therefore subject to the U.K. Sex Discrimination Act, which prohibits sex discrimination with regard to provision of public services.[17] The NEC, by then under the control of Tony Blair, the soon-to-be prime minister, decided not to appeal this decision, instead establishing a working group to identify other ways to maximize women's candidacies. Nonetheless, all 34 of the women placed on all-women shortlists prior to the court challenge were elected, and because Labour women were shortlisted for the most winnable seats and seats with retiring MPs, a record number were swept into government despite the fact that they constituted just a handful more candidates than in 1992. Sixty-four percent—101 of 158 female candidates— were elected.[18] The electoral landslide was key to their success, along with the targeting of "inheritor" and "strong challenger" seats. While the campaign did not highlight women's issues, the presence of women candidates seemed to mobilize unusual support from women and attracted more women voters than ever before, including women over age 55.

Impact on Policy and Leadership

To what extent has electoral success of Labour women brought increased power and leadership roles, as well as the "feminization" of the parliamentary political agenda and style?[19] The general consensus appears to be that while there has been improvement in appointments of women to government roles, few positions have been at the cutting edge of power, limiting women's clout in terms of policy making. For example, there are few, if any, women in the Blair inner circle of power, regardless of formal positions held by women.[20]

In terms of numbers, however, there has been a clear improvement for women's representation. There were no women in Prime Minister Major's first cabinet, in 1990, and only two, or 9 percent, in his second cabinet, which preceded the Blair government. In the Blair government, however, women constituted 23 percent of the total. In addition to filling the backbench in record numbers, Labour women secured key parliamentary leadership posts in the newly elected Labour government: Chief Whip Ann Taylor, House of Commons Leader Margaret Beckett, Speaker Betty Boothroyd, and House of Lords Leader Baroness Jay of Paddington. The party's general secretary also is a woman, and Labour women received appointments as secretaries of state, four as ministers of state, while another nine became parliamentary under-secretaries. Mo Mowlam was named secretary of state for Northern Ireland (subsequently minister for the cabinet office); Margaret Beckett served as the president of the Board of Trade in addition to her parliamentary post; and Dawn Primarolo entered the Treasury in an important role, requiring Treasury to calculate the gender effect of all of its actions.[21] In all, women made up over 20 percent of Labour government appointees. In part, this process represented a continuation of the quota system that mandated at least five places for women in the opposition shadow cabinet, imposed by the Labour party while out of power in the 1980s and 1990s.[22] Margaret Hodge's appointment at the Department for Education and Employment enabled her to have an impact on education and child care, while Patricia Hewitt, minister for small business and e-commerce, and Barbara Roche, one of three ministers of state in the Home Office, have had a role in creating opportunities for women in small business. Tessa Jowell, as minister for public health, has impacted policies on teen pregnancy, and Economic Secretary to the Treasury Patricia Hewitt has influenced welfare reform measures.[23]

Most women in cabinet posts are in traditional fields such as health, education, and international development, far from key areas such as finance and employment.[24] There were grumblings from some that women were not appointed to positions with spending responsibility, but were given "housekeeping" roles instead.[25] For instance, only one woman was put in charge of a parliamentary select committee.[26] Although two party assistant whips were female, no full whips were. The promised Ministry for Women, which would have created a women's cabinet position as outlined in the 1995 and 1996 Labour party resolutions, was limited to cabinet subcommittee status as a Woman's Unit and was never viewed as having the clout of the more powerful "Social Exclusion" unit, whose mission is to fight poverty and social deprivation, primarily through new employment policies.[27] The first minister for women, and head of the Women's Unit, Harriet Harman, was not given a separate ministerial salary and was forced to share this position with her primary role, as minister for social security. Minister Harman's second-in-command, Joan Ruddock, was unpaid during this period. Both women were identified with feminism in Britain and encountered tension between their ideology and the centralized and hierarchical New Labour leadership and structure.

The first major policy controversy centered around the Blair government's decision to reduce the lone-parent rate of benefit, which abolished the single-parent premium. While this action was congruent with spending estimates inherited from the prior Tory government, the announcement of this new policy by Harriet Harman was roundly criticized as inconsistent with the feminist agenda. Harman valiantly defended the prime minister's policy, with which she probably personally disagreed, but in the advent of the intense protest that ensued, she was removed from office.[28] Her successor as minister for women was Baroness Jay, who was not even a member of the House of Commons; her main task was to lead the House of Lords. In the Blair cabinet reshuffle of 1998, there was no woman who held a brief comparable to that which Harman had held in Social Security.[29] This was a dual loss from the perspective of some women observers: Harman's leadership of the important Social Security ministry and the assignment of the Women's Unit to a nonmember of the House of Commons. There has been talk of merging the Women's Unit with the Social Exclusion Unit (to fight poverty and entrenched deprivation, a more central priority of the Blair agenda) and the Sure Start Program under Minister for the Cabinet Office Mowlam, which would mean a loss in the independent status of the Women's Unit.[30]

According to Sylvia Bashevkin and others, the impact of the record numbers of women in the cabinet has been limited under a New Labour government focused more on centralization of power and party modernization than its predecessors.[31] Nonetheless, the minister for women is perceived by many female MPs as providing additional resources without which there would be no priority given to women's concerns and perspectives as part of policy agendas.[32] Efforts to utilize the Women's Unit to "mainstream" policy to other agencies and to dialogue with women and women's groups have disappointed those who hoped for more dramatic change.[33] No leader has emerged as yet in the Blair government who is comparable to Barbara Castle, who, as secretary for employment and productivity in the Wilson Labour government of the late 1960s, was a visible symbol in altering the balance of power between men and women.[34]

With regard to policy-making power, the record is at best mixed and the record-breaking election of women ambiguous in meaning. In categorizing the new bloc of women MPs as "Blair's Babes," the press both trivialized the role of women in politics and created false expectations that these new women MPs would act collectively and create a women's agenda.[35] The reality has been more complex.

The Labour party's successful campaign did not include specific positions on such priority women's movement issues as overhauling equal pay and sex discrimination legislation and creating a national child care program.[36] Women were seen as marginal to Blair's team of all-male advisors. In the highly centralized British party system, backbenchers, a category into which the newly elected women fall, have only a limited policy-making role. Women backbenchers are convinced that public disagreement and voting against party proposals will result in isolation and powerlessness.[37] The costs of speaking out and disagreeing are great and inhibit most from being anything but loyal and quiescent, particularly if individual women aspire to further their own careers.[38]

Although the "Third Way" philosophy of the Blair government has endorsed a number of policies highly beneficial to women, it is reluctant to identify with feminism and promote a pro-woman agenda.[39] For Blair and many of his young advisors, feminism is associated with the old, discredited left; key insiders are more comfortable with strategies that oppose poverty and social exclusion, as well as racism, with women considered as a subgroup.[40] The rights- and change-oriented approach of the liberal left has been replaced by consensus goals, which emphasize inclusiveness and order, family and community, rather than structural inequalities and economic dynamism.[41] In this new "communitarian" value system, group-based oppositional politics in society and party are suspect. It is difficult to build and sustain solidarity among women politicians, even from the same party, where the culture is profoundly individualistic and appointments are by favor.[42] A recent study of New Labour women found that relatively few women representatives perceive their role as primarily involving substantive representation of women's interests, though 40 percent view their role as including such representation.[43] As illustrated in Susan Carroll's chapter, such attitudes reflect the changing mix of representational philosophies among U.S. congresswomen, too, especially since the election of the 104th Congress. Women politicians who are ambitious are caught between supporting party positions and forging their own approaches.

Viewed from this perspective, the overall impact of the unprecedented numbers of cabinet-level women and of those in the House of Commons has been negligible at best . . . "worse than useless."[44] The gap between expectations and the limited visible progress made has heightened the perception that women's achievements to date have not lived up to their advance notices. Women appear unlikely to rebel against party strictures, and newly elected women are more likely to support the government than others.[45] This view has been reinforced by two recent studies reported in the British press, which contend that Labour women have had little impact on policy since their election.[46]

While the institutional rules for nominating and electing women candidates have been transformed, there has been little comparable transformation of the party's male-dominated policy-making structure and "politics as usual" in the House of Commons.[47] Symptomatic of the difficulties in changing the political culture, or the political opportunity structure for policy making, are the obstacles placed before the work of the Modernization Committee in the House of Commons. Established to reform parliamentary procedures to make them more open and women-friendly, the committee has made modest improvements, such as reduced hours of late-night work in order to accommodate family responsibilities, but there has been no effort to create more "family friendly" facilities for women and children.[48]

Other analysts present a more nuanced view of women's impact and the party's policy role. About 50 percent of New Labour women MPs interviewed (34 of the 65) contend that their enhanced presence does permit the articulation of women's concerns in a new way, particularly on such issues as child care, education, equal opportunities, and employment.[49] Women are seen as pressuring ministers to endorse and prioritize policies favorable to women on such issues as education and the welfare state, rather than sponsoring gender-based legislation on their own in the House.[50] In this view, women politicians are not pursuing aggressive, confrontational approaches, but rather seeking to open up dialogue and discussion, stressing cooperation and teamwork, and consultation.[51] They have sought to move away from debates on the floor and use the power of questioning in select committees to raise issues and develop new approaches.[52] They are more likely to attempt to persuade ministers to make changes than to seek to make them themselves.[53] Seen from this perspective, women's most important political role is behind the scenes. This approach to politics means that women's accomplishments, however significant, are unheralded, uncredited, and difficult to discern.

Failure to create a "sea change" in the years since 1997 may also relate to the absence of a "critical mass" among women representatives in the House.[54] The success of bills affecting women is heavily dependent on the proportion of women in a legislative body and their visibility; they must have a large enough or unified enough group so that their attitudes and behaviors will permeate the mainstream.[55] According to Thomas, the minimum percentage for critical mass is probably about 20 percent (the UN Commission on the Status of Women suggests 30 percent). With lower numbers women may feel intimidated and reluctant to maintain a high profile on women's issues.[56] Given the constraints of party, numbers, and political culture, women MPs at present may not be able to participate as a distinctive political group; although if numbers increase, they form a more cohesive unit. However, it is well to recall Drude Dahlrup's suggestion that it may be "critical acts" that count in some instances, rather than a "critical mass."[57]

As suggested above, New Labour women did not espouse particular policy goals related to women. However, women in the House arguably have had an impact on gender-related policy, helping to pave the way for protections for part-time workers, efforts to balance work and family life, "Fairness at Work" and Maternity Review policies and improved maternity pay and parental leave, and better benefits for poor women.[58] No doubt, a number of Labour initiatives also have disproportionately benefited women and are collectively referred to as "family friendly." Perhaps due to the leadership of Harman and Ruddock in the Women's Unit, in 1998 a record increase in child benefit was instituted through the National Childcare Strategy and a child care tax credit was adopted. In 1999, child benefit levels were raised again and spending increased on health education and the elderly. Publicly funded day care has been made available to four-year-olds with the proviso that similar provision will be made for 66 percent of three-year-olds by 2002.[59]

The "Welfare to Work" strategy also benefits women, by moving economically inactive women into the paid labor force. Counseling and training schemes for women (previously primarily for men only) were improved, and more cash made available to lone women parents. The New Deal for Lone Parents provides training for work, and the subsequent Lone Parent Benefit Run On provides two extra weeks of benefits when women move from the program into jobs. A new, second state pension will credit women who care for children under age six as if they were earning £9000 per year. The Working Families Tax Credit was intended to provide more resources to the disproportionately female group within the working poor.[60] Women MPs were instrumental in ensuring that this benefit would be awarded to mothers.[61] Through the National Carers strategy, support for home caring work increased. Other women-friendly policies have included introduction of a national minimum wage, 13-week unpaid parental leave (mandated by the EU) for either parent during the first five years of a child's life, and provisions to aid part-time workers. The Sure Start Maternity grant doubled, and maternity benefits have been extended from 44 weeks to one year; maternity pay is for 8 weeks at full pay (though this remains far lower than what is available in other European nations).[62]

Women in the House were also effective in pressuring the government to increase cash payments to women and children under the Immigration and Asylum Bill, to restore welfare benefits to asylum seekers who need to wait more than six months for their requests to be resolved.[63] Abused wives in their first year of residence in the United Kingdom gained government permission to remain permanently, rather than being deported.[64]

Women have asked oral questions in proportion to their numbers, although it is difficult to assess their impact on select committees, which have a tradition of unanimity. Select committees hold inquiries, issue reports, recommend bills, and exercise oversight over different policy areas. (Only one select committee, Environment, Transport, and Regions, has had a woman chair, Gwyneth Dunwood, through 2000.)[65] According to MP Mactaggart, Labour women MPs have helped to initiate a number of new all-party groups on issues of particular concern to women, including domestic violence and child care.

Perhaps as a function of their newcomer status, women backbenchers appeared more likely than their male counterparts to support the government at least in the first days of the new Labour majority. This practice was of particular importance shortly after the election in the fall 1997 vote on the government bill to reduce the lone-parent benefit premium. While 11 percent of the parliamentary party voted against the proposal, only 7 percent of women did.[66] However, by 1999, among 80 Labour parliamentarians were a handful of newly emboldened backbench Labour women who vigorously opposed and voted against a welfare reform and pensions bill that premised continued support for the unemployed on their willingness to accept training and work. They also protested that tightened eligibility rules for invalid benefit claimants were likely to disproportionately affect women in a negative manner.[67]

Other examples of increasing independence by women MPs and evolving efforts to shift the policy agenda in a women-friendly way are sometimes difficult to discern. Harman and Ruddock may have brought new issues and perspectives to bear on policy making during their brief tenure in the cabinet, particularly with regard to the increased attention to child care with tax credits and the other expanded benefits discussed above.[68] In recent months, women MPs have sought more media coverage of such issues as maternity pay and paid parental leave, with considerable success in putting these policies on the public agenda.[69]

The Future of Women in Elected Roles in Britain

The political opportunity structure with respect to women's representation in Britain continues to evolve. Women constitute 36 percent of the newly established Scottish parliament and 38 percent in the Welsh assembly. The European parliamentary elections of 1999 saw the proportion of women MEPs from Britain rise from 17 to 24 (of 87).[70] These dramatic changes were made through the use of "twinned" constituencies in the absence of incumbents in the newly formed devolved governments, and in the alternation of male and female candidates in the European election. These new procedures are representative of a new, more facilitative approach to women's political equity in Britain, but it is not clear what impact the newly devolved governments at the subnational level, and the European Union at the transnational level, will have on English government in the future.

The future of women in the House of Commons is also uncertain. Increased representation in England in 1997 occurred in large measure due to all-women shortlists as well as targeting winnable seats, but prospects for restoration of the all-women shortlists are dim. In May 2001, Baroness Jay announced that the Labour party would propose a new election law mandating all-women shortlists in all of the parties.[71] A new election law would overturn the unfavorable court ruling and circumvent the strictures of the Sex Discrimination Act, but such changes did not take effect before the June 2001 election. With only one positive action measure remaining in the Labour party rules (i.e., the "one woman on a shortlist" rule),[72] the number of Labour women running for Parliament in 2001 dropped below that of 1997. As a result of the 2001 election, the number of women in the House of Commons declined from 117 to 106, with losses among the Labour women accounting for the lion's share of seats lost for women (101 to 88).

Clearly, in the absence of the adoption of new mechanisms and procedures in selection, it is difficult to expect continued rapid progress in women's candidacies or their electability. Nonetheless, following the June 2001 election, Tony Blair gave cabinet portfolios to seven women. As a result the number of women in the cabinet was at its highest level ever, 30.4 percent, with several appointed to spending positions.[73]

One additional postscript to the 2001 British elections. Some of the Labour women who stood down from their seats had harsh criticism for the institution and its masculine traditions. Tess Kingham, one of the most outspoken critics, explained that she decided not to run again because she wanted "a productive working life, not a cultural experience in a gentleman's club."[74] Jenny Jones, another Labour MP who retired after only four years, cited the physical working conditions, the absence of a daycare center, and the jeering, name-calling, and boorish behavior that characterized many debates.[75] While the huge class of women MPs in 1997 successfully lobbied for improved working hours and better facilities to help members with young children, the climate in Parliament remains a source of discouragement to women MPs.

This analysis has underscored the significance of changing political rules and opportunity structures on women's political representation. However, despite the dramatic increase in the number of women in Parliament and in their appointive ministerial roles, clear policy impact has been more incremental, though not inconsequential. Moreover, the impact on political culture including party ideology, party culture, and parliamentary norms is less clear. Although changes appear to be under way, more dramatic success will be a question for the future.

REPRESENTING WOMEN IN THE UNITED STATES

In 1992, unprecedented numbers of women vied for all levels of U.S. electoral office and were elected in record numbers. By 2000, women's congressional candidacies had increased from 106 to 122, demonstrating steady improvement.[76] Women constituted 13 percent of the Senate, adding four new members in 2000, and 12.6 percent of the House. How do these gains for women in American legislative politics compare with those of their British sisters? What similarities and differences can be seen through the lens of comparative politics?

Clearly, the similarities and differences between the two countries underscore the importance of understanding the political opportunity structures by which lawmakers are chosen and the institutional norms within which they operate to achieve policy goals. The most prominent similarity in the two cases—a visible national political leader who championed new roles for women—is not enough to overcome the chief institutional differences of a parliamentary system built on cohesive, centralized parties as contrasted with a separated system and weak political parties. Moreover, the party structures, which produce differing levels of women's representation and visibility of women in leadership, also generate different possibilities for achievement of policy goals.

Women in U.S. Party Organizations and as Candidates

Because of the power of incumbency, weak parties, and candidate-centered nominations and elections in the United States, change in the political opportunity structure that would create more favorable conditions for increased representation of women is likely to be limited. Moreover, the radical rules changes that transformed women's representation in the British case are highly unlikely in the United States. While some provisions for gender equity in the Democratic party's selection process for the presidential nominating convention have been implemented, efforts to achieve affirmative action in candidacies for women have been rejected as reverse discrimination.[77]

Moreover, the weakness of American political parties would limit the impact of directives designed to achieve greater representation. Parties in the United States are weak organizationally, and cannot control their nominees for office once they are elected. Complicating the matter is the fact that each of the 50 state party organizations have their own rules for nominating candidates for electoral office. In this system of candidate-centered elections, individuals recruit themselves for office, often with group support.[78] Changing the rules in this type of weak party system would have little impact on nominations since parties no longer have exclusive control over the candidate recruitment process.[79]

Nonetheless, party change along feminist lines has occurred to some extent, and to a limited extent, parallels between Britain's New Labour years and the 1990s in the United States are evident. Throughout the 1980s, with the election of Reagan and right-wing dominance in the Republican party, the GOP became less hospitable to feminist interests. The emergence of the gender gap in voting and significant activism within the Democratic party by gender-equality advocates reflected a shift of women to the Democratic party just as women migrated toward Labour in Britain.[80] Many feminist groups viewed positively the eight years of the Clinton administration and the resulting political opportunity structure.[81]

While the influence and financial aid of nonparty groups such as EMILY's List remain of great importance for U.S. female candidates, the initial hostility to women's candidacies by party leaders also has abated, and women, particularly in the Democratic party, are more easily able to gain their party's nomination for office.[82] Evidence of a changing party environment in the United States can be seen, as women have headed each party's national committee; and as of 1978 the Democrats wrote into their rules that there be equal representation for men and women as national convention delegates.[83] As of 2001, Nita Lowey (D-NY) and Patty Murray (D-WA) became the first women to lead House and Senate Democratic campaign committees, respectively.[84] The percentages of women delegates in the Republican party also rose, and women's candidacies were promoted more avidly by both parties after the discovery of the "gender gap" in 1980. The number of female major party nominees for the House doubled between 1972 and 1984, from 32 to 65. Since then it has leveled off, with Republican party nominees accounting for much of the rise. However, since 1992, the Democratic party has nominated twice as many women to the House as Republicans have.[85]

Both parties have provided special funds for female candidates, and have supported training workshops to encourage women to run for office. Counterbalancing EMILY's List, which has attracted about 40,000 contributors since its founding in 1986 to provide seed money to Democratic pro-choice candidates, is the Republican WISH List. In addition, GOPAL (GOP Women's Political Action League) and the Eleanor Roosevelt Fund within the Democratic party were developed in the 1980s to raise money specifically for female candidates.[86]

In spite of these attempts, the major obstacle to women's national electoral opportunities in the United States continues to be the power of incumbency.[87] Moreover, the U.S. system of weak decentralized parties makes it virtually impossible to imagine positive discrimination efforts of the sort described in Britain. While the U.S. women's movement has pressed for election of more women to office at all levels, women's representation seems likely to continue on a slow but steady basis, punctuated periodically by dramatic change as in 1992, and to a lesser extent in 2000.

Leadership Positions

Tony Blair and Bill Clinton are often cast as two similar patrons of greater women's representation in national politics. Where the British press made much ado about "Blair's Babes," women's groups in the United States found the Clinton administration receptive to appeals for prominent appointments. The number of U.S. women in high cabinet level office in the Clinton administration exceeded those in Britain even though the U.S. system of separation of powers and Senate confirmation places more hurdles before the president than parliamentary party leaders face. In his first administration, Clinton appointed women to a record-breaking 27 percent of top executive appointments and to 41 percent of all noncareer executive jobs, as well as to a record 20 percent of judicial appointments,[88] consulting lists of possible female appointees made available to him by feminist groups to make his selections. Early appointments by President George W. Bush suggest a continuation of this pattern, with numerous prominent women in his cabinet.

However, at the congressional level, women have not achieved leadership positions similar to their British sisters in Parliament. Few women have secured positions as chairs of congressional committees and subcommittees or as legislative party leaders. U.S. congresswomen broke into the ranks of leadership as early as 1949 when Representative Chase G. Woodhouse (D-CT) was selected secretary of the House Democratic Caucus, but not until 1985 did the first GOP woman, Representative Lynn Martin (R-IL), break into the leadership ranks as vice chair of the House Republican Conference. In the Senate, Margaret Chase Smith (R-ME) became the first woman to chair the Republican Conference in 1967, but not until 1993 did a Democratic woman, Barbara Mikulski (D-MD), win a leadership position as assistant floor leader. While the number of women in the lower ranks of leadership increased steadily during the 1990s, a second woman did not secure one of the top leadership posts of party floor leader, whip, or conference chair until 2002, when Representative Nancy Pelosi (D-CA) was elected House Democratic whip, the highest ranking leadership post ever held by a woman.[89] (See Rosenthal's closing chapter in this volume for further details on women in leadership.) After the 1998 election, two women, Jennifer Dunn (R-WA) and Rosa DeLauro (D-CT), ran for but lost contests for high-ranking leadership positions. Only two women have ever chaired full Senate committees: the first was in the 1930s; the second was Nancy Landon Kassebaum (R-KS), who chaired the Committee on Labor and Human Resources from 1995 to 1997. Only 10 women have chaired full House committees.[90]

Does Women's Presence Matter? Impact on Policy Agendas

Contrasted with the influence of powerful parties in the United Kingdom, the U.S. policy system is dominated by interest groups, a reflection of the highly decentralized, candidate-centered nature of elections in the United States.[91] Nonetheless, several chapters in this volume suggest that women in Congress, despite their relatively low numbers, have raised awareness of gender-related problems, developed agendas with solutions to those problems, altered the terms of debate, and gotten male colleagues to support those agendas.[92] Women have had an impact on a number of policies, including women's health, abortion, and welfare. By contrast, the dramatic increase of women in the Labour party government since 1997 has produced mixed results even though a more dramatic transformation of the policy agenda was anticipated. Given that both Blair and Clinton were publicly sympathetic to women's issues and that women held more legislative leadership roles in Britain than in the United States, how might the differences in policy achievements be explained?

Clearly a major explanation is the difference between a parliamentary system and a system of separated legislative and executive institutions. Arguably, the looser, candidate-centered U.S. system also has allowed women the chance to impact the policy system to a greater extent than their British sisters, at least to date. To a greater extent than is presently possible in Britain, women in Congress appear to have fewer constraints and cross pressures in advancing feminist legislation, in the absence of strong party directives and pressures to conform. In addition, a tradition of bipartisan women's policy advocacy dates back at least to the founding of the Congressional Caucus for Women's Issues, established in 1977 by 15 of the then

18 women in Congress. Although the caucus was abolished after the 1994 midterm elections, it lives on as an informal nonpartisan caucus with policy-making ability.[93] In 1992, after the election dubbed the "Year of the Woman," the 24 new women elected to Congress again demonstrated their willingness to cross party lines. They held a press conference to announce their commitment to passage of four policy priorities: fully funded Head Start for all eligible children, family and medical leave legislation, a Freedom of Choice Act, and policy addressing workplace sexual harassment.[94] Fully 97 percent of Democratic representatives and 75 percent of Republican women voted for the Freedom of Access (to Abortion) Clinic Entrances Act; the male totals were 80 percent and 19 percent, respectively.[95] While 62 percent of congresswomen were sponsors of the 1992 Freedom of Choice Act of 1992, only 27 percent of congressmen were supporters.[96] Women legislators from both parties appear to feel a special obligation to represent the views of their women constituents (see Carroll in this volume), and by virtue of position and seniority are increasingly able to advocate on behalf of these interests. The question for the future is whether cross-partisan cooperation will continue. Unity on women-related issues may have abated as increasingly right-wing Republican women elected to the House have opposed abortion and espoused policies championed by the religious right.

CONCLUSION

Comparing the cases of Britain and the United States during the 1990s illustrates the importance of the political opportunity structure in each nation for women's representation. Changes in Labour party rules created the conditions that produced a dramatic increase in the number of women in the House of Commons in 1997. At the same time, the political opportunity structure of strong centralized parties in a parliamentary system constrained the achievement of policy outcomes by junior members and backbenchers.

In contrast, the U.S. electoral system of weak parties, powerful incumbents, and candidate-centered elections limits the prospects for significant expansion of women's congressional representation in the United States. The dramatic shift in women's representation in 1992 occurred not because of change in the fundamental opportunity structure but rather because of the convergence of three circumstances: redistricting and reapportionment, intensive mobilization of women in the wake of the Clarence Thomas–Anita

Hill hearing, and voluntary congressional retirements, which, in turn, led to more open seats. Motivated in part by the events surrounding the confirmation of Supreme Court Justice Clarence Thomas, a number of highly qualified women candidates successfully contested open congressional seats.[97]

While other democracies are adopting quota laws and rules similar to those that produced Britain's record class of women parliamentarians, the United States is not likely to embrace positive action any time soon.[98] Nonetheless, there continues to be incremental improvement in women's access to congressional office, as well as a record of policy impact produced by independent-minded women members of Congress less constrained by party strictures than their British sisters.

Emphasizing the political opportunity structure in Britain and the United States, this analysis suggests that women's legislative influence may produce similar, and modest, policy goals, regardless of a dramatic increase in numbers. Viewed in the context of the Anglo-American comparison undertaken in this study, incrementalism can be as significant, if not more so, than giant strides forward at the polls. Even when numbers of women representatives are relatively small (e.g., do not constitute a "critical mass"), institutional realities of congressional seniority and relatively lax party control may yet yield opportunities for lasting impact on policy. By comparison, in the short run, sudden and dramatic increases in the number of women in Parliament did not automatically translate into policy gains. In both cases, women must successfully learn to negotiate the political structures of which they are a part. Enhanced policy impact seems assured only when changes in the political opportunity structure affect both electoral and institutional circumstances, and as of yet, neither the British Parliament nor the U.S. Congress has realized a full transformation of both numbers *and* institutional clout exercised by women members.

NOTES

This research was made possible by visiting scholar positions at the University of London Institute for United States Studies, and the Institute for Gender Studies, London School of Economics, May–June 1999. In addition, I am grateful for funding through a grant from the PSC-CUNY foundation at my home institution, the City University of New York. Finally, I would like to thank two excellent research assistants, Roisin Flood and Hera Cook, for their fine work.

1. Gelb, *Feminism and Politics*, 2.

2. Short, "Women and the Labour Party," 19.

3. O'Connor, Orloff, and Shaver, *States, Markets, and Families,* 214.

4. Childs, "In Their Own Words."

5. Meg Russell, "Women's Representation in UK Politics," 9–11, points to positive action's importance. For example, the Liberal Democrats were the only party to alternate male and female candidates in the 1999 European Parliament elections, which yielded an equal number of male and female MEPs.

6. Mactaggart, *Women in Parliament.*

7. Bashevkin, "From Tough Times to Better Times," 411.

8. Norris, "Women Politicians," 138.

9. Eagle and Lovenduski, *High Time or High Tide for Labour Women,* 5–7

10. Lovenduski and Randall, *Contemporary Feminist Politics,* 8.

11. Norris, "Women Politicians," 132.

12. Ibid., 139.

13. Ibid., 140.

14. Eagle and Lovenduski, *High Time or High Tide for Labour Women,* 5.

15. Ibid., 133, 137.

16. Ibid., 141.

17. Meg Russell, "Women's Representation in UK Politics," 25.

18. Norris, "Women Politicians," 132.

19. Eagle and Lovenduski, *High Time or High Tide for Labour Women,* 7.

20. Childs, "In Their Own Words."

21. Polly Toynbee, interview by author, London, 16 March 2001.

22. Coote, "Women and the Third Way."

23. Fiona Mactaggart, interview by author, May 1999.

24. Coote, "Women and the Third Way."

25. Bashevkin, "From Tough Times to Better Times," 418.

26. Follett, "Women Still Firmly in Their Place," *New Statesman,* 25 September 2000, 20–22.

27. Mactaggart, *Women in Parliament.*

28. Bashevkin, "From Tough Times to Better Times," 421.

29. Ibid., 418.

30. Ibid., 418.

31. Mary Anne Stephenson, interview by author, London, May 1999.

32. Bashevkin, "From Tough Times to Better Times," 416; Benn, "Short March through Institutions," 40.

33. Childs, "In Their Own Words."

34. Ibid.; Benn, "Short March through Institutions."

35. Perkins, "Campaigning in an Era of Consensus," 38.

36. Bashevkin, "From Tough Times to Better Times," 416; Shephard, *Shephard's Watch,* 271.

37. Stephenson, interview by author, May 1999.

38. Bashevkin, "From Tough Times to Better Times," 419; Childs, unpublished manuscript.

39. These tensions have been documented in Coote, ed., *New Gender Agenda*, especially part I, "The Blair Effect," 15–48; Coote, "Gender Parity and the Third Way"; Bashevkin, "From Tough Times to Better Times"; and in numerous other articles by feminists (e.g., Wilkinson et al., "The Day I Fell Out of Love with Blair," *New Statesman*, 7 August 1998).

40. Coote, *New Gender Agenda*, 163.

41. Franklin, "After Modernization," 17.

42. Coote, *New Gender Agenda*, 163.

43. Childs, "In Their Own Words."

44. Wilkinson et al., "The Day I Fell Out of Love with Blair," 9–10; Coote, "Gender Parity and the Third Way"; Childs, "In Their Own Words."

45. Mactaggart interview.

46. Squires and Wickham-Jones, *Women in Parliament*; EOC report and Childs, "Hitting the Target."

47. Childs, "In Their Own Words."

48. Shephard, *Shephard's Watch*, 271.

49. Ibid.; Childs, "Hitting the Target."

50. Childs, "In Their Own Words"; Childs, "Hitting the Target."

51. Ibid.

52. Stephenson, interview by author, May 1999.

53. Mactaggart interview.

54. Joan Ruddock, interview by author, June 1999; Anna Coote, interview by author, June 1999.

55. Thomas, "Introduction," 13.

56. Dolan and Ford, "Are All Women State Legislators Alike?" 77

57. Ruth Lister, communication, 20 May 1999. See also Norton and Walsh chapters, this volume.

58. Mactaggart interview; Mary Anne Stevenson, interview by Roisin Flood, June 1999.

59. Rake, "Gender and New Labour's Social Policies," 219.

60. Stephenson interview, June 1999.

61. Ward, "Learning From the 'Babe' Experience," 23.

62. J. Carvel, "British Parents Getting a Raw Deal," *Guardian*, 20 October 2000, p. 14.

63. Mactaggart, *Women in Parliament*; "Anne Perkins Take Two," *Guardian*, 1 June 1999, pp. 8–9.

64. Ward, "Abused Wives Stay in UK," *Guardian*, 17 June 1999, p. 14.

65. Mactaggart interview.

66. Ibid.; see also Toynbee, "F Stands for Funny and Formidable, but Not Feminism," *Guardian*, 10 November 1998, p. 8.

67. Bashevkin, "From Tough Times to Better Times," 418.

68. Ibid.; Toynbee, "F Stands for Funny and Formidable."

69. Stephenson interview, June 1999.

70. Meg Russell, "Women's Representation in UK Politics," 5.

71. Churcher, Press Association Limited, "Labour to Change Law of All Women Shortlist," 6 May 2001.

72. Eagle and Lovenduski, *High Time or High Tide for Labour Women*, 18.

73. Squires and Wickham-Jones, *Women in Parliament*, 63.

74. Sarah Lyall, "London Journal: With a Parting Swipe, Women of the House Exit," *New York Times*, 18 May 2001, www.nytimes.com/2001/05/18/world/181LOND.html.

75. Ibid.

76. Center for American Women and Politics (CAWP), "Women Candidates for Congress 1974–2000."

77. Norris, *Politics and Sexual Equality*, 132.

78. Burrell, "Party Decline," 292.

79. Norris, "Breaking the Barriers."

80. O'Connor, Orloff, and Shaver, *States, Markets and Families*, 207.

81. With the election of George W. Bush in 2000, the U.S. situation may have reverted once more.

82. McGlen and O'Connor, *Women, Politics, and American Society*, 2nd ed., 87; Darcy, Welch, and Clark, *Women, Elections, and Representation*.

83. CAWP, "Women in Congress: Leadership Roles and Committee Chairs."

84. Ibid.

85. Fox, "Gender and Congressional Elections," 231.

86. Darcy, Welch, and Clark, *Women, Elections, and Representation*, 188.

87. Ibid., 90–92; Fox, "Gender and Congressional Elections," 232.

88. Darcy, Welch, and Clark, *Women, Elections, and Representation*, 93; Costello, Miles, and Stone, eds., *American Woman*, 309.

89. CAWP, "Women in Congress: Leadership Roles and Committee Chairs." See Rosenthal in this volume.

90. Foerstel, *Biographical Dictionary of Congressional Women*.

91. O'Connor, Orloff, and Shaver. *States, Markets, and Families*, 206, and Gelb, *Feminism and Politics*.

92. See in this volume, Walsh, Wolbrecht, Swers, and Kedrowski and Sarow. Also Dodson, "Representing Women's Interests," 138.

93. Primmer, "Congressional Caucus for Women's Issues," 368.

94. Schroedel and Mazumadar, "Into the Twenty-First Century," 207.

95. McGlen and O'Connor, *Women, Politics, and American Society*, 91.

96. Ibid.

97. I am indebted to Cindy Simon Rosenthal for this analytic insight.

98. Norris, "Breaking the Barriers."

CHAPTER SEVENTEEN

Transforming the Future through New Leadership

CINDY SIMON ROSENTHAL

Why do institutions change? More specifically, what factors have brought institutional change to the U.S. Congress since the founding? A substantial literature has attempted to answer these questions, examining the early days of the Republic, the rise of the modern, institutionalized Congress, the reform movement of the 1970s, and most recently the alterations wrought by the Republican party ascension to majority status in 1994.[1] Scholars have posited various theories to explain the tides of stability and reform that periodically have altered this institution, and no single explanation seems satisfactory for the patterns observed. Some students of Congress herald evidence of cyclical change,[2] others point to enduring stability,[3] and still others see congressional change as the product of historical regimes or cultural shifts.[4]

To the original question that motivated this book—are women transforming the U.S. Congress?—we arrive at a summation that is less than definitive. The answer to this straightforward question is a modest, "It depends." In part, the answer depends on whether we look to the substantial contributions made by women in Congress or whether we look to the distance still to travel in reaching representational parity. Women have changed Congress in some important ways, but a dramatic institutional reshaping remains far in the future. In this brief chapter, I revisit the major findings of the book through the lens of institutional change and speculate about the transformative possibilities of women in future congressional leadership.

In one sense, the research in this volume demonstrates how little the basic demography of Congress has changed. The 107th Congress opened with more women members than ever before, but one must look beyond those initial numbers to assess the potential for women changing the institution's composition in the future. The Center for American Women and Politics, which has been tracking steady electoral gains of women in state and federal elections for more than 30 years, reported a decline in seats held by women in state legislatures in 2001.[5] With women's representation in state legislative office hovering around 22 percent since 1997 and term limits producing little or no change in the gender composition of state legislatures,[6] this former primary stepping stone to Congress seems to have become a plateau. Moreover, the United States will not likely institute new election rules or quota laws that have been embraced by other democratic regimes as a means of achieving greater gender representation.

In another sense, these chapters show that while the percentage of women in the U.S. Congress has languished well below 20 percent (and below that in most other Western democracies), women's impact on public policy has been considerable. Congresswomen, women's interest groups, key staff, the media, and a changed societal landscape resulting from the second wave women's movement have combined to transform the congressional public policy agenda and to reshape institutional and policy responses to women as a constituency. The consideration and accommodation of feminalist concerns have altered the agenda, changed the content of policy debate, and affected legislative outcomes regarding reproductive policy, cancer and health care, welfare reform, civil rights, and criminal and economic affairs. In no small part, public policy advances have been achieved because of the commitment to surrogate representation—the sense of obligation felt by congresswomen to act for women beyond their geographic constituency.

While policy achievements are a clear by-product of increased participation by women in Congress, long-standing arrangements of institutional power and norms endure. As Laura Arnold and Barbara King's analysis of Senate committee assignments shows, women in the wake of the 1991 congressional election, the so-called Year of the Woman, briefly seemed to win preferential consideration out of recognition of their underrepresentation. Over the decade of the 1990s, however, Senate practice and traditions went unchanged. Even as the number of women increases incrementally, Congress as an institution remains much as women found it.

Why have policy changes occurred, while institutional transformation seems elusive? Congressional scholar Barbara Hinckley argues that *internal* factors alone do not produce institutional change; rather the institution's membership must change in order to alter the reinforcing dynamic of those who occupy the institution and learn to succeed (or fail) by its norms and rules. For policy change to occur, the defeat of incumbents and the arrival of a handful of feminalist congresswomen are sufficient. Institutional reform requires more than a handful of different faces. Unlike when a critical mass of more liberal and junior House Democrats revolted in the 1970s and achieved organizational reforms, the presence of women in Congress has yet to reach the levels at which they can obtain real organizational power.

Perhaps institutional change may yet occur. Lawrence C. Dodd suggests three dominant theoretical perspectives to shed light on various aspects of the Republican revolution of 1994. These include social choice theory, which emphasizes that members' quest for personal power leads to predictable cycles of partisan and institutional change; social structure theory, which posits that institutional change is produced by larger social forces in society; and social learning theory, which argues that transformation of an institution is shaped largely by the ideas of leaders who provide a philosophical understanding of crises and offer suggestions for experimentation to adapt to those crises.[7] These same theoretical perspectives are useful in illuminating the transformational impact that women might yet have on Congress.

Dodd's three theoretical perspectives provide frames for speculating whether and how soon a congressional transformation might be achieved. Social choice theory, as Dodd suggests, allows members who share common goals to join together for institutional change. Might a unifying commitment to surrogate representation be sufficient to bring women together as a governing force intent on not only policy but institutional change? Probably not in the near term. Susan Carroll reports that as the number of women in Congress has increased, some newer and more conservative women are less motivated by a sense of surrogate representation. Since party remains the unifying organizational construct of Congress and the Congressional Caucus for Women's Issues has been relegated to extra-institutional status, there is little to bind women together as an internal institutional force. Most importantly, the number of congresswomen falls far short of a majority necessary to achieve institutional reforms.

The lens of social structure theory, which reveals the impact of historical and societal forces on an institution, raises the question of how Congress, like many organizations, will adapt to changing gender roles in the 21st century. The substantial influx of women in the House of Commons in 1997 helped move that body to adopt a schedule more friendly to the needs of members with young children and to establish child care to support members' families (see Gelb). But the results of parliamentary elections in 2001 reveal how tenuous such gains can be. Also, Sue Thomas and her coauthors show how little has changed with respect to societal norms about division of family and household duties, which keep women from considering electoral office in greater numbers. The forces of social change that might facilitate a more dramatic institutional transformation by women in Congress appear to be moving glacially slow. Since women do not constitute a critical mass of the membership, let alone a majority, it is perhaps no wonder that more substantial transformation has yet to take hold as a result of women joining Congress.[8]

Finally, social learning theory directs our attention to the question of whether women in congressional leadership roles might be able to facilitate and hasten the pace of institutional change that would accommodate women more effectively. Social learning theory argues that leaders play a key role in shaping a group's response to crisis and then providing the ideas necessary for experimentation and learning that lead to new understandings of politics. Perhaps as some of the current women in Congress succeed to the highest levels of leadership, the institutional norms and practices will change. Other research has shown that strategically placed women in positions of power and leadership can have a transformative impact on an institution.[9] The prospects for women to achieve significant posts of congressional leadership, however, appear uncertain. A detailed look at the current leadership status of women in Congress reveals why.

In an institution that still values and rewards length of service, women generally lack the seniority requisite for the most powerful posts.[10] With the convening of the 107th Congress, Senator Kay Bailey Hutchison (R-TX) is the senior Republican woman, ranking 26th on the GOP seniority list, and Senator Barbara Mikulski (D-MD) ranks 16th in seniority among

Democratic senators. In the House Republican Conference, the three most senior women are Representative Marge Roukema (R-NJ) at 20th, Representative Nancy Johnson (R-CT) at 30th, and Representative Connie Morella (R-MD) at 47th. This degree of seniority will prove short-lived, as Roukema plans to retire in 2002 and Johnson faces a tough reelection against another incumbent due to redistricting. The three most senior women on the Democratic side of the aisle are Representative Marcy Kaptur (D-OH) at 33rd, Representative Nancy Pelosi (D-CA) at 52nd, and Representative Nita Lowey (D-NY) at 57th.

Whether congressional careers lead to party or committee leadership, seniority is the currency for both. As Hinckley points out, the median age of congressional leaders is in the mid-60s, and leadership is typically bestowed after long service (on average 20 years of service between 1903 and 1974).[11] This pattern of leadership tenure, succession, and service has been remarkably stable, with the exception of the ascension of former Speaker Newt Gingrich (R-GA) in 1994 and his ultimate successor Representative J. Dennis Hastert (R-IL). The fundamental pattern of congressional leaders emerging from the ranks of the most senior stratum of the membership is likely to endure, and the reality is that congresswomen are still rare among the most senior members.

Perhaps not surprisingly, women succeeded in securing lesser assistant leadership posts, but rarely did either the House or the Senate elect a woman to serve in one of the top party leadership posts (i.e. Speaker, floor leader, whip, or conference/caucus chair).[12] Representative Chase G. Woodhouse (D-CT) was the first woman selected to a leadership role as House Democratic Caucus secretary in 1949. Almost 40 years later, Representative Lynn Martin (R-IL) became the first GOP congresswoman to hold a leadership job, as vice chair of the House Republican Conference. In 1967, Margaret Chase Smith (R-ME) was elected chair of the Senate Republican Conference, becoming the first woman ever to win a Senate leadership post. Currently, Senator Barbara Mikulski holds the position of conference secretary, after first breaking into the all-male Democratic leadership team in 1992 as assistant floor leader. Across the aisle, Senator Hutchison (R-TX) similarly broke into the all-male party leadership ranks in the 107th Congress as GOP Conference vice chair, and her close relationship with Republican leader Trent Lott (R-MS) is expected to garner her increasing influence.[13] But the life of assistant leaders is not the same as life at the top. As

Representative Susan Molinari (R-NY) lamented, her supposed influence as the vice chair (and then highest ranking woman) of the House Republican Conference in 1997 cast the illusion of power when in reality she had "hit a wall" and never felt like a "real player" in the congressional hierarchy.[14]

In 1998, the first women ran for one of the top three leadership roles in the House but none was successful. Representative Jennifer Dunn (R-WA) lost her bid for the post of majority leader, and Representative Rosa DeLauro (D-CT) fell short in a contest for House Democratic Caucus chair. By all accounts, Dunn was perceived as too moderate for her caucus despite an almost perfect conservative voting record. DeLauro's defeat left the Democratic Caucus leadership as an all-male team, prompting Democratic leader Richard Gephardt (D-MO) to create for her the post of assistant to the Democratic leader.

In 2001, Representative Nancy Pelosi (D-CA) became the first woman ever to crack the top ranks of congressional leadership. Tapped by the Democratic Caucus in October 2001 to become minority whip by a 118–95 vote over Representative Steny Hoyer (D-MD), Representative Pelosi assumed the second-ranking post in the Democratic party leadership in 2002. Four of the nine Democratic whips since World War II have gone on to become Speaker of the House, raising the possibility that Representative Pelosi might someday be addressed as "Madame Speaker." Pelosi built an early lead over Hoyer by securing the support of her female colleagues and fellow Californians, and gender reportedly influenced some in the caucus who felt the absence of women in top leadership was "almost criminal" for a party so dependent on female voters.[15] While her leadership style and goals are to a certain extent not yet tested, Pelosi's prodigious fund-raising ability, media savvy, and passionate policy advocacy are likely to inform her contributions as a leader.[16]

Prospects for more changes in the makeup of congressional leadership depend on which party is considered. In the House Republican Conference, the aforementioned senior women are all political moderates and thus generally out of the mainstream of the party's more conservative leadership. While seniority has earned Representative Nancy Johnson (R-CT) clout as Ways and Means Health Subcommittee chair, Representative Connie Morella (R-MD) serves as chair of the Government Reform Committee's District of Columbia subcommittee, a relatively unimportant though appropriate committee assignment given her district. The most senior Republican woman, Representative Marge Roukema, fell short in her bid to become the first woman to chair a major House committee at the start of the 107th, even though term limits imposed on GOP committee chairs created circumstances for a transformation of the committee power structure. No GOP women were selected to chair a full committee chair even though term limits in 1999 created 14 openings on the 19 major House committees. Across the aisle, Representative Louise Slaughter (D-NY) confronted a similar slight in 1996 when her caucus colleagues shunned her bid to become the ranking member on the Budget Committee even though she was next in line in terms of seniority.[17]

Two women figure most prominently in the House GOP Conference leadership ranks in the 107th: Representative Barbara Cubin (R-WY) was elected to the sixth-ranking post of conference secretary as Representative Deborah Pryce (R-OH) moved up from that job to fill the post of conference vice chair vacated by retiring Representative Tillie Fowler (R-FL).[18] While women make up only 8 percent of the House GOP Conference membership, their share of leadership clout is even thinner: Representatives Cubin and Pryce are the lone women among the 19-member GOP whip team and the 26-person GOP Steering Committee.

Also noteworthy in the 107th Congress, the Democrats achieved two other historic leadership firsts as Senator Patty Murray (D-WA) and Representative Nita Lowey (D-CT) were tapped to head their party's fund-raising committees, the Democratic Senatorial Campaign Committee and the Democratic Congressional Campaign Committee, respectively. While they do not yield power over legislation and policy, the presence of two women atop their party's fund-raising apparatus is heralded as not only symbolically important but politically significant, as these women have "won the right to dole out political checks and favors to Democrats in the House and Senate."[19] Whether they are as successful as their male predecessors is already being scrutinized and analyzed as an indicator "to prove that women can do it."[20]

In the end, change in Congress as an institution defies easy assessment. The three theoretical perspectives, which Dodd finds useful, also expose reasons why internally the institution of Congress seems little transformed by the women who serve in it. Hinckley concludes that the forces of institutional stability are inseparable from the forces of institutional change because of a complex of "reciprocally reinforcing variables," and she argues that the stability of the membership, the structure of norms and influence-producing values, and the system of leadership tends to produce and reinforce existing patterns of action.[21] Women who serve in Congress must adapt to the requisite continuities of the body; they must "go along to get along." While the House Republicans' Contract with America promised to alter institutional norms rewarding seniority and encouraging longevity, its legacy already appears doubtful, and the opportunity for institutional change may be fleeting if the party loses majority status. Even so, GOP congresswomen gained few benefits from committee chair term limits or other procedural reforms wrought by their conference, and they remain one or two steps removed from the main sources of institutional power. The power and opportunity to effect fundamental institutional change continue to be shaped by a congressional system that still recognizes the norm of seniority, which in turn rests on expectations of membership continuity and leadership stability. The harsh reality is that institutional transformation probably depends on congresswomen being sufficiently like-minded in terms of their values, personal styles, and priorities and then securing *both* a critical mass within the membership of the majority party *and* individual seniority to hold key committee and leadership roles. That's a tall order.

Perhaps one other possibility for future change exists. Hertzke and Peters argue that changes in American culture are ultimately the proximate source of influences producing a more atomistic, individualistic, less communal, and seemingly ungovernable Congress.[22] If cultural change leads to institutional change, then perhaps the transformation of gender roles and social relations will produce a consequent redefinition of politics and institutional life in the future. Just as women have transformed the congressional policy agenda in the 20th century, perhaps the 21st century will see men and women participate equally in transforming Congress.

NOTES

1. See, for example, Young, *Washington Community, 1800–1828*; Woodrow Wilson, *Congressional Government*; Polsby, 1968, "Institutionalization of the U.S. House of Representatives"; Ornstein, ed., *Congress in Change*; Cooper and Brady, "Toward a Diachronic Analysis of Change"; Hinckley, *Stability and Change in Congress*; Parker, *Institutional Change, Discretion, and the Making of Modern Congress*; and the continuing series of *Congress Reconsidered*, edited by Dodd and Oppenheimer.

2. Polsby, "Political Change and the Character of the Contemporary Congress."

3. See Hinckley, *Stability and Change in Congress*.

4. See, for example, Hertzke and Peters, *Atomistic Congress*.

5. Center for American Women and Politics (CAWP), "Women in State Legislatures 2001."

6. Carroll and Jenkins, "Unrealized Opportunity?"

7. Dodd, "Re-Envisioning Congress."

8. Kanter, *Men and Women of the Corporation*.

9. Rosenthal, *When Women Lead*.

10. Seniority data were calculated from Nutting and Stern, eds., *CQ's Politics in America 2002*, 1177–81.

11. Hinckley, *Stability and Change in Congress*, 193–94.

12. CAWP, "Women in Congress: Leadership Roles and Committee Chairs."

13. Ibid.; see individual entries for members.

14. Molinari, *Representative Mom*, 260.

15. Charlie Cook, "Whip's Race Is Personal for House Democrats," *National Journal*, 6 October 2001, 3113–14.

16. Karen Foerstel, "Pelosi: A Tireless Fundraiser Sees Herself as a 'Fresh' Face," *CQ Weekly*, 6 October 2001, 2324–25.

17. Brian Blomquist, "Democratic Congresswomen Upset at Budget-Panel Snub; Complain of Being 'Underrepresented,'" *Washington Times*, 22 November 1996, p. A:4.

18. Juliet Eilperin, "House Democrats, GOP Reelect Leaders: Lawmakers in No Mood for Change," *Washington Post*, 15 November 2000, p. A:5.

19. Eliza Newlin Carney, "Stuffing Their Purses," *National Journal*, 16 June 2001, 1794.

20. Ibid., 1798.

21. Hinckley, *Stability and Change in Congress*, 329, 332.

22. Hertzke and Peters, *Atomistic Congress*.

REFERENCES

Abramowitz, Alan I. "A Comparison of Voting for U.S. Senator and Representative in 1978." *American Political Science Review* 74 (1980): 633–40.

Abramson, Paul R., John H. Aldrich, and David W. Rohde. "Progressive Ambition among United States Senators: 1972–1988." *Journal of Politics* 49 (1987): 3–35.

Acker, Joan. "Gendered Institutions: From Sex Roles to Gendered Institutions." *Contemporary Sociology* 21 (1992): 565–69.

Adams, William C. "Candidate Characteristics, Office of Election, and Voter Responses." *Experimental Study of Politics* 4 (1975): 79–91.

Aldrich, John. *Why Parties? The Origin and Transformation of Political Parties in America*. Chicago: University of Chicago Press, 1995.

Aldrich, John, and David Rohde. "Balance of Power: Republican Party Leadership and the Committee System in the 104th House." Paper presented at the annual meeting of the Midwest Political Science Association, Chicago, April 1997.

———. "The Republican Revolution and the House Appropriations Committee." *Journal of Politics* 62, no. 1 (2000): 1–33.

———. "The Transition to Republican Rule in the House: Implications for Theories of Congressional Politics." Paper presented at the annual meeting of the American Political Science Association, Chicago, August 1995.

Alexander, Deborah, and Kristi Andersen. "Gender as a Factor in the Attribution of Leadership Traits." *Political Research Quarterly* 46 (1993): 727–46.

Altman, Roberta. *Waking Up, Fighting Back: The Politics of Breast Cancer*. Boston: Little Brown, 1996.

American Cancer Society. "Cancer Statistics." www.cancer.org/cancerinfo/html.

Aminzade, Ronald. "Between Movement and Party: The Transformation of Mid-Nineteenth-Century French Republicanism." In *The Politics of Social Protest,* edited by J. Craig Jenkins and Bert Klandermans. Minneapolis: University of Minnesota Press, 1995.

Arnold, Douglas. *The Logic of Congressional Action.* New Haven, Conn.: Yale University Press, 1990.

Arnold, Laura W. "The Distribution of Senate Committee Positions: Change or More of the Same?" *Legislative Studies Quarterly.* Forthcoming.

Assendelft, Laura Van, and Karen O'Connor. "Backgrounds, Motivations and Interests: A Comparison of Male and Female Local Party Activists." *Women & Politics* 14 (1994): 77–92.

Austen-Smith, David. "Information Transmission in Debate." *American Journal of Political Science* 34 (1990): 124–52.

Bach, Stanley, and Steven S. Smith. *Managing Uncertainty in the House of Representatives: Adaptation and Innovation in Special Rules.* Washington, D.C.: Brookings Institution, 1988.

Barber, James David. *The Lawmakers.* New Haven, Conn.: Yale University Press, 1965.

Barnett, Rosalind, and Caryl Rivers. "Look Who's Talking about Work and Family." *Ms. Magazine,* July/August 1996, 34–36.

Baron, James N., Brian Mittman, and Andrew E. Newman. "Targets of Opportunity: Organizational and Environmental Determinants of Gender Integration within the California Civil Service, 1979–1985." *American Journal of Sociology* 96, no. 6 (1991): 1362–1401.

Barrett, Edith J. "Gender and Race in the State House: The Legislative Experience." *Social Science Journal* 34, no. 2 (1997): 131–44.

———. "The Policy Priorities of African American Women in State Legislatures." *Legislative Studies Quarterly* 20 (1995): 223–48.

Bashevkin, Sylvia. "From Tough Times to Better Times: Feminism, Public Policy, and New Labour Politics in Britain." *International Political Science Review* 21, no. 4 (2000): 407–31.

Bate, Barbara. *Communication and the Sexes.* New York: Harper & Row, 1988.

Baumgartner, Frank R., and Beth L. Leech. *Basic Interests: The Importance of Groups in Politics and in Political Science.* Princeton, N.J.: Princeton University Press, 1998.

Baylis, Francoise, Jocelyn Downie, and Susan Sherwin. "Reframing Research Involving Humans." In *The Politics of Women's Health: Exemplary Agency and Autonomy,* edited by Susan Sherwin. Philadelphia: Temple University Press, 1998.

Benn, Melissa. "A Short March through the Institutions: Reflections on New Labour's Gender Machinery." In *New Gender Agenda: Why Women Still Want More,* edited by Anna Coote. London: Institute for Public Policy Research, 2000.

Bennett, Stephen E., and Linda M. Bennett. "From Traditional to Modern Conceptions of Gender Equality in Politics—Graduate Change and Lingering Doubts." *Western Political Quarterly* 45, no. 1 (1992): 93–111.

Benze, James G., and Eugene R. Declercq. "Content of Television Political Spot Ads for Female Candidates." *Journalism Quarterly* 62 (1985): 278–83, 288.

Berkman, Michael B., and Robert E. O'Connor. "Do Women Legislators Matter? Female Legislators and State Abortion Policy." *American Politics Quarterly* 21, no. 1 (1993): 102–24.

Bernstein, Robert A. "Might Women Now Have the Edge? Open-Seat House Primaries" *Women and Politics* 17, no. 2 (1997): 1–26.

———. "Why Are So Few Women in the House." *Western Political Quarterly* 39 (1986): 155–65.

Bessette, Joseph M. *The Mild Voice of Reason: Deliberative Democracy and American National Government.* Chicago: University of Chicago Press, 1994.

Bianco, William T. "Strategic Decisions on Candidacy in U.S. Congressional Districts." *Legislative Studies Quarterly* 9 (1984): 351–64.

Bielby, William T., and James N. Baron. "A Woman's Place Is with Other Women." In *Sex Segregation in the Workplace: Trends, Explanations, Remedies*, edited by Barbara F. Reskin. Washington, D.C.: National Academy Press, 1984.

Biersack, Robert, and Paul S. Herrnson. "Political Parties and the Year of the Woman." In *Year of the Woman: Myths and Realities*, edited by Elizabeth Adell Cook, Sue Thomas, and Clyde Wilcox. Boulder, Colo.: Westview Press, 1994.

Binder, Sarah, and Steven Smith. *Politics or Principle? Filibustering in the United States Senate.* Washington, D.C.: Brookings Institution, 1996.

Bingham, Clara. *Women on the Hill: Challenging the Culture of Congress.* New York: Time Books, 1997.

Bisnow, Mark. *In the Shadow of the Dome.* New York: Morrow, 1990.

Black, Gordon S. "A Theory of Professionalization in Politics." *American Political Science Review* 64 (1970): 865–78.

Blair, Diane D., and Jeanie R. Stanley. "Personal Relationships and Legislative Power: Male and Female Perceptions." *Legislative Studies Quarterly* 16 (1991): 495–507.

Blair, Diane Kincaid, and Ann R. Henry. "The Family Factor in State Legislative Turnover." *Legislative Studies Quarterly* 6 (1981): 55–68.

Blau, Francine D., and Marianne A. Ferber. *The Economics of Women, Men and Work.* Englewood Cliffs, N.J.: Prentice Hall, 1986.

Bledsoe, Timothy, and Mary Herring. "Victims of Circumstances: Women in Pursuit of Political Office in America." *American Political Science Review* 84 (1990): 213–24.

Blum, Terry C., Dail L. Fields, and Jodi S. Goodman. "Organization-Level Determinants of Women in Management." *Academy of Management Journal* 37, no. 2 (1994): 241–68.

Boehmer, Ulrike. *The Personal and the Political: Women's Activism in Response to the Breast Cancer and AIDS Epidemic.* Albany: State University of New York Press, 2000.

Bond, Jon, Cary Covington, and Richard Fleisher. "Explaining Challenger Quality in Congressional Elections." *Journal of Politics* 47 (1985): 510–29.

Borger, Gloria. "Judging Thomas." *U.S. News and World Report* 21 October 1991: 32.

Borger, Gloria, and Ted Gest. "The Untold Story." *U.S. News and World Report* 12 October 1992: 28.

Borrelli, Mary Anne, and Janet M. Martin, eds. *The Other Elites: Women, Politics, and Power in the Executive Branch.* Boulder, Colo.: Lynne Rienner, 1997.

Borris, Eileen. "When Work Is Slavery." In *Whose Welfare*, edited by Gwendolyn Mink. Ithaca, N.Y.: Cornell University Press, 1999.

Boxer, Barbara. *Strangers in the Senate.* Washington, D.C.: National Press Books, 1994.

Brace, Paul. "Progressive Ambition in the House: A Probabilistic Approach." *Journal of Politics* 46 (1984): 556–71.

Braden, Marcia. *Women Politicians and the Media.* Lexington: University of Kentucky Press, 1996.

Bratton, Kathleen A., and Kerry L. Haynie. "Agenda Setting and Legislative Success in State Legislatures: The Effects of Gender and Race." *Journal of Politics* 61 (1999): 658–79.

Brennan, Teresa, and Carol Pateman. "'Mere Auxiliaries to the Commonwealth': Women and the Origins of Liberalism." *Philosophical Quarterly* 27, no. 2 (June 1979): 183–200.

Brown, Wendy. *Manhood and Politics.* Totowa, N.J.: Rowman & Littlefield, 1988.

Browne, William. "Multiple Sponsorship and Bill Success in the U.S. State Legislatures." *Legislative Studies Quarterly* 10 (1985): 483–88.

Bryce, Herrington J., and Alan E. Warrick. "Black Women in Electoral Politics." In *Portrait in Marginality: The Political Behavior of American Women*, edited by Marianne Githens and Jewel L. Prestage. New York: D. McKay, 1977.

Bullock, Charles S., III. "Motivations for U.S. Congressional Committee Preferences: Freshmen of the 92nd Congress." *Legislative Studies Quarterly* 1, no. 2 (1976): 201–12.

Bullock, Charles S., III, and John Sprague. "A Research Note on the Committee Reassignments of Southern Democratic Congressmen." *Journal of Politics* 31 (1969): 493–512.

Burden, Barry C., and Aage R. Clausen. "The Unfolding Drama: Party and Ideology in the 104th House." In *Great Theatre: The American Congress in the 1990s*, edited by Herbert F. Weisberg and Samuel C. Patterson, 152–71. Cambridge: Cambridge University Press, 1998.

Burnham, Walter Dean. *Critical Elections and the Mainsprings of American Politics.* New York: Norton, 1970.

Burrell, Barbara. "Campaign Finance: Women's Experience in the Modern Era." In *Women and Elective Office: Past, Present, and Future*, edited by Sue Thomas and Clyde Wilcox. New York: Oxford University Press, 1998.

———. "Party Decline, Party Transformation and Gender Politics: The USA." In *Gender and Party Politics*, edited by Joni Lovenduski and Pippa Norris. London: Sage, 1993.

———. "The Presence and Performance of Women Candidates for the U.S. House of Representatives: 1968–1990." *Legislative Studies Quarterly* 17 (1992): 493–508.

———. *A Woman's Place Is in the House: Campaigning for Congress in the Feminist Era.* Ann Arbor: University of Michigan Press, 1994.

Burstein, Paul. *Discrimination, Jobs, and Politics.* Chicago: University of Chicago Press, 1985.

———. "Interest Organizations, Political Parties, and the Study of Democratic Politics." In *Social Movements and American Political Institutions,* edited by Anne Costain and Andrew McFarland. Lanham, Md.: Rowman & Littlefield, 1998.

Butler, Judith. *Gender Trouble: Feminism and the Subversion of Identity.* New York: Routledge, 1990.

Byrd, Robert C. *The Senate, 1789–1986: Addresses on the History of the United States Senate.* Washington, D.C.: GPO, 1988.

Bystrom, Dianne G. "Candidate Gender and the Presentation of Self: The Videostyles of Men and Women in U.S. Senate Campaigns." Ph.D. diss., University of Oklahoma, 1995.

Bystrom, Dianne G., and Lynda Lee Kaid. "Videostyle and Technology in Political Advertising: An Update on Women Candidates in the 1994 Election." Paper presented at the 82nd Annual Meeting of the Speech Communication Association, San Diego, Calif., 1996.

———. "Videostyles of Women and Men Candidates in U.S. Senate cCampaigns in the 1990s." Paper presented at the "Women Transforming Congress" conference, Norman, Okla., 13–15 April 2000.

Bystrom, Dianne G., Lynda Lee Kaid, and Jerry Miller. "The Evolution of Videostyles for Women Candidates: Advertising as a Form of Debate." Paper presented at the 83rd Annual Meeting of the National Communication Association, Chicago, 1997.

Bystrom, Dianne G., and Jerry Miller. "Gendered Communication Styles and Strategies in Campaign 1996: The Videostyles of Women and Men Candidates." In *The Electronic Election: Perspectives on the 1996 Campaign Communication,* edited by Lynda Lee Kaid and Dianne G. Bystrom. Mahwah, N.J.: Erlbaum, 1999.

Campbell, Karlyn Kohrs. *Man Cannot Speak for Her: A Critical Study of Early Feminist Rhetoric.* Vol. 1. New York: Greenwood Press, 1989.

Canon, David T. *Actors, Athletes, and Astronauts: Political Amateurs in the United States Congress.* Chicago: University of Chicago Press, 1990.

CaP CURE. "Getting Involved: Blue Ribbon." www.capcure.org/getting/blueribbon/html.

———. "Progress Report: Accelerating a Cure 1999–2000." www.capcure.org/publications/index.html.

Carden, Maren Lockwood. *The New Feminist Movement.* New York: Russell Sage Foundation, 1974.

Carey John, Richard Niemi, and Lynda Powell. "Are Women State Legislators Different?" In *Women and Elective Office: Past, Present, and Future,* edited by Thomas Sue and Clyde Wilcox. New York: Oxford University Press, 1998.

Carroll, Susan J. "The Personal Is Political: The Intersection of Private Lives and Public Roles among Women and Men in Elective and Appointive Office." *Women & Politics* 9, no. 2 (1989): 51–67.

———. "The Political Careers of Women Elected Officials: An Assessment and Research Agenda." In *Ambition and Beyond: Career Path of American Politicians,* edited by Shirley Williams and Edward L. Lascher, Jr. Berkeley, Calif.: Institute of Governmental Studies Press, 1993.

———. "The Politics of Difference: Women Public Officials as Agents of Change." *Stanford Law and Policy Review* 5 (spring 1994): 11–20.

———. "Representing Women: Congresswomen's Perceptions of Their Representational Roles." Paper presented at the "Women Transforming Congress" conference, Norman, Okla., 2000.

———. *Women as Candidates in American Politics.* Bloomington: Indiana University Press, 1985.

———. *Women as Candidates in American Politics.* 2nd ed. Bloomington: Indiana University Press, 1994.

Carroll, Susan J., and Krista E. Jenkins. "Unrealized Opportunity? Term Limits and the Representation of Women in State Legislatures." Paper presented at the American Political Science Association meeting, San Francisco, 2001.

Carroll, Susan J., and Wendy S. Strimling, with the assistance of John J. Cohen and Barbara Geiger-Parker. *Women's Routes to Elective Office: A Comparison with Men's.* New Brunswick, N.J.: Center for the American Woman and Politics, 1983.

Casamayou, Maureen. "Nice Girls No More: Grassroots Empowerment and the Politics of Breast Cancer." Paper presented at the annual meeting of the Midwest Political Science Association Meeting, Chicago, April 1996.

Casey, Kathleen J., and Susan J. Carroll. "Wyoming Wolves and Dead-Beat Dads: The Impact of Women Members of Congress on Welfare Reform." Paper presented at the annual meeting of the American Political Science Association, Boston, 1998.

Center for American Women and Politics. *National Information Bank on Women in Public Office.* Database. New Brunswick, N.J.: Eagleton Institute of Politics, Rutgers University. www.cawp.rutgers.edu.

———. "Women Candidates for Congress 1974–2000." Fact Sheet. New Brunswick, N.J.: Eagleton Institute of Politics, Rutgers University, 2000.

———. "Women in Congress: Leadership Roles and Committee Chairs." Fact Sheet. New Brunswick, N.J.: Eagleton Institute of Politics, Rutgers University, 2001.

———. "Women in Elective Office 1994." Fact Sheet. New Brunswick, N.J.: Eagleton Institute of Politics, Rutgers University, 1994.

———. "Women in Elective Office 1995." Fact Sheet. New Brunswick, N.J.: Eagleton Institute of Politics, Rutgers University, 1995.

———. "Women in State Legislatures 2001." Fact Sheet. New Brunswick, N.J.: Eagleton Institute of Politics, Rutgers University, 2001.

———. "Women in the U.S. Congress 2000." Fact Sheet. New Brunswick, N.J.: Eagleton Institute of Politics, Rutgers University, 2000.

———. "Women in the U.S. Congress 2001." Fact Sheet. New Brunswick, N.J.: Eagleton Institute of Politics, Rutgers University, 2001.

Chamberlin, Hope. *A Minority of Members: Women in the U.S. Congress*. New York: New American Library, 1973.

Chaney, Carole, and Barbara Sinclair. "Women and the 1992 House Elections." In *Year of the Woman: Myths and Realities*, edited by Elizabeth Adell Cook, Sue Thomas, and Clyde Wilcox. Boulder, Colo.: Westview Press, 1994.

Cheng, Cliff. *Masculinities in Organizations*. Thousand Oaks, Calif.: Sage, 1996.

Childs, Sarah. "Hitting the Target: Are Labour Women MP's Acting for Women?" *Parliamentary Affairs* 55, no. 1 (2002).

———. "In Their Own Words: New Labour Women and the Substantive Representation of Women." *British Journal of Politics and International Relations* 3, no. 1 (2001): 173–90.

Chodorow, Nancy. *The Reproduction of Mothering*. Berkeley: University of California Press, 1999.

Chong, Dennis. "Creating Common Frames of Reference on Political Issues." In *Political Persuasion and Attitude Change*, edited by Diana C. Mutz, Paul M. Sniderman, and Richard A. Brody. Ann Arbor: University of Michigan Press, 1996.

———. "How People Think, Reason and Feel about Rights and Liberties." *American Journal of Political Science* 37 (1993): 867–99.

Clark, Janet. "Women at the National Level: An Update on Roll Call Voting Behavior." In *Women and Elective Office: Past, Present, and Future*, edited by Sue Thomas and Clyde Wilcox. New York: Oxford, 1998.

Clemmitt, Marcia, Leslie Primmer, and Marjorie Simms. *The Record: Gains and Losses for Women and Families in the 104th Congress*. Washington, D.C.: Women's Policy, 1997.

Cobb, Roger W., and Charles D. Elder. *Participation in American Politics: The Dynamics of Agenda-Building*. 2nd ed. Baltimore: Johns Hopkins University Press, 1983.

Cohen, Richard E. "A Gloomy Day for the GOP." *National Journal* 30, no. 11 (1998): 584.

Coleman, Sally, Jeffrey L. Brudney, and J. Edward Kellough. "Bureaucracy as a Representative Institution: Toward a Reconciliation of Bureaucratic Government and Democratic Theory." *American Journal of Political Science* 42, no. 3 (1998): 717–44.

Common Cause. "Critical Role of Television in Political Campaigns." In *Channeling Influence: The Broadcast Lobby and the $70-Billion Free Ride*. Washington, D.C.: Common Cause, 1997. http://216.147.192.101/publications/040297_rpt.htm

Congressional Caucus for Women's Issues. *Update on Women and Family Issues in Congress* 13 (1993): 1–10.

Congressional Management Foundation. *Setting the Course: A Congressional Management Guide*. Washington, D.C.: CMF Publications, 1994.

————. *Working in Congress: The Staff Perspective*. Washington, D.C.: CMF Publications, 1995.

Congressional Quarterly Almanac. XLVII (1991).

Congressional Quarterly Almanac. XLIX (1993).

Congressional Staff Directory. 54th ed. Washington, D.C.: Congressional Quarterly Press, 1999.

Congressional Quarterly, Inc. *Origins and Development of Congress*. Washington, D.C.: Congressional Quarterly, Inc., 1976.

Connell, R. W. *Gender and Power*. Stanford, Calif.: Stanford University Press, 1987.

————. *Masculinities*. Berkeley: University of California Press, 1995.

Connor, George E., and Bruce I. Oppenheimer. "Deliberation: An Untimed Value in a Timed Game." In *Congress Reconsidered*, edited by Lawrence C. Dodd and Bruce I. Oppenheimer. Washington, D.C.: Congressional Quarterly, 1993.

Conover, Pamela Johnston. "Political Cues and the Perception of Candidates." *American Politics Quarterly* 9 (1981): 427–48.

Conover, Pamela Johnston, and Stanley Feldman. "Candidate Perception in an Ambiguous World: Campaigns, Cues, and Inference Processes." *American Journal of Political Science* 33 (1989): 912–40.

Conrad, Peter, ed. *The Sociology of Health and Illness, Critical Perspectives*. New York: St. Martin's Press, 1997.

Cook, Charlie. "Whip's Race Is Personal for House Democrats." *National Journal*, 6 October 2001, 3113–14.

Cook, Elizabeth Adell. "Voter Response to Women Senate Candidates." In *The Year of the Woman: Myths and Realities*, edited by Elizabeth Adell Cook, Sue Thomas, and Clyde Wilcox. Boulder, Colo.: Westview Press, 1994.

Cook, Elizabeth Adell, Sue Thomas, and Clyde Wilcox, eds. *The Year of the Woman: Myths and Realities*. Boulder, Colo.: Westview Press, 1994.

Cook, Elizabeth Adell, and Clyde Wilcox. "Women Voters in the 'Year of the Woman.'" In *Democracy's Feast: Elections in America*, edited by Herbert F. Weisberg. Chatham, N.J.: Chatham House, 1995.

Cook, Timothy E. *Making Laws and Making News: Media Strategies in the U.S. House of Representatives*. Washington, D.C.: Brookings Institution, 1989.

Cooper, Cary L., and Suzan Lewis. *Managing the New Work Force: The Challenge of Dual-Income Families*. Amsterdam: Pfeiffe, 1994.

Cooper, Joseph, and David W. Brady. "Toward a Diachronic Analysis of Congress." *American Political Science Review* 75 (1981): 988–1006.

Cooper, Joseph, and G. Calvin Mackenzie. *The House at Work*. Austin: University of Texas Press, 1981.

Coote, Anna. "Gender Parity and the Third Way in British Politics." Paper presented at the "Gender Parity and Liberal Tradition" conference at the Center for European Studies, Harvard University, April 1999.

——. "Women and the Third Way." In *Has Liberalism Failed Women? Assuring Equal Representation in Europe and the United States*, edited by Jytte Klausen and Charles Maier, 111–23. New York: Palgrave, 2001.

——, ed. *New Gender Agenda: Why Women Still Want More*. London: Institute for Public Policy Research, 2000.

Corbett, Julia B., and Motim Mori. "Leading and Following: Medical System Influence on Media Coverage of Breast Cancer, 1960–1995." Paper presented at the Association of Education in Journalism and Mass Communication Convention, Chicago, Ill., 1997.

Costain, Anne. "Eliminating Sex Discrimination in Education: Lobbying for Implementation of Title IX." *Policy Studies Journal* 7 (1978): 189–95.

——. *Inviting Women's Rebellion: A Political Process Interpretation of the Women's Movement*. Baltimore: Johns Hopkins University Press, 1992.

——. "Lobbying for Equal Credit." In *Women Organizing*, edited by Bernice Cummings and Victoria Schuck. Metuchen, N.J.: Scarecrow Press, 1979.

——. "Representing Women: The Transition from Social Movement to Interest Group." *Western Political Quarterly* 34 (1981): 100–115.

——. "The Struggle for a National Women's Lobby: Organizing a Diffuse Interest." *Western Political Quarterly* 33 (1980): 476–91.

——. "Women Lobby Congress." In *Social Movements and American Political Institutions*, edited by Anne Costain and Andrew McFarland. Lanham, Md. Rowman & Littlefield, 1998.

——. "The Women's Lobby: Impact of a Movement on Congress." In *Interest Group Politics*, edited by Allan Cigler and Burdett Loomis. Washington, D.C.: Congressional Quarterly Press, 1983.

——. "Women's Movements and Nonviolence." *Political Science and Politics* 33, no. 2 (2000): 175–80.

Costain, Anne, and Heather Fraizer. "Media Portrayal of 'Second Wave' Feminist Groups." In *Deliberation, Democracy, and the Media*, edited by Anne Costain and Simone Chambers. Lanham, Md.: Rowman & Littlefield, 2000.

Costain, Anne, and Steven Majstorovic. "Congress, Social Movements, and Public Opinion: Multiple Origins of Women's Rights Legislation." *Political Research Quarterly* 47 (1994): 111–36.

Costantini, Edmond. "Political Women and Political Ambition: Closing the Gender Gap." *American Journal of Political Science* 34 (1990): 741–70.

Costantini, Edmond, and Kenneth H. Craik. "Women as Politicians: The Social Background, Personality and Political Careers of Female Party Leaders." In *A Portrait of Marginality: The Political Behavior of the American Woman*, edited by Marianne Githens and Jewell Prestage. New York: D. McKay, 1977.

Costello, Cynthia B., Shari E. Miles, and Anne J. Stone. *The American Woman, 1999–2000: A Century of Change—What's Next?* New York: Norton, 1998.

Cott, Nancy F. *The Grounding of Modern Feminism*. New Haven, Conn.: Yale University Press, 1987.

Cox, Gary W., and Mathew D. McCubbins. *Legislative Leviathan: Party Government in the House*. Berkeley: University of California Press, 1994.

Craig v Boren. 429 U.S. 190 (1976).

C-SPAN. "Women and Reflections on Congresssional Life." Broadcast from the Carl B. Albert Center, University of Oklahoma, 20 April 1999.

D'Antonio, Michael. "If I'd Only Known Then What I Know Now: The Inside Scoop from the New Women in Congress." *Redbook*, September 1996, 97–100.

Darcy, R., Susan Welch, and Janet Clark. *Women, Elections, and Representation*. 2nd ed. Lincoln: University of Nebraska Press, 1994.

Davidson, Roger. "Procedures and Politics in Congress." In *The Abortion Dispute and the American System*, edited by Gilbert Steiner. Washington, D.C.: Brookings Institution, 1983.

Dearing, James N., and Everett M. Rogers. "AIDS and the Media Agenda." In *AIDS: A Communication Perspective*, edited by Timothy Edgar, Mary Anne Fitzpatrick, and Vicki S. Freimuth. Hillsdale, N.J.: Erlbaum, 1992.

Deering, Christopher J., and Steven S. Smith. *Committees in Congress*. 3rd ed. Washington, D.C.: Congressional Quarterly, Inc., 1997.

DeGregorio, Christine. *Networks of Champions*. Ann Arbor: University of Michigan Press, 1997.

Dejong, William. "MADD Massachusetts Versus Senator Burke: A Media Advocacy Case Study." *Health Education Quarterly* 23 (1996): 318–29.

Delli Carpini, Michael X., and Scott Keeter. *What Americans Know about Politics and Why It Matters*. New Haven, Conn.: Yale University Press, 1996.

Deutchman, Iva Ellen. "Feminist Theory and the Politics of Empowerment." In *Women in Politics: Outsiders or Insiders?* edited by Lois Lovelace Duke. Englewood Cliffs, N.J.: Prentice Hall, 1996.

Diamond, Irene. *Sex Roles in the State House*. New Haven, Conn.: Yale University Press, 1977.

Dillman, Don. *Mail and Telephone Surveys: The Total Design Method*. New York: Wiley, 1978.

DiStefano, Christine. *Configurations of Masculinity*. Ithaca, N.Y.: Cornell University Press, 1991.

———. "Masculinity as Ideology in Political Theory: Hobbesian Man Reconsidered." *Women's Studies International Forum* 6 (1983): 633–44.

Dodd, Lawrence C. "Re-Envisioning Congress: Theoretical Perspectives on Congressional Change." In *Congress Reconsidered*, 7th ed., edited by Lawrence C. Dodd and Bruce I. Oppenheimer. Washington, D.C.: Congressional Quarterly Press, 2001.

Dodd, Lawrence C., and Bruce I. Oppenheimer, eds. *Congress Reconsidered*. 7th ed. Washington, D.C.: Congressional Quarterly Press, 2001.

Dodson, Debra L. "Change and Continuity in the Relationship between Private Responsibilities and Public Officeholding: The More Things Change, the More They Stay the Same." *Policy Studies Journal* 25, no. 4 (1997): 569–84.

———. *Gender and Policymaking: Studies of Women in Office.* New Brunswick, N.J.: Center for the American Woman and Politics, 1991.

———. "Gender Difference, Institutional Constraints and the Representation of Women's Interests in Congress." Paper presented at the annual meeting of the Midwest Political Science Association, Chicago, April 1997.

———. "Representing Women's Interests in the U.S. House of Representatives." In *Women and Elective Office: Past, Present, and Future*, edited by Sue Thomas and Clyde Wilcox. New York: Oxford, 1998.

———. "What a Difference an Election Makes: Representing Women's Interests on Health Care in the 104th Congress." Paper presented at the annual meeting of the American Political Science Association, Washington, D.C., 1997.

Dodson, Debra L., and Susan J. Carroll. *Reshaping the Agenda: Women in State Legislatures.* New Brunswick, N.J.: Center for American Women and Politics, Eagleton Institute of Politics, Rutgers, the State University of New Jersey, 1991.

Dodson, Debra L., Susan J. Carroll, Ruth B. Mandel, Katherine E. Kleeman, Ronnie Schreiber, and Debra Liebowitz. *Voices, Views, Votes: The Impact of Women in the 103rd Congress.* New Brunswick, N.J.: Center for the American Woman and Politics, 1995.

Doherty, Caroll. "GOP Leaders Scuttle Bipartisan Bill in Nod to House Conservatives." *Congressional Quarterly Weekly Report* 55 (1997): 1324.

Dolan, Julie. "Support for Women's Interests in the 103rd Congress: The Distinct Impact of Congressional Women." *Women and Politics* 18, no. 4 (1997): 81–94.

Dolan, Kathleen. "Determinants of Support for Women Congressional Candidates in the 1990s." Paper presented at the annual meeting of the Midwest Political Science Association, Chicago, April 1997.

———. "Voting for Women in the 'Year of the Woman.'" *American Journal of Political Science* 42 (1998): 272–93.

Dolan, Kathleen, and Lynne E. Ford. "Are All Women State Legislators Alike?" In *Women and Elective Office: Past, Present, and Future*, edited by Sue Thomas and Clyde Wilcox. New York: Oxford University Press, 1998.

———. "Change and Continuity among Women State Legislators: Evidence from Three Decades." *Political Research Quarterly* 50 (1997): 137–51.

———. "Changing Times, Changing Styles: The Professionalization of Women Legislators." Paper presented at the annual meeting of the Midwest Political Science Association, Chicago, April 1993.

———. "Women State Legislators: Experience, Opportunity and Ambition." Paper presented at the annual meeting of the Midwest Political Science Association, Chicago, April 1994.

Donovan, Beth, and Phil Kuntz. "House Panels Recarve Turf; Senators Pick Major Seats." *Congressional Quarterly Weekly Report*, 9 January 1993, 63–65.

DuBois, Ellen Carol. *Feminism and Suffrage*. Ithaca, N.Y.: Cornell University Press, 1978.

Duerst-Lahti, Georgia. "The Bottleneck: Women Becoming Candidates." In *Women and Elective Office: Past, Present, and Future*, edited by Sue Thomas and Clyde Wilcox. New York: Oxford University Press, 1998.

———. "But Women Play the Game Too: Communication Control and Influence in Administrative Decision-Making." *Administration and Society* 22 (1990): 182–205.

———. "Competing Gender Ideologies: The Case of Welfare Reform." Paper presented at the annual meeting of the Midwest Political Science Association, Chicago, April 1998.

———. *Gender Power Relations in Public Bureaucracies*. Ph.D. diss.Dissertation, University of Wisconsin-Madison, 1987.

———. "Making Good Citizens." Paper presented at the annual meeting of the Midwestern Political Science Association, Chicago, 1999.

———. "Reconceiving Theories of Power: Consequences of Masculinism in the Executive Branch." In *The Other Elites: Women, Politics, and Power in the Executive Branch*, edited by Mary Anne Borelli and Janet M. Martin. Boulder, Colo.: Lynne Rienner, 1997.

Duerst-Lahti, Georgia, Cathy Marie Johnson, and Noelle Norton. *Making Masculine Mothers: Gender Ideology in Welfare Reform*. Forthcoming.

Duerst-Lahti, Georgia, and Rita Mae Kelly. "The Study of Gender Power and Its Link to Governance and Leadership." In *Gender Power, Leadership, and Governance*, edited by Georgia Duerst-Lahti and Rita Mae Kelly. Ann Arbor: University of Michigan, 1995.

———, eds. *Gender Power, Leadership, and Governance*. Ann Arbor: University of Michigan Press, 1995.

Duerst-Lahti, Georgia, and Dayna Verstegen. "Making Something of Absence: The 'Year of the Woman' and Women's Representation." In *Gender Power, Leadership, and Governance*, edited by Georgia Duerst-Lahti and Rita Mae Kelly. Ann Arbor: University of Michigan Press, 1995.

Duncan, Phil. "Routines in the House and Family Values." *Congressional Quarterly Weekly Report*, 21 October 1995, 3238.

Duncan, Phil, and Christine Lawrence. *Congressional Quarterly's Politics in America 1996: The 104th Congress*. Washington, D.C.: Congressional Quarterly, Inc., 1995.

Eagle, Maria, and Joni Lovenduski. *High Time or High Tide for Labour Women*. London: Fabian Society, 1998.

Ekstrand, Laurie E., and William A. Eckert. "The Impact of Candidate's Sex on Voter Choice." *Western Political Quarterly* 34 (1981): 78–87.

Elazar, Daniel J. *American Federalism: A View from the States*. 3rd ed. New York: Harper & Row, 1984.

Elkins, Stanley, and Eric McKitrick. "The Founding Fathers: Young Men of the Revolution." *Political Science Quarterly* 76 (1961): 181–216.

Elshtain, Jean Bethke. *Public Man, Private Woman*. Princeton, N.J.: Princeton University Press, 1981.

Endersby, James W., and Karen M. McCurdy. "Committee Assignments in the U.S. Senate." *Legislative Studies Quarterly* 21 (1996): 219–34.

Evans, C. Lawrence, and Walter Oleszek. *Congress under Fire: Reform Politics and the Republican Majority*. Boston: Houghton Mifflin, 1997.

Evans, Sara. *Born for Liberty*. New York: Free Press, 1989.

Feldman, Stanley, and Pamela Johnston Conover. "Candidates, Issues and Voters: The Role of Inference in Political Perception" *Journal of Politics* 45 (1983): 810–39.

Fenno, Richard F., Jr. *Congressmen in Committees*. Boston: Little Brown, 1973.

———. *Home Style: House Members in Their Districts*. Boston: Little Brown, 1978.

———. "The Senate through a Looking Glass: The Debate over Television." *Legislative Studies Quarterly* 14 (1989): 313–48.

Ferguson, Kathy E. *A Feminist Case against Bureaucracy*. Philadelphia: Temple University Press, 1984.

———. *The Man Question: Visions of Subjectivity in Feminist Theory*. Berkeley: University of California Press, 1993.

Ferree, Myra Marx, and Beth B. Hess. *Controversy and Coalition*. Rev. ed. New York: Twayne, 1994.

Fiorina, Morris. *Representatives, Roll Calls, and Constituencies*. Lexington, Mass.: Lexington Books, 1974.

Fiske, Susan T., and Donald R. Kinder. "Involvement, Expertise, and Schema Use: Evidence from Political Cognition." In *Personality, Cognition, and Social Interaction*, edited by Nancy Cantor and John F. Kihlstrom. Hillsdale, N.J.: Erlbaum, 1981.

Flammang, Janet A. *Women's Political Voice: How Women Are Transforming the Practice and Study of Politics*. Philadelphia: Temple University Press, 1997.

Flexner, Eleanor. *Century of Struggle*. New York: Atheneum, 1973.

Foerstel, Karen. *Biographical Dictionary of Congressional Women*. Westwood, Conn.: Greenwood Press, 1999.

———. "Delay Wants Blunt to Succeed Him but Others Want a Whip Less Beholden." *CQ Weekly* 59 (15 December 2001): 2694–95.

———. "Number of Female Departures Means Loss of Seniority." *Congressional Quarterly Weekly Report* 53 (1995): 3760.

———. "Pelosi: A Tireless Fundraiser Sees Herself as a 'Fresh' Face." *CQ Weekly*, 6 October 2001, 2324–25.

Foerstel, Karen, and Herbert N. Foerstel. *Climbing the Hill: Gender Conflict in Congress*. Westport, Conn.: Praeger, 1996.

Foley, Michael. *The New Senate*. New Haven, Conn.: Yale University Press, 1980.

Fox, Harrison W., Jr., and Susan Hammond. *Congressional Staffs: The Invisible Force of American Lawmaking*. New York: Free Press, 1977.

Fox, Richard L. "Gender and Congressional Elections." In *Gender and American Politics*, edited by Sue Tolleson-Rinehart and Jyl Josephson, 227–56. Armonk, N.Y.: M.E. Sharpe, 2000.

————. *Gender Dynamics in Congressional Elections*. Thousand Oaks, Calif.: Sage, 1997.

Fox, Richard L., and Eric R. A. N. Smith. "The Role of Candidate Sex in Voter Decision-Making." *Political Psychology* 19, no. 2 (1998): 405–19.

Francis, Wayne L. *Legislative Committee Game: A Comparative Analysis of Fifty States.* Columbus: Ohio State University Press, 1989.

Franklin, Jane. "After Modernization: Gender, the Third Way and the New Politics." In *New Gender Agenda: Why Women Still Want More*, edited by Anna Coote. London: Institute for Public Policy Research, 2000.

Frankovic, Kathleen A. "Sex and Voting in the U.S. House of Representatives, 1961–1975." *American Politics Quarterly* 5 (1977): 317–30.

Frantzich, Stephen E. "De-Recruitment: The Other Side of the Congressional Equation." *Western Political Quarterly* 31 (1978): 105–26.

Frantzich, Stephen E., and John Sullivan. *The C-SPAN Revolution*. Norman: University of Oklahoma Press, 1996.

Freedman, Allan. "With Child Care Bill, Panel Aims to Influence Welfare Debate." *Congressional Quarterly Weekly Report* 53 (1995): 1507.

Freeman, Jo. *The Politics of Women's Liberation*. New York: D. McKay, 1975.

Friedan, Betty. *The Feminine Mystique*. New York: Dell, 1963.

Friedman, Sally. "Committee Advancement of Women and Blacks in Congress: A Test of the Responsible Legislator Thesis." *Women & Politics* 13, no. 2 (1993): 27–52.

Friedman, Sally, and Robert T. Nakamura. "The Representation of Women on U.S. Senate Committee Staffs." *Legislative Studies Quarterly* 16 (1991): 407–27.

Gaddie, Ronald Keith, and Charles S. Bullock III. "Congressional Elections and the Year of the Woman: Structural and Elite Influence on Female Candidacies." *Social Science Quarterly* 76 (1995): 749–62.

————. *Elections to Open Seats in the U.S. House: Where the Action Is*. Lanham, Md.: Rowman & Littlefield, 2000.

Gaddie, Ronald Keith, Kim U. Hoffman, and Carrie Palmer. "The Role of Gender in Open-Seat Elections, 1982–1998." Paper presented at the annual meeting of the Southwestern Political Science Association, Galveston, Texas, 2000.

Galloway, George B. *History of the House of Representatives*. 2nd ed. New York: Crowell, 1976.

Gamm, Gerald, and Kenneth A. Shepsle. "Emergence of Legislative Institutions: Standing Committees in the House and Senate, 1810–1825." *Legislative Studies Quarterly* 14, no. 1 (1989): 39–66.

Gamson, William. *Talking Politics*. Cambridge: Cambridge University Press, 1992.

Gamson, William, and Kathryn E. Lasch. "The Political Culture of Social Welfare Policy." In *Evaluating the Welfare State: Social and Political Perspectives*, edited by Shimon Spiro and Ephraim Yuchtman-Yaar. New York: Academic Press, 1983.

Garrett, John C., and Charles I. Brooks. "Effect of Ballot Color, Sex of Candidate, and Sex of College Students of Voting Age on Their Voting Behavior." *Psychological Reports* 60, no. 1 (1987): 39–44.

Gehlen, Frieda L. "Legislative Role Performance of Female Legislators." *Sex Roles* 3, no. 1 (1977): 1–17.

———. "Women Members of Congress: A Distinctive Role." In *A Portrait of Marginality: The Political Behavior of the American Woman*, edited by Marianne Githens and Jewel L. Prestage. New York: D. McKay, 1977.

Geiger, S. F., and B. Reeves. "The Effects of Visual Structure and Content Emphasis on the Evaluation and Memory of Political Candidates." In *Psychological Processes*. Vol. 1 of *Television and Political Advertising*, edited by Frank Biocca. Hillsdale, N.J.: Erlbaum, 1991.

Gelb, Joyce. *Feminism and Politics*. Berkeley: University of California Press, 1989.

———. "Feminist Organization Success and the Politics of Engagement." In *Feminist Organizations*, edited by Myra Marx Ferree and Patricia Yancey Martin. Philadelphia: Temple University Press, 1995.

Gelb, Joyce, and Marian Lief Palley. "Women and Interest Group Politics." *American Politics Quarterly* 5 (1977): 331–52.

———. *Women and Public Policies*. Princeton, N.J.: Princeton University Press, 1982.

———. *Women and Public Policies*. Rev. ed. Princeton, N.J.: Princeton University Press, 1987.

———. *Women and Public Policies: Reassessing Gender Politics*. New ed. Charlottesville, Va.: University Press of Virginia, 1996.

Gertzog, Irwin N. *Congressional Women: Their Recruitment, Treatment, and Behavior*. New York: Praeger, 1984.

———. *Congressional Women: Their Recruitment, Integration, and Behavior*. 2nd ed. New York: Praeger, 1995.

———. *Congresswomen in the Breech: The Women's Caucus before and after the 'Republican Revolution.'* 2003.

———. "The Matrimonial Connection: The Nomination of Congressmen's Widows for the House of Representatives." *Journal of Politics* 42 (1980): 820–33.

Gilligan, Carol. *In a Different Voice: Psychological Theory and Women's Development*. Cambridge: Harvard University Press, 1982.

Gimpel, James. *Fulfilling the Contract: The First Hundred Days*. Boston: Allyn & Bacon, 1996.

Githens, Marianne. "Spectators, Agitators or Lawmakers: Women in State Legislatures." In *A Portrait of Marginality: The Political Behavior of the American Woman*, edited by Marianne Githens and Jewell Prestage. New York: D. McKay, 1977.

———. "Women and State Politics: An Assessment." In *Political Women*, edited by Janet A. Flammang. Beverly Hills: Sage, 1984.

Graber, Doris A. *Processing the News: How People Tame the Information Tide*. New York: Longman, 1984.

Granstaff, Bill. *Losing Our Democratic Spirit: Congressional Deliberation and the Dictatorship of Propaganda*. Westport, Conn.: Praeger, 1999.

Groseclose, Tim, and Charles Stewart III. "The Value of Committee Seats in the House, 1947–1991." *American Journal of Political Science* 42 (1998): 453–74.

Gross, Cary P., Gerald F. Anderson, and Neil R. Powe. "The Relation between Funding by the National Institutes of Health and the Burden of Disease." *New England Journal of Medicine* 340, no. 24 (1999): 1881–87.

Guy, Mary E. *Women and Men of the State*. Armonk, N.Y.: M.E. Sharpe, 1992.

Guy, Mary E., and Georgia Duerst-Lahti. "Agency Culture and Its Effect on Managers." In *Women and Men of the State*, edited by Mary E. Guy. Armonk, N.Y.: M.E. Sharpe, 1992.

Hale, Mary M., and Rita Mae Kelly. *Gender, Bureaucracy, and Democracy*. New York: Greenwood Press, 1989.

Hall, Richard L. "Participation and Purpose in Committee Decision Making." *American Political Science Review* 81 (1987): 105–27.

———. *Participation in Congress*. New Haven, Conn.: Yale University Press, 1996.

Hall, Richard L., and C. Lawrence Evans. "The Power of Subcommittees." *Journal of Politics* 52 (1990): 335–54.

Hall, Richard L., and Bernard Grofman. "The Committee Assignment Process and the Conditional Nature of Committee Bias." *American Political Science Review* 84 (1990): 1149–66.

Hardin, John W. "An In-Depth Look at Congressional Committee Jurisdictions Surrounding Health Issues." *Journal of Health Politics, Policy, and Law* 23 (1998): 517–50.

Harris, Fred R., and Paul L. Hain. *America's Legislative Processes*. Glenville, Ill.: Scott, Foresman, 1983.

Harrison, Cynthia. *On Account of Sex: The Politics of Women's Issues, 1945–1968*. Berkeley: University of California Press, 1988.

Hartsock, Nancy C. M. *Money, Sex, and Power*. Boston: Northeastern University Press, 1983.

Hawkesworth, Mary. *Beyond Oppression*. New York: Continuum, 1990.

Hearn, Jeff. *Men in the Public Eye*. London: Routledge, 1992.

Hearn, Jeff, Deborah L. Sheppard, Peta Tancred-Sheriff, and Gibson Burrell. *The Sexuality of Organization*. London: Sage, 1989.

Herrick, Rebekah. "A Reappraisal of the Quality of Women Candidates." *Women & Politics* 15, no. 4 (1995): 25–38.

Herrick, Rebekah, and Michael K. Moore. "Political Ambition's Effect on Legislative Behavior: Schlesinger's Typology Reconsidered and Revised." *Journal of Politics* 55 (1993): 765–76.

Hertzke, Allen, and Ronald M. Peters, Jr. *The Atomistic Congress*. Armonk, N.Y.: M.E. Sharpe, 1992.

Hibbing, John R. *Choosing to Leave*. Washington, D.C.: University Press of America, 1982.

———. *Congressional Careers: Contours of Life in the U.S. House of Representatives*. Chapel Hill: University of North Carolina Press, 1991.

Hickman-Maslin Research. "The New Political Woman Survey." Typescript. Washington, D.C., 1987.

Hill, David B. "Female State Senators as Cue Givers: ERA Roll-Call Voting, 1972–1979." In *Political Women: Current Roles in State and Local Government*, edited by Janet A. Flammang. Beverly Hills, Calif.: Sage, 1984.

———. "Women State Legislators and Party Voting on the ERA." *Social Science Quarterly* 64 (1983): 318–26.

Hinckley, Barbara. "The American Voter in Congressional Elections." *American Political Science Review* 74 (1980): 641–50

———. *Stability and Change in Congress*. New York: Harper & Row, 1971.

———. *Stability and Change in Congress*. 4th ed. New York: Harper & Row, 1988.

Hirschmann, Nancy J., and Richard C. Sinopoli. "Feminism and Liberal Theory." *American Political Science Review* 85 (1991): 221–36.

Hochschild, Arlie. *The Time Bind: When Work Becomes Home and Home Becomes Work*. New York: Metropolitan Books, 1997.

Hochschild, Arlie, with Anne Machung. *The Second Shift: Working Parents and the Revolutions at Home*. New York: Viking, 1989.

Holtzman, Elizabeth, and Shirley Williams. "Women in the Political World: Observations." *Daedalus* 116 (1987): 199–210.

Hoover, Kenneth. *Ideology and Political Life*. 2nd ed. Belmont, Calif.: Wadsworth, 1994.

Huddy, Leonie. "The Political Significance of Voters' Gender Stereotypes." In *Research in Micropolitics: New Directions in Political Psychology*. Greenwich, Conn.: JAI Press, 1994.

Huddy, Leonie, and Nayda Terkildsen. "The Consequences of Gender Stereotypes for Women Candidates." *Political Research Quarterly* 46, no. 3 (1993): 503–25.

———. "Gender Stereotypes and the Perception of Male and Female Candidates." *American Journal of Political Science* 37, no. 1 (1993): 119–47.

Huffman, Matt L. "Who's in Charge? Organizational Influences on Women's Representation in Managerial Positions." *Social Science Quarterly* 80, no. 4 (1999): 738–56.

Idelson, Holly. "Wanted: A Few Good Women." *Congressional Quarterly Weekly Report* 51 (1993): 64.

Iyengar, Shanto. *Is Anyone Responsible? How Television Frames Political Issues*. Chicago: University of Chicago Press, 1992.

Iyengar, Shanto, Nicholas A. Valentino, Stephen Ansolabehere, and Adam F. Simon. "The Effects of Gender Stereotypes on Women's Campaigns?" In *Women, Media, and Politics*, edited by Pippa Norris. New York: Oxford University Press, 1997.

Jacobson, Gary C. *The Electoral Origins of Divided Government: Competition in U.S. House Elections, 1946–1988*. Boulder, Colo.: Westview Press, 1990.

———. *The Politics of Congressional Elections*. 4th ed. New York: Longman, 1997.

———. "Strategic Politicians and the Dynamics of U.S. House Elections, 1946–1986." *American Political Science Review* 83 (1989): 773–94.

Jaffe, Harry. "Dying for Dollars." *Men's Health*, September 1997, 132–39.

James, Edward T., ed. *Notable American Women, 1607–1950*. Cambridge: Harvard University Press, 1973.

Jamieson, Kathleen Hall. *Beyond the Double Bind*. New York: Oxford University Press, 1995.

Jewell, Malcolm E., and Marcia Lynn Whicker. "The Feminization of Leadership." *PS: Political Science and Politics* 26, no. 4 (1993): 705–11.

————. *Legislative Leadership in the American States*. Ann Arbor: University of Michigan Press, 1994.

Jillson, Calvin, and Rick K. Wilson. *Congressional Dynamics*. Stanford, Calif.: Stanford University Press, 1994.

Johannes, John R. "Women as Congressional Staffers: Does It Make a Difference?" *Women & Politics* 4, no. 2 (1984): 69–81.

Johnson, Cathy Marie, and Georgia Duerst-Lahti. "Public Work, Private Lives." In *Women and Men of the States: Public Administrators at the State Level*, edited by Mary E. Guy. Armonk, N.Y.: M.E. Sharpe, 1992.

Johnson, Judith. "Cancer Research: Selected Federal Spending and Morbidity and Mortality Statistics." *CRS Report for Congress* (3 March 1998), No. 96-253. Washington, D.C.: GPO, 1998.

Johnston, Anne, and Anne Barton White. "Communication Styles and Female Candidates: A Study of the Political Advertising during the 1986 Senate Elections." *Journalism Quarterly* 71 (1994): 321–29

Joslyn, R. A. *Mass Media and Elections*. Reading, Mass.: Addison-Wesley, 1984.

Kahn, Kim Fridkin. "Distorted Mirror: Press Coverage of Women Candidates for Statewide Office." *Journal of Politics* 54 (1994): 154–73.

————. "Does Being Male Help? An Investigation of the Effects of Candidate Gender and Campaign Coverage on Evaluations of U.S. Senate Candidates." *Journal of Politics* 54 (1992): 497–517.

————. "Does Gender Make a Difference? An Experimental Examination of Sex Stereotypes and Press Patterns in Statewide Campaigns." *American Journal of Political Science* 38 (1994): 162–95.

————. "Gender Differences in Campaign Messages: The Political Advertisements of Men and Women Candidates for U.S. Senate." *Political Research Quarterly* 46 (1993): 481–502.

————. *The Political Consequences of Being a Woman: How Stereotypes Influence the Conduct and Consequences of Political Campaigns*. New York: Columbia University Press, 1996.

Kahn, Kim Fridkin, and E. N. Goldenberg. "Women Candidates in the News: An Examination of Gender Differences in the U.S. Senate Campaign Coverage." *Public Opinion Quarterly* 55 (1991): 180–99.

Kahn, Kim Fridkin, and Ann Gordon. "How Women Campaign for the U.S. Senate." In *Women, Media and Politics*, edited by Pippa Norris. New York: Oxford University Press, 1997.

Kaid, Lynda Lee. "Ethical Dimensions of Political Advertising." In *Ethical Dimensions of Political Communication*, edited by Robert E. Denton, Jr. New York: Praeger, 1991.

———."Technology and Political Advertising: The Application of Ethical Standards to the 1992 Spots." *Communication Research Reports* 13 (1996): 129–37.

Kaid, Lynda Lee, and Dorothy K. Davidson. "Elements of Videostyle: Candidate Presentations through Television Advertising." In *New Perspectives on Political Advertising*, edited by Lynda Lee Kaid, Dan Nimmo, and Keith R. Sanders. Carbondale: Southern Illinois University Press, 1986.

Kaid, Lynda Lee, and Anne Johnston. *Videostyle in Presidential Campaigns: Style and Content in Televised Political Advertising.* Westport, Conn.: Praeger, 2001.

Kaid, Lynda Lee, and Gary Noggle. "Televised Political Advertising in the 1992 and 1996 Elections: Using Technology to Manipulate Voters." *Southeastern Political Review* 26 (1998): 889–906.

Kann, Mark E. *On the Man Question: Gender and Civic Virtue in America.* Philadelphia: Temple University Press, 1991.

———. *A Republic of Men: The American Founders, Gendered Language, and Patriarchal Politics.* New York: New York University Press, 1998.

Kanter, Rosabeth Moss. *Men and Women of the Corporation.* New York: Basic Books, 1977.

———. "Some Effect of Proportions on Group Life: Skewed Sex Ratios and Responses to Token Women." *American Journal of Sociology* 82 (1977): 965–90.

Kathlene, Lyn. "Alternative Views of Crime: Legislative Policymaking in Gendered Terms." *Journal of Politics* 57 (1995): 696–723.

———. "In a Different Voice: Women and the Policy Process." In *Women and Elective Office: Past, Present, and Future*, edited by Sue Thomas and Clyde Wilcox. New York: Oxford University Press, 1998.

———. "Position Power vs Gender Power: Who Holds the Floor?" In *Gender Power, Leadership, and Governance*, edited by Georgia Duerst-Lahti and Rita Mae Kelly. Ann Arbor: University of Michigan, 1995.

———. "Power and Influence in State Legislative Policymaking: The Interaction of Gender and Position in Committee Hearing Debates." *American Political Science Review* 99, no. 3 (1994): 560–76.

Katz, Jeffrey. "House Passes Welfare Bill; Senate Likely to Alter It." *Congressional Quarterly Weekly Report* 53 (1995): 872–75.

Katz, Jeffrey L., and Carol J. Doherty. "New GOP Leaders' Watchword Is Realism, Not Revolution." *Congressional Quarterly Weekly Report* 56 (1998): 3161–66.

Katz, Jeffrey, and Alissa Rubin. "House Panel Poised to Approve GOP Welfare Overhaul Bill." *Congressional Quarterly Weekly Report* 53 (1995): 689–92.

Katz, Jeffrey, Alissa Rubin, and Peter MacPherson. "Major Aspects of Welfare Bill Approved by Subcommittee." *Congressional Quarterly Weekly Report* 53 (1995): 525–32.

Katzenstein, Mary Fainsod. "Comparing the Feminist Movements of the United States and Western Europe: An Overview." In *The Women's Movements of the United States and Western Europe: Consciousness, Political Opportunity, and Public Policy*, edited by Mary Fainsod Katzenstein and Carol McClurg Mueller. Philadelphia: Temple University Press, 1987.

———. "Discursive Politics and Feminist Activism in the Catholic Church." In *Feminist Organizations*, edited by Myra Marx Ferree and Patricia Yancey Martin. Philadelphia: Temple University Press, 1995.

———. *Faithful and Fearless: Moving Feminist Protest inside the Church and Military*. Princeton, N.J.: Princeton University Press, 1998.

———. "Feminism within American Institutions: Unobtrusive Mobilization in the 1980s." *Signs* 16, no. 1 (1990): 27–54.

Kaufmann, Karen M., and John R. Petrocik. "The Changing Politics of American Men: Understanding the Sources of the Gender Gap." *American Journal of Political Science* 43, no. 3 (1999): 864–87.

Kenney, Sally J. "Field Essay: New Research on Gendered Political Institutions." *Political Research Quarterly* 49, no. 2 (1996): 445–66.

Kerber, Linda K. *No Constitutional Right to Be Ladies*. New York: Hill & Wang, 1998.

———. *Toward an Intellectual History of Women*. Chapel Hill: University of North Carolina Press, 1997.

———. *Women of the Republic: Intellect and Ideology in Revolutionary America*. Chapel Hill: University of North Carolina Press, 1980.

Kern, M. *30-Second Politics: Political Advertising in the 1980s*. New York: Praeger, 1989.

Kessler, Daniel, and Keith Krehbiel. "Dynamics of Cosponsorship." *American Political Science Review* 90 (1996): 555–66.

Kiewiet, D. Roderick, and Mathew McCubbins. *The Logic of Delegation: Congressional Parties and the Appropriations Process*. Chicago: University of Chicago Press, 1991.

Killian, Linda. *The Freshmen: What Happened to the Republican Revolution?* Boulder, Colo.: Westview Press, 1998.

Kimmel, Michael. *Manhood in America: A Cultural History*. New York: Free Press, 1996.

———. Series editor's introduction. In *Masculinities in Organizations*, edited by Cliff Cheng. Thousand Oaks, Calif.: Sage, 1996.

Kinder, Donald R. "Presidential Character Revisited." In *Political Cognition*, edited by Richard Lau and David Sears. Hillsdale, N.J.: Erlbaum, 1986.

Kinder, Donald R., and Thomas R. Palfrey. *Experimental Foundations of Political Science*. Ann Arbor: University of Michigan Press, 1993.

Kinder, Donald R., and Lynn M. Sanders. "Mimicking Political Debate with Survey Questions: The Case of White Opinion on Affirmative Action for Blacks." *Social Cognition* 8, no. 1 (1990): 73–103.

King, Cheryl Simrell. "Sex-Role Identity and Decision Styles: How Gender Helps Explain the Paucity of Women at the Top." In *Gender Power, Leadership, and Governance*, edited by Georgia Duerst-Lahti and Rita Mae Kelly. Ann Arbor: University of Michigan, 1995.

King, Gary. *Unifying Political Methodology: The Likelihood Theory of Statistical Inference*. Cambridge: Cambridge University Press, 1989.

Kingdon, John W. *Agendas, Alternatives, and Public Policies*. Boston: Little Brown, 1984.

Kingsley, J. Donald. *Representative Bureaucracy*. Yellow Springs, Ohio: Antioch Press, 1944.

Kirkpatrick, Jeane. *Political Woman*. New York: Basic Books, 1974.

Klatch, Rebecca E. *Women of the New Right*. Philadelphia: Temple University Press, 1987.

Koch, Jeffrey. "Candidate Gender and Assessments of Senate Candidates." *Social Science Quarterly* 80 (1999): 84–96.

Kofmehl, Kenneth Theodore. *Professional Staffs of Congress*. 3rd ed. West Lafayette, Ind.: Purdue University Press, 1977.

Kommers, Donald P. "Abortion in Six Countries: A Comparative Legal Analysis." In *Abortion, Medicine, and the Law*, 4th ed., edited by Douglas Butler and David F. Walbert. New York: Facts on File, 1992.

Koszczuk, Jackie. "House G.O.P. Freshmen Soften Their Edges." *Congressional Quarterly Weekly Report* 54 (1996): 280–81.

Krasno, Jonathan S., and David Philip Green. "Preempting Quality Challengers in House Elections." *Journal of Politics* 50 (1988): 920–36.

Krehbiel, Keith. "Cosponsors and Wafflers from A to Z." *American Journal of Political Science* 39 (1995): 906–23.

———. *Information and Legislative Organization*. Ann Arbor: University of Michigan Press, 1991.

———. "Why Are Congressional Committees Powerful?" *American Political Science Review* 81 (1987): 929–35.

Krislov, Samuel. *Representative Bureaucracy*. Englewood Cliffs, N.J.: Prentice-Hall, 1974.

Krislov, Samuel, and David H. Rosenbloom. *Representative Bureaucracy and the American Political System*. Westport, Conn.: Greenwood, 1981.

Kuntz, Phil. "Organization of the New Senate Will Look Like the Old One." *Congressional Quarterly Weekly Report* 50 (1992): 3565.

Lake, Celinda C., and Vincent J. Breglio. "Different Voices: Different Views." In *The American Woman 92–93: A Status Report*, edited by Paula Ries and Anne J. Stone. New York: Norton, 1992.

Langdon, Steve. "Debate Shifted from Roe to Late-Term Bill." *Congressional Quarterly Weekly Report* 54 (1996): 2873.

Langer, Amy S. "The Politics of Breast Cancer." *American Medical Women's Association* 47 (1992): 207–209.

Lascher, Edward L., Jr. "The Impact of Job Satisfaction on the Career Decisions of Local Lawmakers." In *Ambition and Beyond: Career Paths of American Politicians*, edited by Shirley Williams and Edward L. Lascher, Jr. Berkeley: University of California, 1993.

Lau, Richard R., and David O. Sears. "Social Cognition and Political Cognition: The Past, the Present and the Future." In *Political Cognition*, edited by Richard R. Lau and David O. Sears. Hillsdale, N.J.: Erlbaum, 1986.

Leader, Shelah Gilbert. "The Policy Impact of Elected Women Officials." In *The Impact of the Electoral Process*, edited by Louis Maisel and Joseph Cooper. Beverly Hills, Calif.: Sage, 1977.

Leeper, Mark S. "The Impact of Prejudice on Female Candidates: An Experimental Look at Voter Inference." *American Politics Quarterly* 19 (1991): 248–61.

Levitt, Steven D., and Catherine D. Wolfram. "Decomposing the Sources of Incumbency Advantage in the U.S. House." *Legislative Studies Quarterly* 22 (1997): 45–60.

Levy, Dena, Charles Tien, and Rachelle Aved. "Do Differences Matter? Women Members of Congress and the Hyde Amendment." *Women and Politics*. Forthcoming.

Lorber, Judith. "Believing Is Seeing: Biology as Ideology." *Gender & Society* 2 (1987): 125–51.

Lovenduski, Joni, and Pippa Norris. "Gender and Party Politics in Britain." In *Gender and Party Politics*, edited by Pippa Norris and Joni Lovenduski, 35–59. Thousand Oaks, Calif.: Sage, 1994.

Lovenduski, Joni, and Vicki Randall. *Contemporary Feminist Politics: Women and Power in Britain*. Oxford: Oxford University Press, 1993.

Lowi, Theodore, J. "American Business, Public Policy, Case-Studies, and Political Theory." *World Politics* 16 (1964): 677–715.

Lublin, David. "The Election of African Americans and Latinos to the U.S. House of Representatives, 1972–1994." *American Politics Quarterly* 25 (1997): 269–86.

Luker, Kristin. *Abortion and the Politics of Motherhood*. Berkeley: University of California Press, 2000.

Mactaggart, Fiona. *Women in Parliament*. Unpublished manuscript. N.d.

Maisel, L. Sandy, and Walter J. Stone. "Determinants of Candidate Emergence in U.S. House Elections: An Exploratory Study." *Legislative Studies Quarterly* 22 (1977): 79–96.

Malbin, Michael. *Unelected Representatives: Congressional Staff and the Future of Representative Government*. New York: Basic Books, 1980.

Maltzman, Forrest. *Competing Principals: Committees, Parties, and the Organization of Congress*. Ann Arbor: University of Michigan Press, 1997.

———. "Maintaining Congressional Committees: Sources of Members Support." *Legislative Studies Quarterly* 23 (1998): 197–218.

Maltzman, Forrest, Lee Sigelman, and Sarah Binder. "Leaving Office Feet First: Death in Congress." *PS: Political Science and Politics* 29 (1996): 665–71.

Maltzman, Forrest, and Steven S. Smith. "The Multiple Principals and Motivations of Congressional Committees." *Legislative Studies Quarterly* 19 (1994): 457–76.

Mansbridge, Jane. "The Many Faces of Representation." Working paper, John F. Kennedy School of Government, Harvard University, 1998.

———. "Should Blacks Represent Blacks and Women Represent Women? A Contingent 'Yes.'" *Journal of Politics* 61 (1999): 628–57.

———. *Why We Lost the ERA*. Chicago: University of Chicago Press, 1986.

March, James G., and Johan P. Olsen. *The Organizational Basis of Politics*. New York: Free Press, 1989.

Margolies-Mezvinsky, Marjorie, with Barbara Feinman. *A Woman's Place: The Freshmen Women Who Changed the Face of Congress*. New York: Crown, 1994.

Markus, Hazel, and Robert B. Zajonc. "The Cognitive Perspective in Social Psychology." In *Handbook of Social Psychology*, edited by Gardner Lindzey and Elliot Aronson. 3rd ed. New York: Random House, 1985.

Martin, Andrew D., and Christina Wolbrecht. "Partisanship and Pre-floor Behavior: The Equal Rights and School Prayer Amendments." *Political Research Quarterly* 53 (2000): 711–20.

Matthews, Donald R. "The Folkways of the United States Senate: Conformity to Group Norms and Legislative Effectiveness." *American Political Science Review* 53 (1959): 1064–89.

———. *The Social Background of Political Decision-Makers*. Garden City, N.J.: Doubleday, 1954.

Mayer, Kenneth R., and David T. Canon. *The Dysfunctional Congress: The Individual Roots of an Institutional Dilemma*. Boulder, Colo.: Westview Press, 1999.

Mayhew, David. *Congress: The Electoral Connection*. New Haven, Conn.: Yale University Press, 1974.

McAdam, Doug. *Political Process and the Development of Black Insurgency, 1930–1970*. Chicago: University of Chicago Press, 1982.

McCarty, Nolan M., Keith T. Poole, and Howard Rosenthal. *Income Redistribution and the Realignment of American Politics*. Washington, D.C.: AEI Press, 1997.

McCombs, Maxwell, and Donald Shaw. "The Agenda Setting Function of the Mass Media." *Public Opinion Quarterly* 36 (1972): 176–87.

McDermott, Monika L. "Voting Cues in Low-Information Elections: Candidate Gender as a Social Information Variable in Contemporary United States Elections." *American Journal of Political Science* 41 (1997): 270–83.

McGlen, Nancy, and Karen O'Connor. *Women, Politics, and American Society*. Upper Saddle River, N.J.: Prentice Hall, 1995.

———. *Women, Politics, and American Society*. 2nd ed. Upper Saddle River, N.J.: Prentice Hall, 1998.

McGlen, Nancy, and Meredith Sarkees. *Women in Foreign Policy: The Insiders*. New York: Routledge, 1993.

McPherson, J. Miller, and Lynn Smith-Lovin. "Sex Segregation in Voluntary Associations." *American Sociological Review* 51 (1986): 61–79.

Men's Health Network. "National Prostate Cancer Coalition Based on the National Breast Cancer Coalition Model" [press release]. www.fathermag.com/htmlmodules/Sep96/xnpcc.html.

Meyer, David S., and Sidney Tarrow. "A Movement Society: Contentious Politics for a New Century." In *The Social Movement Society*, edited by David S. Meyer and Sidney Tarrow. Lanham, Md.: Rowman & Littlefield, 1998.

Mezey, Susan Gluck. "Increasing the Number of Women in Office: Does It Matter?" In *The Year of the Woman: Myths and Realities*, edited by Elizabeth Adell Cook, Sue Thomas, and Clyde Wilcox. Boulder, Colo.: Westview Press, 1994.

———. "Support for Women's Rights Policy: An Analysis of Local Politicians." *American Politics Quarterly* 6 (1978): 485–97.

————. "Women and Representation: The Case of Hawaii." *Journal of Politics* 40 (1978): 367–85.

Mikulski, Barbara, Kay Bailey Hutchinson, Dianne Feinstein, Barbara Boxer, Patty Murray, Olympia Snowe, Susan Collins, Mary Landrieu, Blanche L. Lincoln, with Catherine Whitney. *Nine and Counting: The Women of the U.S. Senate*. New York: Morrow, 2000.

Milkis, Sidney M., and Michael Nelson. *The American Presidency: Origins and Development, 1776–1990*. Washington, D.C.: Congressional Quarterly Press, 1990.

Miller, Karen Czarnecki. "Will These Women Clean House?" *Policy Review* 72 (1995): 77–80.

Mills, Albert J., and Peta Tancred. *Gendering Organizational Analysis*. Newbury Park, Calif.: Sage, 1992.

Mink, Gwendolyn, ed. *Whose Welfare?* Ithaca, N.Y.: Cornell University Press, 1999.

Molinari, Susan, with Elinor Burkett. *Representative Mom*. New York: Doubleday, 1998.

Moncrief, Gary F. "Recruitment and Retention in U.S. Legislatures." *Legislative Studies Quarterly* 24 (1999): 173–208.

Mosher, Frederick. *Democracy and the Public Service*. 2nd ed. New York: Oxford University Press, 1982.

Muller, Edward N., and Karl-Dieter Opp. "Rational Choice and Rebellious Collective Action." *American Political Science Review* 80 (1986): 471–87.

————. "Rebellious Collective Action Revisited." *American Political Science Review* 81 (1987): 561–64.

Munger, Michael C. "Allocation of Desirable Committee Assignments." *American Journal of Political Science* 32 (1988): 317–44.

Murphy, Thomas P. *The New Politics Congress*. Lexington, Mass.: Lexington Books, 1974.

National Cancer Institute. "Historical Budget Information." www.nci.nih.gov/.

————. "Research Dollars by Various Cancers." www.nci.nih.gov/public/factbook 98/varican.htm.

National Center for Health Statistics. "Deaths: Final Data for 1997." *National Vital Statistics Reports* 47, no. 19. www.cdc.gov/nchs/data/nvsr47/nvs47_19pdf.

National Prostate Cancer Coalition. "National Semi-Postal Bill Re-Authorized Without Prostate Cancer Stamp." *Smartbrief* [e-mail newsletter], 28 July 2000.

————. "Prostate Cancer Research Pork Barrel Spending." *Smartbrief* [e-mail newsletter], 30 March 2000.

Nelson, Thomas E., and Donald R. Kinder. "Issue Frames and Group-Centrism in American Public Opinion." *Journal of Politics* 58 (1996): 1055–78.

Newman, Jody. *Perception and Reality: A Study Comparing the Success of Men and Women Candidates*. Washington, D.C.: National Women's Political Caucus, 1994.

Newman, Meredith A., and Mary E. Guy. "Taylor's Triangle, Follett's Web." *Administrative Theory and Praxis* 20, no. 3 (1998): 287–97.

Nippert-Eng, Christina E. *Home and Work*. Chicago: University of Chicago Press, 1995.

Niven, David. "Party Elites and Women Candidates: The Shape of Bias." *Women & Politics* 19, no. 2 (1998): 57–80.

Norrander, Barbara. "The Evolution of the Gender Gap." *Public Opinion Quarterly* 63, no. 4 (1999): 566–76.

Norris, Pippa. "Breaking the Barriers: Positive Discrimination Policies for Women." In *Has Liberalism Failed Women? Assuring Equal Representation in Europe and the United States*, edited by Jyette Klausen and Charles S. Maier. New York: Palgrave, 2001.

———. *Politics and Sexual Equality: The Comparative Position of Women in Western Democracies*. Boulder, Colo.: Lynne Rienner, 1987.

———. *Women, Media, and Politics*. New York: Oxford University Press, 1997.

———. "Women Politicians: Transforming Westminster?" In *Women in Politics*, edited by Joni Lovenduski and Pippa Norris. Oxford: Oxford University Press, 1996.

North, R. C., O. Holsti, M. G. Zanovich, and D. A. Zinnes. *Content Analysis: A Handbook with Applications for the Study of International Crisis*. Evanston, Ill.: Northwestern University Press, 1963.

Norton, Noelle H. "Analyzing Roll-Call Voting Tools for Content: Are Women's Issues Excluded from Legislative Research." *Women in Politics* 17, no. 4 (1997): 47–69.

———. "Committee Influence over Controversial Policy: The Reproductive Policy Case." *Policy Studies Journal* 27, no. 2 (1999): 203–16.

———. "Congressional Committee Power: The Reproductive Policy Inner Circle, 1969–1992." Ph.D. diss., University of California, Santa Barbara, 1994.

———. "Uncovering the Dimensionality of Gender Voting in Congress." *Legislative Studies Quarterly* 23 (1999): 65–85.

———. "Women, It's Not Enough to Be Elected: Committee Position Makes a Difference." In *Gender Power, Leadership, and Governance*, edited by Georgia Duerst-Lahti and Rita Mae Kelly. Ann Arbor: University of Michigan Press, 1995.

Nutting, Brian, and H. Amy Stern, eds. *CQ's Politics in America 2002: The 107th Congress*. Washington, D.C.: Congressional Quarterly Press, 2002.

Nye, Joseph S., Jr., Philip D. Zelikow, and David C. King. *Why People Don't Trust Government*. Cambridge, Mass.: Harvard University Press, 1997.

O'Connor, Julia, Ann Shola Orloff, and Sheila Shaver. *States, Markets, Families*. Cambridge: Cambridge University Press, 1999.

O'Connor, Karen, and Jeffrey A. Segal. "Justice Sandra Day O'Connor and the Supreme Court's Reaction to Its First Female Member." *Women & Politics* 10, no. 2 (1990): 95–104.

Oleszek, Walter. *Congressional Procedures and the Policy Process*. 4th ed. Washington, D.C.: Congressional Quarterly Press, 1996.

Olson, Mancur, Jr. *The Logic of Collective Action: Public Goods and the Theory of Groups*. Cambridge: Harvard University Press, 1965.

O'Neill, William L. *Everyone Was Brave*. New York: Quadrangle, 1969.

Ornstein, Norman J., ed. *Congress in Change*. New York: Praeger, 1975.

Ornstein, Norman, Thomas E. Mann, and Michael Malbin. *Vital Statistics on Congress, 1997–1998*. Washington, D.C.: Congressional Quarterly Press, 1997.

Ota, Alan K. "Well-Choreographed Campaign by Dunn." *Congressional Quarterly Weekly Report* 56 (1998): 3048.

Page, Benjamin, and Robert Shapiro. "Educating and Manipulating the Public." In *Manipulating Public Opinion: Essays on Public Opinion as a Dependent Variable*, edited by Michael Margolis and Gary Mauser. Pacific Grove, Calif.: Brooks/Cole, 1989.

Paolino, Phillip. "Group Salient Issues and Group Representation: Support for Women Candidates in the 1992 Senate Elections." *American Journal of Political Science* 39 (1995): 295–313.

Parker, Glenn R. *Institutional Change, Discretion, and the Making of Modern Congress: An Economic Interpretation*. Ann Arbor: University of Michigan Press, 1992.

Parris, Judith. "The Senate Reorganizes Its Committees." *Political Science Quarterly* 94 (1977): 319–37.

Pateman, Carol. *The Sexual Contract*. Stanford: Stanford University Press, 1988.

Patterson, T. E., and R. D. McClure. *The Unseeing Eye: The Myth of Television Power in National Politics*. New York: Putnam, 1976.

Pearson, Judith C., Lynn H. Turner, and William Todd-Mancillas. *Gender and Communication*. Dubuque, Iowa: Wm. C. Brown, 1991.

Perkins, Anne. "Campaigning in an Era of Consensus: Must Women Wear the Velvet Glove?" In *New Gender Agenda: Why Women Still Want More*, edited by Anna Coote. London: Institute for Public Policy Research, 2000.

Peters, Ronald M. *The American Speakership: The Office in Historical Perspective*. 2nd ed. Baltimore: Johns Hopkins University Press, 1994.

Peterson, Geoffrey, and Mark Wrighton. "The Continuing Puzzle of Committee Outliers: A Methodological Reassessment." *Congress and the Presidency* 25, no. 1 (1998): 67–79.

Piacente, Steve, and Hillary Eigen. *The Almanac of the Unelected*. 12th ed. Washington, D.C.: Bernan Press, 1999.

Pitkin, Hannah. *The Concept of Representation*. Berkeley: University of California Press, 1967.

"The Politics of Breast Cancer." *Science* 259 (1993): 616–17.

Polsby, Nelson W. "Institutionalization in the U.S. House of Representatives." *American Political Science Review* 62 (1968): 144–68.

———. "Political Change and the Character of the Contemporary Congress." In *The New American Political System*, 2nd ed., edited by Anthony King. Washington, D.C.: AEI Press, 1990.

Poole, Keith T., and Howard Rosenthal. *Congress: A Political-Economic History of Roll Call Voting*. New York: Oxford University Press, 1997.

Poole, Keith T., and L. Harmon Zeigler. *Women, Public Opinion, and Politics: The Changing Political Attitudes of American Women*. New York: Longman, 1985.

Popkin, Samuel L. "Information Shortcuts and the Reasoning Voter." In *Information, Participation, and Choice*, edited by Bernard Grofman. Ann Arbor: University of Michigan Press, 1995.

Prewitt, Kenneth, and William Nowlin. "Political Ambitions and the Behavior of Incumbent Politicians." *The Western Political Quarterly* 22 (1969): 298–308.

Primmer, Lesley. "The Congressional Caucus for Women's Issues: Twenty Years of Bipartisan Advocacy for Women." In *The American Woman, 1999–2000*, edited by Cynthia Costello, Shari Miles, and Anne Stone. New York: Norton, 1998.

Prinz, Timothy S. "The Career Paths of Elected Politicians: A Review and Prospectus." In *Ambition and Beyond: Career Path of American Politicians*, edited by Shirley Williams and Edward L. Lascher, Jr. Berkeley: Institute of Governmental Studies Press, 1993.

Rahn, Wendy M. "The Role of Partisan Stereotypes in Information Processing about Political Candidates." *American Journal of Political Science* 37 (1993): 472–96.

Rake, Katherine. "Gender and New Labour's Social Policies." *Journal of Social Policy* 30 (2001): 209–31.

Rapoport, Ronald B., Kelly L. Metcalf, and Jon A. Hartman. "Candidate Traits and Voter Inferences: An Experimental Study." *Journal of Politics* 51 (1989): 917–32.

Regens, James L. "Congressional Cosponsorship of Acid Rain Controls." *Social Sciences Quarterly* 70 (1989): 505–12.

Reingold, Beth. "Concepts of Representation among Female and Male State Legislators." *Legislative Studies Quarterly* 17 (1992): 509–37.

———. "Conflict and Cooperation: Legislative Strategies and Concepts of Power among Female and Male State Legislators." *Journal of Politics* 58 (1996): 464–85.

———. *Representing Women: Sex, Gender, and Legislative Behavior in Arizona and California*. Chapel Hill: University of North Carolina Press, 2000.

Reskin, Barbara. "Sex Segregation in the Workplace." *Annual Review of Sociology* 19 (1993): 241–70.

Riggle, Ellen D. B., Penny M. Miller, Todd G. Shields, and Mitzi M. S. Johnson. "Gender Stereotypes and Decision Context in the Evaluation of Political Candidates." *Women and Politics* 17, no. 3 (1997): 69–88.

Ripley, Randall B. *Power in the Senate*. New York: St. Martin's Press, 1969.

Rogers, M. Everett, James W. Dearing, and S. Chang. "AIDS in the 1990's: The Agenda Setting Process for a Public Issue." *Journalism Monographs* 126 (1991).

Rogers, M. B. "Women in Electoral Politics: A Slow, Steady Climb." *Social Policy* 23, no. 4 (1993): 14–21.

Rohde, David W. "Parties and Committees in the House: Member Motivations, Issues, and Institutional Arrangements." *Legislative Studies Quarterly* 19 (1994): 341–59.

———. *Parties and Leaders in the Postreform House*. Chicago: University of Chicago Press, 1991.

———. "Risk-Bearing and Progressive Ambition: The Case of Members of the United States House of Representatives." *American Journal of Political Science* 23 (1979): 1–26.

Romzek, Barbara S., and Jennifer A. Utter. "Career Dynamics of Congressional Legislative Staff: Preliminary Profile and Research Questions." *Journal of Public Administration Research and Theory* 6 (1996): 415–42.

———. "Congressional Legislative Staff: Political Professionals or Clerks?" *American Journal of Political Science* 41 (1997): 1251–80.

Rosenthal, Alan. "State Legislative Development: Observations from Three Perspectives." *Legislative Studies Quarterly* 21 (1996): 169–95.

Rosenthal, Cindy Simon. "Determinants of Collaborative Leadership: Civic Engagement, Gender, or Organizational Norms?" *Political Research Quarterly* 51, no. 4 (1998): 847–68.

———. "Divided Lives: Revisiting Considerations of the Personal and Political." *Women & Politics* 22, no. 1 (2001): 37–62.

———. "Getting Things Done: Women Committee Chairpersons in State Legislatures." In *Women and Elective Office: Past, Present, and Future*, edited by Sue Thomas and Clyde Wilcox. Oxford: Oxford University Press, 1998.

———. "A View of Their Own: Women's Committee Leadership Styles and State Legislatures." *Policy Studies Journal* 25, no. 4 (1997): 585–600.

———. *When Women Lead: Integrative Leadership in State Legislatures*. New York: Oxford University Press, 1998.

Rosenwasser, Shirley M., and Norma G. Dean. "Gender Role and Political Office: Effects of Perceived Masculinity/Femininity of Candidate and Political Office." *Psychology of Women Quarterly* 13 (1989): 77–85.

Rosenwasser, Shirley M., Robyn R. Rogers, Sheila Fling, Kayla Silvers-Pickens, and John Butemeyer. "Attitudes toward Women and Men in Politics: Perceived Male and Female Candidate Competencies and Participant Personality Characteristics." *Political Psychology* 8 (1987): 191–200.

Rosenwasser, Shirley M., and Jana Seale. "Attitudes toward a Hypothetical Male or Female Presidential Candidate: A Research Note." *Political Psychology* 9 (1988): 591–99.

Rossi, Alice, ed. *The Feminist Papers: From Adams to De Beauvoir*. New York: Columbia University Press, 1973.

Rotundo, E. Anthony. *American Manhood: Transformation in Masculinity from the Revolution to the Modern Era*. New York: Basic Books, 1993.

Rovner, Julie. "Future of Labor-HSS Measure Clouded by Veto Threat." *Congressional Quarterly Weekly Report* 49 (1991): 2624–27.

Rubin, Alissa J. "New Breast Cancer Research Funding . . . Raises Old Questions about Priorities." *Congressional Quarterly Weekly Report* 54 (1996): 1364–65.

Ruddick, Sara. *Maternal Thinking*. Boston: Beacon Press, 1994.

Rule, Wilma. "Why Women Don't Run: The Critical Contextual Factors in Women's Legislative Recruitment." *Western Political Quarterly* 34 (1981): 60–77.

Rundquist, Paul S., Judy Schneider, and Frederick H. Pauls. "Congressional Staff: An Analysis of Their Roles, Functions, and Impacts." Washington, D.C.: Congressional Research Service, 1992.

Rupp, Lelia J., and Verta Taylor. *Survival in the Doldrums: The American Women's Rights Movement, 1945 to the 1960s.* New York: Oxford University Press, 1987.

Russell, Anne, Robert B. Voas, William DeJong, and Marla Chaloupka. "MADD Rates the States: A Media Advocacy Event to Advance the Agenda against Alcohol-Impaired Driving." *Public Health Reports* 110 (1995): 240–46.

Russell, Meg. "Women's Representation in UK Politics: What Can Be Done within the Law?" Constitution Unit, School of Public Policy at University College London, June 2000.

Ryan, Barbara. *Feminism and the Women's Movement.* New York: Routledge, 1992.

Saint-Germain, Michelle. "Does Their Difference Make a Difference? The Impact of Women on Public Policy in the Arizona Legislature." *Social Science Quarterly* 70 (1989): 956–68.

Salant, Priscilla, and Don Dillman. *How to Conduct Your Own Survey.* New York: Wiley, 1994.

Salisbury, Robert, and Kenneth Shepsle. "Staff Turnover and Ties-That-Bind." *American Political Science Review* 75, no. 2 (1981): 381–96.

———. "U.S. Congressman as Enterprise." *Legislative Studies Quarterly* 6 (1981): 559–76.

Sanbonmatsu, Kira. *Gender Equality, Political Parties, and the Politics of Women's Place.* Ann Arbor: University of Michigan Press, 2002.

Sanders, Lynn. "Against Deliberation." *Political Theory* 25, no. 3 (1997): 347–77.

Sapiro, Virginia. "Gender Politics, Gendered Politics: The State of the Field." In *Political Science: Looking to the Future*, edited by William J. Cotty. Evanston, Ill.: Northwestern University Press, 1991.

———. "If Senator Baker Were a Woman: An Experimental Study of Candidate Images." *Political Psychology* 2 (1981–82): 61–83.

———. *The Political Integration of Women: Roles, Socialization, and Politics.* Urbana, Ill.: University of Illinois Press, 1983.

———. "Private Costs of Public Commitments or Public Costs of Private Commitments? Family Roles versus Political Ambition." *American Journal of Political Science* 26 (1982): 265–79.

———. "Research Frontier Essay: When Are Interests Interesting? The Problem of Political Representation of Women." *American Political Science Review* 75 (1981): 701–16.

Sapiro, Virginia, and Barbara G. Farah. "New Pride and Old Prejudice: Political Ambition and Role Orientations among Female Partisan Elites." *Women & Politics* 1, no. 1 (1980): 13–36.

Schank, Roger C., and Robert P. Abelson. *Scripts, Plans, Goals, and Understanding: An Inquiry into Human Knowledge Structures.* Hillsdale, N.J.: Erlbaum, 1977.

Schiller, Wendy J. "Senators as Political Entrepreneurs: Bills Sponsorship to Shape Legislative Agendas." *American Journal of Political Science* 39 (1995): 186–203.

Schlesinger, Joseph A. *Ambition and Politics: Political Careers in the United States.* Chicago: Rand McNally, 1966.

Schlozman, Kay. "Representing Women in Washington: Sisterhood and Pressure Politics." In *Women, Politics, and Change*, edited by Louise Tilly and Patricia Gurin. New York: Russell Sage Foundation, 1990.

Schneider, Anne Larason, and Helen Ingram. *Policy Design for Democracy.* Lawrence: University Press of Kansas, 1997.

———. "Social Construction of Target Populations: Implications for Politics and Policy." *American Political Science Review* 87 (1993): 334–47.

Schochet, Gordon J. *Patriarchalism in Political Thought: The Authoritarian Family and Political Speculation and Attitudes Especially in Seventeenth-Century England.* Oxford: Blackwell, 1975.

Schooler, Caroline, S. Shyam Sundar, and June Flora. "Effects of the Stanford Five-City Project Media Advocacy Program." *Health Education Quarterly* 23 (1996): 240–46.

Schor, Juliet B. *The Overworked American: The Unexpected Decline of Leisure.* New York: Basic Books, 1992.

Schroedel, Jean Reith, and Nicola Mazumadar. "Into the Twenty-First Century: Will Women Break the Political Glass Ceiling?" In *Women and Elective Office: Past, Present, and Future*, edited by Sue Thomas and Clyde Wilcox. New York: Oxford University Press, 1998.

Schroeder, Patricia. *24 Years of House Work and the Place Is Still a Mess: My Life in Politics.* Kansas City: Andrews McMeel, 1999.

Schroeder, Patricia, and Olympia Snowe. "The Politics of Women's Health." In *The American Woman: 1994–95*, edited by Cynthia Costello and Anne J. Stone. New York: Norton, 1994.

Schubert, James N., and Gloria J. Schubert. "The Processing of Women's and Men's Health Policy Issues: Mass Screening Guidelines for Breast and Prostate Cancer." Paper presented at the Political Science Association meeting, Norfolk, Va., 1997.

Schwartz-Shea, Peregrine. "Feminist Empirical Research: Evidence, Explanation, and Persuasion." Paper presented at the annual meeting of the Western Political Science Association, Los Angeles, 1998.

Scott, W. Richard. *Institutions and Organizations.* Thousand Oaks, Calif.: Sage, 1995.

Scully, Roger M., and Samuel C. Patterson. "Ideological Thinking in Legislative Decision Making." Paper presented at the annual meeting of the Midwest Political Science Association, Chicago, April 1997.

Sears, David O. "College Sophomores in the Laboratory: Influences of a Narrow Data Base on Social Psychology's View of Human Nature." *Journal of Personality and Social Psychology* 51 (1986): 515–30.

Selden, Sally. *The Promise of Representative Bureaucracy.* Armonk, N.Y.: M.E. Sharpe, 1997.

Seligman, Lester, et al. *Patterns of Recruitment: A State Chooses Its Lawmakers*. Chicago: Rand McNally, 1974.

Seltzer, Richard A., Jody Newman, and Melissa Voorhees Leighton. *Sex as a Political Variable: Women as Candidates and Voters in U.S. Elections*. Boulder, Colo.: Lynne Rienner, 1997.

Shanks, J. Merrill, and Warren Miller. *The New American Voter*. Cambridge, Mass.: Harvard University Press, 1996.

Shapiro, Robert, and Harpreet Mahajan. "Gender Differences in Policy Preferences: A Summary of Trends from the 1960s to the 1980s." *Public Opinion Quarterly* 50, no. 1 (1986): 42–61.

Shephard, Gillian. *Shephard's Watch: Illusions of Power in British Politics*. London: Politico's, 2000.

Shepsle, Kenneth A. "Institutional Arrangements and Equilibrium in Multidimensional Voting Models." *American Journal of Political Science* 23 (1979): 27–60.

Shepsle, Kenneth A., and Barry R. Weingast. "Why Are Congressional Committees Powerful?" *American Political Science Review* 81 (1985): 935–44.

———. "The Institutional Foundations of Committee Power." *American Political Science Review* 81 (1987): 85–104.

Short, Claire. "Women and the Labour Party." In *Women in Politics*, edited by Pippa Norris and Joni Lovenduski. Oxford: Oxford University Press, 1996.

Sigelman, Lee, and Carol K. Sigelman. "Sexism, Racism, and Ageism in Voting Behavior: An Experimental Analysis." *Social Psychology Quarterly* 45 (1982): 263–69.

Simon, Rita J., and Gloria Danziger. *Women's Movements in America*. New York: Praeger, 1991.

Sinclair, Barbara. "The Distribution of Committee Positions in the U.S. Senate: Explaining Institutional Change." *American Journal of Political Science* 32 (1988): 276–301.

———. *Legislators, Leaders, and Lawmaking: The U.S. House of Representatives in the Postreform Era*. Baltimore: Johns Hopkins University Press, 1995.

———. *The Transformation of the U.S. Senate*. Baltimore: Johns Hopkins University Press, 1989.

Smith, Eric R. A. N., and Richard L. Fox. "The Electoral Fortunes of Women Candidates for Congress." *Political Research Quarterly* 54, no. 1 (2001): 205–21.

Smith, Steven S. *Call to Order: Floor Politics in the House and Senate*. Washington, D.C.: Brookings Institution, 1989.

Smith, Steven S., and Christopher J. Deering. *Committees in Congress*. Washington, D.C.: Congressional Quarterly Press, 1990.

Soule, John W. "Future Political Ambitions and the Behavior of Incumbent State Legislators." *Midwest Journal of Political Science* 13 (1969): 439–54.

Spalter-Roth, Roberta, and Ronnee Schreiber. "Outsider Issues and Insider Tactics: Strategic Tensions in the Women's Policy Network during the 1980s." In *Feminist Organizations: Harvest of the New Women's Movement*, edited by Myra Marx Ferree and Patricia Yancey Martin. New York: Russell Sage Foundation, 1995.

Spohn, Cassia, and Diane Gillespie. "Adolescents' Willingness to Vote for a Woman for President: The Effect of Gender and Race." *Women and Politics* 7, no. 4 (1987): 31–49.

Squire, Peverill. "State Legislative Careers." In *Ambition and Beyond: Career Path of American Politicians,* edited by Shirley Williams and Edward L. Lascher, Jr. Berkeley: Institute of Governmental Studies Press, 1993.

Squires, Judith, and Mark Wickham-Jones. *Women in Parliament: A Comparative Analysis.* Manchester: Equal Opportunities Commission Research Discussion Series, 2001.

Stabiner, Karen. *To Dance with the Devil: The New War on Breast Cancer.* New York: Delacorte Press, 1997.

Stark, Steven. "Gap Politics." *Atlantic Monthly,* July 1996, 70–80.

Steiner, Gilbert. *The Futility of Family Policy.* Washington, D.C.: Brookings Institution, 1981.

Stewart, Charles, III, and Timothy Groseclose. "The Value of Committee Seats in the Senate, 1947–1991." *American Journal of Political Science* 43 (1999): 963–73.

Stivers, Camille. *Gender Images in Public Administration: Legitimacy and the Administrative State.* Newbury Park, Calif.: Sage, 1993.

Stoper, Emily. "Wife and Politician: Role Strain among Women in Public Office." In *Portrait of Marginality: The Political Behavior of the American Woman,* edited by Marianne Githens and Jewell Prestage. New York: D. McKay, 1977.

Strahan, Randall. *New Ways and Means: Reform and Change in a Congressional Committee.* Chapel Hill: University of North Carolina Press, 1990.

Susan G. Komen Foundation. www.komen.org.

Swain, Carol. *Black Faces, Black Interests: The Representation of African Americans in Congress.* Enl. ed. Cambridge: Harvard University Press, 1995.

Swers, Michele L. "Are Women More Likely to Vote for Women's Issue Bills Than Their Male Colleagues?" *Legislative Studies Quarterly* 23 (1998): 435–48.

———. *The Difference Women Make: The Policy Impact of Women in Congress.* Chicago: University of Chicago Press, 2002.

———. "Placing Women's Issues on the National Agenda: An Analysis of Gender Differences in Women's Issue Bill Sponsorship for the 103rd and 104th Congress." Paper presented at the annual meeting of the American Political Science Association, Atlanta, 1999.

Swift, Elaine K. *The Making of an American Senate: Reconstitutive Change in Congress, 1787–1841.* Ann Arbor: University of Michigan Press, 1996.

Tamerius, Karin L. "Sex, Gender, and Leadership in the Representation of Women." In *Gender Power, Leadership, and Governance,* edited by Georgia Duerst-Lahti and Rita Mae Kelly. Ann Arbor: University of Michigan Press, 1995.

Tarrow, Sidney. *Power in Movement: Social Movements, Collective Action and Politics.* Cambridge: Cambridge University Press, 1994.

———. "'The Very Excess of Democracy': State Building and Contentious Politics in America." In *Social Movements and American Political Institutions,* edited by Anne Costain and Andrew McFarland. Lanham, Md.: Rowman & Littlefield, 1998.

Tatalovich, Raymond, and David Schier. "The Persistence of Ideological Cleavage in Voting on Abortion Legislation in the House of Representatives, 1973–1988." *American Politics Quarterly* 21 (1993): 125–39.

Taylor, Andrew. "Hot Button GOP Riders." *Congressional Quarterly Weekly Report* 56 (1998): 2272.

Theodoulou, Stella Z., Gloria Y. Guevara, and Henrik Minnassians. "Myths and Illusions: The Media and AIDS Policy." In *AIDS: The Politics and Policy of Disease*, edited by Stella Theodoulou. Upper Saddle River, N.J.: Prentice Hall, 1996.

Thomas, Sue. "The Effects of Race and Gender on Constituency Service." *Western Political Quarterly* 45, no. 1 (March 1992): 169–80.

———. *How Women Legislate*. New York: Oxford University Press, 1994.

———. "The Impact of Women on State Legislative Policies." *Journal of Politics* 53 (1991): 958–76.

———. Introduction to *Women and Elective Office: Past, Present, and Future*, edited by Sue Thomas and Clyde Wilcox, 1–14. New York: Oxford University Press, 1998.

———. "Voting Patterns in the California Assembly: The Role of Gender." *Women & Politics* 9, no. 4 (1990): 43–56.

———. "Why Gender Matters: The Perceptions of Women Officeholders." *Women & Politics* 17, no. 1 (1997): 27–54.

———. "Women in State Legislatures: One Step at a Time." In *The Year of the Woman: Myths and Realities*, edited by Elizabeth Cook, Sue Thomas, and Clyde Wilcox. Boulder, Colo.: Westview Press, 1994.

Thomas, Sue, and Susan Welch. "The Impact of Gender on Activities and Priorities of State Legislators." *Western Political Quarterly* 5l (1991): 445–56.

Thompson, Seth, and Janie Steckenrider. "The Relative Irrelevance of Candidate Sex." *Women and Politics* 17, no. 4 (1997): 71–92.

Tong, Rosemarie Putnam. *Feminist Thought: A More Comprehensive Introduction*. 2nd ed. Boulder, Colo.: Westview Press, 1998.

Towell, Pat. "House Oks Defense Spending, Minus Curb on Deployments." *Congressional Quarterly Weekly Report* 51 (1993): 2662–67.

———. "$243.7 Billion Compromise Ready for Clinton's Pen." *Congressional Quarterly Weekly Report* 52 (1994): 2818–22.

Trammell, Jeffrey B., and Steve Piacente, eds. *The Almanac of the Unelected*. 7th ed. Washington, D.C.: Almanac, 1994.

———. *The Almanac of the Unelected*. 8th ed. Washington, D.C.: Almanac, 1995.

Traugott, Mark, ed. *Repertoires and Cycles of Collective Action*. Durham, N.C.: Duke University Press, 1995.

Treno, Andrew J., Larry Breed, Harold D. Holder, et al. "Evaluation of Media Advocacy Efforts within a Community Trial to Reduce Alcohol Involved Injury." *Evaluation Review* 20 (1996): 404–23.

Treno, Andrew J., and Harold D. Holder. "Community Mobilization, Organizing, and Media Advocacy: A Discussion of Methodological Issues." *Evaluation Review* 21 (1997): 166–90.

Trent, Judith S., and Teresa Sabourin. "Sex Still Counts: Women's Use of Televised Advertising during the Decade of the 80s." *Journal of Applied Communication* 21, no. 1 (1993): 21–40.

Vega, Arturo, and Juanita M. Firestone. "The Effects of Gender on Congressional Behavior and the Substantive Representation of Women." *Legislative Studies Quarterly* 20 (1995): 213–22.

Wachter, Robert M. "AIDS, Activism, and the Politics of Health." *New England Journal of Medicine* 326 (1992): 128–33.

Waldo, Dwight. "Development of a Theory of Democratic Administration." *American Political Science Review* 46, no. 1 (1952): 81–103.

Wallack, Lawrence. "Media Advocacy: Promoting Health through Mass Communication." In *Health Behavior and Health Education*, edited by Karen Glanz, Frances M. Lewis, and Barbara K. Rimer, 370–86. San Francisco: Jossey-Bass, 1990.

Walsby, Sylvia. *Gender Transformations*. London: Routledge, 1997.

Ward, Lucy. "Learning from the 'Babe' Experience: How the Finest Hour Became a Fiasco." In *New Gender Agenda: Why Women Still Want More*, edited by Anna Coote. London: Institute for Public Policy Research, 2000.

Waters, Malcolm. "Patriarchy and Viriarchy." *Sociology* 23, no. 2 (1989): 193–211.

Webster v Reproductive Health Services. 492 U.S. 490 (1989).

Welch, Susan. "Are Women More Liberal Than Men in the U.S. Congress?" *Legislative Studies Quarterly* 10 (1985): 125–34.

Werner, Emmy E. "Women in Congress: 1917–1964." *Western Political Quarterly* 19 (1966): 16–30.

West, Candace, and Don Zimmerman. "Doing Gender." *Gender & Society* 1 (1987): 125–51.

West, D. M. *Air Wars: Television Advertising in Election Campaigns, 1952–1992*. Washington, D.C.: Congressional Quarterly, Inc., 1993.

Whicker, Marcia Lynn, and Malcolm Jewell. "The Feminization of Leadership in State Legislatures." In *Women and Elective Office: Past, Present, and Future*, edited by Sue Thomas and Clyde Wilcox. Oxford: Oxford University Press, 1998.

Wilcox, Clyde. "Why Was 1992 the 'Year of the Woman?': Explaining Women's Gains in 1992." In *The Year of the Woman: Myths and Realities*, edited by Elizabeth Adel Cook, Sue Thomas, and Clyde Wilcox. Boulder, Colo.: Westview Press, 1994.

Williams, John E., and Deborah L. Best. *Measuring Sex Stereotypes: A Multination Study*. Newbury Park, Calif.: Sage, 1990.

Williams, Melissa. *Voice, Trust, and Memory*. Princeton, N.J.: Princeton University Press, 2000.

Williams, Shirley. Introduction to *Ambition and Beyond: Career Paths of American Politicians*, edited by Shirley Williams and Edward L. Lascher, Jr. Berkeley: Institute of Governmental Studies Press, University of California, 1993.

Wilson, James Q. *The Amateur Democrat: Club Politics in Three Cities*. Chicago: University of Chicago Press, 1962.

Wilson, Rick K., and Cheryl D. Young. "Cosponsorship in the United States Congress." *Legislative Studies Quarterly* 22 (1997): 25–43.

Wilson, Woodrow. *Congressional Government: A Study in American Politics.* Cleveland: Meridian, 1885.

Winsky-Mattei, Laura R. "Gender and Power in American Legislative Discourse." *Journal of Politics* 60 (1998): 440–61.

Witt, Linda, Karen M. Paget, and Glenna Matthews. *Running as a Woman: Gender and Power in American Politics.* New York: Free Press, 1994.

Wolbrecht, Christina. *The Politics of Women's Rights: Parties, Positions, and Change.* Princeton, N.J.: Princeton University Press, 2000.

"Women Break All Congressional Election Records." *Women's Political Times*, winter 1992–93, 1–3.

Women's Policy, Inc. *Special Report: First Session of the 104th Congress.* Washington, D.C.: Women's Policy, Inc., 1996.

Wood, Gordon S. *The Radicalism of the American Revolution.* New York: Vintage, 1991.

Young, James Sterling. *The Washington Community, 1800–1828.* New York: Columbia University Press, 1966.

Zaller, John R. *The Nature and Origins of Mass Opinion.* Cambridge: Cambridge University Press, 1992.

CONTRIBUTORS

Cindy Simon Rosenthal is an associate professor of political science and women's studies at the University of Oklahoma and associate director of the Carl Albert Congressional Research and Studies Center. She is the author of *When Women Lead*, and her research has appeared in *Political Research Quarterly*, *Legislative Studies Quarterly*, *Social Science Quarterly*, and *Women & Politics*. Her current research focuses on women's socialization, mentorship, and institutional constraints on women in legislative leadership.

Laura W. Arnold teaches political science at the University of Missouri at St. Louis. Her research interests include congressional careers, committees, historical perspectives on Congress, and presidential-congressional relations. Her research has appeared in *American Political Science Review*, *Legislative Studies Quarterly*, and *American Politics Quarterly*.

Lauren Cohen Bell is an assistant professor of political science at Randolph-Macon College. Her work has appeared in *Judicature* and *The Almanac of Oklahoma Politics*. She is the author of *Warring Factions: Interest Groups, Money, and the New Politics of Senate Confirmation*. She is a former APSA congressional fellow.

Matthew Braunstein, who received his master's degree in American government from Georgetown University, is legislative director for U.S. Representative Patrick Kennedy (D-RI).

Dianne Bystrom is director of the Carrie Chapman Catt Center for Women and Politics at Iowa State University. She coedited and contributed to *The Lynching of Language: Gender, Politics, and Power in the Hill-Thomas Hearings, The Electronic Election: Perspectives on the 1996 Campaign Communication,* and *Communicating Politics: Engaging the Public in Democratic Life.* Dr. Bystrom teaches in political science, journalism, honors, and women's studies.

Susan J. Carroll is professor of political science at Rutgers University and senior scholar at the Center for American Women and Politics (CAWP) of the Eagleton Institute of Politics. She has authored numerous publications, including *Women as Candidates in American Politics,* and edited *The Impact of Women in Public Office* and *Women and American Politics: New Questions, New Directions.* Her current research focuses on representation by women in Congress, media coverage of women voters and candidates, and the effect of term limits on women's representation in state legislatures.

Anne Costain serves as associate vice president for Human Relations and Risk Management and is professor of political science at the University of Colorado at Boulder. Professor Costain is engaged in research on media coverage of the women's movement. She is author of *Inviting Women's Rebellion: A Political Process Interpretation of the Women's Movement* and coeditor with Simone Chambers of *Deliberation, Democracy, and the Media.*

Georgia Duerst-Lahti is department chair and professor of political science and faculty of women's studies at Beloit College. She recently served as president of the Women's Caucus in Political Science of the American Political Science Association (APSA). With Rita Mae Kelly, she coedited *Gender Power, Leadership, and Governance.* Her research continues to explore gender as protoideology in governing institutions and public policy.

Heather Fraizer is a doctoral student in comparative politics at the University of Colorado at Boulder. She is completing a dissertation looking at social movement use of violent protest in Chile and has done previous research on women's political participation in the former Soviet Union.

Joyce Gelb is the author of *Feminism and Politics* and coauthor of *Women and Public Policies.* She also coedited a volume entitled *Women of Japan and Korea: Continuity and Change* and has written numerous articles on women and public policy in Britain, Japan, and the United States. She is professor of political science at City College and the Graduate Center of the City University of New York.

Irwin N. Gertzog has taught American politics at Yale University, Allegheny College, Princeton University, and Rutgers University. In addition to publishing articles on women in politics, the U.S. Congress, and voter turnout, he is the author of *Congressional Women: Their Recruitment, Integration, and Behavior* and is currently writing a monograph for the CAWP on the Congressional Caucus for Women's Issues.

Rebekah Herrick is an associate professor of political science at Oklahoma State University. Her work has appeared in *Legislative Studies Quarterly, American Politics Quarterly*, and *Social Science Journal*. She has published in the areas of women in politics, Congress and elections, and congressional careers.

Lynda Lee Kaid is senior associate dean and professor of telecommunication in the College of Journalism and Communications at the University of Florida. She was founding director of the Political Communication Center at the University of Oklahoma before assuming this position. With Dianne Bystrom, she coedited *The Electronic Election: Perspectives on the 1996 Campaign*. She is the author of 14 books, including *Political Advertising in Western Democracies* and *Mediated Politics in Two Cultures*.

Karen M. Kedrowski is an associate professor and chair of political science at Winthrop University. She is the author of *Media Entrepreneurs and the Media Enterprise in the U.S. Congress*. Previously she worked as a health policy analyst for Families USA in Washington, D.C.

Barbara M. King is a doctoral student at Southern Illinois University. She is doing additional research on women in the U.S. Senate and curriculum development for the SIU Women's Studies Program. Her dissertation focuses on democratic transition in Eastern Europe since 1989.

David C. King is associate professor of public policy at the Kennedy School of Government at Harvard University. His work has appeared in *American Political Science Review*. He is the author of *Turf Wars: How Congressional Committees Claim Jurisdiction*, which won the Richard F. Fenno book prize from APSA, and a coeditor (with Joseph Nye and Philip Zelikow) of *Why People Don't Trust Government*.

Richard E. Matland is an associate professor of political science at the University of Houston. He is best known for his work on women in politics in comparative settings, including Canada, Scandinavia, and Costa Rica. His work has appeared in *American Journal of Political Science, Journal of Politics, British Journal of Political Science, Political Research Quarterly*, and *Comparative Political Studies*.

Noelle H. Norton is an associate professor of political science and director of the Honors Program at the University of San Diego. Her research can be found in *Legislative Studies Quarterly, Women & Politics, Policy Studies Journal, Journal of the History of Behavioral Sciences*, and in *Gender Power, Leadership, and Governance*. She is currently working on a book about the legislative politics of reproductive policy.

Marilyn Stine Sarow is an associate professor in mass communication at Winthrop University. She previously held various management positions in public affairs and public information at the University of Kentucky Chandler Medical Center and the University of Wisconsin. Her research interests include health information and the Internet, and integrated marketing communication.

Michele L. Swers is an assistant professor of government at Georgetown University. Her book *The Difference Women Make: The Policy Impact of Women in Congress* analyzes the influence of gender on legislators' policy activity during the 1990s. Her work also appears in *Legislative Studies Quarterly, Women & Politics*, and *PS: Political Science*. Her research interests focus on individual legislative decision making and the influence of party leadership, the constituency, and social identity on legislative choices.

Sue Thomas, formerly associate professor and director of women's studies at Georgetown University, is senior policy researcher at Pacific Institute for Research and Evaluation. Her areas of research center on women and politics. Her publications include *How Women Legislate* and *Women and Elective Office: Past, Present, and Future*.

Katherine Cramer Walsh is an assistant professor at the University of Wisconsin. Her work has appeared in *Political Communication* and *The Political Psychologist*. She is currently working on a manuscript on informal political talk, which reflects her research interests in public opinion, political communication, and social identity.

Christina Wolbrecht is an associate professor of political science at the University of Notre Dame. She is the author of *The Politics of Women's Rights: Parties, Positions, and Change*. Her current research focuses on the voting behavior of American women during the period immediately following the granting of suffrage.

Index